Ways of Reading

Second Edition

'*Ways of Reading* is a valuable and immensely usable book . . . its range of text samples is admirably wide-ranging and eclectic.'

John McRae, *Language and Literature*

Ways of Reading is a well-established core textbook that provides the reader with the tools for analysing and interpreting literary and non-literary texts.

Six sections, split into self-contained units with their own activities and notes for further reading, cover:

- problem-solving approaches to texts
- language, text and context
- poetic uses of language
- figures of speech
- story, narrative and narration
- looking beyond the text to authorship, audience, value and performance

This second edition has been extensively updated throughout with a fully revised introduction, new illustrations and two new units: **Literature in performance** looks at oral poetry, drama and theatrical production, and **Ways of reading non-literary texts**, considers examples from journalism as well as political and religious communications.

Martin Montgomery is Reader in Literary Linguistics at the University of Strathclyde, Glasgow; **Alan Durant** is Professor in the School of Humanities and Cultural Studies, Middlesex University, London; **Nigel Fabb** is Professor of Literary Linguistics at the University of Strathclyde, Glasgow; **Tom Furniss** is Senior Lecturer in English Studies, the University of Strathclyde, Glasgow; and **Sara Mills** is Professor in the Department of English Studies at Sheffield Hallam University.

Ways of Reading

Second Edition

Advanced reading skills for students of English literature

Martin Montgomery,
Alan Durant, Nigel Fabb,
Tom Furniss and
Sara Mills

London and New York

First published 1992
Second edition published 2000
by Routledge
11 New Fetter Lane, London EC4P 4EE

Simultaneously published in the USA
and Canada
by Routledge
29 West 35th Street, New York, NY 10001

Reprinted 2001

*Routledge is an imprint of the Taylor &
Francis Group*

© 1992, 2000 Martin Montgomery,
Alan Durant, Nigel Fabb, Tom Furniss
and Sara Mills

Typeset in Times and Futura by
Florence Production Ltd, Stoodleigh, Devon
Printed and bound in Great Britain by
TJ International Ltd, Padstow, Cornwall

*British Library Cataloguing in Publication
Data*
A catalogue record for this book is available
from the British Library.

*Library of Congress Cataloging in Publication
Data*
Ways of reading: advanced reading skills
for students of English literature / Martin
Montgomery . . . [et al.] – 2nd ed.
   p.   cm.
   Includes bibliographical references (p.)
and index.
   1. English literature—History and
criticism —Theory, etc.   2. English
literature—Problems, exercises, etc.
3. Reading (Higher education).
4. Reading comprehension.   5. Books and
reading.   6. College readers.
I. Montgomery, Martin.
PR21.W39 2000
808′.0427–dc21   99–048287

ISBN 0–415–22205–2 (hbk)
ISBN 0–415–22206–0 (pbk)

In memoriam
Gillian Skirrow

Contents

Section 4 Reading figures of speech

Section 5 Aspects of narrative

Section 6 Beyond the literary text

Notes on contributors

Alan Durant is Professor in the School of Humanities and Cultural Studies, Middlesex University, London. His books include *Literary Studies in Action* (co-written with Nigel Fabb, Routledge, 1990), *How to Write Essays, Dissertations and Theses in Literary Studies* (co-written with Nigel Fabb, Longman, 1993), *Ezra Pound: Identity in Crisis* (Harvester/Barnes & Noble, 1981) and *Conditions of Music* (Macmillan/SUNY, 1984). With Nigel Fabb and others he edited the collection of conference papers *The Linguistics of Writing: Arguments between Language and Literature* (Manchester University Press/Routledge, 1987).

Nigel Fabb is a Professor of Literary Linguistics, University of Strathclyde, Glasgow. He is an editor of the *Journal of Linguistics*, and the author of five books, including *Linguistics and Literature: Language in the Verbal Arts of the World* (Blackwell, 1997).

Tom Furniss is Senior Lecturer in English Studies at the University of Strathclyde, Glasgow. His books include *Reading Poetry: An Introduction*, co-written with Michael Bath (Prentice-Hall, 1996).

Sara Mills is Professor in the Department of English Studies at Sheffield Hallam University. Her books include *Feminist Stylistics* (Routledge, 1995) and *Discourse* (Routledge, 1997).

Martin Montgomery is Reader in Literary Linguistics at the University of Strathclyde, Glasgow, where he was head of English Studies. He now heads the Scottish Centre for Journalism Studies. He is the author of *An Introduction to Language and Society* (Routledge, 1995) and is a contributor to several books and journals.

Preface

This is a revised and expanded version of what we believe has been a valuable and usable textbook for students of literature. Many sections have been substantially re-written in the light of experience using the book and in the light of developments in the field. References have been updated. And two completely new units have been added, one on literature in performance and one on journalistic texts.

Preparing the second edition of *Ways of Reading* provided us with a welcome opportunity to reflect upon the origins of the first edition. Looking back, it has become increasingly clear that two particular traditions of work have informed our approach from the outset. *Ways of Reading* was influenced by important developments in literary theory – by discussions concerning, for instance, the nature of narrative, the question of value, or, indeed, the role of the reader. *Ways of Reading* was also, however, significantly informed by the efforts of literary linguistics to bring to bear upon the literary text insights derived from the systematic study of language. The convergence of these traditions in this book lies behind its emphasis on reading as both an active and reflective process.

For reading is, of course, much more than the simple decipherment of words on a page. It involves an active and critical engagement with the text in which readers pose questions of it and attend to details of its form and structure in pursuit of a fuller understanding. To enable or facilitate this process we assembled a set of tools for thinking and for reading with. Many of these 'tools for reading' amount to particular skills of analysis and this helps to explain the structure of the units, each of which moves from exposition of an approach to its application. In this way, the book is not only reader-centred but also student-centred, conceptualizing knowledge as a set of procedures for inquiring about a text rather than as a set of pre-constituted facts.

The book comprises six sections. Section 1 addresses basic issues involved in studying literature and introduces both basic techniques and problem solving.

Section 2 paints a broad picture of the dimensions along which language may vary. It includes attention to questions of language, gender, social position and historical change and examines the way knowledge of such language variation helps in the study of literary and non-literary texts. Section 3 considers aspects of the sound patterning and the grammar of poetry. Section 4 focuses on figures of speech – ways of conveying meaning indirectly by implication and allusion. Section 5 is concerned with aspects of narrative – what makes a story and how stories are told. Section 6, the final section, goes beyond the text itself to address questions of authorship, performance and audience. In addition to its focus on canonical and non-canonical literary texts drawn from various English-speaking countries, the book also explores the relationship between literary and non-literary text by examining examples from the fields of journalism and advertising, film and television.

Above all, however, *Ways of Reading* has been tried and tested for around a decade in many different contexts. It is an extremely practical book. Each unit concludes with a specially designed workshop activity aimed at helping the student extend his or her understanding of critical reading as a broader process where reading the word is part of reading the world.

Martin Montgomery
Department of English Studies
University of Strathclyde

Acknowledgements

The book originated in a course in English Studies developed and taught primarily by the then staff of the Programme in Literary Linguistics, University of Strathclyde, Glasgow. The original planning team for the course also included Gillian Skirrow and Derek Attridge, and *Ways of Reading* owes much to their inspiration. The title itself derives in part from John Berger's book, *Ways of Seeing*; but there was also a course of the same name (though different in aims, scope and constituency) taught by Deirdre Burton and Tom Davis in the English Department at the University of Birmingham.

In writing the book, the authors benefited a great deal both from the responses of students in workshops and also from postgraduates who assisted in the teaching of many of the units – Shân Wareing, Christine Christie, Lena Garry, Linda Jackson, Vassiliki Kolocotroni, Lindsay Hewitt, Luma Al Balaa and others. In addition, we would like to thank Gill Morris and Keith Knightenhelser. Special thanks go to Judit Friedrich and Professor Michael Toolan, who read and commented upon the complete typescript of the book. Its faults, of course, remain our own.

The Publishers and the Authors would like to thank the following for permission to reproduce copyright material: Faber & Faber Ltd and New Directions Publishing Corporation for 'L'art, 1910' by Ezra Pound; 'I, being born a woman and distressed' by Edna St Vincent Millay and Norma Millay Ellis. All rights reserved. Reprinted by permission of Elizabeth Barnett, literary executor; Rogers, Coleridge & White Ltd, Literary Agent for 'On the late late massacres stillbirths ...' by Adrian Henri; Carcarnet Press Limited for 'Message Clear' in Collected Poems by Edwin Morgan; The Society of Authors for '*A Passage to India*' by E. M. Forster; Konecky Associates for 'Time Transfixed, 1938' from *Magritte*, 1988; 'yes is a pleasant country' and 'swi(/across!gold's' are reprinted from *Complete Poems 1904–1962*, edited by George J. Firmage, by permission of W. W. Norton & Company. Copyright © 1991 by the Trustees for the e. e. cummings Trust and George James Firmage;

ACKNOWLEDGEMENTS

Seamus Deane for James Joyce's *Ulysses* and *A Portrait of the Artist as a Young Man*; Carol Cosman for translation of 'I am a young girl' from the Old French, from *The Penguin Book of Women Poets*; Faber & Faber Limited and Farrar, Straus and Giroux, LLC for 'High Windows' by Philip Larkin; Smith and Nephew Consumer Products for 'Lil-lets advertisement'; Lancôme for Plate 38; Van den Berghs for plate 39; you fit into me' from *Power Politics*. Copyright © 1971 by Margaret Atwood. Reprinted by permission of House of Anansi Press Limited; *The Guardian* for Frontcover, 26 March 1999; 'if . . .' Words and Music by Neil Hannon Copyright © BMG Music Publishing Ltd/Damaged Pop Music Ltd. All rights reserved. Used by permission; *The Daily Mail* for Frontcover, 26 March 1999; *The Scottish Sun* for Frontcover, 26 March 1999; *The Daily Telegraph* for Frontcover, 26 March 1999; *The Express* for Frontcover 26 March, 1999; Kamala Das for 'An Introduction' in *The Old Playhouse and Other Poems*, Longman, 1973; Ee Tiang Hong for 'Tranquerah Road'. © Hemingway Foreign Rights Trust for 'A Very Short Story' by Ernest Hemingway.

The publishers would like to thank all individuals and organizations for permission to reproduce material. We have made every effort to contact and acknowledge copyright holders, but if errors have been made we would be happy to correct them at a later printing.

Introduction

Over the last few decades intensive and widespread debates have taken place concerning the nature and purpose of English Studies. These debates have often been conducted in terms of theoretical critique and analysis, and important advances have taken place in our ways of understanding the subject-matter of English. But alongside such critique, and in the wake of it, there is a growing need for materials that can help translate such theoretical and analytic insights into practical methods of study, especially for students in the earlier stages of their work. *Ways of Reading* is designed to provide such materials.

Our perspective in *Ways of Reading* is one which places less emphasis on Literature as such and greater emphasis on exploring relationships between, on the face of it, quite different types of text. Examples in this book will be found from the fields of journalism and advertising, film and television, as well as from the field of Literature as traditionally defined. *Ways of Reading*, then, explores non-literary as well as literary texts, at the same time and in relation to each other. In this respect, our use of the term 'text' may be sometimes puzzling. For one thing, we use it not in the familiar sense of 'set text' – one of the canon of great books. Instead we use it more abstractly to refer to the trace or record of a communicative event, an event which may be performed in words but which may equally take place in images or in a combination of words and images. And so, not only do examples discussed in this book come from everyday life as well as from Literature, some of them also include a significant visual component.

Important changes of critical emphasis follow from broadening the range of texts which we examine. Although the texts which we use for illustration and discussion tend broadly to be playful or persuasive in character, we do not focus particularly on questions of relative value, or on issues of tradition or influence. We focus instead on what might be called the rhetorical organization of texts – on how they work to create meanings in terms of identifiable techniques each of which can be described, analysed, and studied. The ability to identify and recognize modes of patterning and rhetorical organization in text is part and parcel for us of ways of reading.

To this end, the book is composed in terms of discrete units, each of which aims at establishing a technique of analysis and interpretation which should prove useful in reading texts whether they are literary or non-literary, verbal or visual. Each unit not only introduces a concept or technique relevant to critical reading; it is also designed to give crucial practice in its use, by culminating in a concrete activity. These activities at the end of each unit are thus as important as the exposition itself, providing simultaneously a test of the concept's usefulness, and also scope for the reader to extend for him or herself, in a practical fashion, their competence in its application.

Although the units are devoted to discrete topics, they may also be seen as working collectively to furnish tools for use in interpretation. As such, they provide a compendium of critical and analytic strategies to enable critical reading. Critical reading, as we envisage it, examines how texts make sense, what kinds of sense they make, and why they make sense in one way rather than another. This is important because – we believe – the rhetoric of texts contributes to the creation and circulation of meanings in society, to the point that we understand the world and our place within it through the texts which we make and interpret. Hence our concern in *Ways of Reading* to relate readings of the text to readings of the world around the reader.

The book is loosely organized into six main sections. Section 1 deals with basic techniques and problem solving, and addresses the most basic issues involved in studying text. Section 2 presents a broad picture of the dimensions along which language may vary, including attention to issues of historical change, gender, and social position. The units that comprise this second section thus help us to see the range of possibilities that provide the communicative background to the particular features and strategies of a specific text. Section 3 considers aspects of the sound patterning and grammar of poetic texts, including ways in which such texts may break with received patterns of construction. Section 4 focuses more on what might be called figures of speech – ways of making meaning indirectly by implication and allusion. Section 5 is concerned broadly with aspects of narrative – what makes a story and how stories are told. In Section 6, the final section, units explore the text's relation to its author and its audience, ways of reading texts as performance, and ways of extending the books' methodologies to reading non-literary texts.

The book is thus structured in terms of certain kinds of progression – from smaller features of texts (e.g. rhyme) to larger features (e.g. story structure); from poetry to prose; from text to context; from practical questions to theoretical questions. But we would not wish to make too much of these kinds of progression. Instead, each unit may be seen as adding to a network of concepts; and, because each unit opens out upon others in different parts of the book, the reader will find cross-references from one unit to another. At the same time, because many of the units can work in a relatively self-standing fashion, it is possible to study or consult them individually without necessarily referring to other parts of the book. In sum, *Ways of Reading* can be used as a class book; for individual study (working through it topic by topic); or for reference (by consulting the index or contents). In this respect we hope that the book will itself be put to use productively in different ways which none the less contribute to its underlying aim: to develop an awareness of reading as a broader process, where reading the word is a part of reading the world.

Section 1

Basic techniques and problem solving

Unit 1

Asking questions

1.1 What happens when we read?

It is common enough, in everyday conversation, to say that we 'respond' to a text we are reading. In the case of a written text, we might occasionally go on to speculate that what shapes our response is a process of identifying meanings for individual words, and working out relationships between those words by drawing on our implicit knowledge of grammar (see **Unit 3**, **Analysing units of structure**). But readers do far more than simply respond to a text in this rela-tively passive, 'building-bricks' construction-of-meaning way. We approach texts *actively*, with expectations of different kinds and at different levels in mind.

Whether we intend to or not, as we read words and sentences in a written text we are looking for patterns and developing interpretive hypotheses as we go along. We select senses, disambiguate words, decide what particular words or expressions refer to, and establish contexts for features of the text by making decisions about the 'speech situation': about who we think is making the utterance, to whom, when and where. We draw inferences about implied mean-ings, fill in gaps in what is explicitly said and seek to make seemingly disparate elements of the text in some way coherent. As we follow these basic interpretive strategies – which apply to all discourse (not just to literary works) – we are further involved in establishing some form of relationship between the text and what we judge to be its discourse-type, or **genre** (see **Unit 17**). We also develop an idea of the text's possible relationship to specific places, times and other texts, by attending to its explicit references and use of **allusion** (see **Unit 16**).

Such aspects of reading suggest a rather different model of the reading process than simply 'comprehending' a text, in the traditional sense of grasping the meaning of its words and sentences roughly in the form in which they might be taken from a dictionary or grammar book. It seems instead that reading involves two complementary processes or dimensions: not only making sense of various aspects of the language, sounds or images of the text itself, but also continuously constructing possible models of the text's surrounding social and historical context, on the basis of our own views about the world and understanding of other possible or likely views about the world.

What is in question here is not some absolute, fixed, or 'true', relation of the text to the world, which we can read off accurately or correctly. Rather, we ascribe meanings to texts on the basis of an interaction between what we might call textual and contextual material: between kinds of organization or patterning we perceive in a text's formal structures, as a piece of discourse (especially its language structures), and various kinds of background, social knowledge, belief and attitude we bring to it.

Such background material inevitably reflects who we are, including the place and period in which we are reading as well as factors such as our gender, ethnicity, age or social class. Readers from different historical periods, places and social experiences are likely, as a result, to produce different readings of the same words on the page. We also take up different stances towards any given text because of our own particular interest in it at the time we're reading. Are we studying the text? Reading it for pleasure? Skimming it for information? Do we intend to try to remember it, write about it, simply pass the time with it, etc.?

Together, these varying dimensions of the reading process, as well as others introduced later in this book, suggest that we bring an implicit (often completely unacknowledged) *agenda* to any act of reading. Ways of reading on a train or in bed are likely, for this reason, to differ from what you will probably do in a seminar room. Note, though, that this doesn't mean that one kind of reading is necessarily fuller or better than another is.

1.2 Agendas for reading in formal studies

Knowing that ways of reading are always goal-oriented does not in itself help you to start reading a text. In fact, it may act as a deterrent. You may feel, for instance, that your personal circumstances and some kind of personal agenda will be exposed to others the moment you begin to share the processes underlying your reading. But if we are to address any particular text, we need to acknowledge that different situations and purposes are reflected in – and call for – different kinds of question we may need to ask as we read. Making as explicit as possible the kinds of questioning which routinely go on at a subconscious level while reading is an essential stage in relating those questions to more public agendas of literature classes and courses.

Often little help is given in this area by prescribed tasks and examination questions set in institutions of higher education. Such tasks can seem to go off in either of two, equally unhelpful directions. On the one hand, questions are often narrow, comprehension tasks, which emphasize retrieving information from the text but fail to engage with inferential, stylistic or historical aspects of reading. On the other hand, questions can be vague and open-ended invitations for your comments and 'response', while offering little or no structure for you to work in, and no link back to how the text may have prompted or constrained your interpretation.

In such circumstances, even in studying you are likely to have to define your own interest in reading a text, and to investigate the text through a set of questions you yourself decide to ask. Those questions will to an extent reflect your own interests and feelings. At the same time, though, in so far as they are explicit and clearly formulated, your questions should enable you to enter into more productive dialogue with the public, institutional and educational agendas of literary studies.

Many people presented with this do-it-yourself approach to reading will say that they would prefer it if one single route existed for all textual investigations to follow: a search for the text's 'meaning' following some pre-given sequence of procedures or tests. It follows from the points made above, though, that meaning could never be uniform or singular in this way. Looking for the meaning or meanings of a text necessarily involves asking a number of different sorts of question – or alternatively just blocking those different sorts of question off in order to settle on a comfortable but significantly reduced, single interpretation.

Diversity in the types of meaning and effect to be found in a text can function productively, as a catalyst to discussion and theoretical reflection. As a general principle, nevertheless, each of the questions you ask of a text you are reading needs to be as specific as possible. Below we list the main alternative kinds of meaning-question.

1.2.1 The intended meaning?

One way of looking for the meaning of a text is to consider what the author meant by it. To speculate about authorial intention, such as Shakespeare's intention in writing *Hamlet*, involves trying to work from what the text actually says into an imagined set of social circumstances possibly very different from your own. In effect, you try to reconstruct the likely meanings or effects that any given sentence, image, or reference might have had: these may well be the ones the author anticipated. In doing this, you make the imaginative leap of trying to gauge an author's beliefs, emotions, knowledge and attitudes, as well as guessing what the author 'had in mind' at the time of writing.

There are obvious difficulties in looking for a meaning in this way. A persona, or invented voice, might have been deliberately adopted, separating what the speaker or narrator of a text says from the writer's own feelings. In plays, novels, and narrative poems, characters speak as constructs created by the author, not necessarily as mouthpieces for the author's personal voice to come through; even the speaker of a first-person lyric poem (the poetic 'I') can be regarded as an invented speaker. In any case, there is no infallible way of verifying an intention. That is largely why the critics W.K. Wimsatt and M.C. Beardsley (1946) dismissed the quest to discover what the author 'had in mind' as an 'intentional fallacy', or unwarranted shift from what the words of the text appear to mean to what we imagine the author meant by using them. Language can escape our intentions, producing not only meanings which were not anticipated, but also slippages or failures of meaning which can be carefully exposed to undermine any seemingly intended meaning or even any coherent meaning at all (see **Unit 24**, **Authorship and intention**).

1.2.2 The text's own meaning?

In this view of looking for meaning (which some critics have called 'objective' interpretation), features of the text itself are taken to be primarily responsible for guiding interpretation. How the text you are reading is organized (what words and structures it uses, how images and ideas are patterned) directs you towards a specific meaning. In this framework, what is important is to focus on details of the language and form. You examine choices of expression and the use of stylistic devices (such as figurative language, irony, paradox), or contrast the ways the text is presented with other, alternative ways it might have been presented (which would have produced different meanings).

If pursued in isolation, however, the search for a meaning which should be predictable simply from the organization of the text runs into difficulties. The fact that texts are interpreted very differently in different historical periods, and by differing social groups or readerships, challenges the idea of an 'objective' meaning determined by the text alone. Interpretive variation suggests instead that the social circumstances in which a text is produced and interpreted, and the expectations readers bring to it, significantly affect – perhaps affect overwhelmingly – what it will be taken to mean.

1.2.3 An individual meaning?

In this view, the meaning of a text is whatever your personal response is to it: what the text means to you as you read it. Texts are suggestive, and connect with individual experiences, memories and associations for words and images. What is valued, therefore, in this approach, is sensitivity in response and direct personal engagement with the text, reconstructing the text in a new form in the reader's own experience.

But many critics, including Wimsatt and Beardsley (1949), have argued that this sort of reading involves an 'affective fallacy', or over-attention to response at the expense of what the words of the text actually say. Concern with personal resonances of the text can displace attention from its structures and rhetorical organization. In any case, it is quite possible that many of the memories or associations triggered by texts will either be stock responses or idiosyncratic reactions which go off at purely personal tangents.

1.2.4 General properties of meaning?

In this view, meaning is seen as primarily something produced by processes involved in reading. Instead of investigating in detail what a given text means, in order to make a specific interpretation of it, emphasis is placed on the mechanisms or procedures by which texts come to mean whatever meanings are attributed to them (for instance, by identifying and contrasting certain themes, or treating particular elements of a text as symbols, etc.). Interest lies in interpretive conventions and social institutions of reading, as well as in theories of reading. Particular readings are valuable to the extent that they offer evidence of general reading processes. Any given meaning, in this view, is only as interesting as the processes through which it was arrived at.

Reading texts in this way, however, can become merely a process of illustrating more general reading processes. Any other text would be almost equally useful or interesting for this purpose. And while reading clearly does involve general processes (making inferences, applying idiomatic conventions, etc.), reading a given text needs also to attend to particularities of its use of language and form and to draw on the specific background knowledge it takes for granted. Readers bring different expectations and ideologies to bear upon different texts; and so readings cannot be analysed exhaustively in terms of discoverable general codes. Besides, our interest in reading texts is hardly reducible to how interpretation happens in the mind of a reader. It is often prompted by concern with the experiences or topics evidently being represented. An adequate analysis of reading accordingly needs to take into some account how our attitudes, values and social priorities are caught up in particular acts of reading.

1.2.5 Shared social meanings?

What a text means, in this view, is what it has meant to different readerships in the past, together with the different meanings it will have for different groups or communities of readers today. Readers of texts form diverse groups; and the shared meanings of these groups change over time, and between places. Understanding the meaning of a text therefore means not only accounting for individual personal responses, but also placing such responses within the social and historical patterns of reception of that text.

In advertising and market research, groups of readers are classified on the basis of variables such as class, age, gender and income (as As, Bs, ABs, C1s, C2s, etc.). In literary criticism, readers are often distinguished on the basis of their imagined relative taste (élite and mass audiences, for example). But readerships can also be identified on the basis of other considerations, including the function reading a given text serves (for study, as a marker of social accomplishment, as distraction from pain or work, as relaxation, etc.).

What makes investigation of the responses of actual readers or audiences especially interesting are the various insights such work can offer into the different uses readers make of texts: how they appropriate core features or statements of a discourse into their own ways of living and preoccupations. Asking questions about the use of texts can link issues about the meaning or interpretation of the forms of texts with larger patterns of social behaviour within which discourse plays a part.

1.2.6 Critical social meanings?

What might be called critical social meanings are formed where a collision or contradiction arises between your personal responses and the meanings that are being made by other people. As an individual reader, you are always also a specific social subject, with an age, gender, ethnicity, class and educational background. By considering these (and other related) aspects of your identity, you can locate your personal responses within larger, social frameworks of a text's reception. Then you can ask questions from a critical or polemic position about the social significance or effects of taking up different viewpoints, reading as a socially engaged rather than detached reader. You can examine not only a culture's established imagery (how particular topics such as race, sexuality, work, religious belief, social conflict, or money are conventionally represented), but also how such images fit in with or diverge from your own sense of how such topics might or should be represented.

1.3 How to get started in ways of reading

These different senses of the 'meaning' of a text are not completely separable from one another. Rather, they form a network of overlapping but fairly distinct viewpoints, from which any search for meaning in a text can be regarded. Historically, different senses of a text's meanings have been emphasized in different schools of criticism and theories, and embedded in different kinds of reading strategy. Listing principal directions of analysis is useful if it can forestall a tendency to assume that one kind of meaning or approach exhausts the interpretative possibilities available to you with regard to a given text.

In practical terms, however, you may find that what you need is not so much a long list of alternative ways of reading as a focused set of entry-points – especially if the text you are looking at seems to resist your usual ways of getting started. As a checklist of catalysts to reading in any (or any combination) of the directions outlined above, therefore, we offer the following list of more specific questions. Each of the questions should lead you into speculations that have to be assessed finally on the strength of the insights and judgements they make possible.

1.3.1 Textual questions

- Is the piece of text you are looking at the whole of the text?
- Does the text exist in only one version, or many different versions? If in many versions, are there likely to be significant differences between them (e.g. as regards spelling, layout, typeface, or even content)?
- Has the text been cut, edited, or expurgated?
- Has the text been annotated? If so, who provided the annotations, and do the annotations direct you towards a particular way of looking at the text?
- How significant an effect is produced by general features of the particular edition you are using, such as its size, cover illustration, author biography or blurb, illustrations, etc.? Are these features integral to the text itself, or are they part of a repackaging of the text, possibly for a new readership or new market?

1.3.2 Contextual questions

- When, where, and in what circumstances was the text written or produced? (See **Unit 5**, **Language and place**)
- Do aspects of the text (such as elements of its narrative, setting, or themes) have obvious connections, especially parallels or contrasts, with the society contemporaneous with the text being produced? (See **Unit 6**, **Language and context: register**)
- Who was the text originally aimed at? Are you part of that expected or anticipated readership or audience? (See **Unit 23**, **Positioning the reader or spectator**)
- Was the originator of the text (author or producer) male or female? Professional or amateur? Native speaker of English or non-native speaker? (See **Unit 7**, **Language and gender**, **Unit 24**, **Authorship and intention**)
- How old was he/she when the text was produced? How does the particular work you are looking at fit into what you know of the rest of the text producer's output? (See **Unit 25**, **Judgement and value**)

1.3.3 Questions regarding the 'speech situation'

- Who is supposed to be speaking the words of the text?
- From whose point of view is the text (poem, film, etc.) being told?
- Who is the text being spoken to?

(See **Unit 20**, **Narrative point of view**, **Unit 21**, **Narration in film and prose fiction**, **Unit 19**, **Writing, speech and narration**, **Unit 23**, **Positioning the reader or spectator**.)

1.3.4 Referential questions

- Does the text contain quotations?
- Does the text refer to particular social attitudes, facts or suppositions about the world, or to particular interests or geographical knowledge?
- Does the text contain specific references to other literary, media, historical, mythological or religious texts, figures or events? If so, do you know what these references refer to?
- Is it likely to be necessary to understand the precise meanings of the references or allusions, or merely their general origin and flavour?

(See **Unit 5, Language and place, Unit 6, Language and context, Unit 16, Intertextuality and allusion**)

1.3.5 Language questions

- Is the text in its original language, or a translation?
- Is it likely that all the words in the text, especially words used to describe key topics or narrate key moments, mean what you think they mean? (Many words have changed their meanings, and may mean something different now from what they meant in the past.)
- Are the sentences generally of the same length and complexity? If not, is the inequality patterned or distributed in any way that might be significant?
- What sort of vocabulary do the words of the text generally come from (Latinate or Germanic; elevated or colloquial; technical or non-technical; standard or regional, etc.)?
- Were all the words and structures current at the time the text was written, or is it possible that some (e.g. 'thou') are archaisms?
- As regards all of the above, is the text consistent, or are there points of major contrast or change within the text? (For example, do different characters or speakers use language in significantly different ways?)

(See **Unit 4, Language and time, Unit 6, Language and context: register, Unit 11, Parallelism, Unit 12, Deviation**)

1.3.6 Questions of convention

- Should the way you regard the text be guided by conventions about the sort of text it is (e.g. satire, pantomime, sitcom)?
- How realistic do you expect the text to be?
- How appropriate or relevant is it to ask how realistic the particular text is (or is this not a genuine issue as regards the type of text you are reading or viewing)?

(See **Unit 17, Genre, Unit 22, Realism**)

1.3.7 Symbolic questions

- Do names used in the text refer to unique, particular individuals, or do you think they may be representative, standing for general characters or character-types?
- Is it likely that places (mountains, sea), weather, or events (marriage, travel) in the text will have symbolic meanings?
- Is the text concerned to relate a specific set of events, or does it function allegorically, representing one set of concerns in the form of a story about another?
- How far could the text's title be a key to its meaning?

(See **Unit 13**, **Metaphor**, **Unit 16**, **Intertextuality and allusion**)

1.3.8 Affective or identificatory questions

- Do you see significant aspects of yourself in any of the characters, voices, or events depicted?
- Do any of the problems, dilemmas, or issues represented resonate especially with your own experience?
- What kinds of idealization or typical fantasy scenario can you see being constructed in the text?
- Do you think any particular aspect of the text is biased or unfair in its representation of some aspect of social life or experience?
- Do any sections or aspects of the text particularly repel, offend, or embarrass you?

1.3.9 Questions of representation

- Is the text typical – for its time, place, and context of presentation or publication – in terms of how it represents its selected themes, or is it significantly different from other treatments of similar concerns?
- Does the text create images of race, women, industry, money, crime, health, personal success or fulfilment, and other socially central themes? If so, do these images seem to you positive or problematic?
- Does the text omit to mention or deal with any major aspects of the topics it deals with, in ways which appear to restrict or limit the viewpoint that the text is offering? Alternatively, does the text treat these topics in ways that are new to you and instructive?

(See **Unit 7**, **Language and gender**, **Unit 8**, **Language and society**)

1.4 Conclusions

As you ask questions of these different sorts, your attention is likely to be drawn to specific, local details of the text. Some of these details will strike you as illustrations of, or as counter-examples or exceptions to, points you feel you are in the process of developing. Either way, such details should stimulate fresh directions for interpretive enquiry. Also, your answers to the questions you ask – even provisional or negative answers – are likely to be accompanied by informal kinds of reasoning or explanation, based on intuitions you have about the text's language or about how it relates to other texts you are familiar with. (This is especially likely to be the case with questions beginning with 'why'.) Patterns of intuition and justification offer the beginnings of critical argument, and can be written down and linked together into larger interpretative or critical responses. (This is the kind of procedure you are asked to follow in many of the activities in this book.)

Generally, asking questions will demonstrate that you already have a wide range of intuitions about any given text you are looking at, simply by being a language user and because you have been exposed to many texts previously. Not having specific answers to those questions (or information related to them) will feel less of a problem once the reasons for being interested in the particular question are identified. Often, being aware of how specific answers might or might not contribute to an interpretation will help you produce an accurate and insightful reading of a text through a process which is pleasurable and also largely self-reliant. In some cases, there may be no answer to the question you are asking anyway. Formulating the question nevertheless offers you a suitable starting-point into investigating an open-ended, fundamental issue about meaning and interpretation. In this way, the value of formulating questions lies in the way it leads you further into the process of interpretation and analysis and so helps you move from the point at which you started asking your questions in the first place.

ACTIVITY 1.1

1   Make a list of questions you feel it would be useful to ask about the following text. Also list the specific pieces of information you feel it would be helpful to know in order to discuss or comment on the text further. Then arrange the questions and kinds of information in your lists under the various different headings presented in the unit ('Textual questions', 'Contextual questions', etc.). Don't worry about answers to the questions, or even about where such answers might be found. Focus instead on what kinds of questions are worth pursuing.

Tranquerah Road

1

Poor relative, yet well-connected,
same line, same age as Heeren Street
(more or less, who knows?),
the long road comes and goes –
dream, nightmare, retrospect –
through my former house,
self-conscious, nondescript.

2

There was a remnant of a Portuguese settlement,
Kampong Serani, near the market,
where Max Gomes lived, my classmate.

At the end of the road, near *Limbongan*,
the Tranquerah English School,
our *alma mater*, heart of oak.

By a backlane the Methodist Girls' School,
where my sister studied
See me, mother,
Can you see me?
The Lord's Prayer, Psalm 23.

The Japanese came,
and we sang the *Kimigayo*,
learnt some *Nihon Seishin*.

Till their *Greater East Asia Co-Prosperity Sphere*
collapsed, and we had to change
our tune again – God Save the King.
Meliora hic sequamur.

The King died when I was in school,
and then, of course, God Save the Queen.

While *Merdeka* inspired –
for who are so free
as the sons of the brave? –
and so *Negara-ku*

at mammoth rallies
I salute them all
who made it possible.
for better, for worse.

3
A sudden trill,
mosquito whine
like enemy aeroplane
in a blanket stillness,
the heave and fall of snoring sea,
swish and rustle of coconut,
kapok, tamarind, fern-potted,
where *pontianak* perch
by the midnight road.

Wind lifts its haunches off the sea,
shakes dripping mane,
then gallops muffle-hoofed,
a flash of whiteness in sparse bamboo
in a Malay cemetery.

Yet I shall fear no evil
for Thou art with me
though the wind is a horse
is a *jinn* raving free
Thy rod and Thy staff
they comfort me
and fear is only in the mind
as Mother said
why want to be afraid
just say *Omitohood Omitohood Omitohood*
                              Amen.

2   When you have completed your list, read the information about the poem
     given on p. 349 This information is taken (and has been updated) from
     notes provided to accompany the poem in the author's *Selected Poems*.
     Consider how far these pieces of information answer questions you have
     asked (or indirectly imply answers to them). What difference would it
     make to reading the poem whether you had access to such information
     at the time you are reading?

3   Now examine questions which remain *unanswered* by the information provided on p. 349. Some of these questions may simply require specific pieces of information that are not provided in the notes. But how many of your questions involve the word 'why'? Consider whether there is a difference between questions asking 'why' and other kinds of question. If so, how would you describe the difference?

4   Finally, consider a more general issue which is implicit in your analysis of this passage: Do all texts rely, at least to some extent, on background information that will be available to differing extents to readers with different cultural background knowledge and experience, in the way that this poem appears to?

Reading

Belsey, C. (1980) *Critical Practice*, London: Routledge & Kegan Paul, Chapter 1.

Durant, A. and Fabb, N. (1990) *Literary Studies in Action*, London: Routledge, Chapter 4.

Eagleton, T. (1983) *Literary Theory: An Introduction*, Oxford: Blackwell, Chapter 1.

Fabb, N. and Durant, A. (1993) *How to Write Essays, Dissertations and Theses in Literary Studies*, London: Longman, Chapter 1.

Furniss, T.E. and Bath, M. (1996) *Reading Poetry: An Introduction*, London: Prentice-Hall, Chapter 1.

Lodge, D. (1992) *The Art of Fiction*, Harmondsworth: Penguin.

Thwaites, T., Davis L. and Mules W. (1994) *Tools for Cultural Studies: An Introduction*, London: Macmillan.

Wimsatt, W.K. and Beardsley, M.C. (1946) 'The intentional fallacy', in D. Lodge (ed.) (1972) *20th Century Literary Criticism*, Harlow: Longman, pp. 334–44.

Wimsatt, W.K. and Beardsley, M.C. (1949) 'The affective fallacy', in D. Lodge (ed.) (1972) *20th Century Literary Criticism*, Harlow: Longman.

Wray, A., Trott, K. and Bloomer, A. (1998) *Projects in Linguistics: A Practical Guide to Researching Language*, London: Arnold.

Unit 2

Using information sources

2.1 Information and reading

To read a text we must decode what the text literally says but at the same time we must bring our knowledge to the text to determine what the text actually means (to us). The knowledge that we bring can be knowledge of history, of the everyday world, of geography, of zoology or botany, of literature, of science – any kind of knowledge can in principle be relevant in making sense of a literary text. When we read Herman Melville's 1851 novel *Moby Dick*, the text (in a parody of the use of information sources) gives us some of the knowledge about whales and the whaling industry which we might need; but there might be other facts about nineteenth-century America which the text does not tell us and which would nevertheless be useful knowledge in making sense of the text. In 1851 Melville might have assumed that his reader would know enough about the Bible to recognize the first sentence of the first chapter, 'Call me Ishmael.' Today many readers will need to consult an information source to tell them this – either the footnotes of a critical edition of the novel, or perhaps a concordance to the Bible. Information sources are searchable collections of fragments of knowledge. They can be useful for our reading when they help us decode the text (to find the meaning of a particular word for example) but their primary importance is that they can help us bring contextualizing knowledge to the text, particularly when we are separated from texts by history or geography and hence have drifted away from the knowledge which might have been assumed for the original readers of those texts.

2.2 Examples of the use of information sources

Information sources come in many forms and include footnotes to a poem, a dictionary of symbols in the library, the *Encyclopaedia Britannica*, the Modern

Language Association bibliography on CD-ROM, or the Internet search engine Yahoo on www.yahoo.com. Information sources have many uses in literary study, and this chapter illustrates some of them. We begin by looking at some sample problems which can be solved by consulting information sources.

1 An old English folk poem begins 'A frog he would a-wooing go'. One question you might ask about this is: why a frog? A useful type of reference book if you are concerned with the meanings of objects is a dictionary of symbols. For example, if you look up 'frog' in de Vries' *Dictionary of Symbols and Images*, you are given the following meanings:

> a frog is amphibious and therefore often ambivalent in meaning; its natural enemy is the serpent; it has a number of favourable meanings – it symbolises fertility and lasciviousness, creation, the highest form of evolution (hence princes turn into frogs), wisdom, and poetic inspiration; it also has unfavourable meanings – in religious terms it is considered unclean, and it is said to have a powerful voice but no strength.

This dictionary also tells us that 'Frogs are great wooers': there are several songs about frogs who go 'a-wooing' a mouse; perhaps a spinning song as the mouse itself is referred to as 'spinning' several times. So we have our answer: frogs are symbols of fertility and lasciviousness, hence wooers. The other meanings do not seem to be relevant here (e.g. creation, wisdom, uncleanness). The next question we could ask is: why does he woo a mouse? To begin to answer this, we could return to the dictionary of symbols. In general, dictionaries of symbols are useful in opening up meanings in a text. Symbol dictionaries are most useful if the symbol appears in a text which is part of a particular interpretive tradition (e.g. many medieval texts use a consistent system of symbolism), because in these cases the symbol dictionary guides the reader towards stereotyped interpretations which would have been characteristic of original readers. Otherwise symbol dictionaries need to be used with appropriate caution; a symbol dictionary which is devoted for example to psychoanalytic symbolism will offer possibilities for interpretation which are suited to a particular way of reading. As a general guide, it is often worth using a dictionary of symbolism to investigate the symbolic implications of natural things which are mentioned in texts: body parts, animals and plants, planets and stars, weather, geographical phenomena, etc.

2 A sonnet by Christina Rossetti (1881) begins with the following lines:

> 'I, if I perish, perish' – Esther spake:
> And bride of life or death she made her fair.

In order to understand the poem, the reader needs to know that Esther is a historical character and to realize who she is. Some editions of the poem will explain this in a footnote, but if there is no footnote, what do you do? Many information sources are useful for finding out about names. A Classical Dictionary lists all the names from Greek and Roman mythology; a Bible Concordance lists all the names from the Bible; and many names are also listed in general reference works like *Brewer's Dictionary of Phrase and Fable*. You need to guess which reference source will be useful. As it happens, *Brewer's* has nothing about Esther, but the Bible Concordance does (i.e. it is a name from the Bible). If you look up 'Esther' in a Bible Concordance you see all the lines listed which include this name, with references to the parts of the Bible where the lines are found; in fact they all occur in the Book of Esther, and you could look at this part of the Bible in order to find out about the character. You might also notice that one line listed in the concordance under 'Esther' is 'and Esther spake yet again', which is echoed in Rossetti's poem in the words 'Esther spake'. So you have found a biblical **allusion** (see **Unit 16**) in the language as well as finding out who the character is.

3 Shakespeare's play *The Tempest*, written in 1611–12, has among its themes those of sea travel, bad weather, the wrecking of ships (and loss of travellers), and the discovery of strange things in distant places. If you want to place these themes in their historical context, you could use an annals, which is a list of events, organized by date. For example, if you look up 1611 in *The Teach Yourself Encyclopaedia of Dates and Events*, you find that in this year the Dutch began trading with Japan, the British explorer Hudson was lost in Hudson Bay in North America, and there were publications of a scientific explanation of the rainbow, a book of maps of Britain, and an autobiographical travel book by Thomas Coryate. These facts may or may not be significant; the point is that it is very easy to find them using this information source (you would have to decide whether to investigate any which seem to be particularly relevant).

Because information sources are random collections of fragmentary knowledge, the risk in consulting an information source (that you are wasting your time) is balanced by the possible rewards (that you might find a richly rewarding clue for very little effort).

2.3 Adapting an information source to your needs: the *OED*

In this section we look at some of the uses of the *Oxford English Dictionary*, the largest dictionary of English vocabulary, first published by Oxford University Press in 1888 as *A New English Dictionary on Historical Principles*. The full version of the *Oxford English Dictionary*, or *OED*, now exists as a second edition in three forms, identical in content: as a collection of twenty volumes published in 1989, as a single volume with tiny print (and a magni-fying glass), and as a CD-ROM.

The *Oxford English Dictionary* is a list of English words which, in certain respects, is very complete (it is most complete for Southern British English); for each word, a number of meanings (all those the word has had in its history) are distinguished, and quotations are given showing the word in use, including the earliest known use. Dictionaries are usually used as guides to the current usage (meaning, spelling or pronunciation) of difficult words, but the *OED* can be adapted to many other uses. We can illustrate this by looking at the first stanza of Percy Bysshe Shelley's 'To a Skylark' (1820):

Hail to thee, blithe spirit!
Bird thou never wert,
That from heaven, or near it,
Pourest thy full heart
In profuse strains of unpremeditated art.

If you look up 'blithe' in the *OED* you will find two appropriate meanings:

Meaning 2: exhibiting gladness ... In ballads frequently coupled with 'gay'. Rare in modern English prose or speech; the last quotation with this meaning is 1807.
Meaning 3: Of men, their heart, spirit etc.: joyous ... Rare in English prose or colloquial use since 16th century but frequent in poetry.

This dictionary entry acts as more than just a definition of the word; it tells us a number of interesting things relating to the poem. First, the word is used primarily in poetry – though in Shelley's poem it might have seemed a little old-fashioned (since 1807 is the date of the last citation for meaning 2). Second, the word is typically used in ballads; a significant fact when we consider that Romantic poets like Shelley were influenced by folk poetry of this kind. Third, it is explicitly associated with the word 'spirit' in the entry under mean-ing 3; the only quotation given which supports this association is in fact one from 1871, but nevertheless there may have been a traditional co-occurrence of these two words which Shelley drew upon. (It is also worth remembering that the *OED*, like any information source, provides only fragments and clues: there might be earlier or later uses of words which are not recorded in the dictionary.)

We could do the same with most of the words in this stanza; we might, for example, wonder how 'hail' was generally used (what does it tell us about the spirit?), what meanings 'spirit' had, how necessarily religious the word 'heaven' was at this time, what the significance of combining 'unpremeditated' with 'art' was, and so on. It often happens that we may have one reason for looking a word up, but will find something unexpected in the process (e.g. with 'blithe' I expected the term to have been old-fashioned, but I did not expect the link with ballads or with 'spirit').

The *OED*, like other dictionaries, can also be used as a 'brainstorming' aid when starting out on a research project. For example, if you were interested in the notion of 'spirit' in Romantic poetry, it would be a good and easy start to look up 'spirit' in the *OED* to see who used the word, what its history up to that time had been, how religious or otherwise its meanings were, and so on. By doing this you are adapting the *OED* to a new goal: you are using it as an admittedly partial guide to culture, as embodied in language use.

Other information sources can also be adapted in a similar way. A concordance, for example, can be used as a specialized dictionary of quotations (all from the same author), or an indication of the words which an author tends to combine together (a Shelley Concordance would tell us instantly whether Shelley uses 'blithe spirit' elsewhere), or an indication of the meaning which a particular word has for an author. Often you need to interpret the facts which the information source presents to you, and use them as a guide to further research.

2.4 Information sources and computers

Information can be stored in a 'hard' copy, such as a book, where it is laid out in a fixed order to be used in particular ways. But increasingly, information is also available in a 'soft' form, as files stored on a CD-ROM or on the Internet. The advantage of using computers to access information rather than reference books can be shown by comparing a Shakespeare Concordance in book form with Shakespeare's complete works on CD-ROM. Both the concordance and the CD-ROM contain the same information (basically, all the lines from Shakespeare's works), but the concordance organizes it in a fixed way – as a list of almost all the words from the plays, each word then having a list under it of all the lines which use that word. Using a concordance, you can find a quotation (if you know one word from the quotation), you can get a guide to where Shakespeare uses a specific word in his plays, and what sorts of meanings the word has for him. The CD-ROM containing all the plays can also be thought of as a compilation of all the lines, and by using appropriate software you can use it as a concordance. The advantage of the CD-ROM, however, is that you can do more complicated things just as easily – for example, you can restrict the type of searches that you ask the computer to do for you: to find all the uses of a word in the Tragedies, or, assuming that the software is sophisticated enough, you could find all the uses of a word in speeches by women, and so on. As another example, many Shakespeare Concordances will not include words like 'and' as key words, but you might be interested in how often and in what patterns Shakespeare uses 'and'. Because the CD-ROM has not been pre-organized as rigidly as the printed concordance, you could search for this word as easily as any other. With computer-searched information, you have greater power to decide for yourself how to organize the information (though you are still governed by the possibilities of the searching software); with a book the information is already organized for you. In many cases, it will not make a lot of difference; it may be more convenient to use the book. But for more complicated or bigger tasks, a computer is useful, since information on a computer can be moved around easily, and you can copy the relevant part of the information source onto your own computer disc or print it out.

2.5 The Internet as an information source

When this book, *Ways of Reading*, was first published in 1992, there was no mention of the Internet in this chapter; though it was possible to use the Internet as a research tool at that time, it was relatively inaccessible to most people. Now it is very widely accessible, there is much more information available, and it can be very useful; in writing this chapter I consulted the Internet (specifically the website of Oxford University Press) to find out how many volumes make up the second edition of the *Oxford English Dictionary*.

The experience of using the Internet is that you sit in front of a networked computer, click on parts of the screen or type in commands or addresses, and as a result receive texts, images, and sounds on your computer. The texts, images, and sounds are all computer files which have been sent to your computer by a computer somewhere else on the network (and in principle on the other side of the world); 'browsing' or 'surfing the net', despite the impression that they give of you as a traveller across the Internet, are actually the opposite – they bring files to your computer rather than send you somewhere else. To obtain a file from a distant computer, your computer needs to send out a request for that file, by stating the file's address, called its URL (uniform resource locator); an example of a URL is *http://homepages.strath.ac.uk/~chcs03 /wor2info.html* which uniquely identifies a particular file which you can copy to your computer by requesting it by its address. You might type that address into a box on the screen or you might click on a part of the screen which automatically states the address; for example, a link on a page contains the address of the file to which you are linking, so if you click on the link you automatically state the address at the same time.

There are millions of texts, pictures and sounds available on the Internet. There are files about authors, recordings of authors speaking, files which contain whole novels or poems which you can copy, pictures of original printings of texts, and of course files which just give any kind of relevant general knowledge. Library catalogues and the sites of bookshops and publishers can help fill out information about a particular book. Contents of journals, abstracts of articles, and lists of articles cited can be found at particular sites. The cost of this richness of information is that you have to know how to find the files you need. One approach to this is to consult a source (printed or on the Internet) which lists the addresses of files which are relevant to your interests; your library might have some suggestions of places to start. The second approach is to embrace the randomness of the Internet by using a search engine. A search engine offers you a file through which you can search for other files by typing in keywords or phrases. You might for example ask the search engine to find files with the phrase 'Call me Ishmael' in them. I have just tried this and have located 451 files containing this phrase; I could now ask for any of these files to be sent to me. The first ten files include: an advertisement for a hotel, a tourism site about Bedford, Massachusetts, an annotated bibliography about Melville, and a page about an artist's installation relating to *Moby Dick*. Within a minute I have found at least one possibly relevant site for the study of the novel (i.e. the annotated bibliography). Searching for a single phrase or word is one possibility, but it is also possible to conduct a Boolean search (i.e. a search for a combination of words or phrases). So we might use the search engine to look for a file which has the words 'frog', 'wooing' and 'mouse' in it; I have just tried this and in about two minutes have located a file which offers me a version of this song and includes a sound file which plays me a traditional melody for the song.

2.6 The unreliability of information sources

All information sources have some inevitable flaws which mean that they have to be used with some caution. Even the biggest information source (the Internet, conceived of as a whole) is a selection from a much larger range of things which might be included; information sources are always selective, and hence fragmentary and to some extent random. And the information that goes into information sources has to be selected by someone, and hence the information is filtered through someone's value judgements and can be altered through someone's error. Thus the basic flaws of information sources are: they are partial, they are partisan, and they may misinform.

The partisan aspects of information sources make them interesting; information sources are themselves cultural artefacts which are worth study in their own right. In Samuel Johnson's *A Dictionary of the English Language* (1755), the choice of words to include, the definitions of words, and the choice of quotations to illustrate them carry value judgements which may be used as a guide to issues in the language and society of the period. The same applies to all dictionaries and other information sources – all are to some extent partisan, though few make this explicit. One information source which does make its partisan nature explicit is Kramarae and Treichler's *A Feminist Dictionary* (1996), where quotations are used as the major form of information about words, and are selected to question the conventional meanings of words as well as to inform about them.

2.7 Information as a hindrance rather than a help?

Information sources are resources to be drawn upon, and can help us in solving problems raised by texts. But there are some cases in which information sources can restrict us. For example, there is a poem by John Donne called 'Community' (1633) about the relations between men and women, which includes the lines:

> If then at first wise Nature had
> Made women either good or bad,
> > Then some we might hate, and some choose,
> But since she did them so create,
> That we may neither love, nor hate,
> > Only this rests, All, all may use.

This poem contains a line which includes the clause 'All, all may use'; one edition of the poem provides a footnote which suggests that the line means 'All men may use all women' in order to clarify what might otherwise seem an ambiguity (it could perhaps have meant 'All women may use all men' or 'All people may use all people'). The footnote here is an information source, but there is a problem in that it may be removing from the poem part of its meaning and effect (it may be that the confusion of gender is part of the poem's meaning – an effect which is potentially destroyed by the footnote).

Some might argue that the use of information sources to direct the reader is illegitimate in all cases, because it interferes with the flow and immediacy of the reading process, and denies the reader the right to interpret a text in any way in which she or he sees fit. Part of the problem with such a view comes from the fact that many texts are read in a context very different – geographically, socially or historically – from that in which they were written, and information which the author originally could assume the reader to know may now not be common knowledge. Christina Rossetti would have been able to assume that her readers would recognize that Esther was a biblical figure and might even have expected them to spot the allusion; but this is now not likely to be true for many readers of the poem. The necessity and role of information sources thus depend on who you are as a reader, as well as on your goals in working on literary texts.

ACTIVITY 2.1

Practice in using information sources generally means working in the library; however, it is possible to prepare speculatively for such work. This activity (which can be done without information resources) focuses on preparation.

Read the following poem by Charlotte Smith (1749–1806):

> Queen of the silver bow! – by thy pale beam,
> Alone and pensive, I delight to stray,
> And watch thy shadow trembling in the stream,
> Or mask the floating clouds that cross thy way.
> And while I gaze, thy mild and placid light
> Sheds a soft calm upon my troubled breast;
> And oft I think – fair planet of the night,
> That in thy orb, the wretched may have rest:
> The sufferers of the earth perhaps may go,
> Released by death – to thy benignant sphere,
> And the sad children of despair and woe
> Forget in thee, their cup of sorrow here.
> Oh! that I soon may reach thy world serene,
> Poor wearied pilgrim – in this toiling scene!
>
> (from *Elegiac Sonnets*, 1784)

Listed below is a selection of reference books, which may be of use when thinking about various aspects of this poem.

1   *Dictionary of Symbols and Images*, by A. de Vries. Select two words in the poem which would be worth looking up in this dictionary, and explain briefly in each case why you think this might be worth doing.

2   *The Oxford English Dictionary*. Each word in this dictionary is given a definition or definitions, and illustrative uses from a range of authors, all dated, including the first known use. Select two words in the poem which would be worth looking up in this dictionary and explain why you think this might be worth doing.

3   *The Collins Dictionary of Quotations*, ed. D. Fraser. Like most dictionaries of quotations, this is organized around key words. Select two words in the poem which would be worth looking up in this dictionary, and explain why you think this might be worth doing.

4   *Dictionary of British and American Women Writers, 1660–1800*, ed. J. Todd. Suggest what you might possibly find in a short biographical entry about Charlotte Smith which would be useful in thinking about the poem.

5   *The Modern Language Association International Bibliography of Books and Articles on the Modern Languages and Literatures*. This is a comprehensive list of critical, descriptive and theoretical publications organized under author and under general topic (you will find it in book and CD-

ROM form in some libraries). One obvious place to look would be under 'Charlotte Smith', to see what work has been done on this author. But you could also search for critical discussions of particular topics; suggest one topic which might be worth looking up references for in order to extend your understanding of the poem.

6   An annals, such as *The Teach Yourself Encyclopaedia of Dates and Events*. List some aspects of the poem which might be illuminated by looking up the dates 1774–1784 (i.e. the ten years up to the publication of the poem).

7   An Internet search engine. What phrase might you search for? What pair of words might you do a Boolean search for? What reason would there be for making either of these searches?

This activity has asked you to speculate about the possible directions you might take, using information sources to investigate this poem. Ideally, you should now go to the library and try out some of your hunches.

Reading

Anderson, E.A. (1982) *English Poetry, 1900–1950: A Guide to Information Sources*, Detroit: Gale Research Company. This is chosen as an example of a large number of books, all subtitled 'a guide to information sources' and published by Gale, which are useful resources for literary studies.

Baker, N.L. (1989) *A Research Guide for Undergraduate Students (English and American Literature)*, New York: MLA Publications.

Durant, A. and Fabb, N. (1990) *Literary Studies in Action*, London: Routledge, Chapter 4.

Harner, J.L. (1993) *Literary Research Guide: A Guide to Reference Sources for the Study of Literatures in English and Related Topics*, 2nd edn, New York: Modern Languages Association of America.

Kirkham, S. (1989) *How to Find Information in the Humanities*, London: Library Association.

Kramarae, C. and Treichler, P.A. (1996) *A Feminist Dictionary*, Illinois: University of Illinois Press.

Thompson, J. (1971) *English Studies: A Guide for Librarians to the Sources and their Organisation*, London: Bingley, pp. 49–74.

Todd, A. and Loder, C. (1990) *Finding Facts Fast: How to Find Out What You Want and Need to Know*, Harmondsworth: Penguin.

Todd, J. (ed.) (1985) *A Dictionary of British and American Women Writers, 1660–1800*, Totowa, NJ: Rowman & Allanheld.

Todd, J. (ed.) (1989) *A Dictionary of British Women Writers*, London: Routledge.

Williams, R. (1988) *Keywords: A Vocabulary of Culture and Society*, London: Collins, Introduction, pp. 11–26.

Analysing units of structure

When we read, see or hear a text, our understanding is guided by a sense of the elements which make up the text (its constituent parts) and how they fit together. In Unit 1, we saw that this sense of constituents is by no means the only factor in reading and understanding, but it is nevertheless one central and important factor. Our intuitive judgement about the constitutive elements of a text provides a basis for larger interpretative hunches and critical reactions. So we can say that texts have a sort of 'mechanics'; they are constructed or built for a purpose and with anticipated meanings. In many cases, the arrangement of textual components involves interesting regularities and patterns, which work towards the creation of meanings and significance. Because of this, it is worth finding out about the units of structure from which texts can be built. The field of stylistics – whether discourse stylistics generally, or literary stylistics – is based on this insight: that interpretations are shaped and guided to a significant extent by perceptions of constituent structure which can be described.

Consider the twelve-bar blues as an illustration. The blues form consists, with some variation, of the following units (among others): three groupings of words, as lines, with the second line a repeat of the first, and with each line harmonically accompanied by particular chords in a given sequence of bars (thus lines, chords, and bars are important units of structure for the twelve-bar blues). Here is a verse from a twelve-bar blues in the key of C.

chords:	C	/ F		/ C	/ C7 /
line 1:	Early one mornin',	/ on my way to the penal	/ farm		
bars:	[1]	/ [2]		/ [3]	/ [4] /

chords:	F	/ F		/ C	/ C7 /
line 2:	Early one mornin',	/ on my way to the penal	/ farm		
bars:	[5]	/ [6]		/ [7]	/ [8] /
chords:	G7	/ F7		/ C	/ G7 /

line 3:   Baby, all locked up / and ain't doin' nothin' / wrong.
bars: [9]   / [10]   / [11]   / [12] /
(Francis Blockwall, written c. 1910–20)

We cannot, of course, be certain that the labelling offered here offers a 'correct' description of the units, or that the list presented is exhaustive or comprehensive. Nor can we take it for granted that the grouping of elements as units matches real distinctions or divisions, rather than simply reflecting categories we choose to impose. Without some notion of units of structure (lines, chords, bars), however, it seems impossible to describe patterning or regularities which distinguish what we recognize as the blues from other forms which would prompt fairly consistent judgements that, whatever they are, they are not blues.

3.1 'Form' and 'structure'

Units of structure are also called **formal elements** or **formal properties**. The terms 'structure' and 'form' are used here to describe the arrangement of elements in a text. But it should be noted that these terms are used in various different ways in the discussion of aesthetic objects and texts.

3.1.1 'Form' as coherence and unity

A different sense of 'form', which has a long history in philosophy since Plato, considers form as an underlying essence or ideal of something which exists beyond its physical manifestation. 'Form' in this sense is something inherent and beyond analysis. The poet Samuel Taylor Coleridge (1772–1834) developed the term 'organic form' to capture the idea that aesthetic form occurs or grows of itself, naturally, rather than being a human or social construct. In New Criticism (an American literary theory at its height from the 1930s to the 1960s), the idea of organic form in literature takes on an added dimension: poetic 'form' is said to involve a complex balancing of potentially conflicting elements (hence New Criticism's stress on irony, paradox, and ambiguity). What unites this sense of form with the Platonic sense is that, in both cases, formal elements are seen as in some sense inseparable from the text as a whole. By contrast, when we refer to formal elements in this unit, we assume that it is possible to extract and examine individual formal elements.

3.1.2 'Structure'

We use the term 'structure' here to refer to the 'insides' of a text: its network of underlying relations which can be discovered by analysis. But it is worth remembering that there is another use of the term 'structure' too, which refers to the text itself (just as a house or a bridge can be called a structure).

3.2 Grammars of language

The most basic way in which a written (or spoken) text is structured is by means of a set of organizing principles called a 'grammar'. The descriptive grammar of a language is a theory of how words can be thought of as different kinds of unit, how those units fit together into larger units (called phrases), and how these larger units combine into sentences. The grammar of English (like all other human languages) appears to be quite complicated, and parts of it are still not well understood. But it is possible, by looking at the most basic elements of the system – words and the different parts of speech which they can be grouped into – to begin to see the scope and power of grammatical description.

If we were to build up a grammatical description of our own, we might begin with a basic rule that says that a sentence is made up of a sequence of units called 'words'. This seems adequate for the following sentence:

(1)   someone lived in a pretty little town

But if we re-order these words, our basic grammatical rule turns out to be only partly reliable:

(2)   someone pretty lived in a little town

(3)   someone lived a in pretty little town

We can recognize that sentence (2) is an acceptable sentence, while sentence (3) is not. Our theory of units, as it stands, cannot explain why (3) is not an acceptable sentence. So, in order to understand why changing the order of words gives these different results, we need to distinguish between different kinds of words on the basis of their different functions in sentences. In other words, we need to divide the basic unit 'word' into a number of sub-units, such as 'noun', 'verb', 'adjective', 'article', and so on. These different sub-units, or types of words, are called **parts of speech**.

Using available distinctions between parts of speech, we can now analyse our original sentence as follows:

(4)   someone   lived   in   a   pretty   little   town
       (noun)   (verb)   (preposition) (article)   (adjective) (adjective)   (noun)

In sentence (3) above, the problem seems to lie in the sequence 'a in pretty'. Using the analysis of parts of speech, this sequence takes the following form: article–preposition–adjective. Since this sequence does not make sense in the above example, we might add a provisional descriptive rule which says that *a preposition does not come between an article and an adjective*.

Rules are only useful, however, if they apply in most cases. So we would now have to try out our rule using other words in the article–preposition–adjective positions. The sequence 'the of happy', for example, also turns out to be a combination which is never found in a normal-sounding English sentence. In fact, we have found a general grammatical rule in English, and so we can safely predict that prepositions never appear in between an article and an adjective.

Not all grammatical rules are as straightforward or as general in their application as this one. But the process of discovering them would be essentially the same. By analysing sequences, formulating provisional rules, testing them out with different combinations of words, and modifying the rules where necessary, we could build up our own descriptive grammar of English and learn important things about the structure and possibilities of the language in the process.

The system of units called 'parts of speech' has been studied since classical times. Some fairly generally accepted names for different parts of speech, together with examples, are set out in Table 3.1 (note that this list of parts of speech is not exhaustive).

Table 3.1 Parts of speech

Name of unit	Examples
Verb	go, went, seemed, give, have, be, am, eat, break
Noun	thing, book, theory, beauty, universe, destruction
Adjective	happy, destructive, beautiful, seeming, broken
Adverb	fast, quickly, seemingly, probably, unfortunately
Preposition	in, on, beside, up, after, towards, at, underneath
Article	the, a
Demonstrative	this, that, those, these
Modal	should, could, need, must, might, can, shall, would
Degree word	how, very, rather, quite
Quantifier	some, every, all

3.3 Literary applications of grammatical description

Analysing a text into its constituent elements becomes useful when it illuminates how the writing of any given text is working. Rather like an action replay, descriptive analysis can examine in slow motion and close detail a process which in composition or spontaneous reading occurs without conscious attention.

3.3.1 Descriptive analysis

The most basic usefulness of the analysis of units of structure in literary texts is simply that it enables us to describe how a text works. Take the first stanza of William Blake's 'London' (1794), for example:

> I wander thro' each charter'd street,
> Near where the charter'd Thames does flow,
> And mark in every face I meet
> Marks of weakness, marks of woe.

This textual fragment could be analysed and described in terms of a range of different units: stanza, sentence, line, phrase, word, parts of speech, etc. An account of the poem might want to describe and discuss the repetition of the word 'mark' in the third and fourth lines of the first stanza; but it would be more accurate and useful to note that 'mark' in line 3 is being used as a verb meaning to see or to notice, while in line 4 it is used (in the plural) as a noun. The analysis would not stop here, of course. It might go on to ask why these 'marks' are being linked through the verbal echo with the speaker's act of seeing ('marking') them. The point here is simply that any such discussion would be facilitated by the analysis and description of units of structure.

3.3.2 Parallelism

By identifying units in a text we can make visible the structure of certain kinds of **parallelism** (see **Unit 11**), for example, the repetition of grammatical structures. Blake's 'London' is highly structured by verbal and grammatical parallelism (as again in the fourth line, for instance: 'marks of weakness, marks of woe').

3.3.3 Descriptions of style

By analysing large stretches of text (or a large number of texts), it is possible to identify characteristic linguistic choices made by individual writers. A writer may show a predisposition towards adverbs, complex sentences, or relative clauses, etc. On the basis of detailed analysis of recurrent structures, it is possible for editors to ascribe a text of unknown origin to a particular author, especially with the help of the sorts of computer analysis of a large number of texts outlined in **Unit 2**, **Using information sources**. Or it is possible to begin to describe exactly why the styles of different authors feel different, irrespective of what is being written about (e.g. the perceptible differences between the writing of Ernest Hemingway and Virginia Woolf could be accounted for in grammatical terms).

3.3.4 Deviation

A grammar of a language is the set of rules for combining units (parts of speech) into sequences. But it is always possible to break these rules in order to achieve certain effects (see **Unit 12**, **Deviation**). Rule-breaking texts can be analysed by looking at which rules have been broken and considering what the individual effects are of each transgression. Consider for example the first line of a poem by e.e. cummings (1940):

anyone lived in a pretty how town

This line seems odd. But we can begin to explain its oddity by showing which grammatical rules it deviates from. The sequence 'a pretty how town' is odd because 'how' is a degree word (see Table 3.1) which appears here in a place where we would usually expect an adjective (e.g. nice, awful, etc.). In fact, the sequence article–adjective–degree word–noun is not a possible one in English. (A parallel example would be 'the stone very houses'.)

The other obvious problem in this line is 'anyone'. 'Anyone' is an indefinite pronoun, and as such might potentially fit into the place it appears in. The pronouns 'it' or 'someone', for example, would be perfectly acceptable before the verb 'lived'. But users of English instinctively realize that 'anyone' does not make sense in the actual sequence of words that cummings has used.

At this point, the reader might either abandon the poem as nonsensical or might try other ways of reading it. For example, it might help to try rearranging the words in order to 'make sense' of them:

how anyone lived in a pretty town

In this new sequence, 'anyone' does make sense in the position preceding the verb 'lived'; and we seem to have the beginnings of an interpretation which would go something like 'how anyone lived in a pretty town like that is a mystery to me'. But if we try to match this interpretation with the rest of the poem, we find that it doesn't seem to work and so probably needs to be abandoned. Alternatively, there is another way we can use the analysis of units of structure in order to deal with this grammatical problem. If we look at the other uses of 'anyone' in the poem, we discover a consistent pattern:

> anyone's any was all to her (line 16)
> one day anyone died i guess (line 25)

Although neither of these makes grammatical sense, we can see that 'anyone' consistently appears in a position in sequences where we would normally expect to find expressions which refer to particular entities in a definite way (e.g. proper names; noun phrases, such as 'the woman'; or pronouns, such as 'he' or 'she'):

> one day (he/she/the man/the woman/Bill/Alice) died i guess

In fact, a close reading of the poem in this way suggests that 'anyone' was a man who lived in a pretty town and married a woman referred to as 'noone' and that they were eventually buried side by side. Thus, we can make a sort of sense of the poem on the basis that it works by grammatical substitution: indefinite pronouns are being used as if they were definite pronouns referring to particular people. The next step in this way of reading the poem would be to ask why it is written like this and what effects it has as a result. The para-phrase given above suggests that if we substituted definite nouns in the place of 'anyone' and 'noone', the poem would seem quite banal. The effect of using 'anyone' and 'noone' is to make the poem ambiguous and poignant. On the one hand, these figures and their experience are given more general signifi-cance (they stand for every man and every woman), while on the other they are anonymous and emptied of individual significance (they are both anyone and no one).

3.4 Extending the notion of grammar

Our discussion so far suggests that the grammar underlying a text governs how it is constructed. We have also suggested that a text's grammatical organiza-tion constrains how it will be interpreted. Accordingly, notions of grammar are essential to the activity of structural analysis, which seeks to make explicit orga-nizing principles which are in our everyday practice of reading texts simply acted on spontaneously and taken for granted.

If we think of a grammatical sequence as a set of slots which can be filled by different items, we can also extend the notion of grammar to other things besides language, such as the possible combinations of clothes. It is possible, for example, to divide the body into zones, each of which can be thought of as a 'slot' within the clothing system: head, upper torso, legs, feet, etc. Each of these areas can be covered with an item of clothing, chosen from a set of available possibilities. These individual items of clothing are the 'fillers' of the slots (e.g. for the feet: boots, shoes, sandals, nothing at all). By examining combinations of items selected, specific styles can be described on the basis of consistency between selections. Deviations from conventional clothing 'statements' can also be described (e.g. the wearing of Wellington boots and a headscarf with a suit).

Or consider a narrative film. The film as a whole will have a number of slots or units of structure: its credit sequence (and possibly pre-credit sequence); the main body of the narrative (including sub-units such as establishing shots, dialogue, car chase sequences, etc.); and end credits. Each of these can be handled in different ways by a director through selecting different options to fill slots and sub-slots (car chases can end in the death of the person chased, loss of the person being followed, etc.). An overall style is produced by manipulating possibilities within each paradigm. By the same token, styles can be analysed by attending to how they use film grammar.

The study of the units of structure (slots and fillers) of a wide range of cultural texts, institutions and ideas (from literature and photography through to the fashion system and what people eat) forms a central part of **structuralism**, a theoretical movement which developed in the late 1950s and which has been very influential in literary studies (see Culler, 1975). The grammar of narrative, for example, which allows us to describe the range of possible slots and fillers for any narrative, has received particular attention (see **Unit 18**, **Narrative**, and **Unit 21**, **Narration in film and prose fiction**).

The rules of what might be called the 'cultural grammars' proposed by structuralism are often described as 'constitutive'. This means that the grammatical rules do not just regulate an already existing system, but fundamentally define what can count as allowable elements within a conventional system that only comes into being on the basis of those rules. It is only by invoking the particular conventions or rules of a game of chess or football, or social behaviour such as greeting or eating in a restaurant, that you are able to recognize the activity as whatever you know that it is. The same may be thought to apply to social institutions such as weddings, birthday parties, money, or law. Structuralism's descriptions gained much of their power and interest not only from this sense of being able to isolate and describe basic structures of how conventional social codes operate, but from two further widespread claims. The first claim is the suggestion, made by many thinkers, that the formulation of grammatical rules in terms of layers of often two-way (binary) oppositions has deep origins in human psychology. The second claim is that the means for describing such systems – considered to be available in linguistic techniques for analysing the grammar of language – would be similar across a very wide range of sign systems.

3.5 Possibilities for analysis

Why should we analyse form or structure? Reasons range from the need to understand how a form comes to have a particular meaning, to the desire to create new forms on the basis of old forms. In many areas of analysis, little work has been done in terms of naming relevant units and working out their possible combinations. So it is often the case that when you analyse a text you can invent your own units and your own rules of combination, if these can be justified in terms of the new ideas and insights they make possible. There are only the beginnings of a grammar of pop songs, for example. In creating such a grammar, we might think of units called intro, verse, chorus, bridge or middle 8, fade, as well as units at other musical levels (riffs, solo, drum fills, hook), and so on. Having available a clearer and more precise vocabulary for describing how such songs are organized than exists at present would be interesting and useful. This unit has suggested that developing one would depend on the same general procedures of analysis (including tests of replacement and movement to identify units and how they function) that have long been used in descriptions of English grammar.

ACTIVITY 3.1 ■■

This activity is based on a plot summary of Charles Dickens's novel *Oliver Twist* (1837). The fifteen sentences which make up the summary have been jumbled up into the sequence which appears below. Each of the sentences describes an event in the novel (so the unit of structure here is the sentence and/or event). To contrast that level with a different level of analysis, sentence 1 in the jumbled sequence has itself been jumbled up.

You are asked to carry out two tasks: first, to rearrange the first, jumbled sentence into an order which makes grammatical and narrative sense; second, to rearrange the sentences/events into an order which makes narrative sense and respects signals presented in the sentences about how they are linked together. The most important part of the activity, however, is that you should justify the decisions you make in your reordering. (The original ordering is given on pp. 349–50.)

1   Try to construct a possible sentence out of the jumbled words of sentence 1 below. Use all the words, and do not use any word twice. Keep a record of how you are able to do this on a more systematic basis than simply guesswork (e.g. which words, or parts of speech, can follow which others; which words are usually found together, as fixed idioms, etc.).

    1   escape and tries Nancy's cry to following hue the death Sikes

2   Now work out a plausible sequence for the fifteen jumbled events listed below. Again, keep a list of the kinds of evidence – especially particular words or expressions, or possible and impossible sequences of events – that you use to help you decide in favour of one particular order rather than another. (It may help if you photocopy the page and actually cut the copy with scissors into fifteen strips, with one event on each, so that you can physically reorder the events.)

When you have done this, try rearranging the fifteen events into a new order, which tells the story in a different way. In doing this, think only of what happens, not the particular wording of the events as they appear in the account of them you have been given. You can refer to a single event more than once (for example, you may want to insert other events into the description of a particular event in order to create a 'flash-back').

Finally, consider how different your new narrative structure is from the one created by the summary you assembled earlier. What are its differences at other levels of structure (for which relevant units of analysis might also be developed): point of view; suspense; thematic interest; chronology; genre; effect?

1   [Write your rearranged version of sentence 1 here.]

2   Keen to take advantage of these offers, the gang of thieves kidnap Oliver from Mr Brownlow

3   The thieves try to convert Oliver into a thief.

4   Nancy discovers that Monks knows about Oliver's true parentage; having developed redeeming traits, she informs Rose of the danger Oliver is in.

5   With Sikes dead, the rest of the gang are captured; Fagin is executed.

6   Oliver accompanies Sikes on a burglary, but receives a gunshot wound.

7   Nancy's efforts are discovered by the gang, and she is brutally murdered by Bill Sikes.

8   Oliver runs away and is looked after by benevolent Mr Brownlow.

9   The thieves become especially interested in Oliver, because they receive offers concerning him from a sinister person named Monks.

10 Found and threatened with exposure, Monks confesses that he is Oliver's half-brother, and has pursued his ruin in order to acquire the whole of his father's property.

11 Oliver falls into the hands of a gang of thieves, including Bill Sikes, Nancy and the Artful Dodger, and headed by a rogue called Fagin.

12 Suffering pain from the gunshot wound, Oliver is captured by Mrs Maylie and her protégée Rose, who brings him up for a time.

13 Monks emigrates and dies in prison; Oliver rejoins Mr Brownlow and is adopted by him.

14 He accidentally hangs himself in the process.

15 Oliver Twist, a pauper of unknown parentage, runs away to London.

Reading

Aitchison, J. (1972) *Teach Yourself Linguistics*, London: Hodder.
Culler, J. (1975) *Structuralist Poetics*, London: Routledge & Kegan Paul, Chapter 1.
Fabb, N. (1994) *Sentence Structure*, London: Routledge.
xLeech, G. and Short, M. (1981) *Style in Fiction*, London: Longman, Chapter 1.
Leech, G. and Svartvik, J. (1975) *A Communicative Grammar of English*, 2nd edn, London: Addison-Wesley, Longman.
Quirk, R. and Greenbaum, S. (1973) *A University Grammar of English*, Harlow: Longman.

Section 2

Dimensions of
language variation

Unit 4

Language and time

All languages change over the course of time. Within a language group, these changes may develop to the extent that the language use of a particular community is significantly different to that of other users. This language use may then be described as a dialect (if those changes are at the level of small differences in grammar and vocabulary), and as a separate language (if those grammatical and lexical differences are significant). The fact of language change is relevant to the study of texts in several ways. A text may be a force for language change or it may attempt to retard a change. A text may become difficult because of language change: it may have meanings, for example, those carried by the use of words and phrases that have become **archaisms**, which rely on an understanding of what the state of the language was at any given time. A modern text may also deliberately use archaisms for particular effects.

4.1 Theories of language change

There are various different accounts of why and how language changes over time.

4.1.1 Formalist theories: change as an anonymous process

Many linguists have described language change as being caused by and working according to structural pressures which are internal to the language itself. For example, between 1500 and 1700 many of the vowel sounds of English changed into other vowel sounds in a process called the Great Vowel Shift. The modern English word 'make', for example, was pronounced in the sixteenth century with a different vowel, a little like the one you get in the modern English word 'mack' if you stretch the vowel out. In pronouncing these words, the tongue is higher and therefore nearer to the roof of the mouth in 'make' than it is in 'mack', so we can say that the vowel was 'raised' from its sixteenth-century pronunciation to its modern pronunciation. Many linguists, from nineteenth-century philologists to contemporary generative linguists, have investigated how these changes relate to each other and to the larger structures of the language. For example, one might classify vowels as 'high', 'mid' and 'low' on the basis of the height of the tongue when it makes them, and we could then say that, in the above example, a low vowel becomes a mid vowel. This change seems to have 'pushed' the old mid vowel to become a modern high vowel (modern 'meat' changed from a sixteenth-century word sounding like 'mate') and the older high vowel to have become a modern low vowel (modern 'ride' was once pronounced like 'reed'). What interests linguists, then, is that there seems to have been a system of interrelated changes which can be understood in relation to one another. Such linguists give a **formalist** account of these changes in language (that is, an explanation in terms of the form or units of structure of the language).

4.1.2 A functionalist account: change as a politically motivated process

There is another view of language change and how to study and explain it which suggests that changes in language result from social activity, in particular from political struggle. Dick Leith (1983) accounts for the Great Vowel Shift by suggesting that the migration of workers into London in the period produced a clash of dialects which induced Londoners to distinguish their speech from the immigrants by changing their vowel system. This particular functionalist account therefore claims that language change is socially motivated, rather than being solely motivated by the formal system of the language itself. A functionalist way of looking at language therefore analyses language change from the perspective of the social values carried by certain usages at specific points in time.

It is possible to combine functionalist and formalist accounts; for example, the Great Vowel Shift may have been triggered and supported in general terms by a struggle for linguistic identity, but the details of the shift – for example, which vowels changed and how they changed – might best be explained in formalist terms.

Political, economic and social change can result in words being pronounced in new ways and given new meanings, and can lead to new words being invented. And it should be remembered that rarely, if ever, do words have one single fixed meaning or pronunciation. According to some Marxist accounts of language, the pronunciation and meaning of words can be a 'site of struggle' when two or more social groups or interests have a political stake in enforcing one meaning of a word or phrase (see **Unit 8, Language and society**). For example, the local government tax levied on property in Britain in the 1980s was termed 'the community charge' by the Conservative

government which introduced it, and 'the poll tax' by those opposed to its introduction. The latter term was coined because it has political implications in
English history. The *Oxford English Dictionary* tells us that 'poll' used to mean
'head' (the current usage associated with voting comes from the poll as a
counting of heads); one reason for reviving the archaism 'poll tax' is because
it is levied on all 'heads' – i.e. on everyone of a voting age. But the term poll
tax is also a specific allusion to the Peasants' Revolt of 1381 which, *Brewer's
Dictionary of Phrase and Fable* notes, was 'immediately occasioned by an
unpopular poll-tax at a time when there was a growing spirit of social revolt'
in England. Thus, the revival of the term poll tax was a politically motivated
gesture which seemed to make an analogy between 1381 and the situation at
the time of the introduction of the property tax. (Ironically enough, the *OED*
informs us that an archaic meaning of poll was 'to plunder by . . . excessive
taxation; to pillage, rob, fleece'.) The success of the opposition to the new tax
can be judged in part by how widely and by whom the alternative name 'poll
tax' was used during the controversy and is still now used, since even on the
radio and television news programmes the terms 'community charge' and 'poll
tax' seem to be used interchangeably, and only the government uses the term
community charge consistently.

4.2 Change and linguistic media

The main linguistic media – the mediums in which verbal language is used –
are **speech** and **writing** (see **Unit 19**), together with various other techno-
logically enabled forms (language can be broadcast, recorded, telephoned,
e-mailed, etc.).

4.2.1 Writing

Before the seventeenth century, written texts varied enormously in terms of
spelling and punctuation. This arose partly from the lack of a central standardization of spelling, partly from the variability and rapid changes of
pronunciation, and partly from typesetting practices like the symbolic use of
capital letters to indicate importance and the insertion of letters to fill out a
line. From the seventeenth century onwards, however, printed texts began to
look more like modern English texts because standards were instituted which
still hold. One of the results of this is that while spellings have stabilized,
pronunciations have continued to change, so that spellings which once corre-
sponded to pronunciation no longer do so. This is one of the many reasons for
the difficulties which all English speakers encounter when writing, since when
English spelling was formalized, it resulted in a rift between the way words
were spelt and pronounced in the seventeenth century and the way the pronunciation of words changed over time.

4.2.2 Speech

It has only recently become possible to record speech as sound; our evidence for how English was spoken in the past is generally in the form of: (a) the reports of contemporary linguists; (b) transcripts of speech, as in trial transcripts; (c) representations of speech in literature and drama; (d) indirect evidence from sound patterns in literature (e.g. rhymes); (e) indirect evidence from informal writing such as diaries and letters.

Speech seems to change more rapidly than writing, partly because it is not codified in the same way, and partly because it is open to much wider cultural variation. Youth subcultures generate a large number of new terms and phrases to mark membership of groups, and more importantly to mark non-membership. Such subculture words and phrases filter into mainstream spoken English or into the written standard only very occasionally. Consider, for example, the word 'wicked' as meaning something exceptionally good which appeared in mainstream pop music via African American youth subculture groups several years ago; today, however, the term no longer appears in the mainstream, except parodically. In the 1960s' subcultures, one of the key distinctions was that between 'heads' (those who took drugs and shared a set of radical beliefs about the world) and 'straights' (those who did neither of these). Today, these terms seem archaic, and indeed, 'straight' has now changed its reference to mean 'heterosexual'.

4.2.3 Twentieth-century technologies and linguistic change

New technologies have brought new ways of using English. This is most obvious with specialized languages like those used for short-wave radio or for telegrams. But it is also true of linguistic practices developed for talking on the telephone or for being a radio DJ. So-called 'BBC English' was a pronunciation standard developed for radio and television.

Electronic mail has resulted in a number of changes mainly centring on questions of register. Because e-mail messages are generally short and sent immediately, a style of writing has developed which is more informal than letters or memos and which does not include formulae such as 'Dear Sir/Madam' and 'Yours faithfully', and so on. Grammatical and typographical errors are often left uncorrected on e-mail messages. E-mail style has more in common with informal notes left for friends or family, and this informality seems to be used even when the person you are addressing is not known to you. This new informality very much accords with recent work by Norman Fairclough which suggests that within British English in general the use of more informal and seemingly more personalized forms of expression is becoming more widespread (Fairclough, 1992). However, other commentators have begun to complain about the supposedly detrimental effects on language usage of 'e-mail English'.

4.3 Some types of language change

4.3.1 Sound

We have seen that many of the English vowel sounds (particularly long vowels) changed as a result of the Great Vowel Shift. But the relics of older pronunciations are still preserved in the spellings of English words which were codified before the Shift was completed. For example, the related words 'meet' and 'met' are spelt with the same vowel letter (because they were originally pronounced with the same vowel sound), but are now pronounced with different vowel sounds. A more extreme example would be the word 'knight', whose spelling reflects a very different pronunciation from the current one; if we go back 500 years we have evidence that the 'k' was pronounced, that the vowel was pronounced more like the vowel in 'neat', and that the 'gh' was pronounced like the 'ch' of 'Bach'.

4.3.2 The arrangement and interrelationships of words (syntax)

In the early form of English known as Anglo-Saxon or Old English (spoken in much of Britain, in various dialects, from about AD 400 into the early Middle Ages), word order was fairly flexible. Some aspects of this flexibility survived into the modern English of the seventeenth century – such as allowing particular parts of sentences (such as the verb or an object) to be moved to the front of sentences. But the fact that this flexibility seems to have survived only in literary texts (it is difficult to find examples of this in non-literary documentary evidence such as letters and diaries) provides one example of the way that literature uses archaism to create literary effects. Vestiges of this flexibility in word order can be found in Wordsworth's writing in the eighteenth century. The first stanza of 'The Last of the Flock' (1798) is given an archaic feel by repeatedly placing before the verb elements (italicized in the extract) which would normally follow it:

> *In distant countries* I have been,
> And yet I have not often seen
> A healthy man, a man full grown,
> Weep in the public roads alone.
> But such a one, *on English ground*,
> *And in the broad high-way*, I met;
> *Along the broad high-way* he came,
> His cheeks *with tears* were wet.

In the first line, for example, a more usual sequence in modern English would be:

I	have been	in distant countries
(subject)	(verb)	(complement)

This can also be thought of as a literary **deviation** (see **Unit 12**) from more usual syntactical sequences.

4.3.3 Pronouns

The history of the distinction between the second-person pronouns 'thou' and 'you' is a revealing example of how language change relates to social change. The *Oxford English Dictionary* tells us that early forms of 'thou' (plus 'thee', 'thine' and 'thy') and 'you' (plus 'ye', 'your' and 'yours') were both used in ordinary speech in Old English, where the distinction was primarily a grammatical one. In Middle English 'you' began to be used as a mark of respect when addressing a superior and (later) an equal, while 'thou' was retained for addressing an inferior. This distinction between 'thou' and 'you' was related to the rigid stratification of society in the Middle Ages. It allowed an aristocratic speaker to distinguish between an equal (referred to as 'you') and someone inferior in social standing (referred to as 'thou'), or to signal intimacy. The lower orders, on the other hand, were required to address aristocrats as 'you' as a mark of deference. In the fifteenth century, the rising merchant classes began using 'thou' to the lower orders. Increasing social mobility and competition between this merchant class and the aristocracy meant that by Shakespeare's time there was widespread confusion about who should use the term 'thou' to whom. The seventeenth-century radical Quaker movement seized on the confusion about 'thou' and 'you' by using 'thou' for everyone, as a political act of levelling. The distinction eventually collapsed, and only 'you' survived. 'Thou' only appears now in archaizing registers, including those of poetry and religion, where it functions, curiously enough, as a marker of respect rather than of inferiority. The King James Authorized Version of the Bible (1611) perhaps influenced this change in the function of 'thou' by having biblical characters address God as 'thou'.

A second distinction between 'thou' and 'you' was one of **register** (see **Unit 6**), since 'thou' was a familiar form of address, whereas 'you' was more formal. Shakespeare's texts often seem to mix 'you' and 'thou' indiscriminately, but the distinction is important in the following exchange between Hamlet and his mother:

Queen. Hamlet, thou hast thy father much offended.
Hamlet. Mother, you have my father much offended.
Queen. Come, come, you answer with an idle tongue.
Hamlet. Go, go, you question with a wicked tongue.

(Hamlet, c. 1600, III, 4, 10–14)

The queen's initial use of 'thou' to Hamlet and his 'you' in return are quite standard choices for parent-to-offspring and offspring-to-parent, respectively. It is the queen's follow-up 'you' which is significant; annoyed by Hamlet's caustic rejoinder, she switches icily to a distancing 'you'.

4.3.4 Lexis or vocabulary (words and their meanings)

The vocabulary of a language can change through the introduction of new terms on the model of older forms (for example, 'personal stereo' describes a new machine by using a combination of already existing words; 'air rage' describes a form of violent behaviour on aeroplanes on the model of word-combinations such as 'road rage'), or through adopting foreign language forms, such as 'pizza' or 'segue'. Vocabulary changes often result from pressures from social change or because of new technological inventions. The vocabulary of computers has been very productive in introducing new terms into mainstream usage (e.g. 'log in/out', 'interface', 'to access', etc.).

4.4 Archaism

A linguistic **archaism** is the use of a particular pronunciation, word, or way of combining words, which is no longer in current usage. The term comes from the New Latin word *archaismus*, meaning to model one's style upon that of ancient writers (*Collins' English Dictionary*). Thus, an archaism is an anachronistic use of a word or phrase. Certain registers are characterized in part by their use of archaism, particularly registers associated with institutions, such as the Church or the legal system.

The Bible exists in a number of different English translations. Until recently, the King James Authorized Version (1611) was the most widely used translation. Many Christian groups and churches have now adopted more recent translations such as *The New English Bible* (1961), partly because it seems more 'up to date' and accessible. A measure of the difference between them can be seen by comparing the language of equivalent passages (I Corinthians 15: 53):

King James Version: For this corruptible must put on incorruption, and this
mortall must put on immortalitie.

New English Bible: This perishable being must be clothed with the imperishable,
and what is mortal must be clothed with immortality.

Although the new version is easier to understand, the old version is still preferred by some Christians, in part because its archaic language seems more mysterious and appropriate to religious experience. Perhaps it is precisely because it is different from everyday language and more difficult to understand that this type of language is deemed more appropriate.

English legal texts are also characterized by archaism. If we take the English Copyright (Amendment) Act 1983 as an example, we find archaisms like 'be it enacted', 'shall have effect', and 'cinematograph film'. The extensive use of archaism in legal texts arises partly from the fact that the law was the last institution to stop using the French and Latin of the Norman occupation (French was still used in the law into the eighteenth century). But it is also due to the fact that legal language has to be seen to be distinct from ordinary usage; lawyers would argue that it needs to be more precise and less open to ambiguity, but it might also be due to the fact that one of the jobs of the legal profession is to be the paid interpreters of this archaic language. (For a more extended discussion of the legal register, see **Unit 6, Language and context: register.**)

There is a long tradition of poetic texts using archaism. Edmund Spenser, writing in the late sixteenth century, developed a vocabulary for poems like *The Faerie Queene* by copying archaic words from Chaucer (writing 200 years earlier). Spenser's language was itself imitated by later writers – especially by Romantic poets such as Keats in the early nineteenth century. Because of this, most attempts to define a poetic register would probably include some archaism as a component feature. Here, for example, is a line from Walter Scott's 'The song of the Reim-kennar' (1822): 'Enough of woe hast thou wrought on the ocean'. Archaisms here include the syntax (word-order) – a modern English word order would probably be 'You have brought enough' – and words such as 'thou', 'hast' and 'wrought'. A more recent poem which exploits archaism is W.H. Auden's 'The Wanderer' (1930), which is explicitly modelled on an Anglo-Saxon poem of the same name and uses Anglo-Saxon word formation patterns, such as 'place-keepers' or 'stone-haunting', and alliterative patterns common in Anglo-Saxon poetry. The first line of the poem is: '*D*oom is *d*ark and *d*eeper than any sea-*d*ingle' which uses a repeated 'd' sound on stressed syllables (see **Unit 9, Rhyme and sound patterning**). In using such archaisms, the poem may seem to explore meanings and values which give the impression of transcending time and place.

It should be added, however, that there is a problem with the identification of archaism, since 'archaisms' are sometimes not archaic in the register in which they are used. For example, 'thee' or 'thou' are not archaic forms in a certain type of poetic register; they are archaic only in relation to our contemporary day-to-day speech. Thus the use of an archaism can be interpreted as either conforming to a register or looking back to the past (or both). One of the questions you should ask, therefore, in reading a text which seems to be using archaisms is whether they are archaic relative to our current usage, or whether they would have been archaisms in literature at the time the text was written. Only by using a dictionary such as the *Oxford English Dictionary*, which is a historical dictionary, giving the meanings of words over time, will you be able to find out whether certain words were current or archaic at the time of writing.

4.5 Feminist changes to language

Recent writers on the relation between language and political and social power, such as Michel Foucault (1978), stress the fact that language is both an instrument of social constraint and a means of resisting that constraint.

This is most clearly seen in recent feminist theory, where language is identified as one of the means through which patriarchal values are both maintained and resisted (for a fuller discussion of this, see **Unit 7**, **Language and gender**). Feminists such as Dale Spender (1980) draw our attention to the fact that there are many elements in language which are sexist and which offend women. Jane Mills' *Womanwords* (1989) is a dictionary which demonstrates the way that words associated with women often have a revealing history of meanings. For example, the word 'glamour' once meant 'magical strength', and was used to refer to both men and women; however, when the word began to be used for women alone it took on sexual and trivializing connotations, as in 'glamour girl'. A similar trajectory can be noted for words like 'witch', which was once used for both men and women and started to acquire negative connotations once its usage was restricted to referring to women. It would be hard to identify a particular individual or group responsible for such changes; rather, we interpret them as occasioned by the ideological and discursive structures which make up what feminists generally call 'patriarchy' (i.e. the economic, social and political norms within a society whose end result is that women are treated as if inferior to men).

To counter this verbal discrimination against women, some feminists have attempted to reform the language in a variety of ways. For example, offensive or discriminatory terms can be replaced by more neutral terms: 'chairperson' can be used instead of 'chairman'; 'humankind' instead of 'mankind'; 'staff' instead of 'manpower', and so on. A different strategy adopted by other feminists is to modify existing words (e.g. 'wimmin' to refer to women, so that the term does not appear to have been formed with reference to 'men') or to coin new words (such as 'herstory' rather than 'history' – his story) in order to mark the separation of their work and themselves from patriarchal forms of thought. Mary Daly (1978) argues that old derogatory words should be used in new positive ways: for example, she uses the words 'crone', 'dyke' and 'virago' to refer to strong women and lesbians. In Daly's work especially, this process is quite playful and shows little respect for conventional etymology.

However, as Deborah Cameron (1985) has noted, although it is possible to make changes in language on a small scale, getting the changes adopted more generally is not so easy. This is partly because the changes have to go through what she calls 'the gatekeepers of language' – i.e. institutions such as the media, education, the government, lexicographers, and so on – which tend to be resistant to the type of changes feminists wish to introduce. Changes which feminists wish to make may also be labelled mere 'political correctness' by their detractors (Dunant, 1994). However, as Cameron makes clear, one of the effects of this debate about the negative connotations of gendered terms is that within the public sphere at least sexist terms are now largely unacceptable. In addition, those who wish to continue to use terms such as 'chairman' for women will be viewed as making clear statements about their beliefs:

> By coining alternatives to traditional usage, the radicals have effectively politicised all the terms. They have made it impossible for anyone to speak or write without appearing to take up a political position for which they can then be held accountable.
>
> (Cameron, 1994: 31)

The more general point which emerges from this is that, for the most part, changes in language occur outside the conscious control of particular individuals or groups. Even when 'the gatekeepers of language' attempt to resist or introduce change there is no guarantee that they will be successful: British and American history furnishes many examples of failed attempts to reform the language according to some arbitrarily imposed standard (see Cameron, 1995). The concerted efforts by anti-racist, feminist and gay and lesbian activists, however, have shown that pressure groups can effect change in language, though not necessarily bringing about precisely the changes that they envisaged or hoped for.

ACTIVITY 4.1

This activity uses two poems (Lord Byron's 'If that high world' of 1814, and Philip Larkin's 'High windows' of 1974) in order to make some provisional observations about differences in language and poetic conventions between 1814 and 1974.

1   On the evidence of Byron's poem (printed below), list the language-related conventions which appear to have held for poetry around 1814 (e.g. use of archaism, choice of words, order of words, metre, rhyme, visual layout of the lines, etc.).

2   On the evidence of Larkin's poem (printed below), list language-related conventions which appear to have held for poetry in 1974.

3   Using the evidence you have gathered, make a list of the changes in poetic
     language between the two poems and a list of what does not seem to
     have changed.

4   Prevailing conventions constrain what we say, but they also enable us to
     say things in particular ways. Compare the two sets of conventions, and
     try to classify them for each poet into limiting and enabling conventions;
     in each case justify your decision (e.g. if you think Byron's use of rhyme
     is enabling while Larkin's use of rhyme is limiting, explain why).

If that high world

I

If that high world, which lies beyond
Our own, surviving Love endears;
If there the cherished heart be fond,
The eye the same, except in tears –
How welcome those untrodden spheres!
How sweet this very hour to die!
To soar from earth and find all fears
Lost in thy light – Eternity!

II

It must be so: 'tis not for self
That we so tremble on the brink;
And striving to o'erleap the gulf,
Yet cling to Being's severing link.
Oh! in that future let us think
To hold, each heart, the heart that shares;
With them the immortal waters to drink,
And soul in soul, grow deathless theirs!

                              (Lord Byron, 1814)

High windows

When I see a couple of kids
And guess he's fucking her and she's
Taking pills or wearing a diaphragm,
I know this is paradise

Everyone old has dreamed of all their lives –
Bonds and gestures pushed to one side
Like an outdated combine harvester,
And everyone young going down the long slide

To happiness, endlessly. I wonder if
Anyone looked at me, forty years back,
And thought, *That'll be the life;*
No God anymore, or sweating in the dark

About hell and that, or having to hide
What you think of the priest. He
And his lot will all go down the long slide
Like free bloody birds. And immediately

Rather than words comes the thought of high windows:
The sun-comprehending glass,
And beyond it, the deep blue air, that shows
Nothing, and is nowhere, and is endless.

(Philip Larkin, 1974)

Reading

Barber, C. (1976) *Early Modern English*, London: André Deutsch.

Cameron, D. (1985) *Feminism and Linguistic Theory*, London: Macmillan, pp. 79–90.

Cameron, D. (1994) 'Words, words, words: the power of language', in S. Dunant (ed.) *The War of the Words: The Political Correctness Debate*, London: Virago, pp. 15–35.

Cameron, D. (1995) *Verbal Hygiene*, London: Routledge.

Daly, M. (1978) *Gyn/ecology*, London: Women's Press.

Dunant, S. (ed.) (1994) *The War of the Words: The Political Correctness Debate*, London: Virago.

Fairclough, N. (1992) *Discourse and Social Change*, London: Polity Press.

Foucault, M. (1978) *The History of Sexuality*, vol. 1, Harmondsworth: Penguin.

Jeffers, R. and Lehiste, I. (1979) *Principles and Methods for Historical Linguistics*, Cambridge, MA: MIT Press.

Leech, G. (1969) *A Linguistic Guide to English Poetry*, London: Longman, pp. 1–19.

Leith, D. (1983) *A Social History of English*, London: Routledge & Kegan Paul, pp. 32–57.

Mills, J. (1989) *Womanwords*, London: Longman.

Spender, D. (1980) *Man Made Language*, London: Routledge & Kegan Paul, pp. 28–36.

Vološinov, V.N. (1973) *Marxism and the Philosophy of Language*, New York: Seminar Press.

Unit 5

Language and place

Texts can create a sense of place in two main ways. They can describe places, as happens most clearly in various types of travel writing. In novels, the effect of description of this general kind is what we think of as 'setting'. In many cases, such as the description of Egdon Heath at the beginning of Thomas Hardy's *The Return of the Native* (1878), or Emily Brontë's Yorkshire Moors in *Wuthering Heights* (1847), place provides both a geographical background and a major symbolic dimension of the narrative. Alternatively, place can be represented in texts through the particular ways in which characters (and some-times narrators or poetic personae) are made to speak. This latter way of representing place is possible because of connections we typically make, as readers or listeners, between distinctive properties of voices (in terms of accent and dialect) and the places with which they are associated.

Creating a sense of place in texts by incorporating regional mannerisms of speech can be more problematic than descriptions of place. The represen-tation, in a written text, of different kinds of regional voice calls on our ability to recognize differences of grammar, vocabulary and pronunciation. It also asks us to make associations between these differences and the way speakers are supposed to speak in different places. Representation of dialect or accent thus draws on conventional images and connotations for the varieties of language we encounter, since it is these images and connotations which make possible our response to imagined sounds of speech in terms of a (sometimes very vivid) sense of place. Such images are nevertheless inevitably to some extent stereo-typical. They not only permit an association of voice with place, but also trade on received ideas that some regional voices are more naïve, stranger, rougher, more erotic, or more authoritative than others.

To investigate how we read this conventional 'imagery' of different voices in texts, we need to examine how variation in language correlates with place. Then we can explore how such variation is manipulated in literary, non-literary and media texts as a significant resource or technique.

5.1 Language variation and varieties

The many languages of the world are related to each other in families (Indo-European, Dravidian, etc.). The family structure of languages involves overlapping and historically connected varieties, which in many cases have loaned each other words, sounds and structures. Even within what is called a single language, there is typically variation from region to region, as well as between classes, ethnic groups, and genders.

5.1.1 Dialect and accent

Variation within a language can involve differences in the sound system, when speakers from a particular region (or social group) consistently pronounce words in different ways from other groups. Examples of this type of variation are the words 'rather', 'farmer' and 'such', which are all pronounced differently in different parts of Britain. 'Tomato', 'vase' and 'dynasty' differ between British and American English; and 'nothing', 'hotel' and 'west' all differ between British English and Indian English.

Alongside differences in pronunciation, there can also be consistent differences in other aspects of the language. Different words are used in different places to refer to equivalent things or ideas. The word 'throat', for example, varies with 'gullet', 'throttle', 'thropple' and 'quilter' in different parts of Britain. A 'faucet' is what American English speakers call a 'tap'; 'pants' are 'trousers'; 'suspenders' are equivalent to 'braces'. A 'cot' in India is an adult 'bed', not, as in British English, a child's bed. In South Africa, a 'robot' is a traffic light, as well as an automaton. 'Outwith' in Scotland means the same as 'outside' or 'beyond' in England. Dialect maps of such variation can be drawn to show the traditional geographical distribution of different words representing the same (or closely similar) meanings.

Differences also occur in grammar. Scottish English 'the potatoes need peeled' matches Southern English English 'the potatoes need to be peeled'. Yorkshire 'thou knowest' parallels Southern English English 'you know'. American English 'they did it Monday' parallels British English 'they did it on Monday'. British English 'I didn't like it either' matches Indian English 'I didn't like it also'.

When variations according to place are found exclusively in pronunciation, we speak of different **accents**; when variation according to region occurs simultaneously at the level of sound, vocabulary and grammar, we speak of different **dialects**. It is possible, therefore, to speak of a Yorkshire accent, if we are referring only to pronunciation, or of a Yorkshire dialect if we are referring to all the ways language in Yorkshire varies in relation to other regions. Similarly, we can speak of a 'West of Scotland' accent or dialect, and of a 'South East of England' accent or dialect.

The issue is complicated, however, by the fact that language also varies according to class (and to a lesser degree, according to subculture and profession). Because these variations affect vocabulary and grammar as well as pronunciation, it is therefore also possible to speak of class dialects and social dialects, as well as accents (see **Unit 8, Language and society**). The relation between regional dialects and social dialects is variable. Sometimes they reinforce one another; sometimes one will override the other. For example, the language of the upper classes in Scotland is likely to have more in common with that of the equivalent social group in England than with that of working-class speakers in Scotland.

5.1.2 Attitudes towards variation

What makes issues of accent and dialect important, both in social interaction and as regards ways of reading, is that attitudes to different varieties are not equivalent. Such attitudes are often based on stereotypical contrasts between the localities the accents are historically associated with, for instance the contrast between rural and industrial. They also rely on our ability to 'place' a language variety in such conventionalized terms. (When this is not possible, and judgement is made simply on the basis of the sound itself rather than on the basis of attached social knowledge, such stereotypical views tend to evaporate.) Conventional attitudes towards different language varieties also rely on a notion of 'standard' pronunciation or grammar. The 'standard' variety is the one which is given most prestige. Pronunciation or grammar that are thought to stray from it are implicitly compared with it, and as a result perceived as 'non-standard'.

One limitation of stereotypical views about accent and dialect is that, although they seem to be attuned to variation, they tend to be insensitive towards actual variations: do all working-class people really sound the same? Or all Americans? Or all Scots? Or all Nigerians? Or all English people? The further from a person's own experience someone else's variety is, the less precise intuitions about it – and about the contrasts it enters into with other varieties – are likely to be. (This insight is easily tested by considering how much accent differentiation you can confidently match with social distinctions in television programmes or films produced in some part of the English-speaking world relatively distant from where you live.)

5.1.3 Variety-switching: the repertoire available to individual speakers

While it seems clear that language varies according to the regional and social identity of the user, this does not mean that there is strict consistency in the variety which an individual speaker or writer uses. In different situations, or when talking about different topics, a speaker will automatically modify his or her language. Speakers shift – in response to subtle changes in situation and relationship – between different areas of the linguistic repertoire available to them. Variations which arise according to situation of use, rather than according to the identity of the user, are known as **registers** (see **Unit 6**). Speakers who are able to use more than one dialect are in fact able to manipulate these dialects as if they were registers, changing between them to achieve specific effects in any given situation (e.g. of appropriacy or marked inappropriacy). This type of shifting is especially common between a regional and a 'standard' variety (for a literary example of this, see the discussion of *Lady Chatterley's Lover* in **Unit 8**, **Language and society**).

5.2 Variations and varieties of English

Disparities in attitudes towards varieties of English are partly a consequence of the history of the language. Virtually all languages involve hierarchies between regional varieties, but the detail is different in each case. Variation is created by, and later remains left over from, historical, social and political changes in the society; and different amounts of prestige (as well as the social benefits which follow from such prestige), or what has been called symbolic capital (Bourdieu, 1991), attach to the respective varieties. As we saw in **Unit 4**, **Language and time**, the linguistic and social dimensions of language variation are deeply entangled.

5.2.1 History: the British Isles

Throughout their history, the British Isles have been host to many different languages, including Gaelic, Welsh, Anglo-Saxon, Latin, Norman French, Punjabi, Chinese, etc. The number of languages in regular use (as well as the number of users of each language) has been reduced at different times by military conquest, by legal and educational suppression, and by the emerging prestige of one language or variety as compared with others.

During the sixteenth and seventeenth centuries, English spelling was regularized and aspects of the grammar were codified, bringing the question of language standardization itself openly into critical debate. The continuing complexity of relations between varieties of English in modern times bears the marks of this history, even though present users of the language are generally familiar only with contrasts between current varieties, not with the history which brought them into being or determined their relative status (see McCrum *et al.*, 1986).

5.2.2 History and geography: the English-speaking world

In the English-speaking world beyond Britain, variation within Indian English, American English, Nigerian English and Jamaican English – to take only a few instances – correlates not only with regional differences (and, in cases of bilingualism, with the first languages of the speakers); it also relates to social and educational inequalities between metropolitan and outlying regions, and between industrialized urban classes and rural classes. In many of these societies, the presence of English results from an imperial history which imposed English on the indigenous population. But processes of decolonization have led to changes in language which give new prestige to regional varieties, so producing new standard varieties (such as American English or Indian English) which are nevertheless divergent from British English.

The legitimacy of these emergent 'standard' varieties is not universally recognized. In many of these countries, in fact, continuing tensions surround the use of English, which is widely viewed as being at a crossroads between residual prestige (as a left-over, imposed colonial language), and an ascendent prestige (as an increasingly essential, global language of access to information and communication technologies). Within many such countries, despite these continuing conflicts over linguistic and cultural values, English functions as a crucial marker of class and agent of social mobility.

5.2.3 Received Pronunciation

In terms of pronunciation, the major phase of standardization in English comes much later than it does in spelling, grammar or punctuation. It is only during the nineteenth century – mainly through the influence of English public school education, and the role of the army officer corps – that one accent emerges as a non-regional prestige form: 'Received Pronunciation'. This accent, which is itself undergoing changes (and has taken on increasingly negative connotations in the context of the changing social and class structures of the society), is most closely connected with the dialect of English spoken in south-east England ('Educated Southern British English'). In this respect, standardization in speech has followed the pattern established by earlier standardization of the written system (influenced as that was by the location of the royal court, and the political, legal and commercial institutions).

5.3 Language variety in literary texts

Historically, the language in which literary texts might be written in Britain has been a troubled question. Quite apart from the issue of Welsh and Gaelic, it is also worth noting that, before the sixteenth century, Latin and French were serious competitors to English; and in the sixteenth century itself, English was not always thought good enough for literary work (though writing in it did take place).

During the period of the late Elizabethans and early Jacobeans, the attitude that English might not be good enough for literary work gradually changed (partly in celebration of existing writing in English, partly because of attitudes towards Latin during the Reformation). A major part was played in increasing the relative prestige of English as a literary language by Sir Philip Sidney's *An Apology for Poetry* (1595), which explicitly argued that, while England had only produced a small number of poets of merit writing in English, the language was nevertheless a good enough language (in fact, the most apt of what Sidney calls the 'vulgar' languages) for poetry to be written in. Little more than a century after Sidney, English was widely believed to have produced an especially eminent literature. Many of the (often vigorous) arguments about which language to use in many parts of the world today thus have, despite their otherwise vast differences, an analogue in the circumstances of English in Britain during the later medieval and early Renaissance period.

5.3.1 Dialect representation

In the history of literary writing in English, there have been clear but shifting constraints on which variety or varieties might be used and how. A criterion of decorum was often invoked as a standard of appropriate style within a **genre** (see **Unit 17**), so excluding a wide range of voices from serious literary writing. On the basis of conventions of this kind, dialect speakers were represented in many works only as comic characters, with jokes (including many jokes specifically about dialect) made at their expense.

As regards the representation of regional voices in written texts, it is of course important to remember that accent and dialect are primarily features of speech rather than writing. The representation of speech in writing does not reproduce the way people actually speak, but instead draws on a set of conventions which produce an illusion of speech (see **Unit 19**, **Writing, speech and narration** and **Unit 26**, **Literature in performance**). Representation of dialect speech in writing draws on a further set of specialized (but never formalized) conventions, including non-standard spellings, which are meant to signal that a character's speech is different from that of other characters in the text.

Conventions surrounding dialect representation do not only concern the manner of representing particular sounds, however. Differences in the way 'standard' and 'non-standard' voices are represented tend to set up a hierarchy of voices within a literary work. In nineteenth-century novels, for instance, the narrator and central characters will usually use 'standard' English, while regional or working-class characters – often minor characters in narrative and thematic terms – may speak with an accent or in dialect. This raises the question whether non-standard speech is used in order to reproduce the way such people actually spoke in the place where the novel is set, or whether such use aims simply to give an aura of authenticity or to signify a difference of class or moral authority (see **Unit 8**, **Language and society**).

Consider the novels of Thomas Hardy in this respect. In Hardy's novels the construction of a sense of place is central; they are set in 'Wessex' – his fictional name for the Southwest of England – and are peopled with rural characters who speak in West Country dialect. Within this setting, however, Hardy typically explores the fate and fortune of middle-class characters whose speech is more standard than that of the rural characters. *The Mayor of Casterbridge* (1886), for example, centres on the rise and fall of Michael Henchard (from destitute rural worker, to mayor, and back to destitution). In the following scene, Henchard chastises one of the workers on his farm for being late in the mornings:

> Then Henchard . . . declared with an oath that this was the last time; that if he were behind once more, by God, he would come and drag him out o' bed.
>
> 'There is sommit wrong in my make, your worshipful!' said Abel, '. . . I never enjoy my bed at all, for no sooner do I lie down than I be asleep, and afore I be awake I be up. I've fretted my gizzard green about it, maister, but what can I do? . . .'
>
> 'I don't want to hear it!' roared Henchard. 'To-morrow the waggons must start at four, and if you're not here, stand clear. I'll mortify thy flesh for thee!'

The worker's dialect is rendered here through non-standard spelling ('maister'), non-standard grammar ('no sooner do I lie down than I be asleep'), and dialect phrases ('I've fretted my gizzard'). But of more interest is that Henchard, in his anger, 'lapses' into dialect (and/or biblical language) in a way that reminds us of his origins ('thee' and 'thy' remain in use in dialects long after their disappearance from Standard English). The narrative voice reinforces this, by introducing Henchard's first comments in standard English using **indirect speech** ('Henchard . . . declared with an oath that this was the last time') and then switching into **free indirect speech** in order to let Henchard's own, non-standard speech come through: 'by God, he would come and drag him out o' bed'. (For a discussion of 'indirect' and 'free indirect speech' see **Unit 19, Writing, speech and narration**.)

5.3.2 Modernist polyphony

It is one of the distinctive features of Modernist writing that a wider range of voices is sometimes presented than was usual (or even possible) in earlier literary works in English. In many cases, this introduction of a wider range of voices takes the form of variety switching (as in James Joyce's *Ulysses* (1922)), or of juxtaposition (as in T.S. Eliot's *The Waste Land* (1922)). But a fundamental question about dialect representation then arises: do these texts introduce representation (or mimicry) of regional and class voices as a fundamentally new kind of polyphony, in which each voice has become equal? Or do they simply present a wider range of voices in order for those voices to be finally subordinated to, or refined or distilled into, a reaffirmed, authoritative standard voice of the narrator or poetic persona? (The second of these alternatives is directly arguable with respect to T.S. Eliot's *The Waste Land*; for a discussion of this issue in *Ulysses*, see **Unit 6, Language and context: register** and **Unit 15, Juxtaposition**.)

What seems especially significant in experimental writing of this period is that regional varieties are often used as much to create a visible (or 'visible–audible'), schematic contrast between standard and non-standard English as for their own qualities. Only in forms of dialect writing linked to an expressed sense of regional identity (as in much twentieth-century Scottish writing) does dialect function less in terms of contrast with the established standard than in order to affirm a distinct regional idiom.

5.3.3 Dialect and accent in media

Film and television have inherited, and helped maintain, the legacy of associating character stereotypes with particular accents or dialects. The simple fact of mass exposure in media, however, can alter the standing of entire dialects and accents. Soundtracks of Hollywood films in the 1930s, for instance, were sometimes thought incomprehensible in Britain – a fact hardly believable now. US radio announcers imitated British accents until around 1930, before the conventions of what has come to be called the 'network standard' variety of American English were established. It is only more recently, most obviously in contemporary pop music, that the trend of transatlantic influence has been to some extent reversed (though many pop songs continue to be sung in a 'mid-Atlantic' voice).

As regards British dialects and accents in particular, exposure to regional and class varieties on radio and television is still increasing, largely as a consequence of reduced use of – and changing public attitudes towards – Received Pronunciation (the 'BBC accent'). This shift is reinforced by a more general shift in perception of broadcast discourse from being viewed as public, mass address to the nation towards being seen as informal voices being allowed or welcomed into a viewer's or listener's home. Received Pronunciation, coupled with a formal register of public speaking, appears less well suited to these developments in TV and radio broadcasting.

Changes such as these have already had a significant effect on accent connotations and stereotypes. Despite the overall trend in programme output as a whole towards including increased amounts of dialect speech, however, news broadcasting is still mostly presented by speakers who approximate to Received Pronunciation, even on regional television. It remains unclear how emergent, multi-channel television environments will affect the complex network of accent and dialect significance in future.

5.3.4 Accents, dialects and the future

Given the increasing pervasiveness of media, some critics argue that distinctions created by accent are likely to be minimized – and may even disappear – following increased exposure to a wide range of class and regional voices in radio, television, and other media. Perhaps equally likely, though, is that accents may only alter in relative prestige and connotation, taking on new and different meanings as a result of changes in the images of self and social class to which people aspire, rather than losing such distinctions altogether. The network of attitudes towards accent and dialect in societies at large will almost certainly continue to be reflected – as well as challenged in many kinds of dramatic work, polemical or oppositional music and song, comedy and satire – across the range of media programming.

5.4 Writing in English

In many post-colonial societies whose current use of English is largely a legacy of British imperialism, the idea of using English at all in creative writing is contentious. Some writers, such as the Kenyan novelist and dramatist Ngugi wa Thiong'o, have argued that using the former colonial language reinforces the power of emerging neo-colonial élites at the expense of developing a self-confident and emancipated local or national literature. Building local readerships, in this view, is thought more valuable than representing (in this case African) social experience to a predominantly non-African audience spread around the English-using world. Other writers have argued, by contrast, that the linking function of a language like English enables different communities (including different African communities) to become more aware of each other. In this view, using English in literary and other contexts opens up new possibilities for redefining the relations between African communities in a way which would be impossible if they were to remain separated by walls of linguistic incomprehensibility.

Traditions of writing in English which use and affirm a value for dialect voices – as in a great deal of writing in India, Anglophone Africa, the Philippines, Malaysia, the Caribbean, and many other places – engage in different ways with these complex issues. New, often more complex and polyglot notions of self-expression are created; and new techniques for representing places and ways of life are devised.

In some cases, critical arguments for using dialect are formulated in terms of an idea of authenticity, or aspiration to present an accurate or true representation of the writer's own identity (see **Unit 24**, **Authorship and intention**). In other, contrasting cases, dialect is viewed more as a kind of anti-language, or mode of expression deliberately adopted to mark it off from other, dominant traditions of writing that are implicitly being rejected. In both cases, texts using such varieties – in this respect like any text – are viewed differently when they are read by readers in places outside the region or country in which the variety represented is used.

In Britain, dialect writing – and writing which mixes across the range of varieties which make up the collective linguistic experience of the population – challenge established ideas that it is only standard forms of the language which are appropriate to serious creative work. The regional, class and ethnic diversity of the British population ensures that there are many quite different experiences of place, as well as changing and unpredictable connections between voice, region and sense of identity.

Reading off a sense of place from a represented accent or dialect, accordingly, rarely involves a simple act of locating the writer, in the way that depictions of landscape or scenery may. Instead, it involves engaging with a set of complex relationships between the variety represented, conventional attitudes towards that variety, the reader's own attitudes and variety, and the way the variety in question is used either to reinforce or to disrupt conventional treatments of the subject-matter it represents.

ACTIVITY 5.1 ━━━━━━━━━━━━━━━━━━━━━━━━━━━━━━━━━━━

It could be argued that, although dialects are associated with place (among other things), they do not actually represent place. After all, people move from place to place, and take their dialect with them. So even though a dialect may evoke a place for a listener or reader, it is more a characteristic of the speaker or writer than of the fixed place the speaker notionally comes from. You are asked to explore this issue in this activity.

The two contrasting passages reproduced below are both from poems representing aspects of Indian life. One describes in detail a scene or 'setting'; the other focuses on how language may represent – and also misrepresent – a kind of 'Indianness' which may be perceived to underlie Indian life.

Passage 1

The painted streets alive with hum of noon,
The traders cross-legged 'mid their spice and grain,
The buyers with their money in the cloth,
The war of words to cheapen this or that,
The shout to clear the road, the huge stone wheels,
The strong slow oxen and their rustling loads,
The singing bearers with the palanquins,
The broad-necked hamals sweating in the sun,
The housewives bearing water from the well

With balanced chatties, and athwart their hips
The black-eyed babies; the fly-swarmed sweetmeat shops,
The weaver at his loom, the cotton-bow
Twanging, the millstones grinding meal, the dogs
Prowling for orts, the skilful armourer
With tong and hammer linking shirts of mail,
The blacksmith with a mattock and a spear
Reddening together in his coals, the school
Where round their Guru, in a grave half-moon,
The Sakya children sang the mantras through,
And learned the greater and the lesser gods . . .

(From *The Light of Asia*,
by Sir Edwin Arnold (1832–1904))

Passage 2

I don't know politics but I know the names
Of those in power, and can repeat them like
Days of the week, or names of the months, beginning with
Nehru. I am Indian, very brown, born in
Malabar, I speak three languages, write in
Two, dream in one. Don't write in English, they said,
English is not your mother-tongue. Why not leave
Me alone, critics, friends, visiting cousins,
Every one of You? Why not let me speak in
Any language I like? The language I speak
Becomes mine, its distortions, its queernesses
All mine, mine alone. It is half English, half
Indian, funny perhaps, but it is honest,
It is as human as I am human, don't
You see? It voices my joys, my longings, my
Hopes, and it is as useful to me as cawing
Is to crows, or roaring to the lions, it
Is human speech, the speech of the mind that is
Here and not there, a mind that sees and hears and
Is aware. Not the deaf, blind speech
Of trees in storm or of monsoon clouds or of rain or the
Incoherent mutterings of the blazing
Funeral pyre.

(from 'An Introduction', by Kamala Das,
Collected Poems, vol. 1, 1984)

1   For each passage, make a list of words and/or grammatical constructions which are not part of your own dialect. In the case of individual words outwith your own dialect, do you know what they mean or refer to? Are such words associated with any particular place or way of life?

2   Which of the two passages in your view contains more locally specific vocabulary? (One way of judging this – though not the only way – is to see which of your lists contains more words that are not part of your own dialect.)

3   Do the two passages give equal attention to difficulties which arise in using language to establish either a sense of place or a sense of belonging to a place? If not, which do you feel focuses on this issue more?

4   In the light of your answers to Question 1, does your answer to Question 3 surprise you? If so, why? If not, why not?

5   How important is it, in representing experience or life in a place, to be careful about the particular linguistic variety used in that description (e.g. in terms of its relative social prestige or authority)?

6   Sir Edwin Arnold was a nineteenth-century British Orientalist scholar, as well as being a poet; Kamala Das is a twentieth-century Indian writer. How far do you think their different historical, geographical and cultural origins affect the means by which they seek to represent their relationship to India?

Reading

Bourdieu, P. (1991) *Language and Symbolic Power*, Oxford: Blackwell.
Cameron, D. (1995) *Verbal Hygiene*, London: Routledge.
Kachru, B. (1982) *The Other Tongue: English across Cultures*, Oxford: Pergamon.
Leith, D. (1983) *A Social History of English*, London: Routledge & Kegan Paul.
McCrum, R., Cran, W. and McNeil, R. (1986) *The Story of English*, London: Faber & Faber and BBC Publications.
Montgomery, M. (1995) *An Introduction to Language and Society*, London: Routledge & Kegan Paul, pp. 61–92.
Ngugi wa Thiong'o (1986) *Decolonising the Mind: The Politics of Language in African Literature*, London: Currey.
Strang, B. (1970) *A History of English*, London: Methuen.

Unit 6

Language and context: register

The term 'register' is used by linguists to describe the fact that the kind of language we use is affected by the context in which we use it, to such an extent that certain kinds of language usage become conventionally associated with particular situations. Our tacit knowledge of such conventions of usage enables us to judge whether what someone says or writes is 'appropriate' to its context. This is highlighted by our reactions when a text deviates from its appropriate register – as happens towards the end of the following announcement by a guard on a train:

> May I have your attention please, ladies and gentlemen. The train is now approaching Lancaster. Passengers for the Liverpool boat train should alight here and cross to platform one. Delays are being experienced on this train and passengers intending to use this service should consult the notice board on platform one *to find out what the score is*.

The comic effect of this arises basically through a sudden (and presumably unintentional) switch of register (in the last italicized phrase). For the most part the announcement is typical of the formal language we have come to associate with train announcements, though we may feel that it is a little too 'high-flown' for what is after all only information about trains and platforms. The unintended humour arises when the announcer **juxtaposes** (see **Unit 15**) the formal opening of the announcement with the much less formal conclusion ('to find out what the score is') and thereby comically undercuts what has gone before.

The most obvious way in which a text 'registers' the effect of its context is in the selection of vocabulary. Our experience of language in context allows us to recognize that vocabulary items such as 'alight' and 'consult' are characteristic of the professional idiom which the railway company has selected for communicating to the public, and we are equally sensitive to the fact that 'to find out what the score is' does not belong to that idiom. But differences in register involve differences in grammar as well as in vocabulary. For example, in the phrase 'Delays are being experienced', the use of the impersonal passive construction contributes as much as the vocabulary choice to the formality of the rail announcement register.

Each of us experiences a variety of language situations every day and from moment to moment: speaking in a tutorial, talking on the phone to a bank manager, chatting to friends in a coffee bar, writing a letter. In response to these contexts, each of us switches from one register to another without effort and we are able to recognize when others do the same. By the same token, as we have seen in the railway announcement example, we are all sensitive to deviation in register.

6.1 Contexts which affect register

It is possible to isolate three different aspects of any context or situation which will affect the register of a text:

1   the medium of communication (e.g. whether the language is spoken or written);
2   the social relationships of participants in the situation (which determines the tone);
3   the purpose for which the language is being employed, which typically derives from the field in which it is employed.

6.1.1 Medium

The register of a text is partly constituted by the **medium** which is adopted for communication. The medium of a text is the substance from which the text is made, or through which it is transmitted, or in which it is stored. For register, the most prominent difference in medium is between **speech** and **writing** (see **Unit 19**). Speech is usually made up on the spot and interpreted as it is heard. Writing, on the other hand, may involve long periods of composition and revision and the resultant text may be read and re-read at leisure in circumstances quite remote – both in time and place – from that in which it was written. Written texts, therefore, tend to be more formal than spoken texts, which, by contrast, tend to be looser and more provisional in their structure and to feel less formal. In public settings, of course, spoken texts may be carefully prepared in advance and may take on the formal characteristics of the written mode. Our rail announcement begins in this fashion before slipping into something much closer to everyday speech.

6.1.2 Tone

A second aspect of the context which affects register relates to the social roles which are prescribed for, or adopted by, participants in the communication situation. Differences in the text will result from whether the relationships between participants are informal or formal, familiar or polite, personal or impersonal. Thus, the **tone** of the text can indicate the attitude or position adopted by the writer or speaker towards the reader or listener. In the rail announcement, for example, 'ladies and gentlemen' constitutes a marker of social distance signalling politeness; the intricate syntax, together with words such as 'attention', 'approaching', and 'alight', signals formality; and the passive voice (avoiding reference to human agency – as in 'Delays are being experienced') are all features of the impersonal register. The suggestion that passengers should 'find out what the score is', on the other hand, assumes a much more informal and familiar relation between speaker and addressee – one which seems to clash with the context which has been previously set up.

6.1.3 Field and role

A third aspect of the context which affects register is the **role** of the communication. Language can be used for a variety of different purposes (to convey information, to express feelings, to cajole, to seduce, to pray, to produce aesthetic effects, to intimidate, etc.), each of which will leave its mark on what is said and the way it is said. In addition, a wide range of human activities have developed their own characteristic registers because they employ 'field-specific' vocabularies. **Fields** in this sense include those occupied by the legal profession, the scientific community, the culinary arts, religious institutions, academic disciplines, advertising, football commentary (and the list could be extended almost indefinitely). All employ terms which are particular to themselves, the use of which thereby invokes particular situations.

6.2 The social distribution of registers

It is important to remember that each of us is able to control the appropriate register for a wide variety of contexts and we each have, in addition, a passive familiarity with a range of others (e.g. of advertising, of income tax returns, of legal documents) which we are rarely called upon to actively use. But the range of registers we feel comfortable with (both actively and passively) will be affected by a number of factors, including our age, social background, education, gender, race, and work status. Register positions, or can be used to position, the participants of a dialogue differently according to who those participants are. Thus the conventional distinction between register and dialect as that between *language according to use* and *language according to user* (see **Unit 5**, **Language and place**) seems to break down when considering how the relative social roles in any communication situation govern, or are governed by, the register adopted. The registers we become familiar with and learn how to manipulate in higher education, for example, might well be alienating to those who have not had access to them. (In fact, one of the purposes of any degree course is to familiarize the student with the special register of the discipline being studied. In the study of literature, students are generally required to write essays in a formal and impersonal register which includes the use of a specialized critical vocabulary and excludes words and phrases which they might be accustomed to using in other contexts.)

Although linguistic usages usually change with time, some historical periods, societies, or professions try to preserve the 'purity' of particular registers and maintain rigorous hierarchical distinctions between registers. In the early twenty-first century it is possible to see how institutions such as the Church and the law have been relatively successful in maintaining their field-specific registers virtually unchanged across the centuries. Consider, for example, the following extract from a legal notice printed in the *Glasgow Herald*:

> Notice is Hereby Given, That ... the sheriff at Campbeltown, by Interlocutor dated 30th December, 1986, ordered all parties desirous to lodge Answers in the hands of the Sheriff Clerk at Castlehill, Campbeltown within 8 days after intimation, advertisement or service, and in the meantime, until the prayer of the Petition had been granted or refused, nominated Alistair White to be Provisional Liquidator of the said Company on his finding caution before extract.

From this example, we can see that the legal register is relatively opaque to the non-specialist. It is possible to offer different reasons why this should be so: one response might be to say that the legal profession maintains its register in order to intimidate the general public and so forces us to employ lawyers and solicitors to represent us in legal matters; another response might argue that such intricate and highly specific language is necessary in order to prevent potentially costly or crucial ambiguities. (See the discussion of archaism in the legal register in **Unit 4, Language and time**.)

Leaving these questions aside, however, a brief analysis of some of the features of the legal register that are displayed in this text can serve as a model for the way we might analyse any register:

- *Vocabulary*: The most obvious feature of this text is its field-specific words and phrases, as seen in 'Provisional Liquidator' and 'finding caution before extract'. There are also archaisms ('desirous'), and highly Latinate vocabulary (Interlocutor, intimation, Petition, nominated, Provisional, caution, extract).
- *Syntax* (sentence structure): Syntax makes an equal contribution to this register: remarkably, the complete notice is made up of a single complex

sentence with an array of subordinate clauses whose interrelations with each other are acutely difficult to follow.

- *Typography* (the appearance of the printing): Archaic typography is also a feature of this register, since it makes extensive use of capitalization for words which are no longer capitalized in modern English.

Institutions which seek to preserve their particular registers in this way and to isolate them from the linguistic changes taking place in the society surrounding them may be said to employ 'conservative' registers. Compared with these, areas such as advertising, journalism, pop music, and TV have more 'open' or 'liberal' registers which change frequently and continually borrow from each other and from the 'conservative' registers which surround them.

6.3 Literature and register

Looking at the history of literature, it seems that literature has sometimes maintained a conservative register and sometimes a liberal one. Interestingly, the shifts between liberal and conservative registers seem to parallel shifts in society and in the place literature has in society (roughly indicated by whether poets think poetry is a way of preserving the language or of rejuvenating it). In the eighteenth century, for example – an age dominated by reason, politeness, and rigid social distinctions – literature was governed, for the most part, by notions of decorum; its language is educated, polite, upper middle class. Its assumptions about what kind of language is appropriate to literature are best summed up by Alexander Pope in 1711: 'Expression is the dress of thought, and still / Appears more decent, as more suitable' (*An Essay on Criticism*, II, 318–19). But at the end of the eighteenth century, when ideas of democracy and revolution began to challenge the stabilities of the neo-classical period, there was a parallel revolution in the register thought appropriate to literature. In the 'Preface to *Lyrical Ballads*' (1800), Wordsworth explains that *Lyrical Ballads* 'was published as an experiment . . . to ascertain, how far . . . a selection of the real language of men in a state of vivid sensation' might be a suitable language for poetry, and he indicates that the language 'of low and rustic life' – suitably adopted and 'purified' – was chosen because 'such men . . . convey their feelings and notions in simple and unelaborated expressions'. Romanticism can therefore be seen as a movement which attempts to change the register considered appropriate to poetry and so participates in a struggle over literature's role in society (raising questions such as whether it should be the preserve of an élite or be as widely available and accessible as possible).

In the twentieth century literature has become particularly open to other registers. James Joyce's *Ulysses* (1922) epitomizes this openness; its pages often seem like a rag-bag of odds and ends taken from a huge variety of different and usually incongruous registers. But although, as we might expect, this mixing of registers is often used for comic effect, it also seems to have more far-reaching implications. In the following paragraph, for example, one of the central characters of the novel, Leopold Bloom, has invited the other main male character, Stephen Dedalus, back to his house for tea after a bizarre night on the town; it is late, and Bloom has to move carefully in order not to wake his wife sleeping upstairs. The places where the register changes have been numbered:

[1] What did Bloom do?

[2] He ... drew two spoonseat deal chairs to the hearthstone, one for Stephen with its back to the area window, the other for himself when necessary, [3] knelt on one knee, composed in the grate a pyre [4] of crosslaid resintipped sticks and various coloured papers and irregular polygons [5] of best Abram coal at twentyone shillings a ton from the yard of Messrs Flower and M'Donald of 14 D'Olier street, [6] kindled it at three projecting points of paper with one ignited lucifer match, [7] thereby releasing the potential energy contained in the fuel by allowing its carbon and hydrogen elements to enter into free union with the oxygen of the air.

[8] Of what similar apparitions did Stephen think? ...

In order to identify the various registers here, we need to imagine the context in which each one would usually occur. Tentative names for these registers are

Table 6.1 Identifying registers in an extract from *Ulysses*

Portion of text	Provisional name	Usual context	Textual evidence
1	catechism	Christian teaching	question and answer
2	descriptive prose	realist novel	use of simple past tense ('He . . . drew')
3	religious	description of ceremony	'knelt', 'pyre'
4	technical description	report	'irregular polygons'
5	language of commerce	advertisement	'best Abram coal'
6	technical description, as 4	report	'ignited lucifer match'
7	scientific description	textbook or journal	'potential energy', 'carbon and hydrogen'
8	catechism, as 1	Christian teaching	question and answer

given in Table 6.1, together with the textual features which provide evidence for such decisions.

According to the above analysis, this short passage contains six different registers. Part of its comedy depends upon our sensitivity to a number of clashes between language and context – e.g. the incongruity of describing the act of lighting a fire in a terraced house in Dublin in the early part of the twentieth century in various registers (the religious, the technical, the scientific) which seem too 'elevated' or too precise for this humble action. But note that each of these registers would be appropriate for describing the lighting of a fire in a different context (e.g. in a religious ceremony or in a scientific experiment). A second context to be considered is that of the novel genre itself: in a realist novel (see **Unit 22**, **Realism**) we would expect the scene to be narrated in register 2 rather than in registers 3–6. Furthermore, we do not expect a novel to be narrated in a series of questions and answers (as this whole chapter is) – this procedure is, in fact, more appropriate to religious instruction by catechism in the Christian Church.

The mixing of registers in this passage not only produces comic effects but raises a series of unsettling speculations. The description of this commonplace action in the religious register seems to invite us to recall the spiritual significance of fire, while the scientific register forces us to remember that fire is a process of chemical transformation. Thus we could argue that these incongruous registers **defamiliarize** a process which has become so familiar that we hardly think about it any more. Conversely, it could be argued that the 'conservative' registers of the Church and science are being undermined in so far as they are shown to employ 'pretentious' terminology to describe the most commonplace of events (the interweaving of the commercial register perhaps adds to this by undercutting the religious and technical registers which precede it). The passage is unsettling, however, in that it gives us no clues about which of these readings is 'correct'. Hence it becomes impossible to decide whether the 'elevated' registers are meant to have more authority than the 'low' register of commerce or vice versa. This is partly because the text seems to abdicate the authority which realist texts usually maintain through a clearly defined narrative voice. The register of narrative prose 2 is simply one register among others in this passage, without any special authority. And although the narrative is presented through a technique reminiscent of the Christian catechism, the mixing of registers undercuts the potential authority of both question and answer. By undermining or rejecting the register thought appropriate for narrating novels, *Ulysses* can be interpreted either as attempting to rejuvenate the novel genre, or as rejecting the genre's claims to be a special or elevated discourse.

Ulysses and T.S. Eliot's *The Waste Land* (both published in 1922) are two of the best examples of the way twentieth-century literature exploits the range of potential effects of register mixing. But we should be wary of suggesting that playing with or exploiting the possibilities generated by register is peculiar to twentieth-century literature. In fact, it could be argued that the recycling and mixing of registers are central to the literary process and its effects in general. One simple but revealing example of this is that parody is a genre which depends upon the notion that certain kinds of language are conventionally associated with particular genres and themes. Alexander Pope, who was cited above as arguing that poetic language should be 'suitable', can also exploit the possibilities set up by this notion in order to produce comic irony; in *The Rape of the Lock* (1712/1714), the humorous effect depends precisely upon the reader's familiarity with the register used in epic poetry and consequent ability to recognize the mismatch between Pope's use of this 'high' register and the 'low' subject-matter of the poem. In just the same way, a novel such as *Ulysses* depends upon the notion of appropriateness built into the fact of register in order to achieve its effect – whether this be to challenge established ideas about literature, or make a joke, or both.

We might summarize this discussion by making a number of general observations about the way literature draws upon the possibilities opened up by register:

1   Literature seems to continually renew or change its register by borrowing from other registers or by recycling the registers of previous literature.
2   Through unusual juxtaposition, parody, irony, and so on, it can draw attention to the notion of register by foregrounding the features of particular registers.
3   In this way, literature can show how arbitrary and often absurd certain registers can be.
4   By being so open to the registers which surround it, literature seems to challenge the strict distinctions maintained by conservative registers and seems ultimately to question the idea that literature itself is a privileged or special discourse.

ACTIVITY 6.1

The two poems for this activity (a 'neoclassical' sonnet by Thomas Gray and a 'romantic' sonnet by William Wordsworth) were written according to different views about the appropriate language for poetry: i.e. what constitutes a 'poetic register' is different in each text. Wordsworth quotes the Gray poem in the Preface to *Lyrical Ballads* as an example of 'bad' (i.e. neoclassical) poetic register in contrast to his own practice.

> In vain to me the smiling Mornings shine,
> And redd'ning Phoebus lifts his golden fire:
> The birds in vain their amorous descant join;
> Or chearful fields resume their green attire:
> These ears, alas! for other notes repine,

A different object do these eyes require.
My lonely anguish melts no heart but mine;
And in my breast the imperfect joys expire.
Yet morning smiles the busy race to chear,
And new-born pleasure brings to happier men:
The fields to all their wonted tribute bear:
To warm their little loves the birds complain:
I fruitless mourn to him, that cannot hear,
And weep the more, because I weep in vain.
> (Gray, 'Sonnet on the death of Richard West',
> written 1742, published 1775)

Surprised by joy – impatient as the Wind
I turned to share the transport – Oh! with whom
But Thee, deep buried in the silent tomb,
That spot which no vicissitude can find?
Love, faithful love, recalled thee to my mind –
But how could I forget thee? Through what power,
Even for the least division of an hour,
Have I been so beguiled as to be blind
To my most grievous loss? – That thought's return
Was the worst pang that sorrow ever bore,
Save one, one only, when I stood forlorn,
Knowing my heart's best treasure was no more;
That neither present time, nor years unborn
Could to my sight that heavenly face restore.
> (Wordsworth, no title, published 1815)

1   Using the two poems as evidence, describe as precisely as possible (a) the conventions of the poetic register used by Gray; and (b) the conventions of the poetic register used by Wordsworth. (You will find it helpful to look at the detail of how sentences are put together.)

2   In order to further explore the two registers, attempt to rewrite:

(a)   the first four lines of the Gray poem in the register used by Wordsworth;

(b)   the first four lines of the Wordsworth poem in the register used by Gray.

3   Is Wordsworth's poetic register at all recognizable as a (historical) development of the register used by Gray – that is, are there any shared elements – or are there no connections at all?

4   Do the different registers of the two poems relate at all to any difference in function which you see between the two poems?

Reading

Furniss, T.E. and Bath, M. (1996) *Reading Poetry: An Introduction*, London: Prentice-Hall, pp. 3–24.

Gregory, M. and Carroll, S. (1978) *Language and Situation*, London: Routledge & Kegan Paul.

Halliday, M.A.K. (1978) *Language as Social Semiotic: The Social Interpretation of Language and Meaning*, London: Arnold.

Leech, G. (1969) *A Linguistic Guide to English Poetry*, London: Longman, pp. 9–12, 49–51.

Montgomery, M. (1995) *An Introduction to Language and Society*, 2nd edn, London: Routledge.

Nowottny, W. (1962) *The Language Poets Use*, London: Athlone Press.

Unit 7

Language and gender

That language plays an important role in shaping the parameters of the social scene and constructing social identities can be seen particularly in the area of gender – the socially constructed differences of behaviour and belief considered appropriate to the two sexes. For many of us, most of the time, language seems like a neutral tool for expressing ideas and conveying information. In the domain of gender, however, as in other important areas of social life, careful analysis can reveal that language operates sometimes to disguise distinctions, sometimes to reinforce them, and sometimes actively to produce them.

7.1 Male as the norm

Within the English language, reference to human beings is often made as if all humans were male. This happens partly through the operation of the noun 'man', when it is used generically to stand for the species, but also through the use of 'he' as a generic pronoun (generic means general rather than specific – the generic 'he' is therefore supposed to include females as well as males). But, as Rosalind Coward and Maria Black (1990) have pointed out, if generic 'man' is genuinely inclusive then both of the following sentences should sound equally odd:

(1)   Man's vital interests are food, shelter, and access to females.

(2)   Man, unlike other mammals, has difficulties in giving birth.

In practice, however, sentences like (1) are more likely to be produced and accepted unreflectingly than sentences like (2). Even when operating generically, therefore, words such as 'he' and 'man' carry their masculine connotations with them. This tendency also operates at more restricted levels of reference, when generic 'he' is not intended to refer to the human species as a whole but to some non-gender specific group within it, as, for example, in the following:

(3)   When the police officer has completed his investigation, he files a report.

(4)   The modern reader may at first feel baffled by the overpunctuation, as it will feel to him that there are too many commas.

The conventions of usage of the generic pronoun say that we should understand the use of 'he' and 'his' in (3) as referring to all police officers (that is, including female officers). Similarly, in (4) the conventions of usage suggest that both male and female readers are being included in the reference. However, research has revealed that readers of sentences containing generic pronouns often do not read them as having general reference, but in fact read them as referring strictly to males. Kidd (1971), for instance, has demonstrated that when students are asked to visualize the referent of a generic pronoun, they almost invariably draw a male referent, even when the intended referent seems at first sight to be general.

A similar process may be seen at work in the following caption from an advertisement for Lufthansa airlines: 'What does today's business traveller expect of his airline?' Most people would read 'his' as having generic reference here, since it follows a generic noun 'business traveller'. But the picture which accompanies this advertisement makes it clear that the reference is only to males, since it shows a plane full of male business travellers relaxing on board an aeroplane, the only female on board being the steward who is serving them drinks. Thus, so-called generic nouns and pronouns are quite commonly not truly generic in practice: apparently non-gender specific, they often turn out to be referring actually to males. As a consequence of this, feminists such as Spender (1979) have argued that general categories of persons and indeed of the human species are often constructed through the language in male-oriented or androcentric terms. This process serves to make women less visible in social and cultural activity; the use, for instance, of the generic 'he' in example (3), or in the advertisement, serves to erase the fact that there are women who work as police officers, or who travel on business.

In some ways generic nouns (such as 'business travellers') which masquerade as non-gender specific terms are more insidious than the generic pronoun, 'he'. This is partly because there are so many of them, and partly because – unlike 'he' – they do not give any explicit signals that they might be excluding women. Because of this they become powerful ways of carving up social reality in implicitly masculine ways without announcing that they are doing so. Cameron (1985), for instance, shows that even expressions such as 'astronaut', 'firefighter', 'lecturer', 'shop assistant', 'scientist', and so on, disguise a tendency to refer only to men – despite their apparently neutral generic potential. Cameron cites two newspaper reports:

(5)   The lack of vitality is aggravated by the fact that there are so few able-
bodied young adults about. They have all gone off to work or look for
work, leaving behind the old, the disabled, the women and the children.
(*The Sunday Times*)

(6)   A coloured South African who was subjected to racial abuse by his
neighbours went berserk with a machete and killed his next-door
neighbour's wife, Birmingham Crown Court heard yesterday.
(*The Guardian*)

In example (5), the generic expression is 'able-bodied young adults', yet it is
clear from the rest of the sentence that what is really meant is 'able-bodied
young men', since women and children are subsequently excluded from its
reference. In the second example (6), the generic expression is 'next-door
neighbour' since this word ostensibly means both male and female neighbours,
and yet it is clear that when it is used to refer to women it needs to be modified to 'neighbour's wife'. Thus, neighbour, rather than being a generic in this
context, is in fact only referring to male neighbours. In the following headline
from *The Observer*, 'Top people told: Take a mistress' (where top male civil
servants are advised to take a mistress with them on foreign business trips to
avoid contracting AIDS from prostitutes), it is significant that a generic is used
('top people'), only to reveal that in fact it refers solely to males, since
'mistresses' are not normally 'taken' by women.

It can clearly be seen that generic nouns often refer solely to men in the
fact that women doing a job which is conventionally seen as stereotypically
male are sometimes described as 'lady doctor', 'female engineer', 'woman pilot'.
One assumes that as more and more women take up jobs which have been
conventionally seen as male, the most salient feature of their work will not
continue to be their gender.

Apart from the discrimination entailed within generic nouns and
pronouns, they can also be ambiguous in their reference, as, for example, in
the following sentence:

(7)   The more education an individual attains the better his occupation is likely
to be.

It is unclear here whether the 'individual' is supposed to be a man or whether
this is indeed a generic use (this is not cleared up by 'his' – which may also be
generic). Because the reference of generic nouns and pronouns is ambiguous
and because they serve to make women seem invisible, feminists such as Dale
Spender (1979), Casey Miller and Kate Swift (1979) have objected to their use.
Since the 1970s, feminists have been active in campaigning against their use in
official documents so that in the public sphere, at least, their use is becoming
much less common, and it is now seen as acceptable to object to such usage.

There are a number of different ways around the problem of the generic pronoun and generic reference: some writers have begun to avoid using generic 'he' entirely, since it can alienate readers and listeners. The 'he' can be avoided by using the passivized form, as in the following:

(8)   When a police officer has finished an investigation, a report should be filed.

Or the 'he' can be avoided by using the plural 'they':

(9)   When police officers have finished their investigation, they should file a report.

In these sentences, it is clear that the reference is truly generic. But it is also possible to signal more positively that there may be female as well as male police officers:

(10)   When the police officer has finished the investigation, he or she should file a report.

Some writers even use 'she' throughout their work to draw attention to the problems with generic 'he' usage, or they use a plural 'they' after a singular subject for example:

(11)   When the police officer has finished the investigation, they should file a report.

These forms are often contested, particularly examples (10) and (11), and even though usage has changed greatly in the last five years, since nearly all publishers, educational institutions and organizations have issued their staff with guidelines on language use to cover reference to gender and race, the subject of the use of generics is still contested and debated.

7.2 Female as downgraded or derogated

There are a range of words which are used solely for males or females and are therefore *gender-specific*. Many of these words have a slightly archaic feel about them now – this is an indicator of the way language has been changing rapidly in this area in recent years (see **Unit 4**, **Language and time**). So, for example, the word 'poetess' is only used for women, and the word 'courtier' is usually only used for men. Many female actors, particularly those who are at the top of the profession, do not use the word actress to describe themselves, preferring to use the generic 'actor'; this indicates the extent to which actress is seen to be a demeaning word which describes someone who is not serious about her profession.

Analysis reveals that there are significant patterns in the use of gender-specific language, in that pairs of gender-specific nouns are not always symmetrical; instead, they tend to downgrade (or derogate) women by treating them as if they were only sexual objects rather than full human beings. This emerges in the following sets of pairs:

master/mistress
courtier/courtesan
host/hostess
king/queen

Most of the terms on the male side have positive connotations and seem to refer solely to an occupation, whereas the female equivalents often have negative sexual connotations. There is a further asymmetry in the way that women are often referred to as 'girls'. In the following advertisement from *The Guardian*, 'girl' is used as if it were the female equivalent of 'man', whereas 'girl' generally refers to female children rather than adults:

EFL TEACHERS: required first week in February. Girl with driving licence for Italy; Man with experience and girl with degree in German for Germany.

This usage is also common in sports commentaries, where adult women athletes are often described as 'girls' (or as 'ladies').

Jane Mills (1989) has noted that there are many more words to refer to women in sexual terms than there are for men. For example, even the words 'laundress' and 'nun' have been used at some stage to refer to a woman who is suspected of being a prostitute. In a similar way, insult terms for women are greater in number than insult words for men, and they tend to be concerned with women's sexuality and appearance (slag, tart, dog), whereas insult terms for men seem to be more centred around questions of intelligence or ability (wanker, dickhead, dork). Women's sexual availability and marital status are also signalled by the use of the terms Mrs and Miss for which there are no current male equivalents (Mr does not indicate whether a man is married or single). To resist this, the term Ms was introduced in the 1970s and 1980s and has become much more general in recent years, despite a great deal of opposition. Yet, some women still feel wary about using it since it is associated with feminism or is assumed to refer to women who are divorced or separated. Nevertheless, a surprisingly large number of companies and institutions now offer Ms as an option for women to refer to themselves on forms and documents.

Analysis also reveals a covert asymmetry in the way that women are referred to in tabloid newspapers, where they are frequently identified by their marital or family status (wife, mother, grandmother) rather than by their profession. This is clear in a headline from the *Daily Star*: 'MAD GUNMAN HUNT AS WIFE IS SHOT'. It is also quite common in tabloid newspapers for women to be described in terms of their physical appearance (hair colour, body shape, and so on), whereas men are usually described with reference to their jobs and age.

This type of discrimination can be seen at work not only in the way that males and females are described but also in the way that scientific reports are written, for example in assertions made about the activity of eggs and sperm (Martin, 1997) or when describing animals in nature programmes (Crowther and Leith, 1995). Martin describes the way that scientific reports tend to draw on stereotypical notions of male and female activity and passivity when analysing sperm and eggs; she claims that:

> The egg is seen as large and passive. It does not move or journey, but passively 'is transported', 'is swept' or even 'drifts' along the fallopian tube. In utter contrast, sperm are small, 'streamlined' and invariably active. They 'deliver' their genes to the egg, 'activate the developmental program of the egg' and have a velocity which is often remarked upon. Their tails are strong and efficiently powered.
>
> (Martin, 1997: 87)

Despite the fact that both egg and sperm play an active role in conception and both move, scientists still tend to represent conception in terms which accord with the notion of the female element being passive. In a similar way, Crowther and Leith have found that, in nature programmes on television, in descriptions of the way that lions organize themselves in social groups, terms such as 'harems' have been used to describe a situation where the female lions in a pride allow one male lion to mate with them, excluding all others. In this way, the stereotypes of female passivity associated with the term harem are carried over to the way lion communities are described.

7.3 The potential for reform

Some feminists, such as Dale Spender (1979), see such asymmetries in language as demeaning to women and urge that language should be reformed accordingly; others, such as Deborah Cameron (1985), argue that sexism is so deep-rooted within the language that it is impossible to change it by reforming individual language items. (See also **Unit 4**, **Language and time**.)

7.4 Women's speech

Much early feminist research in sociolinguistics was concerned with investigating whether women speak differently from men. Robin Lakoff (1975), for example, claimed that women use different words to men (e.g. 'pretty' and 'cute') and different sentence structures (e.g. tag questions: 'This is hard to understand, isn't it?'). She characterizes women's language as being prone to hesitation, and as being repetitive and disjointed. This sociolinguistic work has now been questioned, since it is clear that women are not a unified grouping: there are many hierarchies within the grouping 'women', such as differences of class, race, economic power, education, and so on, with the consequence that groups of women speakers differ from other female speakers (see Bergvall *et al.*, 1996 for an overview). The speech patterns of the former Prime Minister, Margaret Thatcher, or current Minister, Margaret Beckett, bear greater similarities to the speech of males in similar positions of power than they do, say, to working-class women's speech.

However, there are certain elements of speech which we can classify as stereotypically 'feminine': that is, those elements which signify lack of confidence or assertiveness. These may be drawn on by both women and men in certain situations, particularly within the public sphere. O'Barr and Atkins (1982) have shown that within a court room setting both men and women from low-income groups are likely to adopt what they term 'powerless speech', that is, speech which bears a strong resemblance to Lakoff's definition of women's speech: hesitant, repetitive, disjointed, and so on. Thus it is probable that when discussing 'women's speech', theorists have been describing 'powerless speech' (see also **Unit 8**, **Language and society**).

7.5 The female sentence: a woman's writing?

Work on female speech has been echoed by work on women's writing, since many theorists claim that women's writing is qualitatively different from men's writing. For example, Virginia Woolf proposed that Dorothy Richardson's writing had developed a new way of using language, which Woolf termed 'a woman's sentence'. Woolf did not describe in detail what this 'psychological sentence of the feminine gender' consisted of, but if we compare the following two extracts by Anita Brookner and Malcolm Lowry, it seems quite easy to argue that Brookner is using a 'feminine' style while Lowry is using a 'masculine' style:

> From the window all that could be seen was a receding area of grey. It was to be supposed that beyond the grey garden, which seemed to sprout nothing but the stiffish leaves of some unfamiliar plant, lay the vast grey

lake, spreading like an anaesthetic towards the invisible further shore, and beyond that, in imagination only, yet verified by the brochure, the peak of the Dent d'Oche, on which snow might already be slightly and silently falling.

(Anita Brookner, *Hôtel du Lac* (1984))

Two mountain chains traverse the republic roughly from north to south, forming between them a number of valleys and plateaux. Overlooking one of these valleys, which is dominated by two volcanoes, lies, six thousand feet above sea-level, the town of Quauhnahuac. It is situated well south of the Tropic of Cancer, to be exact on the nineteenth parallel, in about the same latitude as the Revillagigedo Islands to the west in the Pacific, or very much farther west, the southernmost tip of Hawaii – and as the port of Tzucox to the east on the S. Atlantic seaboard of Yucatan near the border of British Honduras, or very much farther east, the town of Juggernaut, in India, on the Bay of Bengal.

(Malcolm Lowry, *Under the Volcano* (1967))

The Brookner passage describes the landscape from a particular point of view, that is, as seen from a character's perspective rather than from an omniscient narrator's standpoint. This personalized account consists of descriptions of colours, and the effect these colours have on the character. There seems to be a certain vagueness about the description; instead of facts, this account is concerned with what 'was supposed to be', what 'seemed' and what 'might be' happening. This modification or tentativeness is conventionally said to characterize a feminine style. In contrast, the Lowry passage seems far more distanced and at the same time precise; the information emanates not from an identifiable character but from a seemingly objective, omniscient narrator. In fact, the style used is reminiscent of the **register** (see **Unit 6**) of guidebooks or of geographical descriptions.

For many readers, these two passages may seem to characterize a feminine and masculine style respectively – one a personalized style, describing in detail relationships and the actions of characters, and the other more concerned with factual descriptions of the world. This accords with assertions made by Deborah Tannen that women tend to adopt certain strategies in speech which she calls rapport talk, while men adopt those strategies which she terms report talk (Tannen, 1991). However, it is clear that these distinctions, although fairly easy to make, are based on stereotypical notions of gender difference (women are supposed to be vague, interested in colours, and concerned with relationships, whereas men are supposed to be interested in facts and are precise). Not all male writers write like Lowry, and not all women writers write as Brookner does here. Iris Murdoch, for example, often writes in a manner more akin to Lowry's writing, and frequently uses a male narrator. And it should be noted that much of the imprecision of the Brookner passage arises from the fact that she is focusing on the impressions of a character who is unfamiliar with the landscape (the character has a 'brochure' of the area).

Thus, the idea that there is a masculine style and a feminine style appears to be based more on stereotypical notions of sexual difference than on any inevitable textual difference in the way men and women write. Although the way a person uses language (in writing as in speech) will be influenced by conventional stereotypes about gender, and although readers often apply those same stereotypes when reading literature, it is important to remember that these stereotypes are neither natural nor inevitable. If women do sometimes use language differently, this is related to the way that women are derogated in language and the way that social pressures may encourage them to adopt 'powerless' speech. At the same time, however, women writers (like their male counterparts) may adopt different linguistic styles for particular artistic and political ends. Feminist critics and writers often employ language in ways which challenge the gender biases embedded in language and resist the derogation and disempowering of women. On the other hand, early twentieth-century writers, such as Woolf, Richardson, and Rosamond Lehmann, can be seen as adopting a 'feminine' style precisely in order to subvert or question the assumptions of 'masculine' objectivity.

ACTIVITY 7.1

1   Read the text below from the 'Heartsearch' column of the *New Statesman* (May, 1987), and underline the words that reveal or hint at the sex of the writer.

2   Put a circle round all uses of generic nouns (e.g. terms like 'scientist', which seems to refer to all scientists, regardless of whether they are male or female).

3   Are there any differences between the way that male and female writers use generic nouns in these advertisements?

4   What other linguistic differences are there which relate either to the sex of the writer or the sex of the person being sought?

5   Are there any possible confusions with generic uses here?

> CAMBRIDGE GRADUATE: vaguely academic; likes films, opera, Europe, old things. Lithe, fit, 6', sporty. Still attractive despite thinning hair.

INCURABLE ROMANTIC, charming, uncomplicated, attractive woman, not slim, not young, feminine, wide interests, seeks personable caring, retired male, sixty plus, middle brow for commitment.

GOOD-LOOKING German writer, early 30s, wishes to indulge in voyeuristic fantasy with young couple or single FORUM minded female.

LADY, ATTRACTIVE, intelligent, independent mind and means, seeks similar man 40–50. Devon Cornwall only.

Rich 1948 Claret with firm strong body sensuous flavour and adventurous bouquet, handsomely bottled, seeks younger crisp and frisky Chablis, equally well-packaged, for mulled fun, including weekends and holidays abroad with a view to durable casting. Photo appreciated.

SENSITIVE HIPPY, 24, seeks sincere and caring female for loving relationship.

Reading

Bergvall, V., Bing, J. and Fried, A. (eds) (1996) *Rethinking Language and Gender Research: Theory and Practice*, London: Longman.

Cameron, D. (1985) *Feminism and Linguistic Theory*, London: Macmillan.

Cameron, D. (ed.) (1990) *The Feminist Critique of Language*, rev.edn, London: Routledge.

Cameron, D. and Coates, J. (1989) *Women in their Speech Communities*, London: Longman.

Coward, R. and Black, M. (1981/1990) 'Linguistic, social and sexual relations: a review of Dale Spender's *Man Made Language*', in D. Cameron (ed.) (1990) *The Feminist Critique of Language*, London: Routledge.

Crowther, B. and Leith, D. (1995) 'Feminism, language and the rhetoric of television wildlife programmes', in S. Mills (ed.) *Language and Gender: Interdisciplinary Perspectives*, London: Longman, pp. 207–26.

Daly, M. (1978) *Gyn/ecology*, London: Women's Press.

Kidd, V. (1971) 'A study of the images produced through the use of the male pronoun as generic', *Moments in Contemporary Rhetoric and Communication*: 1: 25–30.'

Lakoff, R. (1975) *Language and Woman's Place*, New York: Harper Colophon.

Martin, E. (1997) 'The egg and the sperm: how science has constructed a romance based on stereotypical male–female roles', in L. Lamphere, H. Ragone and P. Zavella (eds) *Situated Lives: Gender and Culture in Everyday Life*, London: Routledge, pp. 85–99.

Miller, C. and Swift, K. (1979) *Words and Women*, Harmondsworth, Penguin.

Mills, J. (1989) *Womanwords*, London: Longman.

Mills, S. (1987) 'The male sentence', *Language and Communication*, 189–98.

Mills, S. (1996) *Feminist Stylistics*, London: Routledge.

O'Barr W.F. and Atkins (1982) 'Women's speech or powerless speech', in S. McConnell-Ginet *et al.* (eds) *Women and Language in Literature and Society*, New York: Praeger.

Spender, D. (1980) *Man Made Language*, London: Routledge & Kegan Paul.

Tannen, D. (1991) *You Just Don't Understand: Women and Men in Conversation*, London: Virago.

Woolf, V. (1979) 'Women and writing', in D. Cameron (ed.) (1990) *The Feminist Critique of Language*, London: Routledge.

Unit 8

Language and society

The myriad social exchanges that go to make up society largely depend on language. It is difficult to become a fully integrated member of a society or a group without taking on and developing a competence in its language. Indeed the acquisition of language in childhood is intimately bound up with becoming a social being, for in learning to communicate through words the child takes on the concepts, values and modes of relationship of the society into which it is born. The child is assigned and begins to construct for itself its own sense of identity through language. Thus language is crucial to the creation and maintenance both of social relationships and social identities. Because of this, the way we use language (our accent, our vocabulary, etc.) carries with it important signals about the social order and our own place within it.

8.1 Language and social reality

8.1.1 Language as a set of shared social conventions

Linguistic signs (spoken or written words, the gestures which make up the sign language of the deaf, etc.) have meanings only by virtue of a communal agreement among the users of a language. There is no intrinsic reason why the idea of 'tree' should be represented (in English) by the letters t,r,e,e (or the sounds /t/, /r/, /i:/). This is shown by the fact that other languages choose quite different sounds and letters to represent the same idea. The relationship, therefore, between the signifier (the sounds or letters) and what is signified (ideas, concepts) seems wholly arbitrary. Because of this, words only become meaningful through convention. Language works because its users implicitly agree to adhere to the conventions that underpin every aspect of its organization and which pre-exist the individual's entry into the system. In so far as the system of signs belongs not to the individual but to the community it is social rather than individual in its origins. The users of a particular language are thus parties to an implicit agreement to a set of socially held conventions. By virtue of this agreement they are also party to the way their language assigns significance and social values to the world they live in.

8.1.2 Language as a site of social struggle

These conventions, however, though basic to the way in which language works, are not shared equally or uniformly throughout society. What we find instead is that ways of speaking and using the language vary according to social differences and operate differently in different social domains. The adoption of particular habits of speaking leads to distinct ways of seeing and representing the world. At the level of vocabulary we can detect this in pairings such as *heart attack* versus *cardiac arrest*. These are not straightforwardly synonyms for each other, nor is the second simply a euphemistic version of the first. Instead, *cardiac arrest* is likely to be used by a particular social grouping (doctors, etc.) and involves a different way of seeing the phenomenon than that shared by the majority of people. In discussing the effects of war, the phrase *collateral damage* has quite different implications and effects than *civilian casualties*. Selection of one term rather than another often entails choosing particular modes of conceptualizing the reality in question. Adopting a phrase such as *collateral damage* makes it more likely that one will also select phrases such as *surgical strikes* with *80 per cent success rate* or *degrading the enemy's war machine* because they all serve to represent war from a particular perspective. In adopting the linguistic currency of military strategists and tacticians, it is difficult to avoid adopting their frames of reference and priorities. Vocabularies such as these thus entail particular ways of looking at the world and particular ways of defining reality which have social and political consequences. Particular linguistic choices, then, can often involve adopting certain positions regarding contentious issues and rejecting others. For this reason language becomes an arena and a means of social struggle – as, for instance, in the case of **Language and gender** (see **Unit 7**).

8.1.3 Language as a record of social history

A term such as *family* (which became important in political debates in Britain in the 1980s) has in fact a long and complex history of change (see Raymond Williams, 1988). It first entered English from Latin in the late fourteenth century, at which time it tended to refer to a household (incorporating not only blood-relations but also servants living together under one roof). It was then extended to include the notion of house formed by descent from a common ancestor. The specialization of the term to refer to a small kin-group living in a single house is a fairly late development in the history of the word in English (it happened between the seventeenth and nineteenth centuries), and is related

– Williams claims – to the growing importance of the family as an economic unit in developing capitalism. Thus the term *family* has meant significantly different things in the 600 years since it entered the English language. Even now it means different things to different social groupings in contemporary society. A single-parent family is different from the extended family common in the Asian community in Britain, and both are different from the two-parent-two-child family presented in TV advertisements as the 'happy norm'. The word 'family', therefore, is not only inextricably bound up with the ideological struggles of the past but can become a stake in present struggles. (For further discussion of this see **Unit 4, Language and time**.)

One of the reasons why linguistic signs change their meanings through history is because they reflect both the transformations of social structures and the fact that society is not a single entity but differentiated along lines of class, race, and gender. The use of the term 'the family' in recent political debate emphasizes the heterosexual, parenting couple as a self-contained economic unit living in its own home independently of state and social support (the 'nuclear family') – a sense which tends to exclude single parents, unmarried parents, and so on. The fact that such a definition does not accord with the way the majority of people live in Britain in the early twenty-first century goes some way to demonstrating the ideological work to which language can be recruited in an attempt to promote or legitimate particular versions of reality. It seems as if language cannot escape becoming the site of social and political contestation. It gives us categories for organizing experience and understanding the world which may seem neutral and unbiased but are inevitably partial and particular.

8.2 The social implications of syntax

The way language organizes experience for us is not restricted to the meanings of individual words. Significant orderings of experience are also carried out by the way in which we put the words together into sentences. Not only vocabulary but also grammatical construction help to represent social realities in determinate ways. One important kind of grammatical construction is that which linguists call **transitivity**. Transitivity is a way of describing the relationship between participants and processes in the construction of clauses – basically, 'who (or what) does what to whom (or what)'. Transitivity relations and the roles of participants depend upon the kind of process encoded by the main verb in a clause. For English, four fundamental types of process may be distinguished (but for more complete and complex treatments see Fawcett, 1980; Simpson, 1993; Halliday, 1996; and Thompson, 1996).

1 *Material action processes* (realized by verbs such as 'break', 'wipe', 'dig', 'unbolt') involve roles such as an **agent** (someone or something to perform the

action), and the **affected** (someone or something on the receiving end of the action):

John		broke		the lock
AGENT		PROCESS		AFFECTED

The agent in a clause is not always the grammatical 'subject' of the verb (i.e. the phrase which precedes the verb). In the **passive** form, the subject is the affected:

The lock		was broken		by John
AFFECTED		PROCESS		AGENT
Subject		Verb		

The passive focuses attention on the affected (rather than upon the agent). It also allows the agent to be omitted:

The lock		was broken
AFFECTED		PROCESS

2 *Mental processes* (realized by verbs such as 'know', 'feel', 'think', 'believe') involve roles such as the **senser** (the one who performs the act of 'knowing', 'thinking', or 'feeling') and the **phenomenon** (that which is known or thought about by the senser):

James		considered		the problem
SENSER		PROCESS		PHENOMENON

Mary		understood		the message
SENSER		PROCESS		PHENOMENON

The message		amazed		me
PHENOMENON		PROCESS		SENSER

3 *Verbal processes* are processes of saying (signalled by terms such as 'suggest', 'promise', 'enquire', 'tell', 'inform', etc.). Typical participant roles are **sayer**, **message** and **recipient**:

I		said		it was time to leave
SAYER		PROCESS		MESSAGE

I		told		him		it was time to leave
SAYER		PROCESS		RECIPIENT		MESSAGE

4 *Relational processes* in their simplest form involve some entity which is identified by reference to one of its attributes. The process may be realized by verbs such as 'become', 'seem', 'be', 'have' and typical roles are **carrier** and **attribute**:

The sky		is		blue
CARRIER		PROCESS		ATTRIBUTE

Other important roles in relational processes are those of **possessor** and **possessed**:

He		had		no money
POSSESSOR		PROCESS		POSSESSED

Any event or relationship in the 'real world' is filtered through and given linguistic shape by means of one or other of the types of process outlined above. Transitivity relations, therefore, go to the heart of the linguistic construction and mediation of experience. The patterning of transitivity choices in a text can reveal its predispositions to construct experience along certain lines rather than others. The analysis of transitivity, therefore, becomes a useful way of exploring the ideological dimension of texts.

In the coverage of the 1983 miners' strike, for instance, the action of picketing was constructed in quite different linguistic ways by different newspapers, depending on their political perspective. The *Daily Mail*, which generally supported the government position, described events on the picket line in sentences such as the following:

41 policemen had been treated in hospital
police horses and their riders were stoned
five policehorses were also injured
pickets demolished a wall
pickets bombarded the police

Using the categories of transitivity given above, we find that in material action processes 'the police' figure in the accounts mainly in the role of the affected (of usually violent actions). Where 'picketing miners' appear in action clauses it is usually as agents, mostly of (violent) actions performed against the police.

In contrast to the *Daily Mail*, a newspaper such as the *Morning Star*, whose support for the miners was unwavering throughout the strike, described events on the picket line in sentences such as:

police attacked isolated groups of miners
several miners were hit with truncheons
one miner was pounced upon by other policemen

the miners massed around the entrance
3000 pickets yesterday gathered outside Cortonwood Colliery

Here, police become agents of (violent) actions by which the miners are affected. And whilst the miners are sometimes presented as agents, it usually involves processes of non-violent movement (as in 'the miners massed around the entrance').

This brief analysis shows that the actual events of the picketing are constructed in quite different ways through the transitivity choices adopted in the respective newspapers. The choices in the *Daily Mail* present the industrial dispute as one in which the police are defenders of civil order in the face of a threat from the miners. The choices in the *Morning Star*, by contrast, present the dispute as working-class solidarity in the face of state provocation. These different ideological viewpoints are not simply reflected in the language; they are produced and constructed through these different patterns of grammatical organization.

The concept of transitivity is not only useful for understanding ways in which social realities are constructed in the language of the media. It also provides a way of examining the fictional construction of reality. A study of the transitivity choices in Sylvia Plath's *The Bell Jar* (see Burton, 1982) shows how the first-person narrator's own language choices typically present her as an affected entity rather than as the agent of actions that affect others. This is particularly apparent as she moves into mental crisis and begins to lose control of her life. Burton's point here is that the structures of language themselves – the character's habitual patterns of linguistic choice – contribute to her crisis precisely because they are disenabling rather than empowering. The social and political implications of this analysis are significant, since it suggests that members of marginalized social groups will potentially adopt linguistic choices which both reflect and reinforce their disempowerment (see the discussion of 'powerless speech' in **Unit 7**, **Language and gender**).

8.3 Language and social structure in the novel

The novel is a literary genre which is more overtly 'social' than poetry (or even drama). This is partly to do with its form (by definition it includes a range of different voices rather than the single consciousness often present in poetry), partly to do with the themes it was used to treat in the nineteenth century (typically the tensions between different classes), and partly to do with its origins (as a means of representing the rising middle classes in the eighteenth century).

The nineteenth-century 'realist' novel in Britain often dramatizes the (usually fraught) relations between three classes – the upper class, the middle class, and the working class. These distinctions and struggles are typically registered through a sociology of language as well as in themes, characters and plots. Charles Dickens's *Great Expectations* (1860–61), for example, explores these issues through having a character (the narrator Pip) cross the boundaries of social class. Pip is brought up in a working-class household by his sister and her husband Joe Gargery, a blacksmith with whom he develops strong ties in the first third of the novel. Through the support of a mysterious benefactor, however, Pip becomes a 'gentleman', takes rooms in London, and begins to regard his humble past as an embarrassment. Thus when he receives word that Joe intends to visit him in London, Pip anticipates meeting his old friend 'with considerable disturbance, some mortification, and a keen sense of incongruity':

> As the time approached I should have liked to run away, but ... presently I heard Joe on the staircase. I knew it was Joe, by his clumsy manner of coming up-stairs – his state boots being always too big for him – and by the time it took him to read the names on the other floors in the course of his ascent. When at last he stopped outside our door, I could hear his finger tracing over the painted letters of my name ... Finally he gave a faint single rap, and Pepper ... announced 'Mr Gargery!' I thought he never would have done wiping his feet ... but at last he came in.
>
> 'Joe, how are you, Joe?'
>
> 'Pip, how AIR you, Pip?'
>
> ...
>
> 'I am glad to see you, Joe. Give me your hat.'
>
> But Joe ... wouldn't hear of parting with that piece of property, and persisted in standing talking over it in a most uncomfortable way.
>
> 'Which you have that growed,' said Joe, 'and that swelled, and that gentle-folked'; Joe considered a little before he discovered this word; 'as to be sure you are a honour to your king and country.'
>
> 'And you, Joe, look wonderfully well.'
>
> (Chapter 27)

Dickens uses a number of devices here to indicate the social distance which has arisen between these characters. Apart from registering Joe's uneasiness through the way he wipes his feet and holds his hat – not to mention Pip's equally revealing attention to these details – the social difference between Pip and Joe is indicated by their different relations to language. Joe's difficulty with the written language is foregrounded through Pip's acute consciousness of his ponderous attempts to read the names on the doors. But more to the point here is the way Joe speaks. While Pip conceals his unease behind the **register** (see **Unit 6**) of polite affability, Joe precisely reveals his sense of awkwardness in echoing Pip. In attempting to imitate his young friend's speech, Joe 'hyper-corrects' (see Montgomery, 1995) his own accent by revealingly overdoing the 'proper' pronunciation of 'are' (as 'AIR'). Joe quickly 'forgets himself' by 'lapsing' into his normal accent in what we may take as a flood of genuine feeling and admiration. Pip, by contrast, continues in a polite register which signals his inability to respond to his old friend and maintains the social stratification through language which this passage dramatizes.

In the twentieth-century novel, such socio-linguistic stratifications are often challenged or undermined. D.H. Lawrence's fiction typically attempts to reverse the kind of hierarchy set up in the Dickens passage above. This can be seen in several places in *Lady Chatterley's Lover* (1928), including the following exchange between Lady Chatterley and her lover (who is a gamekeeper on her estate):

'Tha mun come one naight ter th'cottage, afore tha goos; sholl ter?' he asked, lifting his eyebrows as he looked at her, his hands dangling between his knees.

'Sholl ter?' she echoed, teasing.

He smiled.

'Ay, sholl ter?' he repeated.

'Ay!' she said, imitating the dialect sound.

. . .

' 'Appen Sunday,' she said.

' 'Appen a' Sunday! Ay!'

He laughed at her quickly.

'Nay, tha canna,' he protested.

'Why canna I?' she said.

He laughed. Her attempts at the dialect were so ludicrous, somehow.

(Chapter 12)

On one level, this presents a tender scene between the two lovers in which the social difference in their ways of speaking becomes material for a lovers' game. At the same time, however, the social significance of this difference cannot be overlooked. At several points in the novel, Mellors, the gamekeeper, uses the fact that he can move at will between one way of speaking and the other as a weapon in a class war against the upper-class family which employs him. Lady Chatterley's attempt to imitate the dialect of a 'lower' social class (which reverses the situation in *Great Expectations* examined above) can be read as a bid to escape from the restrictions of her own class. This is reinforced by the fact that the gamekeeper's dialect is treated throughout the novel as if it were the authentic expression of desire in contrast to the coldly mental, sexless language of the upper classes. In this respect, Lady Chatterley's imitation of her gamekeeper's dialect – which is an amusing failure in Mellors's eyes – becomes symptomatic of a wider failure in the novel's terms to achieve an authentic modality for the enactment of desire across the divide of social class. (For a fuller discussion of accent and dialect, see **Unit 5, Language and place**.)

ACTIVITY 8.1 ▬▬▬▬▬▬▬▬▬▬▬▬▬▬▬▬▬▬▬▬▬▬▬▬▬▬

1   Read the following passage from Elizabeth Gaskell's *North and South* (1854–5). The central character, Margaret Hale, has recently moved from the south of England to Manchester (one of the main centres of industrial development in the nineteenth century) and is discussing an impending strike at a local mill with a poverty-stricken leader of the union, Nicholas Higgins ('to clem' is a dialect term for 'to starve'):

> 'Why do you strike?' asked Margaret. 'Striking is leaving off work till you get your own rate of wages, is it not? You must not wonder at my ignorance; where I come from I never heard of a strike.'
>
> . . .
>
> 'Why yo' see, there's five or six masters who have set themselves again paying the wages they've been paying these two years past, and flourishing upon, and getting richer upon. And now they come to us, and say we're to take less. And we won't. We'll just clem to death first; and see who'll work for 'em then.'
>
> . . .
>
> 'And so you plan dying, in order to be revenged upon them!'
>
> 'No,' said he, 'I dunnot. I just look forward to the chance of dying at my post sooner than yield. That's what folk call fine and honourable in a soldier, and why not in a poor weaver-chap?'
>
> 'But,' said Margaret, 'a soldier dies in the cause of the Nation – in the cause of others.'
>
> '. . . Dun yo' think it's for mysel' I'm striking work at this time? It's just as much in the cause of others as yon soldier . . . I take up John Boucher's cause, as lives next door but one, wi' a sickly wife, and eight childer, . . . I take up th' cause o' justice. . . .'
>
> . . .
>
> 'But,' said Margaret, . . . 'the state of trade may be such as not to enable them to give you the same remuneration.'
>
> 'State o' trade! That's just a piece o' masters' humbug. It's rate o' wages I was talking of. Th' masters keep th' state o' trade in their own hands; and just walk it forward like a black bug-a-boo, to frighten naughty children with into being good.'
>
> (from Chapter 17, 'What is a Strike?')

2   Make a list of all the words and phrases which Higgins uses to describe: (a) the mill owners; (b) the workers; (c) himself; (d) the mill owners' actions; (e) the workers' actions; (f) his own actions. From this evidence, try to describe Higgins's view of the strike (for example, by considering who does what to whom).

3   Make a list of all the words and phrases which Margaret uses to describe:
     (a) the mill owners' possible actions; (b) Higgins's description of his own
     role; (c) the actions of workers in a strike. From this evidence, try to
     describe Margaret's view of the strike.

4   What is the difference between Margaret's suggestion that 'the state of
     trade' might not allow the owners to give the workers the same 'remu-
     neration', and Higgins's response that he is not talking about the state of
     trade but 'rate o' wages'? How, in Higgins's view, do the owners use the
     term 'state of trade'?

5   What is the effect of the fact that Higgins speaks in a working-class
     northern dialect, while Margaret speaks in Standard English? Does it
     make his view of the strike more credible? less credible? more authentic?
     less authoritative?

Reading

Burton, D. (1982) 'Through glass darkly: through dark glasses', in R. Carter (ed.)
     Language and Literature: An Introductory Reader in Stylistics, London: George
     Allen & Unwin, pp. 195–214.
Fawcett, R. (1980) *Cognitive Linguistics and Social Interaction*, Heidelberg: Julius Groos.
Halliday, M.A.K. (1996) *An Introduction to Functional Grammar*, 2nd edn, London:
     Arnold.
Montgomery, M. (1995) *An Introduction to Language and Society*, 2nd edn, London:
     Routledge.
Simpson, P. (1993) *Language, Ideology and Point of View*, London: Routledge.
Thompson, G. (1996) *Introducing Functional Grammar*, London: Arnold.
Vološinov, V.N. (1973) *Marxism and the Philosophy of Language*, London: Academic
     Press.
Williams, R. (1988) *Keywords: A Vocabulary of Culture and Society*, London: Collins.

Analysing poetic form

Unit 9

Rhyme and sound patterning

In the process of reading words on a page, we translate visual marks (letters) into mental representations of sounds (phones, or **phonemes**). English uses a 'phonetic-alphabetic script' in which letters stand for sounds, or serve to represent particular patterns of sound. For example, the letter 'p' in 'pin' stands for a single sound (which we write phonetically as 'p'); the two letters 'th' in 'thin' stand for a single sound (which we write phonetically as 'θ'); the letter 'i' in 'time' stands for a combination of sounds called a diphthong (which we write phonetically as 'aɪ'). We can represent the way a word is made up of sounds using a phonetic script, and so can compare the letter-spelling of a word with the phonetic structure of the word:

letter-spelling:	thing	queen	come
phonetic structure:	θɪŋ	kwiːn	kʌm

In this unit we are interested in the phonetic structure of words rather than their spelling. Because of the relatively small number of distinct sounds used in a language, the sounds of a text inevitably occur and recur as we read. As they do so, they make up a kaleidoscope of repetitions and permutations. In casual conversation and most kinds of written texts, this repetition of sounds occurs for the most part apparently randomly, ordered only by the historical accidents governing which sounds make up which words. But it is also possible for speakers and writers to organize the sounds of utterances in more systematic ways – ranging from motivated but irregular instances through to fully predictable patterns – in order to achieve certain effects. Many different types of discourse employ such sound patterning: poetry; jokes; slogans; proverbs; advertising copy; sound-bites in political speeches and interviews; pop lyrics; rapping; etc.

9.1 The structure of the syllable

In order to be able to analyse the various sound patterns which can occur between words, it is useful to be able to describe the structure of the syllables which make up words. The structure of a **syllable** can be described as C–V–C, where C stands for a **consonant cluster** (i.e. any number of consonants, including none) and V stands for one vowel or one diphthong. This simple notation can be used to describe syllables as shown in Table 9.1 (phonetic symbols are used on the left to represent the words on the right):

Table 9.1

C	V	C	
b	aɪ	t	bite
sp	ɔ	t	spot
spl	æ	t	splat
m	əʊ	st	most
	ɪ	n	in
p	eɪ		pay
	aɪ		l

The above words all consist of just one syllable (they are monosyllabic). But words may consist of a number of syllables put together (see Table 9.2).

Table 9.2

C	V	C	C	V	C	C	V	C	
p	eɪ		m	ɑː		st	ə		paymaster
p	eɪ		m	ə	nt				payment
	e		l	ɪ		f	ə	nt	elephant

9.2 Types of sound pattern

Sound patterns are formed when there is some form of 'echo' between syllables in words that occur close enough to one another in space or time to be perceived by a reader or listener (e.g. next to each other, or in the same line as each other, or in the same place in different lines). The various names which literary criticism has used to refer to particular kinds of local sound patterning are simply conventional labels for different kinds of repetition and **parallelism** (see **Unit 11**). The nature of the echo can be analysed by indicating which elements in the C–V–C structure of the relevant syllables are similar. Developing a description presented in Leech (1969), we can say that there are six basic kinds of pattern:

1   Alliteration [**C**–V–C] occurs when there is a repetition of sounds made by the initial consonants or consonant clusters of nearby words (e.g. 'boat', 'big', 'bad'; or 'grow', 'grand', 'greed'). Alliteration can also occur where there is a repetition of the first stressed segment within a word ('aggression', 'ungrateful', etc.).

A number of further points are worth noting about alliteration:

(a)   As with all the patterns, it is sounds, not letters, which produce the effect. So 'city' alliterates with 'sandwich', not with 'cauliflower'.

(b)   Alliteration can exist between the initial sound of a word and a sound at the beginning of a stressed syllable within another word. So 'song' alliterates with 'unseen' and 'dissociate', but not with 'dancing' (because the stress in 'dancing' is on the first syllable – see **Unit 10**, **Verse and metre**).

(c)   Alliteration was a major organizing device in Old and Middle English 'alliterative metre', which required that most or all of the stressed syllables in any line of verse were made up of the same word-initial sound. An example of a line of fifteenth-century alliterative verse is: 'Stark strokes thei stryken on a stelyd stokke'. This form of patterning was gradually displaced in later poetry in English by sound patterns at the end of lines (especially rhyme).

(d)   Alliteration is usually said to occur in the case of word-initial sound clusters (e.g. 'spl', 'tr', 'pl') only when the entire cluster is repeated, not when only one part recurs. So 'glad' alliterates with 'glimmer', not with 'go' or 'grow'.

(e)   One way of remembering some of these features of alliteration is to think of the so-called 'three Rs': 'reading, writing and arithmetic'. These three words are generally heard as alliterative. But alliteration between 'reading' and 'writing' illustrates that the effect is produced by sound rather than spelling (because the letters 'wr' are different from the letter 'r', but both correspond to the same sound). 'Arithmetic' alliterates with both 'reading' and 'writing' because its 'r' sound occurs in the first stressed syllable, rather than the first syllable of the word as a whole (which is unstressed).

2   Assonance [C–**V**–C] occurs when there is a repetition of the same vowel sound – especially in stressed syllables – embedded within nearby words. So 'light' is assonant with 'wide' and 'sign'.

3   Consonance [C–V–**C**] occurs when there is a repetition of sounds made by the final consonants or consonant groups of nearby words, as in 'bad' and 'good', or 'treats' and 'floats'. (Note, however, that some critics have argued that use of the term consonance is only justified when both the initial and final consonants are repeated, as in 'read' and 'ride'; this is then equivalent to what we call pararhyme in this classification; see 5 below.)

4   Reverse rhyme [**C–V**–C] occurs when the sounds of both the initial consonant or consonant group and the vowel are repeated in nearby words, as in 'cash' and 'carry', or 'stand' and 'stamp'.

5   Pararhyme [**C**–V–**C**] occurs when the sounds of both the initial and the final consonant or consonant groups in nearby words are repeated, as in 'send' and 'sound', or 'beat' and 'bite'. (Notice that this effect is what some critics refer to as consonance – see point 3 above.)

6   Rhyme [C–**V–C**] occurs when the vowel sound and the sound of the final consonant or consonant group are repeated in nearby words: 'cloud' rhymes with 'shroud'; 'bending' with 'sending'; and 'demonstrate' with 'remonstrate'. Rhyme can occur either within a line of verse (where it is called 'internal rhyme') or at the end ('end rhymes'). The term rhyme is sometimes also used to describe repetition of a V–C combination which is not at the end of a word, as in 'action pack'.

A number of further points are worth noting about rhyme:

(a)   Some apparent approximations to rhyme result from historical changes in how words are pronounced, as with 'line' and 'join', or 'day' and 'tea' (which more or less rhymed with each other during the eighteenth century).

(b)   Sounds, not spellings, produce rhyme. So 'cough' rhymes with 'off', not with 'plough'. (Words like 'cough' and 'plough', whose spelling suggests they ought to rhyme, are called 'eye-rhymes'.)

(c)   In some traditional literary criticism, the term 'masculine rhyme' is used where the rhyme consists of a single stressed syllable ('round' and 'sound'). The term 'feminine rhyme' in the same vocabulary means a rhyme involving two syllables ('yellow' and 'fellow'). An alternative, and possibly more useful, terminology is 'single rhyme' and 'double rhyme', since it also permits 'triple rhyme' for a rhyme involving three syllables.

(d)   Rhymes at the end of lines of poetry are usually organized into patterns, or rhyme schemes. A poem's rhyme scheme can be worked out by marking 'a' against the last word of the first line and against all the end words which rhyme with it; 'b' is then used to mark the next rhyme, and so on. Typical patterns which emerge are: abab, abba, abcabc, etc. Some poetic genres are defined partly on the basis of their rhyme schemes (e.g. the sonnet, the ballad).

(e) Metrical poetry which does not have end rhymes is called blank verse (this should be distinguished from 'free verse'; see **Unit 10, Verse and metre**).

9.3 The significance of sound patterns

So far, we have simply identified possible patterns and presented ways of describing them. In order to investigate how such patterns work as a stylistic resource, we need now to consider what kind of significance or function they might have. Five alternative possibilities are presented below. Each possibility should be considered for each case of sound patterning identified in a text.

1   Patterning may serve no particular function, and be simply the accidental result of a random distribution of the small number of distinct sounds which make up the language. This is especially likely in spontaneous conversation. It is also likely where there is some distance in the text between instances of the sound taken to create the effect: functional sound patterning depends on proximity between the words involved, since readers (or listeners) are unlikely to recognize sounds repeated far apart. Moving to a more formal type of description (see Fabb, 1997), we can express this another way by saying that a distance constraint seems to operate on some or all kinds of sound patterning, and that this distance constraint seems required in order to ensure that such patterning is noticeable or perceptually 'salient'.

2   Patterning may serve a **cohesive** function, bonding words together as formulaic, fixed phrases or units. This extra bonding at the level of sound can enhance the memorability of an utterance, as in riddles, catch phrases, and proverbs ('action pack'; 'a stitch in time saves nine'; 'be Indian, buy Indian', etc.).

3   Patterning may have the effect of emphasizing or **foregrounding** some aspect of the text. Sometimes patterning which involves repetition serves to make a passage seem as though it expresses great feeling, as is often the case in political rhetoric. Sometimes the physical existence of the utterance as a linguistic construct is emphasized, as in the case of tongue twisters such as the alliterative 'Peter Piper picked a pot of pickled peppercorns'.

4   Patterning may have the effect of creating or reinforcing a parallelism. In this case, words which are linked together on the basis of shared sounds will also be linked in terms of their meanings (they typically have similar or opposite meanings). This technique is common in jokes, advertising, and some types of poetry (e.g. Augustan verse). Consider, from this point of view, such phrases as 'chalk and cheese' and 'cash and carry'; or recall Blake's 'marks of weakness, marks of woe', for an example of this effect in Romantic poetry (see **Unit 3**, **Analysing units of structure**).

5   Patterning may contribute to a level of **sound symbolism**. Such effects are based on a belief that the sounds which make up words are not arbitrarily related to their meaning, as most linguists think, but are motivated in some way by being loaded with resonance or connotational value.

A number of further points are worth noting about the notion of sound symbolism:

(a)   The linguistic view that the sounds of language are arbitrary is supported by evidence such as the fact that the same meaning is expressed in different languages by words with very different sounds ('tree', 'arbre', 'Baum', etc.), and that the sounds of words change over time. Such evidence suggests that sounds are merely conventional aspects of the formal system of a language.

(b)   The view that sounds in language may have symbolic meanings or expressive effects, on the other hand, is based on a musical belief that sound itself carries meaning, as well as on the idea that individual sounds are felt differently because the way we make them with the voice differs for each sound. Consider three types of much-discussed evidence for this:

(i)   Here are three imaginary but possible 'words': 'la', 'li', and 'lor'. If you had three tables of different sizes to label with these words, which would you call which? Research has shown that most people – across a wide range of different cultures – label the small table 'li', the middle-sized one 'la' and the largest 'lor'. This tendency probably reflects the fact that sounds are made differently in the mouth: 'lor' is a 'big' sound (mouth open, tongue back, large mouth cavity); 'li', by contrast, is a 'small' sound (mouth relatively closed, tongue up and forward, etc.).

(ii)   Some groups of words have both their sound and their general area of meaning in common (this effect is traditionally called **onomatopoeia**): 'clatter', 'clang' and 'clash' all suggest one thing striking against another; 'sneeze', 'snore', 'snooze' and 'sniffle' are all to do with breathing through the nose and might be considered to sound like the actions they refer to (though consider 'snow' and 'snap' as counter-examples).

(iii)   Consider the hypothesis of a gradience of linguistic sounds, from 'hard' through to 'soft'. The so-called hardest sounds include 'p', 'b', 't', 'd', 'k' and 'g' (which all involve completely stopping breath coming out of the mouth, then releasing it suddenly). The so-called softest sounds are the vowels (which do not impede the air-flow out of the mouth at all, but simply reshape it), plus sounds like those commonly produced from the letters 'w' and 'l'. The idea that words contain hard and soft sounds is sometimes then used as the basis for making an equation between sound and meaning.

(c)   Sound symbolism involves attributing conventional meanings or resonances to sound patterns. In Keats's famous line in 'To Autumn' (1820), 'Thou watchest the last oozings hours by hours', the repeated 's' and 'z' sounds are often taken to represent the oozing of cider in the press. In an equally well-known line from Tennyson, 'The murmuring of innumerable bees' ('The Princess' [1853]), the repeated 'm' sounds are taken to represent the sound of bees. These associations of sound and meaning are not fixed, however: the sounds 's' and 'z' could equally be taken to stand for the buzzing of bees if they were in a poem about bees. Meaning thus contributes significantly to the apparent effect of sound symbolism in a poem.

9.4 Making interpretations on the basis of sound patterns

Having looked at how sound patterns may function, we need to consider how the identification of sound patterning can be used in ways of reading, and to assess some of the possibilities and problems involved in doing this.

Understanding the conventions of many idioms or genres requires that we recognize aspects of their use of sound patterning. Contemporary rapping involves rhyming as one of its main organizational principles; and headlines and advertising slogans have characteristic ways of using sound patterns. Many texts written within established literary traditions draw on conventions of sound patterning (and sometimes sound symbolism) as a conventional compositional resource. Traditions of interpretation of these texts also draw on the same network of conventions.

The conventional register of poetic language has itself fluctuated throughout its history in terms of its use of sound patterning. Some periods and poets have preferred highly complex effects, such as Gerard Manley Hopkins, whose sound patterning is evident in the opening lines of 'The Windhover' (written 1877, published 1918):

I caught this morning morning's minion, king

    dom of daylight's dauphin, dapple-dawn-drawn Falcon, in his riding

    Of the rolling level underneath him steady air, and striding

High there, how he rung upon the rein of a wimpling wing

In his ecstasy!

Such complexity of sound patterning contrasts strongly with, for instance, Wordsworth's aspiration for poetic language (or 'diction') to approximate to the ordinary language of speech, famously presented in the 'Preface to *Lyrical Ballads* (1800) roughly half a century earlier. We should nevertheless be careful about generalizations about the contribution made by sound patterning to poetic styles. This is partly because sound patterning intersects in complex ways with rhythm and other aspects of register; it is also partly because writers are not always consistent in their practice.

Wordsworth's co-authorship of the *Lyrical Ballads* with Samuel Taylor Coleridge, for instance, did not stop Coleridge less than two decades later producing one of the most celebrated instances of intricate sound patterning in English verse – the first lines of 'Kubla Khan' (1816):

In Xanadu did Kubla Khan

    A stately pleasure-dome decree:

Where Alph, the sacred river, ran

Through caverns measureless to man

    Down to a sunless sea.

Earlier in this unit, we listed six types of local sound patterns which can be formed by neighbouring words in a text. These distinctions and labels are useful if they help us to describe sound patterning. But in the actual analysis of texts it often seems that there are no clear-cut boundaries between sound effects. Rhyme, assonance and consonance are mixed together not as a repertoire of separate devices but in a texture of complex and interconnected patterning. Consider the lines from 'Kubla Khan' above in this respect. If you try simply to list instances of sound patterning, you quickly run into difficulties (including difficulties which are the result of language variation as well as language change). Does the vowel in 'Khan' in the first line, for instance, assonate with 'Kubla' (and possibly with 'Xanadu')? Or does it rhyme with the first vowel in 'Xanadu'?

In attempting to interpret sound patterns, it is useful to distinguish between fairly systematic and predictable patterns which serve to define a form (such as rhyme schemes and local kinds of ornamentation), and patterns which have locally marked effects and seem to have expressive or symbolic functions (such as extra memorability or special suggestiveness). One problem with trying to interpret this second kind of pattern is that the expressive or symbolic significance of sound effects cannot simply be read off from a text in a series of mechanical equations between sound and sense (see the examples from Keats and Tennyson above). A sequence of words beginning with the same sound may suggest one thing in one context and quite a different thing in another. The context and meanings of words which appear to create local, expressive effects should therefore take priority. Only after considering these is it safe to suggest ways in which the sound might support (or perhaps undercut) the sense.

More generally, it is rarely, if ever, possible to prove an effect of sound patterning or sound symbolism. Caution is therefore needed in putting forward interpretative arguments based on the connotations or symbolic qualities of sounds. Arguments regarding the expressive or symbolic qualities of sound in a text are persuasive only when they are based on some mutual reinforcement that can be shown between properties of the text at different levels (e.g. between its sounds, grammatical structures, vocabulary, etc.), rather than when appeals are made either directly to fixed symbolic values for sounds, or to a reader's personal sense of a sound's resonance.

Finally, when writing about a text, there is little point in simply listing aspects of its sound patterning (e.g. its rhyme scheme, or the fact that two words alliterate). Comments along these lines only become interesting when linked to one of two kinds of argument: either as a contribution to the identification of a genre or form, where for some reason this is in question or worth establishing; or else to support a case for some local interpretation, where the evocative effect of the sound connects with other indicators of what is meant.

ACTIVITY 9.1

1   Read the three passages given below.

A. (from a letter)

O dear Sir Raph, – I am sory to be the mesinger of so dismall news, for por London is almost burnt down. It began on Saterday night, & has burnt ever sence and is at this tim more fears than ever; it did begin in pudding lan at a backers, whar a Duch rog lay, & burnt to the bridge & all fish street and all crasus stret, & Lumber Stret and the old exchang & canans stret & so all that way to the reaver and bilinsgat sid, & now tis com to chep sid and banescasell, & tis thought flet stret will be burnt by tomorow, thar is nothing left in any hous thar, nor in the Tempell, thar was never so sad a sight, nor so dolefull a cry hard, my hart is not abell to expres the tenth nay the thousenth part of it, thar is all the carts within ten mils round, & cars & drays run about night and day, & thousens of men & women carrying burdens.

> (from a letter by Lady Hobart to Sir Ralph Verney, dated
> 3 Sept 1666, telling him about the Great Fire of London)

B. (from a lyric poem)

> I did not live until this time
> Crown'd my felicity,
> When I could say without a crime,
> I am not thine but Thee.
>
> This carcass breath'd, and walkt, and slept,
> So that the World believ'd
> There was a soul the motions kept;
> But they were all deceiv'd.

(from Katherine Philips, 'To my Excellent Lucasia,
on our Friendship' [pub. 1667], in the Oxford
Book of Seventeenth Century Verse)

C. (from a popular song)

> It was the Frogge in the well,
> Humble-dum, humble-dum.
> And the merrie Mouse in the Mill,
> tweedle, tweedle twino.
>
> The Frogge would a woing ride,
> humble-dum, humble-dum.
> Sword and buckler by his side,
> tweedle, tweedle twino.
>
> When he was upon his high horse set,
> humble dum, humble dum.
> His boots they shone as black as jet,
> tweedle, tweedle twino.

(from 'The Marriage of the Frogge and the Mouse'
[1611], in Opie, The Oxford Dictionary of Nursery Rhymes)

2   Fill in the following grid by giving one example of each type of sound pattern from each passage (if there are any noticeable or perceptually salient instances). (We have filled in the first box for you.)

3   For each of your examples, try to describe the particular effect(s) – if you think there *are* any – conveyed by the sound patterning when the text is read aloud. As a way of doing this, work through the list of different kinds of possible significance for sound patterns provided above.

4   Now consider the following three variants (taken from a dictionary of proverbs) of the common proverb, 'A friend in need is a friend indeed'.

	Text A	Text B	Text C
Alliteration	so sad a sight		
Assonance			
Consonance			
Reverse rhyme			
Pararhyme			
Rhyme			
Rhyme scheme			

Using a grid based on the one given above for the other passages, describe as precisely as you can the different sorts of sound patterning in each version. Again, decide whether it is reasonable to attribute particular psychological, emotive, or aesthetic effects to the patterning you notice.

(a)   The very and trewe frend is fond in the extreme nede.
          (William Caxton's translation, *Fables of Esope* [1484])

(b)   A freende is neuer knowen tyll a man haue neede.
      Before I had neede, my most present foes
      Semed my most freends, but thus the world goes.
                    (John Heywood, *Proverbs* [1546])

(c)   A friend in need is a friend in deed.
                    (John Ray, *English Proverbs* [1678])

5   Sound patterning is a matter of sounds, not written forms. But because many of the extracts presented in this activity were written before the conventions of modern spelling were fully established, some of the words may seem odd to you in the written forms in which they are reproduced here. This strangeness may create difficulties as you try to assess possible sound patterns. Make a note of specific kinds of difficulties you encounter as a result of spellings in the passages.

Reading

Attridge, D. (1982) *The Rhythms of English Poetry*, Harlow: Longman, Chapter 9.
Fabb, N. (1997) *Linguistics and Literature*, Oxford: Blackwell.
Furniss, T.E. and Bath, M. (1996) *Reading Poetry: An Introduction*, London: Prentice-Hall, Chapter 4.
Leech, G. (1969) *A Linguistic Guide to English Poetry*, London: Longman, Chapter 6.

Unit 10

Verse and metre

10.1 Verse

A text which is divided into lines is called **verse**. A line is a specific kind of unit of structure, typically having one of the following characteristics:

(a)   Its internal structure (specifically its prosodic phonological structure, see below) is governed by a metre.

(b)   Its internal structure (usually its syntactic structure or possibly the choice of words) is in canonic parallelism with another line (see **Unit 11**, **Parallelism**).

(c)   It is a single coherent utterance, usually followed by a pause.

(d)   There are characteristic ways in which it begins (e.g. with alliteration) or ends (e.g. with rhyme).

(e)   It is printed on the page as a unit.

Sometimes, verse lines in a particular tradition have more than one of these characteristics. Thus for example in some verse traditions, the lines are both metrical and are single utterances followed by pauses; and if they are written down they are written as distinct units on the page. Some kinds of lines are prototypical; others are less good examples of lines and there are limit cases, lines which are barely distinct as units within the text (as in some kinds of free verse, where there might be ambiguity as to the organization of the poem into lines).

Verse always has lines, and if these are the basic unit of structure in the text, the text is called **stichic**. Epic verse tends to be stichic (in classical and folk traditions as well as in literary epics such as Milton's *Paradise Lost*). If the lines are organized into larger regularly repeated units (stanzas), the text is called **strophic** (ballads are good examples of strophic verse). Lines can also be organized in other ways; thus verse allows for a range of different kinds of units of structure above the line.

10.2 Prosodic phonological structure

The phonological structure of a text is the sequence and organization of sounds which constitute the text. What linguists call **prosodic phonological structure** is the larger-scale organization of sounds, which in English involves the grouping of sounds into syllables and the placement of stress on syllables. All texts, whether literary or not, and whether verse or not, have prosodic phonological structure when they are spoken or sung. A metre governs specific components of the prosodic phonological structure of a text.

A word is made from individual sounds, and all sounds are grouped into syllables. Some sounds make natural 'syllable peaks' (the central sound in the syllable); these include vowels and some consonants such as [l] or [n]; other sounds fit next to the peak in the syllable. It is relatively straightforward to count syllables in a word, by listening for the number of peaks; if you aren't sure, try beating out the syllables as you say the word. It is difficult to say a three-syllable word (for instance) over four beats; it will generally be easier if the number of beats you make also matches the number of syllables.

Words of one syllable are called monosyllables. Some examples are

in, up, man, heart, score, feet, words, smelt, death, wheat, hope

Polysyllables are words of more than one syllable; these are of particular importance for English metres.

2 syllables:	re**a**dy, p**ie**ces, ups**e**t, **a**pple, with**ou**t, **e**nding, f**ea**rsome, Sc**o**tland
3 syllables:	re**a**diness, **e**verywhere, undert**a**ke, m**a**nicure, r**a**ndomness, g**e**ntlemen
4 syllables:	monstr**o**sity, rep**u**lsiveness, men**a**gerie, telesc**o**pic, dissert**a**tion
5 syllables:	unre**a**lity, fortific**a**tion, str**u**cturalism, Winnepes**au**kee, philos**o**phical
6 syllables:	encyclop**ae**dia, poststr**u**cturalism, psychotherap**eu**tic

Some words have alternative numbers of syllables (e.g. 'literature' usually has 3 but can be pronounced with 4; 'Wednesday' can be pronounced with 2 or 3).

Although all syllables peak, some syllables peak more than others – these might be louder, longer or higher, and are called **stressed syllables**. Stressed syllables are relatively 'strong', with unstressed syllables being relatively 'weak'; we introduce this notion of strength because metrical verse tends to be best thought of in terms of strength rather than in terms of stress alone, as we will shortly see. Within a word, the pattern of stressed and unstressed syllables is always the same, with some differences between accents. (The realizations of stress are also different in different accents; in Scottish English for example, there are less marked differences between stressed and unstressed syllables, giving a different sense of stress, though more abstractly the patterns of stress within the word are usually identical to those of other accents.) In the words above, where I think the strongest stresses are in each word this is shown in bold type (I show the syllable peak – sometimes written as a single vowel and sometimes written as two vowels). You can usually check whether you have the syllable count and stress of a word right if you look in a dictionary (or a dictionary of pronunciation); remember, though, that accents differ sometimes in where the stresses are placed within a word.

10.3 Metre

In metrical verse, the prosodic phonological structure of a line is **governed** by the metre. There are various ways of doing this, found in different literatures. In some literary traditions (e.g. Welsh, Irish, French) a syllabic metre governs the number of syllables in the line. In other literary traditions (e.g. Old English) an accentual metre governs the number of strongly stressed (= accented) syllables in the line. Many of the metres of literary poetry in English govern two things – the number of syllables and also the relative placement of stressed syllables – and this dual function is marked by giving them a dual name: they are **accentual-syllabic** metres.

In metrical verse, all the lines can be governed by the same metre; the text is then said to be isometric. Most English poetry is **isometric**, in that the poem has the same metre throughout. But it is also possible for different lines to be governed by different metres, and if this occurs then the text is called **heterometric.** Heterometric verse is quite rare in English and where it exists it tends to vary the metre in terms of the number of syllables in the line (rather than in the placement of stresses), giving rise to longer and shorter lines within the same poem. These lines from Wordsworth's 'Intimations of Immortality from Recollections of Early Childhood' (1807) are heterometric:

		no. of syllables
1	Our birth is but a sleep and a forgetting:	11
2	The Soul that rises with us, our life's Star,	10
3	Hath had elsewhere its setting	7
4	And cometh from afar	6
5	Not in entire forgetfulness	8
6	And not in utter nakedness	8
7	But trailing clouds of glory do we come	10
8	from God who is our home:	6

Lines 1 and 2 are in iambic pentameter, lines 3 and 4 iambic trimeter; lines 5 and 6 iambic tetrameter; line 7 iambic pentameter; line 8 iambic trimeter. (Note the extra syllables in lines 1 and 3, examples of 'extrametricality' to be discussed shortly.)

The prosodic phonological structure of a text is fixed in certain respects, but in other respects it can be altered in performance. The aspects of the text which are fixed are (a) the number of syllables in the text, and (b) the stress patterns inside (polysyllabic) words. It is these two fixed aspects of texts which are most commonly governed by a metre. The major aspects of an English language text's prosodic phonological structure which can be altered in performance are: (a) the distribution and relative strength of stresses across a whole utterance; (b) the length of syllables (which can be stretched out or compressed); and (c) the pitch of syllables (altered for example in singing a melody). While these aspects of an English language text are not normally governed by the metre, they might be governed by other means, for example by pre-existing musical rhythm or melody into which the text is fitted.

10.4 Iambic pentameter and other accentual-syllabic metres of English

An accentual-syllabic metre governs the number of syllables in the line and also governs the placement of some of the stressed (or 'accented') syllables in the line. To illustrate, consider the following poem, Shakespeare's Sonnet 40 (1609):

> Take all my loves, my love, yea, take them all;
> What hast thou then more than thou hadst before?
> No love, my love, that thou mayst true love call;
> 4   All mine was thine **before** thou hadst this more.
> Then if for my love thou my love **receivest**,
> I **cannot** blame thee for my love thou **usest**;
> But yet be blamed, if thou **thyself deceivest**
> 8   By **wilful** taste of what **thyself refusest**.
> I do **forgive** thy **robbery**, **gentle** thief,
> **Although** thou steal thee all my **poverty**;
> And yet, love knows, it is a **greater** grief
> 12   To bear love's wrong than hate's known **injury**.
> **Lascivious** grace, in whom all ill well shows,
> Kill me with spites; yet we must not be foes.

Note first the characteristics of the lines. Each line is governed by a metre; there is a tendency for a pause at the end of the line and sentences have a loose tendency to end here; and it is of course printed in lines. (Some metrical verse is not printed in lines, incidentally; it has been argued by Morris Halle and others that some of the Hebrew psalms are divided into metrical lines though they were originally written down as continuous prose.)

The metre does two things. First, it requires each line to have ten syllables. This is why lines 1–4, and 10–14 have ten syllables. Why, then do lines 5–8 have eleven syllables, if they are required by the metre to have ten? This is a common phenomenon called **extrametricality**. Some parts of the line – usually the very end of the line – fall outside the control of the metre (hence are extra-metrical); it is as though the metre does not exhaustively govern the verse line, leaving a residue. It has been argued that the Italian endecasillabo metre, close to iambic pentameter and used by Petrarch and Dante, where there are between ten and twelve syllables in the line but usually eleven, is in fact a ten-syllable metre with frequent extrametricality. Thus we see that the metre has limited exceptions. There is in fact another limited exception on show in line 9, where the three-syllable word 'robbery' adds an extra syllable to the line, giving eleven syllables again. This is probably not a case of extra-metricality because the word is in the middle of the line and not 'out of view' of the metre as it would be if it were at the end of the line. Instead, this is most likely to be a case where two syllables '-ery' are counted as one for the purposes of the metre (a phenomenon sometimes called **resolution** and again fairly common in English and other metres). Given extrametricality and resolution, we can now see that all the lines are governed by a ten-syllable metre.

The second thing which the metre does is to govern the placement of certain stressed syllables. In an iambic metre, there is a general tendency for the stressed syllables to be in even positions in the line (e.g. here, we would expect stressed syllables to be in positions 2, 4, 6, 8, and 10). This does not mean that every even position is filled by a stressed syllable, but it does mean that we might expect a stressed syllable to be in an even position. This is clearest when we look at words which have an unvarying stress pattern – that is, polysyllables (words containing more than one syllable). If we look at the polysyllabic words in the poem (in boldface), we can see that the stressed syllables (in italics) in the polysyllables are all in even positions – second in lines 6, 8, 10, 13; fourth in line 9; sixth in lines 4 and 9; eighth in lines 7, 8, 9, 11, 12, and tenth in lines 5, 6, 7. What about monosyllabic words (words of one syllable)? Many monosyllables can be stressed, or not, depending on the performance of the verse; this means that the metre has less control over them, but there is nevertheless a loose pattern where stressed monosyllables have a slight tendency to be in even positions. In the poem quoted above, all the stresses in polysyllabic words are aligned exactly as the metre would predict. However, there is a fairly common variation, which is found at the beginning of the line; here it is possible for a stressed syllable in a polysyllabic word to be in the first position (i.e. not an even position), a phenomenon called **trochaic inversion** and seen in the following line (also from Shakespeare):

Bearing the **wanton burthen** of the prime

In this line the second and third polysyllables have their stressed syllables in even positions, but the first has its stressed syllable in an odd position (the first). Trochaic inversion seems to involve some loosening of the metre's grip at the beginning of the line; the fact that the metre is looser at the beginning is very common in all metrical verse throughout the world (just as extrametrical effects are), and may reflect something about the way metrical composition and reception work at a psychological level.

So far we have concentrated on polysyllables at the expense of monosyllables. Monosyllables are counted by the syllable counting part of the metre, but because they do not have internal stress patterns there is little which can be controlled by the stress part of the metre. There is a general tendency for important monosyllabic words to be in even positions, but this cannot be a basic metrical fact since it is not based on prosodic phonological characteristics of the words. It may be the result of something slightly different, which is a tendency to perform the lines with a regular rhythm, placing greater stress on even syllables (which the metre conspires with when polysyllables are involved). Note, however, that any regularity of the rhythm in performance, while it might be supported by the metre, is not itself a requirement of the metre. The metre controls only the structure of the text, not how it is performed.

Why is the metre of Shakespeare's text called 'iambic pentameter'? The term comes from a way of conceptualizing how the metre works. It assumes that the metre is a complex structure, consisting of a sequence of five iambic feet, where an iambic foot is made from two metrical positions with the second metrical position in each case being metrically strong. The metre governs the number of syllables by requiring that each syllable matches a single metrical position (there are $5 \times 2 = 10$ metrical positions, hence ten syllables). And the metre requires that stressed syllables in polysyllabic words fit metrically strong positions (hence even-numbered metrical positions).

foot		foot		foot		foot		foot	
w	s	w	s	w	s	w	s	w	s
Although		thou	steal	thee	all	my		**poverty**;	

Different kinds of metre can involve different numbers of feet, and differently structured feet, but the basic principle of matching syllables and stressed syllables is the same. A trimeter has three feet; tetrameter has four feet; pentameter has five feet; hexameter has six feet, etc. An iambic foot is a two-position foot with the second one metrically strong; a trochaic foot is a two-position foot with the first one metrically strong. An anapaestic foot is a three-position foot with the third metrically strong; a dactylic foot is a three-position foot with the first metrically strong; and so on. The number of metrical positions (and hence of syllables) is calculated by multiplying the number of feet by the number of metrical positions in each foot. It is worth noting that the heterometric text we saw earlier varies the number of feet in the line rather than the number of syllables.

10.5 Songs

There are various kinds of similarity between musical structure, on the one hand, and prosodic phonological structure and metrical structure, on the other; these include the division into constituents and the distinction between strong and weak constituents. These similarities raise questions about the influence of musical structure on songs, which are texts which are set to music.

It is particularly relevant to compare the small musical constituents – musical notes – with syllables and metrical positions. If we consider just English songs, there are major differences between different sorts of song. In some cases, there might be a tendency to match a single note with a single syllable; in other cases several syllables might fit into a single note, or a single syllable might be spread over a range of notes. In addition to the matching of syllables to notes, the timing of the notes might also be important (would longer notes fit two syllables, or one syllable stretched over the long note?). In principle, we might find that for a particular song there is a requirement that the text be composed from syllables which will match the notes from which the song is constructed; thus the musical structure might to some extent govern the structure of the text, if the text is composed to fit the music. If the text is also metrical, then it might be influenced from two directions – by the requirements of the music on the one hand, and the requirements of the metre on the other.

The issue is complicated further by stress, and accentual or accentual-syllabic metres. If, for example, we take a text which is governed by iambic pentameter, this means that the stressed syllables in polysyllabic words will be in specific places in each metrical line. Is the setting of such a text to music also sensitive to these stressed syllables in polysyllabic words which are so important for the metre? Do they, for example, match to the first (accented) beat in a bar? Do they match notes which are emphasized in other ways, such as by marked length or pitch? Or does the setting of text to music ignore these important stressed syllables, or alternatively exploit tensions which might be felt when these important stressed syllables are placed in musically weak positions? Many questions arise, which would need to be answered on a case-by-case basis; it is possible that different composers would exploit different strategies for coping with the stress patterns of metrical texts in setting them to music.

Some kinds of text might have their characteristics shaped entirely by being sung, with no role played by a metre. Consider, for example, the first two lines of a ballad:

I'll tell you a Tale of my Love and I,
How we did often a milking goe.

In saying these lines aloud, there is a tendency to put four strong stresses into each line:

I'll **tell** you a **Ta**le of my **Lo**ve and **I**,
How **we** did **of**ten a **mi**lking **goe**.

However, this is not a matter of metre, but of the performance of the text according to a regular beat. As originally composed, this text would have been put to music, presumably with four beats to the musical phrase, and it is this which shapes the text and its performance, rather than a metre. In the history of English verse, there are genuinely accentual metres, which govern only stress and not syllable counting. These metres control aspects of the prosodic phonological structure of the line in more restricted ways than those found in folksongs (and in addition may place other requirements such as alliteration on the line). They include the metres of Old English (such as that of the eighth-century poem *Beowulf*) and some medieval verse (such as the fourteenth-century poem *Sir Gawain and the Green Knight*).

10.6 Free verse

Until the nineteenth century, most English verse was either governed by a metre or by being matched to a musical structure. The consequence of this is that this verse tends to be divided into lines which are regular in terms of their prosodic phonological structure. Particularly in the twentieth century, much verse has been written where the lines do not have regular prosodic phono-logical structure because they are unconstrained by a metre (or by a regular musical structure). This is **free verse**; an important early example is provided by Whitman's *Leaves of Grass* (1855):

Suddenly out of its stale and drowsy lair, the lair of slaves,
Like lightning it le'pt forth half startled at itself,
Its feet upon the ashes and the rags, its hand tight to the throats
    of kings.

Sections of these lines resemble metrical verse – there are coherent sequences which resemble iambic pentameter here (e.g. the first half of the third line could be a complete iambic pentameter line), as well as sequences of anapaestic feet (the beginning). But within each line there is no overriding regularity in the prosodic phonological structure. Instead, the lines are defined as constituents not by a metre but by other principles: the visual layout on the page, the syntactic structure of the sentences, a general principle of allowing each line to be declaimed as a single utterance followed by a pause (i.e. the line as a unit defined by what the poet Allen Ginsberg referred to as 'bardic breath').

10.7 What to look for in verse

Verse is interesting for a number of reasons. Metrical verse is characterized by a degree of formal complexity perhaps greater than that found in any other aspect of literature; for this reason, some researchers have suggested that the possibility of composing metrical verse reflects deep aspects of how we process language. This is much debated, and there is still no general agreement on how best to understand how metres work.

In the reading of specific verse texts, one of the questions often worth asking is whether the different kinds of constituent structure match or mismatch. In verse, the major constituent is the line. The language of the text is also divided into major constituents – sentence, subordinate clauses, and phrases – and it is worth asking whether in a particular text line endings are matched with major linguistic constituent endings. Matches or mismatches might give rise to aesthetic effects of coherence or complexity, and their use might reflect the aesthetic attitudes of the time. An example of mismatch, where the line ending interrupts a syntactic constituent (a phenomenon called **enjamb-ment**) can be found in Wordsworth's *The Prelude* (1805):

> And there, with fingers interwoven, both hands
> Press'd closely, palm to palm, and to his mouth
> Uplifted, . . .

In both first and second lines a noun phrase is interrupted, with the noun coming at the end of the line and a modifying phrase (contained in the same phrase as the noun) coming at the beginning of the next line. Mismatches between syntactic and line structure are common in this text, but much less common in poetry of the preceding century, with its different aesthetic aims. Compare the following lines from a poem by John Brown published in 1776:

> . . . Now every eye,
> Oppressed with toil, was drowned in deep repose;

Here, too, we have a noun separated from its modifier by a line break. Though superficially similar, the major difference is that the modifying phrase is separated from the noun by a comma, and in fact constitutes additional information about an already established phrase 'every eye'. Thus it is not as coherently bound to the preceding noun as the modifiers in the Wordsworth text, where the modifiers crucially express what the body parts are doing and hence are very tightly bound to the noun in the preceding line. Thus there is no reason to describe the Brown text as involving enjambment.

These are two poems by Matthew Arnold, originally printed in distinct lines, but rewritten as continuous text for the purposes of this exercise. You can check your answers to (3) and (6) by looking up the originals; text B in particular is widely anthologized.

A. Part of 'To Marguerite' (1852)

> But when the moon their hollows lights and they are swept by balms of spring, and in their glens, on starry nights, the nightingales divinely sing; and lovely notes, from shore to shore, across the sounds and channels pour;

B. All of 'Dover Beach' (1867)

> The sea is calm to-night. The tide is full, the moon lies fair upon the Straits; – on the French coast, the light gleams, and is gone; the cliffs of England stand, glimmering and vast, out in the tranquil bay. Come to the window, sweet is the night air! Only, from the long line of spray where the ebb meets the moon-blanch'd sand, listen! you hear the grating roar of pebbles which the waves suck back, and fling, at their return, up the high strand, begin, and cease, and then again begin, with tremulous cadence slow, and bring the eternal note of sadness in. Sophocles long ago heard it on the Aegean, and it brought into his mind the turbid ebb and flow of human misery; we find also in the sound a thought, hearing it by this distant northern sea. The sea of faith was once, too, at the full, and round earth's shore lay like the folds of a bright girdle furl'd; but now I only hear its melancholy, long, withdrawing roar, retreating to the breath of the night-wind down the vast edges drear and naked shingles of the world. Ah, love, let us be true to one another! For the world, which seems to lie before us like a land of dreams, so various, so beautiful, so new, hath really neither joy, nor love, nor light, nor certitude, nor peace, nor help for pain; and we are here as on a darkling plain swept with confused alarms of struggle and flight, where ignorant armies clash by night.

1   What evidence is there that text A is verse?

2   What evidence is there that text A is in a metre which controls its rhythm (e.g. an iambic metre)?

3   Try to reconstruct the original printed line-divisions of text A.

4   What evidence is there that text B is verse?

5   What evidence is there that text B is in a metre which controls its rhythm (e.g. an iambic metre)?

6   Try to reconstruct the original printed line-divisions of text B.

7   Try to reconstruct the stanza divisions within text B, and explain what evidence you are using.

8   Why are these tasks more difficult for text B than for text A, and why did Arnold write text B in a way which creates these difficulties? (Remember that he wrote both poems in lines on the page, not as here.)

Reading

Attridge, D. (1982) *The Rhythms of English Poetry*, Harlow: Longman.

Attridge, D. (1995) *Poetic Rhythm: An Introduction*, Cambridge: Cambridge University Press.

Fabb, N. (1997) *Linguistics and Literature*, Oxford: Blackwell, Chapters 2–4.

Furniss, T.E. and Bath, M. (1996) *Reading Poetry: An Introduction*, London: Prentice-Hall, Chapter 2.

Fussell, P. (1979) *Poetic Meter and Poetic Form*, New York: McGraw-Hill.

Halle, M. (1987) 'A biblical pattern poem', in N.D. Fabb, A. Durant and C. McCabe (eds) *The Linguistics of Writing: Arguments between Language and Literature*, Manchester: Manchester University Press.

Hayes, B. (1995) *Metrical Stress Theory*, Chicago: University of Chicago Press.

Wimsatt, W.K. (ed.) (1972) *Versification: Major Language Types: Sixteen Essays*, New York: MLA and New York University Press.

Unit 11

Parallelism

Parallelism exists in a text when some component of the form or the meaning of a text is similar to some other component at some abstract level of description. The following example from Blake's *Poetical Sketches* (1783) illustrates parallelisms in form and in meaning:

> He caught me in his silken net,
> And shut me in his golden cage.

The two lines are formally parallel because they are the same at a particular abstract level of description: the level of sentence structure (= 'syntactic structure'). The structure of the first line is pronoun ('he') + verb + pronoun ('me') + preposition ('in') + pronoun ('his') + adjective + noun. The second line has exactly the same structure except that it begins with 'and' and drops the first pronoun (which is implied). They are formally identical as a sequence of categories from the verb onwards, and thus formally identical at an abstract level, even though on the surface they differ (in the verbs 'caught' and 'shut', in the adjectives 'silken' and 'golden', in the nouns 'net' and 'cage'). The two lines also show two distinct parallelisms in meaning. Each line describes a 'pleasant' imprisonment; this abstraction from the meaning is the same between the lines, whereas the specific meaning differs between the lines. And the words 'caught' and 'shut' (and the other pairs), though they are different words, are parallel because they belong to the same more abstract area of meaning ('semantic field', see below), which we might call 'entrapment' vocabulary.

While it is always true to say that there is some abstract identity between two parallel sections of text, we might further distinguish **polar parallelisms** from **non-polar parallelisms**. 'Polar' in this sense means 'consisting of two opposed elements' (like the north vs. the south pole). Polar parallelisms include for example 'love' and 'hate' where the two words belong to the same semantic field (and so at this abstract level are the same) but are opposites within that

123

field. If the parallelism was instead between 'hate' and 'dislike' then this would be a non-polar parallelism between two words in the same semantic field. The syntactic parallelism in Blake's lines is non-polar because the same syntactic components are in the same order; there is no opposition. In contrast the following line from Thomas Gray's 'Elegy Written in a Country Churchyard' (1751) illustrates a polar syntactic parallelism:

> Large was his bounty and his soul sincere.

Here the two halves of the line are parallel: their abstract similarity is that they both consist of an adjective ('large' and 'sincere') and a noun phrase with a possessive pronoun ('his bounty' and 'his soul'). However, while the components at this abstract level are in non-polar parallelism as components, they are in polar parallelism in order: AB sequence in the first half and BA sequence in the second half (with A = adjective, and B = noun phrase). This is called **chiasmus**. Note that there is another kind of difference between the two half lines, in that the first half has the copula 'was' and the second half lacks it; this is a common practice in syntactic parallelism, where some components are omitted rather than repeated – it is called **ellipsis**.

There is a special case of parallelism, where the two components of the text are identical on the surface; this is **repetition**. Thus the final two lines of Robert Frost's poem 'Stopping by Woods on a Snowy Evening' are identical. However, though the lines are the same formally and in meaning, they nevertheless do differ in one respect, which is that they are in different places in the poem. Thus even exact repetition falls under the more general case of parallelism whereby there is some difference on the surface between components which are identical at some abstract level.

There is a fundamental difference between parallelism and metre (**Unit 10**), despite superficial similarities between them. Superficially, lines in a metrical poem seem to be parallel to each other, in that they differ on the surface but are identical at some abstract level (in their metrical structure). In the broadest definition of parallelism (such as that used by Roman Jakobson, discussed below), lines of metrical verse are thus instances of parallelism. However, this very broad approach misses a fundamental difference between parallelism and metre. In metrical verse, the lines are similar to one another but only because all the lines are measured against the same external model (the metre); thus the similarity between lines is not primary but is derived from something else. This is why verse can be heterometric, where the lines are metrical but do not necessarily resemble one another (but each metrical line matches its own external model). In contrast, in parallelism, each section of text matches another section of text directly (at some level of abstraction), with no external model forcing the section into a particular pattern. The difference between metre vs. parallelism is similar to the difference between two different copies of the same text printed off the same machine vs. an original and a photocopy.

11.1 Kinds of parallelism

In this section we review some of the different kinds of parallelism, illustrating some of them from the following poem by Margaret Cavendish, Duchess of Newcastle (1653):

The Clasp

1   Give me the free and noble style,
2   Which seems uncurbed, though it be wild:
3   Though it runs wild about, it cares not where;
4   It shows more courage, then it doth of fear.
5   Give me a style that nature frames, not art:
6   For art doth seem to take the pedants part.
7   And that seems noble, which is easy, free,
8   Not to be bound with ore-nice pedantry.   [ore = over]

Lexical parallelism is a parallelism in meaning, involving words (hence 'lexical'). Typically, lexical parallelism involves two or more words which belong to the same basic area of meaning, called a **semantic field**. The words can be in non-polar relation (roughly similar meanings) or in polar opposition (opposite meanings). There are a number of semantic fields in operation here, including:

field 1.   free – uncurbed – wild – easy
field 2.   frames – bound
field 3.   wild – nature
field 4.   art – pedants, pedantry
field 5.   seems – shows – frames – art
field 6.   clasp (title) – frames

Notice that the semantic fields overlap, and can also be fitted into larger semantic fields. 1 and 3 form one field (concerning freedom and being natural); 2, 4, 5, and 6 form another (concerning the idea of being framed – in more than one sense – by artifice). Although they are polar opposites, 1 and 2 form another kind of field (concerning the idea of being bound or unbound). From this, we can see that the semantic fields in the text involve general thematic parallelisms between art and restriction, and between nature and freedom. (Thus an examination of parallelism may be used to highlight the 'value-system' which a text is assuming or promoting: here, nature is being associated with freedom and is preferred over the restrictions of art.) Notice that the decision that certain words belong together in a semantic field is an interpretive decision, partly guided by the various kinds of parallelisms in the poem (hence, 'noble' can be put into the semantic field with 'free', etc., guided by the syntactic parallelism). In addition to parallelism involving semantic fields between different words, this poem also has lexical parallelism in the repetition of identical words in different places. If we count the uses of repeated words by writing a number above each occurrence, we see that the most common of the 'important' words is 'seems' (3 uses), and that 'wild', 'style', 'art', 'noble', and 'free' are each repeated twice. This use of lexical repetition (a subtype of lexical parallelism) draws attention to important notions in the poem, helping us to its meaning.

Syntactic parallelism (parallelism in sentence structure) is a parallelism in form. This is a parallelism between two sections of text which have the same syntactic components. As we saw in the previous section, it is possible to have the components in the same order, or to reverse the orders (or other possibilities). Furthermore, components can be omitted by ellipsis in the parallel sections. Syntactic parallelism is fairly common in poetry, particularly in metrical verse, between lines or between half-lines. It is typically combined with lexical parallelism, where words from the same semantic field are found in similar syntactic positions. In the text above, pattern of syntactic parallelism can be seen in lines 2 and 7, both internal to each line and between the lines. Line 2 has two instances of the components verb + adjective: 'seems uncurbed' and 'be wild'; line 7 has the same internal parallelism with a variant: 'seems noble' and 'is easy, free'. Note that there is also a lexical parallelism here, involving a semantic field into which 'uncurbed', 'wild', 'easy' and 'free' fall, and by implication into which 'noble' should also be put – thus we are forced into certain interpretations (noble = free) by the parallelisms in the poem.

Phonological parallelism is parallelism involving sounds ('phonological units'). There are basically two kinds of phonological parallelism. The most common type of phonological parallelism in English literature involves coherent 'clumps' of sound, and is exemplified by rhyme and alliteration. In rhyme and alliteration, individual sounds parallel other individual sounds, or small coherent sequences of sounds parallel other small coherent sequences. Most of the rhymes in the poem are line-final (in couplets), with one possible internal rhyme 'me' and 'free'; there is alliteration at least in 'pedants' and 'part'. There is little to say about these phonological parallelisms in this text; however, in some texts, words which are phonologically parallel can also be interpreted as lexically parallel, a further example of a reinforcement of one type of parallelism by another. We might argue that some kinds of rhyme (and in some traditions, alliteration) can fall outside parallelism proper, and instead are like metre in matching the sound-structure of the text to some external model. Thus, for example, Shakespeare's sonnets have a rhyme scheme of ABABCDCDEFEFGG; here it seems that the sounds could be said not to rhyme with each other directly but to be matched against some external model. There is another type of phonological parallelism, which is developed systematically in some literary traditions; this is a parallelism between two longer, more dispersed, sequences of sounds and could be called **sound-pattern**

parallelism. Examples of this are found in the technique of *cynghanedd* in Welsh poetry, where a sequence of consonants in the first half of the line is repeated in the second half of the line; the Welsh-born poet Gerard Manley Hopkins adapted this technique in some of his English-language poems.

We now turn to kinds of parallelism which are common in narratives, both basically parallelisms of meaning. The component parts of a narrative include distinct subplots, episodes, characters and narrative props, and all of these types of component can be involved in parallelism – either non-polar or polar. Thus for example it is not uncommon for a sub-plot to parallel a main plot (as for example in Shakespeare's *A Midsummer Night's Dream* (1596)). A narrative might be organized into groups of parallel episodes, possibly stacked up according to some numerical rule (e.g. three incidents of one kind, followed by three incidents of another). And it is common to have characters in a narrative who are similar at some level of abstract description but who are opposites on the surface; there may be a polar parallelism between the hero and the villain.

There are many other potential kinds of parallelism. Wherever superficial aspects of a text are subject to a more abstract level of analysis, it is possible for different superficial aspects to be the same at a more abstract level, and hence for parallelism to emerge. Thus for example there might be parallelisms involving shape or colour between two different images in a film, or parallelisms between shape and interpretation in a pattern-poem (like George Herbert's poem 'Easter Wings' (1633)).

11.2 How parallelism is identified and interpreted in a text

It is possible to distinguish between an occasional parallelism and a more systematic kind of parallelism which is technically called **canonic parallelism**. Roman Jakobson (Fox, 1977) introduced the term 'canonic parallelism' while pointing out that many of the world's written and oral literatures have systematic (i.e. canonic) parallelism as a fundamental formal characteristic. These parallelisms tend to be syntactic parallelisms or lexical parallelisms, though phonological parallelisms (of the sound-pattern parallelism type) are also found. In these literatures, there is a general expectation that for large sections of the text, segments of text will be parallel to other segments of text; thus for example we might expect every second line to be syntactically or lexically parallel to the preceding line. Canonic parallelisms of this kind are characteristic of some of the literatures of Central America, Indonesia, the ancient Near East, and traditional Northern literatures stretching from Finland to Mongolia. In these literatures, parallelism appears to constitute the fundamental structuring principle in verse, which is played by metre in metrical literatures (verse in these canonic parallelism traditions is in many cases not metrical).

It is difficult to find good examples of canonic parallelism in literature in English; if canonic parallelism existed then we should be able to come to a text with an expectation of a high degree of fairly systematic and uniform parallelistic structure. But even in types of verse which have a lot of parallelism (e.g. eighteenth-century verse), parallelism is never found consistently in line after line. Literature in English tends to have the occasional type of parallelism instead; that is, parallelisms exist somewhat intermittently and unpredictably. In this type of occasional parallelism, we might come to the text with a loose expectation of parallelism, but will identify it in the text on a case-by-case basis, and might in principle disagree whether certain patterns are obvious enough or closely enough repeated to count as parallelism. Parallelism is thus again different from metre; in English verse, every line in a text is usually metrical, but parallelism will be sometimes present and sometimes absent.

Where two parts of a literary text are parallel, this can guide us in our interpretation of the text. We saw this in the discussion of the Cavendish poem. The idea that parallelism is somehow significant, and guides meaning, can be exploited by writers to produce complex effects. Thus Douglas Oliver's *The Diagram Poems* (1979) places text and diagram on opposing sides of the open book; there are clues which suggest that the text of the poem and the diagram are parallel at some abstract level, but the clues are somewhat indeterminate, such that there are various possible directions for interpretation. The point is that the decision that a parallelism exists, which is strongly supported by the book, is a licence to interpret the text in one of a number of ways. Similarly John Ashbery's poem 'A wave' (1981) consists of two simultaneous texts, parallel to one another by placement on the page, but about apparently very different things; the placement, however, suggests that there is some level at which the texts are similar, and sets the reader the difficult task of reading the poem as a whole by finding the basis for the implied parallelism.

Parallelisms in a text can also draw upon parallelisms which are built into the culture, through the classifications and distinctions which are commonly made by our vocabulary and our social practices. Thus for example our culture might offer us a range of polar oppositions (each based on an abstract parallelism) between male and female, between nature and culture, between the country and the city, between the organic and the mechanical, between the animal and the human, between the oriental and the western, between the sane and the mad, between writing and speech, etc. A value is often placed on the two poles, such that one pole is seen as better or more important than the other. Any of these cultural parallelisms can be exploited in literary parallelisms (most obviously in lexical parallelisms and in parallelisms in narratives). Cultural parallelisms have an interesting characteristic, which is that individual polar oppositions can be related to one another, with the horizontal pair of two-part (polar) parallelisms forming a larger non-polar vertical parallelism:

culture	vs.	nature
the city	vs.	the country
the mechanical	vs.	the organic

Literature can also build on these larger-scale parallelisms built from basic oppositions; in particular this opposition between the country and the city, with all the sub-oppositions which it invokes, is widespread in British literature.

11.3 Functions of parallelism

There are probably a large number of functions which parallelism can play; in this section we consider some of the basic functions for parallelism.

Parallelism holds a text together by setting up formal relations between its various parts. In this way parallelism is a kind of textual glue. In advertisements made up of a photograph and writing, for example, the different media are typically yoked together by some kind of parallelism (see **Unit 15**, **Juxtaposition**). Our analysis of the Cavendish poem suggests that poems can be 'glued' together in a number of different ways through parallelism. We might say that 'The Clasp' has a high 'density' of parallelism both formally (the frequency and variety of sound-based parallelisms) and semantically (the large number of words which relate to binding/freedom and art/nature). There are a number of ways in which we could think about the density of parallelism in 'The Clasp'. We might ask whether it is unusually dense for poems of its time, or whether, as a representative poem from the mid-seventeenth century, it differs in density from a representative poem from a century earlier or a century later. This might assist an investigation of how poetic register differs in different periods. If we were interested in possible differences between women's and men's writing, we might compare its density with the density of a male-authored poem of the same time. Or a reader might ask whether the highly-organized patterns of parallelism in the poem contradict its speaker's celebration of 'the free and noble style'. Thus the density of parallelisms within poetry is not just a general and obvious fact, but a subtle and interesting issue in its own right.

Parallelism contributes to the way texts create meanings and draw upon parallelisms operating in the culture which surrounds them. In 'The Clasp', for example, the parallelisms build a repeated thematic opposition (itself a parallelism) between Nature and Art, which is made parallel in the poem to another thematic opposition between unboundedness and boundedness. These are meanings created by the text, but they draw upon parallelisms which exist in the cultural context: the opposition of Nature and Art is a fundamental one in British culture (though the way it is understood varies through history), and the poem is simply adopting this already-existing parallelism and putting it to use. (Remember this opposition when you do the activity at the end of this unit.) When a text brings two words or phrases together in formal parallelism it stimulates us to consider whether there are parallelisms in their meanings; for example, in these lines from 'Epilogue to the Satires' by Alexander Pope (1738), 'Shame' and 'Fame' are formally parallel (they rhyme), and this invites us to consider the possible parallelism between these usually very different concepts (see **Unit 9**, **Rhyme and sound patterning**):

> Let humble ALLEN, with an awkward Shame,
> Do good by stealth, and blush to find it Fame.

This function of parallelism suggests that the conventional distinction between form and content is a problematic one.

Parallelism can make a text easier to remember (e.g. a chorus, a repeated phrase or refrain, a patterning of events). This is particularly important in oral literature, where texts exist only by virtue of being remembered; it is also particularly true for canonic parallelism, where parallelism may take on a mnemonic function elsewhere played by metre.

Parallelism can create expectation and excitement and is often used for emotive and persuasive effects; this rhetorical function is clear in the syntactic and intonational parallelism of political speeches:

> No government owns the law. It is the law of the land, the heritage of the people. No man is above the law and no man is below it. . . . Obedience to the law is demanded as a right, not asked as a favour.
>
> (British Prime Minister Margaret Thatcher,
> Party Conference Speech 1984)

Shakespeare often reproduces this feature of political speeches. In *Henry V* (1589), the king rouses his troops before the battle of Agincourt (against overwhelming odds) by first offering money to any man who wishes to go home, saying that

> We would not die in that man's company
> That fears his fellowship to die with us.

This is, of course, an attempt to persuade the soldiers that it would be honourable to die in such company, and its use of parallelism contributes to that end; this is reinforced shortly afterwards by the king's most persuasive (and parallelistic) description of those who will join him in battle: 'We few, we happy few, we band of brothers' (for the whole speech, see IV, ii, 18–67). In a Christian context, influenced by the Bible, syntactic parallelism is also associated with authority and divine inspiration; this is because Hebrew poetry has parallelism to a degree which might constitute canonic parallelism and English translations of the Bible often retain this feature (in fact, the earliest critical analysis of parallelism was an eighteenth-century discussion of the Bible). The Psalms provide good examples of this:

> They have mouths, but they speak not;
> Eyes have they, but they see not;
> They have ears, but they hear not
> > (from Psalm 135)

Much of our current understanding of parallelism in the world's literatures comes from the work of Roman Jakobson, who pointed out how extensive parallelism (specifically canonic parallelism) is in the literatures of the world. Jakobson related the widespread use of parallelism to fundamental characteristics of literary language. He suggested that, of the various functions of language, the 'poetic function' which is dominant in literature requires that the reader or hearer's attention is drawn to the language of the text itself (he called this a 'focus on the message', with the 'message' being the actual text itself). This can be achieved in various ways, but linguistic parallelisms (parallelisms involving language) – syntactic parallelism, lexical parallelism, and phonological parallelism – are very effective means of drawing attention to form, because the recognition of a parallelism requires that we go beneath the surface of the text to some more abstract representation of the text (i.e. to some level of linguistic form). Thus parallelism has a central place in literature because it is ideally placed to carry out one of the basic functions of literary language – to draw attention to the linguistic form of the text.

ACTIVITY 11.1

To the Ladies

Wife and servant are the same,
But only differ in the name:
For when that fatal knot is tied,
Which nothing, nothing can divide,
When she the word *Obey* has said,
And man by law supreme has made,
Then all that's kind is laid aside,
And nothing left but state and pride.
Fierce as an eastern prince he grows,
And all his innate rigour shows:
Then but to look, to laugh, or speak,
Will the nuptial contract break.
Like mutes, she signs alone must make,
And never any freedom take,

But still be governed by a nod,
And fear her husband as her god:
Him still must serve, him still obey,
And nothing act, and nothing say,
But what her haughty lord thinks fit,
Who, with the power, has all the wit.
Then shun, oh! shun that wretched state,
And all the fawning flatt'rers hate.
Value yourselves, and men despise:
You must be proud if you'll be wise.
                    (Lady Mary Chudleigh, 1703)

1   List some examples of parallelism between:

   (a)   lines which are adjacent (next to each other)
   (b)   first and second parts of individual lines (i.e. within the line)

   In this text is parallelism more common between lines (a) or inside the
   line (b)?

2   List some examples of the following:

   (a)   lexical parallelism
   (b)   phonological parallelism
   (c)   syntactic parallelism

   Is any kind of parallelism particularly dominant in the text? Do the
   different kinds of parallelism interact (give examples)?

3   List examples of the following:

   (a)   chiasmus
   (b)   ellipsis

4   Indicate the cases of exact repetition in the poem, and explain why exact
   repetition is used when it is. How does repetition interact with parallelism
   in the poem?

5   The beginning and the ending of any text are 'hot spots', places of particular significance. Does parallelism have any particularly important
   function at the beginning and end of the text, and does it differ between
   beginning and end?

6   Give examples of polar and non-polar parallelism in this text. Which is
   more common, and why?

7   Which already-existing parallelisms in the culture does this poem draw upon?

8   Why does this poem use parallelism so extensively? (There might be several reasons.)

Reading

Fabb, N. (1997) *Linguistics and Literature*, Oxford: Blackwell, Chapter 6.

Fox, J.J. (1977) 'Roman Jakobson and the comparative study of parallelism', in C.H. von Schooneveld and D. Armstrong (eds) *Roman Jakobson: Echoes of His Scholarship*, Lisse: Peter de Ridder Press, pp. 59–90.

Fox, J.J. (ed.) (1988) *To Speak in Pairs: Essays on the Ritual Languages of Eastern Indonesia*, Cambridge: Cambridge University Press.

Furniss, T.E. and Bath, M. (1996) *Reading Poetry: An Introduction*, London: Prentice-Hall, Chapter 4.

Jakobson, R. (1988) 'Linguistics and poetics', in D. Lodge (ed.) *Modern Criticism and Theory*, London: Longman, pp. 32–57.

Leech, G. (1969) *A Linguistic Guide to English Poetry*, London: Longman, Chapter 5.

Williams, R. (1973) *The Country and the City*, London: Chatto & Windus.

Deviation

12.1 Introduction

In this unit we explore one common feature of the language of literature – a tendency to deviate from everyday norms of communication. Literary language, especially in poetry, distinguishes itself from everyday language by breaking linguistic rules. We consider briefly the types of linguistic rule whose observance is necessary for ordinary communication and then explore ways in which these are breached in literary communication. The unit concludes with a consideration of what purpose is served in literary communication by the breaking of linguistic rules.

12.2 Convention and deviation in everyday language

Words need to be combined in structures or patterns that conform to the underlying rules (or grammar) of the language that we share with our interlocutors in order for us to communicate intelligibly. (See **Unit 3**, **Analysing units of structure**.) Accordingly, when linguists study a language, their aim is to describe all the permissible patterns of combination and to formulate them as the abstract rules that underlie everyday linguistic behaviour. These rules are designed to account for our mutual intelligibility when we are using the same language with each other and should be distinguished from prescriptions such as 'don't split your infinitives', 'don't drop your aitches' or 'say "it is I" rather than "it is me"'. Such prescriptions amount to a kind of linguistic etiquette and bear little relation to the underlying grammar that makes communication possible.

12.1.1 Components of grammar and types of linguistic rule

Linguists commonly distinguish three levels in the way a language operates: substance, form and meaning. Substance refers to the physical medium in which expression takes place – articulated sounds in speech or marks on paper in writing. Form refers to how these sounds become organized into words, and words into sentences. Meaning refers to what we encode in form and substance. Each level has a different subsection of the grammar associated with it, each subsection being constituted by different kinds of rules. Substance (sounds or letters) is analysed in terms of phonological or graphological rules (pronunciation and spelling). Form – the patterning of words into sentences – is analysed in terms of syntactic rules. And meaning is studied through semantics. The overall picture may be summed up in Table 12.1.

Table 12.1 Levels of grammar

G R A M M A R	Substance	Articulated sounds	Phonology
		Marks on paper	Graphology
	Form	Words	Vocabulary
		Words combined into sentences	Syntax
	Meaning	Propositions	Semantics

For the linguist, formulating the grammar for a language ultimately consists of stating what rules govern its operation at each of the three main levels. Thus, there are phonological or graphological rules which state permissible patterns at the level of substance: in English, for instance, we do not find the sound /n/ followed immediately by /g/ at the beginning of a word. There are rules of syntax that govern how words combine into sentences: in English, for instance, definite articles ('the') come before the noun, not after ('the car', not 'car the'). And there are semantic rules governing how to formulate propositions.

For various reasons, of course, the grammar, or rule system, is not always observed. In rapid speech, for instance, we constantly make mistakes – slips of the tongue, false starts, unfinished sentences, and other kinds of production error. Even so, it is our background awareness of the rule system that helps us decipher or edit out the mistakes so that often we do not even hear them as such.

Children provide another example of deviation. When learning their first language, they build up the adult grammar or rule system over time, making interesting mistakes on the way. These mistakes (e.g. 'me go home') can be thought of as productive errors rather than as production errors, marking progress into full control of the language. Finally, particular kinds of cognitive impairment (such as aphasia or dyslexia) can have disruptive effects on parts of the rule system. In all these cases, however, the linguistic errors or deviations that result are unintended; and speakers attempt to avoid them.

In addition to these cases there is, however, a further kind of error which is of a qualitatively different kind – the playful error that is appreciated precisely for the way it deliberately subverts the rule system. Although this kind of deliberate, rule-breaking playfulness undoubtedly occurs in everyday contexts of communication, it is particularly common in literature. Indeed, the language of literature can be seen as dominated by two overarching principles, rule-breaking on the one hand and rule-making on the other. In Units 9–11 (Rhyme and sound patterning, Verse and metre, Parallelism), we have looked in detail at rule-making or the superimposition of extrapatterning in the language of literature. In the remainder of the present unit we focus on its antithesis – rule-breaking, or deviation.

12.3 Convention and deviation in literature

As we have just suggested, literature often appears to separate itself from other uses of language by deliberately distorting the rules of everyday communication. This is not invariably the case. The literary institution could be seen as operating within a spectrum constituted by degrees of linguistic deviation, so that some authors, periods and genres are more deviant than others. The first half of the twentieth century, for instance, has probably seen more conscious linguistic experimentation, and hence deviation, in literature than, say, the first half of the eighteenth century.

The pleasure we experience from linguistic deviation in everyday language depends upon our knowledge of the norms or conventions of ordinary usage: deviation only becomes pleasurable and interesting when we know what it deviates from. The same is true of deviation in literature. In this case, however, there is a complicating factor. In literature, deviation may operate against the background of two sets of norms:

1   the conventions or norms of ordinary usage;
2   the conventions or norms of the literary system itself.

Indeed, what is at first deviant and 'original' in literature can quickly become conventional – which is why writers continually invent new kinds of deviations in the attempt, as Ezra Pound put it, to 'make it new'.

We will now examine some common types of linguistic deviation in literature, considering examples of deviation in substance, form and meaning.

12.3.1 Deviation in rules of substance

In modern as opposed to traditional, pre-literate societies, literature exists
primarily as a body of printed works rather than as a set of oral performances.
Since its principal mode of expression is written rather than spoken, it follows
that where we get deviation at the level of substance this is primarily a matter
of typography, layout, punctuation and spelling. Poetry routinely adopts modes
of layout that are peculiar to itself – relatively short lines indented on the page,
and so on. But this has itself become a poetic convention against which even
more extreme deviations can be measured. The following poem by Edwin
Morgan, for example, takes liberties with many aspects of substance simultaneously – principally features of typography, layout, and punctuation:

Message clear

```
    am              i
                              if
 i am                    he
      he r         o
      h     ur    t
      the re             and
      he      re     and
      he re
  a                   n   d
     th  e   r              e
 i am     r                 ife
                i n
           s       ion and
 i                       d    i e
   am   e res    ect
   am   e res    ection
                     o         f
       the                     life
                     o         f
     m    e           n
             su  re
       the               d    i e
  i          s
             s    e  t     and
 i am the    sur          d
   a   t    res    t
                     o         life
  i am  he r                   e
  i a            ct
  i         r   u      n
```

```
i  m   e e      t
i               t              i e
i          s    t    and
i am th              o       th
i am     r             a
i am the   su       n
i am the   s       on
i am the   e   rect on         e if
i am     re           n     t
i am       s           a        fe
i am       s   e   n     t
i    he e                d
i    t e  s     t
i          re          a d
  a   th re          a d
  a        s    t on            e
  a  t   re          a d
  a   th r        on            e
i          resurrect
                      a       life
i am                i n       life
i am     resurrection
i am the resurrection and
i am
i am the resurrection and the life
```

Perhaps the most deviant feature of this text is the way in which the conventional method of indicating the boundaries between words in the written medium has been violated by using spaces within words as well as between them. Moreover, not only do the spaces seem to be randomly distributed with no respect for word-boundaries, they also vary in length. This deviation may seem trivial in itself, but it makes the text initially difficult to read and understand, because the conventional signals about how letters combine together to make up words have been abandoned. It is only as we approach the final line – perhaps on a second or third reading – that we recognize that all the previous lines are variations on the last line in that they delete some of its letters, leaving blank spaces instead. The letters which remain in each line are thus placed in exactly the same position as they appear in the last line. Yet if the resulting irregular spacings are carefully negotiated these apparently random letters can be read as words and phrases. By doing this, we discover that every line anticipates the last line not only by drawing its letters from it, but also by making a series of statements ('i act', 'i am the sun', etc.). These, it turns out, can be interpreted as partial but congruent versions of the message of the final line – 'I am the resurrection and the life'. The title, 'Message Clear', initially might seem to be an ironic comment on the struggling reader, but by adopting a different way of reading the deviations begin to make sense so that the 'message' finally begins to become 'clear'.

Deviation of substance is not restricted to poetry but may also be found in novels – as you will see if you leaf through novels such as Laurence Sterne's *Tristram Shandy* (1759–67), James Joyce's *Finnegans Wake* (1939), or Alasdair Gray's *Lanark* (1981).

12.3.2 Deviation in rules of form: vocabulary

This occurs in literature when new words are deliberately created for particular effect. This may be done in various ways, but the most straightforward strategy is simply the pasting of words or elements of words together into new combinations. Many words in English have been formed in this way:

> fortunate = fortune+ate
> unfortunate = un+fortune+ate
> unfortunately = un+fortune+ate+ly
> unusually = un+usual+ly
> breakfast = break+fast
> straightforward = straight+forward

We can see from these examples that even the small elements or affixes – such as un-, -ate, and -ly – can have a fairly predictable meaning in the structure of a word: the affix un- usually means 'not'; -ate usually suggests 'quality'; and -ly usually suggests 'manner'. These basic patterns of meaning and word construction allow us to make sense of words that we have never encountered before. When the Victorian religious poet, Gerard Manley Hopkins, refers in *The Wreck of the Deutschland* (1875) to the sea as 'widow-making, unchilding, unfathering deeps' he is using affixation and compounding to form neologisms or new words. This enables him to emphasize in a particularly compressed fashion the way in which the sea can take husbands from their wives, children from their parents, and fathers from their children. Similarly, when T.S.Eliot in *The Waste Land* (1922) puts a neologism in the mouth of the blind seer Tiresias, so that he says 'And I Tiresias have foresuffered all', our knowledge of the conventional function of 'fore-' means that we are able to derive a meaning for 'foresuffer'. (Tiresias is presumably claiming that his prophetic powers mean that he not only 'foresees' events but also suffers or endures them before they occur.) Thus, we make sense of neologisms in the same way that we make sense of other kinds of deviation – through using our implicit knowledge of the underlying conventions of the language. These principles enable the production and understanding of puns in everyday life, and they help us to at least attempt to interpret the radical deviations in word formation found in *Finnegans Wake*:

I have just (let us suppraise) been reading in a (suppressed) book – it is notwithstempting by measures long and limited – the latterpress is eminently leglibile and the paper, so he eagerly seized upon, has scarsely been buttered in works of previous publicity wholebeit in keener notcase would I turf aside for pasturcuration.

(p. 356)

In this relatively mild example of the novel's lexical deviations, Joyce employs what Humpty Dumpty called 'portmanteau' words (because they pack several meanings into one word): 'notwithstempting', for example, can be read as containing both 'notwithstanding' and 'not tempting'.

12.3.3 Deviation in rules of form: syntax

Intelligible communication depends not only on the choice of words but on how they are arranged in sentences. Indeed, there are strong constraints on the ways in which words can be put together into sentences if they are to make sense. (See **Unit 3**, **Analysing units of structure**.) These constraints are called the syntax of the language and all language users are subject to them. The importance of syntactic conventions in English can be demonstrated by how relatively small shifts in word order and combination can significantly alter the meaning of sentences. In the following example the change from a statement to a question is brought about by a simple change in the order of the initial two items:

This is the ten o'clock news.
Is this the ten o'clock news?

Poets, no less than other language-users, have to subscribe to syntactic constraints if they are to be understood; even when they deviate from them, they depend upon our knowledge of the conventions they break in order to achieve their effects. In poetry, inversions from the normal order are quite common, may be motivated by considerations of rhyme and rhythm, and are tolerated as such if not too blatantly intrusive. Consider the following:

Silent is the house: all are laid asleep:
One alone looks out o'er the snow-wreaths deep.
(Emily Brontë, 'The Visionary', 1846)

A more straightforward (but less effective) order would be:

The house is silent: all are laid asleep:
One alone looks out over the deep snow-wreaths.

These are fairly minor deviations from normal word order when compared with the following poem by e.e. cummings:

swi(
          across!gold's

rouNdly
)ftblac
kl(ness)y

a-motion-upo-nmotio-n

Less?
          thE
(against
is
)Swi

mming

(w-a)s
bIr

d,

This is not an easy text to make sense of at first, since it is deviant on more than one level. At the level of substance, for instance, the normal conventions of graphology and typography have been subjected to severe distortion. At the level of form, affixes, such as -ness, -ly and -less, have become detached from the items with which they (most probably) fit, and words have become interrupted internally by other words. In addition, the sequences of conventional syntax have been severely disrupted, so much so that it is difficult to reconstruct an easily intelligible alternative with any degree of confidence. But one plausible order would be as follows:

The bird is/was a black motion swimming swiftly against/across/upon gold's motionless roundness.

If we assume it to be a poem about a bird silhouetted in flight against the orb of the setting sun ('gold's roundness'), what has been gained by scrambling the more normal word order that could have been adopted? In literature, such extreme disruption of syntax conventionally suggests psychological immediacy – the rendering of the actual process of perception or cognition as it happens. This seems to be the case here: it is as if the process of unravelling the syntax mimics the process of recognizing – out of a jumble of impressions – the flight of a bird across the face of the sun.

12.3.4 Deviation in meaning: semantics

All the earlier cases of deviation that we have considered have consequences for meaning and interpretation; breaking the rules of punctuation, for instance, affects the way we read and make sense of the text in which it occurs. However, it is also possible to find cases of direct manipulation of conventional meanings in themselves. Joseph Heller's novel, *Catch 22* (1961), is particularly rich in this kind of deviation. Set during the Second World War, it gets its title from the famous paradox (Catch 22) which is used by the authorities in the novel to keep American fliers flying an ever increasing number of bombing missions. Although fliers can appeal to be grounded on grounds of insanity:

> There was only one catch and that was Catch 22, which specified that a concern for one's own safety in the face of dangers that were real and immediate was the process of a rational mind. Orr was crazy and could be grounded. All he had to do was ask; and as soon as he did, he would no longer be crazy and would have to fly more missions. Orr would be crazy to fly more missions and sane if he didn't, but if he was sane he would have to fly them. If he flew them he was crazy and didn't have to; but if he didn't want to he was sane and had to.

Conventionally, the expressions 'sane' and 'crazy' are opposite in meaning. Part of the fascination (and the humour) of *Catch 22* is the way in which it constructs conditions under which such opposites can both be true at the same time. Love and hate are conventionally opposite, yet the novel tells us that 'Dunbar loved shooting skeet because he hated every minute of it and the time passed so slowly.' Many examples of semantic deviation in the novel are structured like jokes in two parts:

> Doc Daneeka was Yossarian's friend
> and would do just about nothing in his power to help him.

This profusion of semantic anomalies in the opening chapters of *Catch 22* helps to create the impression of a world in which war has undermined the rational basis of social and moral action.

Another, more fundamental, way in which literature produces and exploits semantic deviation in meaning is through its use of figurative language, since figures of speech can be thought of as deviations from literal meaning (see **Unit 13**, **Metaphor**, and **Unit 14**, **Irony**). Figures of speech play a large part in other kinds of discourse, but they tend to become conventional and we lose our sense of their 'deviance'. In literature, on the other hand, figurative language tends to be unusual and makes us aware of the way it deviates from literal usage or conventional figures.

12.3.5 Literature as deviant discourse

Perhaps the most fundamental kind of deviation which characterizes literature stems not so much from its manipulation of linguistic conventions, but from peculiarities in the way it relates to the world at large. These peculiarities include:

- the way that literary texts construct imagined worlds;
- the way that literary texts construct imagined speakers;
- the way that literary texts address imagined addressees.

Most kinds of discourse – news, problem-pages, research reports, gossip, even advertising – operate under certain conditions of truth; we expect their assertions to be true, or at least to amount to a reasonable claim. Literature, on the other hand, is full of things that look like assertions about the world but which actually contradict our everyday sense of what the world is like. Literary discourse, then, is deviant in the sense that it is non-referential, and even when it claims to refer to things in the world, we are not expected to take those claims seriously. Take, for instance, the opening sentence of George Orwell's novel, *Nineteen Eighty-Four* (1949):

It was a bright cold day in April and the clocks were striking thirteen.

To a British readership, the notion of there being a bright cold day in April may be completely unremarkable, but the fact that the same sentence tells us that 'the clocks were striking thirteen' serves to place the events of the novel outside that readership's everyday world (since clocks in Britain don't habitually strike thirteen). Furthermore, although for many years the title of the book (written 1948, published 1949) looked forward to a date in the future, the past tense of the first sentence refers backwards as if to events which have already happened. Yet most readers would not interpret the first sentence as the beginning of a factual record of events that had really happened but would realize that Orwell's point was that such events could conceivably come to pass.

But it is not just the way that literature refers to non-existent entities that marks its peculiarity as a discourse. The narrators of novels and the speakers of poems are as fictional as the events which are presented. When Julian Barnes uses a woodworm to retell the biblical story of Noah's Ark from an unusual angle in *A History of the World in 10½ Chapters* (1989), he follows a long tradition of using non-human narrators in literary narratives. The speaker of Sylvia Plath's poem 'Elm' (1962) is a tree.

In the case of poetry in particular, literature's whole mode of address turns out to be deviant since it typically addresses someone (or something) other than the reader. During the Romantic period, for instance, there are poems which directly address a rose, a skylark, and even a piece of pottery (a Grecian urn):

O Rose, thou art sick
                    (Blake, 'The Sick Rose')

Hail to thee blithe spirit!
                    (Shelley, 'Ode to a Skylark')

Thou still unravished bride of quietness
                    (Keats, 'Ode on a Grecian Urn')

Addressing entities that are incapable of talking back may have become a fairly unremarkable literary convention (known as 'apostrophe'), but it is worth noting how deviant this is by comparison with everyday conditions of discourse. We might swear at the cat when it gets under our feet, but we don't write an elaborate note to it – not, at least, unless we're writing poetry.

12.4 Effects and implications of literary deviation: defamiliarization

We have seen that literature is a discourse which reworks the conventions and codes of the language and is potentially deviant in a range of different dimensions. But this does not mean that literature has nothing to say about the ordinary world we live in. On the contrary, its use of deviation allows us to see that world from unfamiliar and revealing angles (Russian Formalist critics called this effect defamiliarization). The philosopher Ludwig Wittgenstein is credited with saying that 'the limits of my language are the limits of my world'. In everyday communication we are usually content to leave intact the limits of our language and therefore of our world. Literature, by contrast, extends the boundaries of our taken-for-granted world and allows us to think and feel it afresh by systematically deviating from conventional linguistic practices and habitual modes of expression. Literature may be seen as a domain of linguistic experiment in how to say new things by bending the rules of the system. By subverting the common-sense bonds between utterances and their situations of use it allows us to explore new kinds of identity and forms of relationship.

1   Choose an appropiate word (or phrase) to fill the blank in the context of
the phrases which are given.

       _____ is a pleasant country
       _____ is wintry
    let's open the _____
       _____ is the very weather,
    (not _____)
    love is a deeper _____

2   Now compare your choices with those made in the following poem by
e.e. cummings.

       yes is a pleasant country:
       if's wintry
       (my lovely)
       let's open the year

       both is the very weather
       (not either)
       my treasure,
       when violets appear

       love is a deeper season
       than reason;
       my sweet one
       (and april's where we're)

3   Circle all the deviant words and answer the following questions.

    (a)   Do any of the deviant words have anything in common with each
other (e.g. what kinds of words are they)?
    (b)   What are the differences between the phrases you made and those
in the poem?

4   In addition to these semantic deviations (deviations in rules of meaning),
list any deviations in:

    (a)   rules of substance (i.e. in the letters and punctuation);
    (b)   rules of form (i.e. how the words are combined together).

5   Are all features of the poem deviant? Do any of the following features appear conventional or fall into regular patterns?

   (a)   rhythm;
   (b)   rhyme;
   (c)   address;
   (d)   punctuation;
   (e)   syntax.

6   Assuming that you find some aspects of the poem deviant and some conventional or regular, think of answers to the following:

   (a)   Why does the poem use deviation at all?
   (b)   Why isn't everything in the poem deviant?
   (c)   What is the effect of using deviation in some aspects and being conventional or regular in others?

Reading

Erlich, V. (1969) *Russian Formalism: History – Doctrine*, The Hague: Mouton.
Garvin, P. (ed. and trans.) (1964) *A Prague School Reader in Aesthetics, Literary Structure and Style*, Washington, DC: Georgetown University Press.
Leech, G. (1969) *A Linguistic Guide to English Poetry*, London: Longman, Chapters 2 and 3.
Lemon, L.T. and Reis, M.J. (eds) (1965) *Russian Formalist Criticism*, Lincoln: University of Nebraska Press, especially the chapter by Shklovsky (1921) 'Sterne's *Tristram Shandy*: stylistic commentary', pp. 25–57.
Widdowson, H.G. (1975) *Stylistics and the Teaching of Literature*, London: Longman.
Widdowson, H.G. (1992) *Practical Stylistics: An Approach to Poetry*, Oxford: Oxford University Press.

Reading figures
of speech

Unit 13

Metaphor

What numbers for those charming features pine,
If blooming acres round her temples twine!
Her lip the strawberry, and her eyes more bright
Than sparkling Venus in a frosty night;
              ('An Essay on Woman', Mary Leapor (1751))

These lines contain several **figures of speech** (two metaphors and a simile) which are kinds of **figurative language**. Figurative language is a kind of non-literalness, and in this unit we examine why non-literalness of this kind is possible in language, we distinguish between kinds of non-literal language (e.g. between the metaphors and the simile in the above example), and consider why non-literal language is so widespread in literature.

   Consider for example the sentence 'blooming acres round her temples twine'. The words of a language always have a **literal meaning**, the meaning which is fixed in association with each word as part of the vocabulary of the language. When words are combined into a sentence, their literal meanings combine to produce a literal meaning for the sentence as a whole. If we take 'temples' with its meaning of 'forehead', the sentence 'blooming acres round her temples twine' has a literal meaning which cannot be true: acres of flowers cannot twine round a woman's head. Because the literal meaning cannot be true, this sentence – if it makes any sense at all – must be interpreted as having meaning other than its literal meaning; that is, it must have a **non-literal meaning**. We can examine how sentences get to have non-literal meanings by considering the non-literal meaning of 'blooming acres round her temples twine'. A possible non-literal meaning of this sentence is 'she has abundant, beautiful and curling hair'. Notice that none of these notions are literally expressed by the sentence, which does not have words which literally mean beauty, curls or hair; thus the non-literal meaning is not derived directly from the sentence. Instead, it is separately made up by the hearer or reader and then

149

attached to the sentence with some degree of confidence. Why would a hearer or reader have any confidence that this meaning can be attached to this sentence? The answer comes from the assumption that the sentence has a potentially true meaning; since the literal meaning cannot be true, the hearer/reader must invent a meaning which is plausible for the sentence. Plausibility depends on a number of factors: the meaning must be capable of being true, it must fit with the rest of the text, and it must have some relation with what is actually said (i.e. the non-literal meaning must have some relation with the literal meaning). In this case, the non-literal meaning 'she has abundant, beautiful and curling hair' is capable of being true, it fits with the rest of the text which describes a range of beautiful features for a woman, and it has some relation with what is actually said. The relation is as follows: (a) acres of flowers (literal) are abundant (non-literal); (b) flowers (literal) are beautiful (non-literal); (c) something which twines (literal) is curly (non-literal); (d) the thing which twines around the temples of the head (literal) is hair (non-literal).

The processes of working out the literal meaning and the non-literal meaning of a text are very different from one another. When we work out the literal meaning of the text we decode the text, applying our knowledge of the code (i.e. the pairing of word and meaning which makes up the vocabulary of the language). But when we work out the non-literal meaning, we are guessing, using the available evidence, at the most plausible meaning which might be attached to the text. This process of assigning a meaning by guessing, using evidence from the text and other sources, is called **inferencing**. All speakers of the same language should decode the same literal meaning from the same text, but speakers of the same language might differ in the non-literal meaning which they infer from the text. This has several consequences for non-literal meanings. First, a range of non-literal meanings might all be plausible for the same text; sometimes these meanings are compatible with one another, and sometimes they are not. Sometimes the non-literal meaning is very easy to derive and sometimes quite difficult, perhaps because it is only weakly evidenced by the text. In the case of 'blooming acres round her temple twine', other possible non-literal meanings might be inferred: perhaps the non-literal meaning is 'she wears a crown of flowers'. This other non-literal meaning is not entirely compatible with the first, though they both have a similar implication: that the woman is beautiful (an implication supported by the rest of the text). Which meaning is right? There is probably no certain way of deciding; we can only go with what we think is the best evidence. Metaphor – and figurative language more generally – is thus a way of generating indeterminacy in a text, which might be an important part of the aesthetic effect of the text.

13.1 Types of metaphor: metaphor, simile, metonymy, synecdoche

13.1.1 Metaphor

'Blooming acres round her temples twine' is an example of a metaphor. The word **metaphor** comes from a Greek word *metaphora*, 'to transfer' or 'carry over'. Metaphor occurs when a word or phrase in a passage is clearly out of place in the topic being dealt with but nevertheless makes sense because of some similarity between it and what is being talked about. To interpret the word or phrase, we automatically look for the element of similarity and transfer it into the new context. In doing this, we interpret metaphorically.

When Paul Simon sings 'I am a rock' we are unlikely to think that he is made of stone or wonder how a rock can sing. Rather, we select those aspects of a rock which might also characterize how the singer may feel or want to represent himself and transfer them to the new context. The metaphor which results is effective because, in describing psychological experience in terms of a 'rock', it vividly transfers our associations of rock – such as hardness, isolation, imperviousness – to the singer.

Analogously, in the statement 'by the year 2010 manufacturing will be dominated by industries now at an embryonic stage', the word 'embryonic' does not initially appear to fit in a discussion of industry and manufacturing (because literally it is a term for the offspring of an animal before birth or emergence from an egg). To make sense of 'embryonic' in this unusual context, we select those parts of its meaning which allow us to interpret the word in a discussion about industry. 'At an embryonic stage' becomes a figurative way of saying that the industries of the future are at a rudimentary level of development. The idea of natural gestation is also transferred into the new context, however, and we are therefore invited to see the development of industry as in some way a natural process; this offers us a reassuring sense that the new industries are to be welcomed. In this way, metaphor can significantly affect how we perceive or respond to what is being described.

13.1.2 Simile

Simile is a subdivision of metaphor in that, as its name suggests, it draws attention to a similarity between two terms. But whereas in metaphor the link between the terms is implied, in simile it is made through an explicit textual signal ('like', 'as', etc.). Simile does not, strictly speaking, always entail figurative language, since both terms of a simile can often be understood literally. The simile 'the sky is like a polished mirror', for example, invites the listener or reader to imagine how the sky might actually appear like a polished mirror. This difference between simile and metaphor can be demonstrated by turning the simile into a metaphor. If we say 'the sky is a polished mirror' this formulation can no longer be understood literally. We know that the sky is not really a polished mirror, though it might look like one, and therefore 'polished mirror' has to be read metaphorically. In the lines cited at the beginning of this chapter, 'her eyes [are] more bright than sparkling Venus in a frosty night' is a simile comparing the brightness of her eyes to Venus. What makes this a simile is the explicit expression of comparison in the construction 'more . . . than'. The close relation between metaphor and simile can be seen in another example of figurative language in this poem, 'her lip the strawberry'. In order to make any sense of this text we must assume that a proposition is being communicated, but it is not entirely clear whether the proposition is 'her lip is the strawberry' in which case this is not capable of being literally true and is a metaphor, or 'her lip is like the strawberry' which is capable of being literally true and is a simile.

13.1.3 Metonymy

Metonymy (Greek for 'a change of name') is distinguished from metaphor in that, whereas metaphor works through similarity, metonymy works through other kinds of association (e.g. cause–effect, attribute, containment, etc.).

The sentence 'Moscow made a short statement' makes sense only if we understand it figuratively, taking 'Moscow' to stand for the leaders of the Russian Federation. This figure is possible not because of any obvious similarity between the two, but because the two are associated with each other (the leadership is based in the city). Metonymies can be formed through many different kinds of associative link. Typical dress, for example, can be used metonymically to stand for those who wear it: if someone says 'a lot of big wigs came to the party', we understand 'big wigs' to refer to 'important people' (a metonymy which probably derives from the fashion among the upper classes in earlier centuries in Europe of wearing elaborate wigs in public – a practice still followed by judges and barristers in court).

13.1.4 Synecdoche

Synecdoche (Greek for 'taking together') is a sub-branch of metonymy. It occurs when the association between the figurative and literal senses is that between a part and the whole to which it belongs. 'Farm hands' is a common synecdoche for workers on a farm; 'a new motor' comes to mean 'a new car' by using one part of the car, its engine, to stand for the whole. (Note that the big wig is not a part of the person to which it belongs, and so would not be called synecdoche; instead, it is simply associated with the person.)

13.2 Analysing metaphors

13.2.1 Tenor, vehicle, ground

I.A. Richards suggested some useful terminology to distinguish the component parts of a metaphor. The literal meaning is the **vehicle** of the metaphor; the non-literal meaning is the **tenor** of the metaphor; and the relation between them is the **grounds** of the metaphor. In Leapor's lines, we have a metaphor consisting of the vehicle 'blooming acres round her temple twine', the tenor 'she has abundant, beautiful and curling hair', and the grounds (the similarity between blooming acres and abundant hair). If we treat 'her lip the strawberry' as a metaphor by spelling it out as 'her lip is the strawberry', then the vehicle is 'the strawberry', the tenor is 'something red which you might want to put to your lips', and the ground is that a strawberry is something red which you might want to put to your lips. The literal meaning 'her lip is the strawberry' is thus dispensed with in favour of the potentially true non-literal meaning 'her lip is "something red which you might want to put to your lips"'.

In a metaphor, the vehicle is part of the literal meaning and the tenor is part of the non-literal meaning; the grounds will often not be explicit. In a simile, there may only be a literal meaning, and the parts of the simile which correspond to vehicle and tenor may both be part of the literal meaning of the sentence. In the simile 'her eyes [are] more bright than sparkling Venus in a frosty night', the part which is analogous to the vehicle (sparkling Venus) and the part which is analogous to the tenor (her eyes) are both part of the literal meaning; note furthermore that the grounds (extreme brightness) are also part of the literal meaning.

13.2.2 Metaphors as different parts of speech

In many cases, the vehicle of a metaphor is a noun, with the tenor also being a noun (in general, vehicle and tenor will be of the same part of speech, since there is a relation of substitution between them). However, all parts of speech can participate in a metaphor. Consider the phrase, addressed to Spring (in Blake's *To Spring* 1783), 'let our winds kiss thy perfumed garments'. Here the verb phrase 'kiss thy perfumed garments' functions as a vehicle in a metaphor whose tenor might be 'blow lightly over the fragrant flowers (of spring)'. Within this metaphor, the verb 'kiss' is a vehicle with 'blow lightly' as its tenor, the adjective 'perfumed' is a vehicle with 'fragranced' (or some similarly plausible term for the smell of flowers) as its tenor; and the noun 'garments' is a vehicle with 'flowers' as its tenor.

13.2.3 Classifying metaphors

Besides classifying metaphors according to the parts of speech they involve, it is also possible to classify them according to the types of transference of meaning they employ (see Leech, 1969). A **concretive metaphor** uses a concrete term to talk about an abstract thing. Examples include *the burden of responsibility* and *every cloud has a silver lining*. Religious discourse often uses concretive metaphors to make abstract ideas more vivid: heaven is frequently referred to as if it were a place or a building – 'In my Father's house there are many mansions.' An **animistic metaphor** uses a term usually associated with animate things (living creatures) to talk about an inanimate thing. Examples include *the leg of the table* and *killing a bottle*. A **humanizing metaphor** or anthropomorphic metaphor (sometimes called personification) uses a term usually associated with human beings to talk about a non-human thing. Examples include *the hands of the clock* and *the kettle's sad song*. Humanizing metaphor is connected with the **pathetic fallacy** (the idea that the world reflects or participates in one's emotions); *the kettle's sad song* might be used as a way of indicating a character's mood by implicitly describing how he or she perceives the kettle's sound.

13.2.4 Extended metaphor

When a piece of language uses several vehicles from the same area of thought, it is possible to speak of extended metaphor. Extended metaphor is a common literary device. Marvell, in 'A Dialogue Between the Soul and Body' (1681), talks of the soul's relation to the body as follows:

> O who shall from this dungeon raise
> A soul enslaved so many ways?
> With bolts of bones, that fettered stands
> In feet; and manacled in hands.

Taking the once commonplace metaphor of the body as a prison of the soul, Marvell extends it by selecting a series of vehicles concerned with imprisonment ('dungeon', 'enslaved', 'bolts', 'fettered', 'manacled') and transferring them to the human body. In extended metaphors, there are linked vehicles, grounds and tenors, which provides aid in interpreting each new metaphor in the sequence as it arrives. Thus the poem with which we began this unit begins with the line 'Woman, a pleasing but a short lived flower', and then extends the pairing of flowers (vehicles) with the woman's body (tenors) throughout the next few lines.

The vocabulary of a language is often pervaded by collections of dead metaphors which constitute extended metaphors. These are what Lakoff and Johnson call the 'metaphors we live by'. Thus English has many metaphors which are part of an extended chain based on the metaphor 'life is a journey'; these metaphors appear both in everday language, as when we say that someone is 'reaching the end of the road' or 'in a cul-de-sac', and are also exploited in new ways in poetry, as in Frost's poem 'Stopping by Woods on a Snowy Evening', which ends by suggesting that on his life's journey the speaker has 'miles to go' before he sleeps (= dies).

13.2.5 Mixed metaphor

Books on 'good style' generally condemn the use of mixed metaphor (the combination of two or more metaphors whose vehicles come from different and incongruous areas) because they can have unintentionly ludicrous effects. For precisely this reason, jokes often exploit mixed metaphor (e.g. 'I shall make no bones about the skeletons in the cupboard'). Abrams (1988) claims that mixed metaphor in poetry can have a functional effect – as in the following lines from *Hamlet* III, i, 56–9 (1601):

> To be, or not to be: that is the question:
> Whether 'tis nobler in the mind to suffer
> The slings and arrows of outrageous fortune,
> Or to take arms against a sea of troubles
> And by opposing end them.

Hamlet mixes his metaphors in this passage since he represents the struggle between the individual and fortune as a battle (fortune has its 'slings and arrows' and the individual may 'take arms'), but takes his next metaphor ('sea') from a completely different area. In literal terms it is evidently ludicrous to imagine taking a sword to fight the sea. But Abrams suggests that this mixing of metaphors might be a symptom of Hamlet's troubled mind. It is also possible to suggest that it underlines the futility of trying to resist 'outrageous fortune'.

13.3 Why use metaphors?

Non-literal meanings are more difficult to arrive at than literal meanings, since they involve some inferencing in addition to the decoding process required for literal meanings. Furthermore, non-literal meanings are always hypotheses – unlike literal meanings, a reader or hearer can never be certain that a particular non-literal meaning can be attached to an utterance or sentence. Thus there are disadvantages in principle to the use of metaphor. In this section we look at some of the advantages which outweigh those disadvantages.

13.3.1 Metaphor and language change

Metaphor is crucial to the way language changes, and can be seen as a process of change in action. New metaphors are constantly being developed, whenever a new area of experience or thought needs new descriptive terms.

When a new term is needed, the tendency is to make the unfamiliar familiar by borrowing terms from other fields (so forming metaphors) rather than inventing new terms. 'The greenhouse effect' involves a metaphor which figures the earth as a giant greenhouse (this might help us to understand an unfamiliar idea, but it may also work to domesticate the effect in question and thereby reduce our sense of alarm). Gradually, however, metaphors become over-familiar and cease to be recognized as metaphors at all. When this happens, they lose their power to confront us with their effects as metaphors. Everyday language is full of terms which would once have required a metaphorical interpretation, but which are now so familiar that they produce no effect at all. A speaker of English would not normally be conscious of producing two (very different) metaphors in claiming that 'things are looking up for the team since the landslide victory last week'. Yet both 'things are looking up' and 'landslide' have to be understood as metaphors since they cannot be taken literally in the context. Words and phrases which are metaphorical, but cease to be treated as if they are, are called dead metaphors (notice, incidentally, that the phrase 'dead metaphor' is itself a dead metaphor). Some dead metaphors can be revived, nevertheless, if we draw attention to the fact that they are metaphors. We can temporarily revive the metaphorical nature of 'made my blood boil' by extending the metaphor: 'it made my blood boil and steam came out of my ears'.

It is sometimes suggested that literature can be distinguished from non-literary discourse because literature uses language metaphorically, while non-literary discourse uses it literally. A more useful way of thinking about how metaphor is used, however, is to imagine a 'spectrum' of language types, ranging from discourses which consist mostly of literal usages and dead metaphors through to discourses which are highly conscious in their use of metaphor.

13.3.2 The persuasive effects of metaphor

Metaphors can be used to reinforce our images of the world or to challenge them. Figurative language can significantly affect our attitude towards the topic under discussion, and is capable of affecting us even (or perhaps especially) if we do not consciously recognize that it is being used. This is possibly why it is so common in advertising, politics, and journalism. The rhetorical purpose or implication of a metaphor can usually be grasped, nevertheless, by thinking about the connotations it brings to its new context, and then asking what effects those connotations are likely to have on the way we perceive or respond to what is being talked about (see the examples of 'embryonic' and 'greenhouse' examined above).

Terms of address used primarily or exclusively by men to address women include 'honey', 'babe', 'doll', 'hen', etc. – dead metaphors which figure women as food, immature, playthings, animals, etc. These metaphors figure women in ways which reinforce conventional images and attitudes, and therefore both reflect and reproduce those conventions. Drawing out the implications of such metaphorical 'terms of endearment' can contribute to exposing the way such conventions are embedded in our language in a wide range of dead metaphors.

When metaphor works against convention, on the other hand, it can operate as a powerful challenge to established ways of thinking. Wallace Stevens puts the point the other way round: 'Reality is a cliché from which we escape by metaphor'. Rather than promoting a conventional way of seeing the world, a metaphor which draws attention to itself as a metaphor can make demands on our powers of creative interpretation. Each time such challenging metaphors are produced, the way language maps the world is altered. Domains which the language usually keeps separate are momentarily fused, and new meanings are brought into existence.

13.3.3 Metaphor in history

Historically, metaphor has served both radical and conservative purposes. This is reflected in shifting attitudes towards it in the history of literature in English.

In the Neoclassical period (*c.* 1660–1800), poetry was widely thought of as a process of re-telling truths which were generally shared and accepted – or, as Pope puts it in his *Essay on Criticism* (1709), 'What oft was thought, but ne'er so well expressed'. This outlook can be thought of as a conservative one in that it emphasizes the reflection of existing meanings rather than the creation of new ones. In this period, metaphor was distrusted as a potentially falsifying device whose use ought to be sanctioned by social convention or 'decorum'. Although metaphor could be used to 'dress' or embellish accepted and acceptable truths, care was to be taken to keep it subservient to that end. It was even suggested in 1670 that an Act of Parliament should be introduced forbidding the use of 'fulsome and luscious' metaphors.

The Romantic poets, by contrast, thought of metaphor not as an embellishment of thought but as the means of imaginative thought itself. They argued that poetry should not be restricted to saying old things in new ways, but could be made capable of creating new thoughts and ideas; this view was influentially formulated in Shelley's 'A Defence of Poetry' (1821):

[The language of poets] is vitally metaphorical; that is, it marks the before unapprehended relations of things, and perpetuates their apprehension, ... if no new poets should arise to create afresh the associations which have been thus disorganized, language will be dead to all the nobler purposes of human intercourse.

In this view, thoughts and ideas do not exist prior to metaphor; rather, they are produced by metaphor. Far from presenting what oft was thought, poetic metaphor 'disorganizes' conventional analogies in order to reveal relations which were 'unapprehended' beforehand. As such, metaphor can be seen as an agency through which it becomes possible significantly to transform our perceptions of the world. And since 'poetic' metaphor, in Shelley's sense, is not necessarily confined to poetry, it is possible to generalize from his suggestion to the idea that producing, responding to and analysing metaphor is a form of active participation in the circulation and criticism of meanings in society.

ACTIVITY 13.1

The texts for this activity are three translations of a short epigram (book 3 number 43) by the Roman poet Martial (who lived *c.* 40–103). These translations come from the useful anthology *Martial in English*, edited by J.P. Sullivan and A.J. Boyle (Penguin 1996). The original Latin text and a translation of it by Keith Nightenhelser are provided for reference.

> original
> > mentiris iuvenem tinctis, Laetine, capillis,
> > tam subito corvus, qui modo cycnus eras.
> > non omnes fallis; scit te Proserpina canum:
> > personam capiti detrahet illa tuo.
> > > (Martial)

> You pretend to be a young man, Laetinus, by dyeing your hair.
> All of a sudden you're a raven, who were just now a swan.
> You aren't fooling everyone: Proserpine knows that you're gray,
> she'll pull the mask off your head for you!

> translation A
> > *Against Lentinus*
> > Thou dyest thy hair to seem a younger man,
> > And turns't a Crow, that lately wert a Swan.
> > All are not cousen'd; hell's queen knows thee grey.
> > She'll take the vizor from thy head away.
> > > (Thomas May, 1629)

translation B

> Thou that not many months ago
> Wast white as Swan, or driven Snow,
> Now blacker far than *Aesop*'s Crow,
> Thanks to thy Wig, set'st up for Beau.
> > Faith *Harry*, thou'rt i'the wrong box,
> Old Age these vain endeavours mocks,
> And time that knows thou'st hoary locks,
> Will pluck thy Mask off with a pox.
> > > > (Thomas Brown, 1700)

translation C

> Why should'st thou try to hide thy self in youth?
> Impartial *Proserpine* beholds the truth,
> And laughing at so fond and vain a task,
> Will strip thy hoary noddle of its mask.
> > > > (Joseph Addison, 1705)

cousen'd = tricked; Proserpine = 'hell's queen' = queen of the underworld in Greek mythology; vizor = a mask to conceal the face; pox = disease (usually implying venereal disease); hoary = white-haired; noddle = back of the head (where a wig goes; cf. 'noddle-case' = wig); 'Aesop's Crow' = in Aesop's tale of Raven (= Crow) and Swan, Raven tries to change its colour to match the white Swan, imitating the life of the Swan (moving from altars where it fed to pools and rivers), and consequently dies from starvation.

1   Identify all metaphors and all similes in translations A, B and C.

2   Using the terminology of 'vehicle', 'tenor' and 'ground', analyse the metaphors/similes involving the swan and the crow in translations A and B.

3   What situation does each translation describe? Do they differ in what they describe?

4   In what ways do the three translations differ in their use of metaphor and simile, and in what ways are they similar? What possible reasons might there be for the differences in the use of metaphor and simile between the three translations?

Reading

Abrams, M.H. (1988) *A Glossary of Literary Terms*, 5th edn, New York: Holt, Rinehart & Winston.

Furniss, T.E. and Bath, M. (1996) *Reading Poetry: An Introduction*, London: Prentice-Hall, Chapters 5–6.

Hawkes, T. (1972) *Metaphor*, London: Methuen.

Jakobson, R. (1988) 'Two aspects of language and two types of aphasic disturbances', extracted in D. Lodge (ed.) *Modern Criticism and Theory*, London: Longman.

Lakoff, G. and Johnson, M. (1980) *Metaphors We Live By*, Chicago: University of Chicago Press, especially pp. 3–40.

Leech, G. (1969) *A Linguistic Guide to English Poetry*, London: Longman, pp. 147–65.

Lodge, D. (1977) *The Modes of Modern Writing: Metaphor, Metonymy and the Typology of Modern Literature*, London: Arnold.

Richards, I.A. (1936) *Philosophy of Rhetoric*, Oxford: Oxford University Press, Chapters 5–6.

Sacks, S. (ed.) (1979) *On Metaphor*, Chicago: University of Chicago Press.

Unit 14

Irony

14.1 Verbal irony

Verbal irony is one of the ways of using language where we mean something different from what we say or write, though there is a relation between what we say and what we mean. Verbal irony is thus a 'loose' or 'non-literal' kind of communication, in company with metaphor (these loose kinds of communication are traditionally called tropes). The approach to verbal irony taken in this chapter is based on Sperber and Wilson's 'Relevance Theory' (see Reading).

To understand how verbal irony works, we need to consider the composition of the meanings we communicate. A communicated meaning can be analysed into two component parts: a proposition and an attitude towards that proposition. A **proposition** is a statement about the real world or about some fictional world. The sentences we produce typically encode propositions by containing specific words in a specific order; to be able to speak and understand sentences of a language is to be able to encode and decode a proposition into and from the sentences of that language. However, our thoughts, and the meanings we communicate (which are based on our thoughts), consist of something more than just basic propositions; attached to each proposition is an **attitude**, which expresses the speaker's or writer's relation to that proposition. The most common attitude is belief, but there are other attitudes as well – differing in strength (e.g. basic belief as opposed to strong commitment) as well as in polarity (e.g. belief as opposed to disbelief). If I have an attitude of belief towards a proposition, then that proposition is true for me.

This is relevant for irony, because in irony a speaker or writer produces a proposition which is *not* true for him or her. In normal (non-ironic) communication, I communicate two things: a proposition and my attitude towards that proposition: that I believe the proposition to be true. In verbal irony, I communicate a proposition and a different kind of attitude: that I do not believe the proposition to be true. There is no difference in the proposition itself; the difference is in the attitude which I communicate. Verbal irony is successful when the writer or speaker provides sufficient evidence to indicate that his or her attitude is one of disbelief rather than the expected attitude of belief.

Here is an example of verbal irony, from Solomon Northup's auto-biography *Twelve Years a Slave* (1854):

> The softest couches in the world are not to be found in the log mansion of the slaves. The one where I reclined year after year was a plank twelve inches wide and ten feet long.

If we take the first sentence, we can distinguish two (linked) ironies, both of which require us to work out some propositions from the text which are not directly stated. The first irony is in the phrase:

> 'the log mansion of the slaves'

We can straightforwardly derive various propositions from this including:

> Slaves live in a mansion made of logs.

The irony here does not directly arise from the obvious falseness of this statement; instead it arises because the writer communicates that he does not believe this statement to be true (by making a statement which cannot sensibly be believed). The other irony requires some interpretation of the first sentence, which states a literal truth to which the writer is clearly committed:

> 'The softest couches in the world are not to be found in the log mansion of the slaves.'

To get at the irony we must infer another proposition (or a range of propositions) from this literally encoded one. The proposition which is apparently presupposed by this sentence is:

> There are soft couches to be found in the log mansion of the slaves.

And there is another reasonable inference from the sentence, which is:

> I am being informative when I tell you that the softest couches of the world are not to be found in the log mansion of the slaves.

This is a reasonable inference about anything anyone says – that they are being informative in telling us this. Both of these propositions, both derived by straightforward processes from the actual sentence, are propositions which are clearly disbelieved by the writer, and hence constitute examples of irony.

For irony to work, the writer or speaker must be sure that the reader or hearer will be able to recognize that an attitude of disbelief is being communicated; since this is not the normal state of affairs, there must be something odd about the text in order to give clues that the author disbelieves what she is saying. We will consider some ways in which the text might be made odd in a later part of this unit. In the passage just discussed, the oddness comes from the contradiction between what we actually know about slavery (they do not live in log mansions, and there are no soft couches in them) and what we are being told. The dissonance between what we know and what we are being told is a clue that the writer also does not believe his statements to be true.

So far we have described irony as involving the speaker/writer communicating that he or she does not believe the proposition. In fact, something slightly more complex might be happening. We might interpret the speaker/writer to be saying not only that he or she does not believe the proposition but that someone else might believe it to be true. Thus the ironist communicates both his or her own attitude (of disbelief) along with implying another attitude (of belief) attributed to someone else – whether that someone else is identifiable or not. In the case of the slavery irony cited above, we might interpret Northup as communicating not simply his own disbelief in the propositions expressed but also as attributing to someone else a belief in these propositions; that someone else might perhaps be an apologist for slavery.

There are different varieties of verbal irony, though all work in basically the same way: an attitude of disbelief is implicitly communicated. Sarcasm is a kind of verbal irony in which, typically, a very marked tone of voice very obviously communicates the attitude of disbelief. In irony in general, it is important that the attitude of disbelief is implicitly communicated rather than explicitly communicated. If I say 'I do not believe that slaves live in a log mansion' I am explicitly communicating disbelief and this is not irony; it is irony only if I say 'Slaves live in a log mansion' and implicitly communicate my disbelief. Irony thus involves some tension between what is said and what is meant.

(A final comment: note that 'verbal' means 'using language' and does not mean the same as 'oral' which means 'using spoken language'; hence verbal irony exists in both speech and writing.)

14.2 Situational irony

The difference between verbal irony and **situational irony** can be illustrated by the following example of situational irony from Aphra Behn's play *The Rover* (1677):

Pedro: Sure I had dwelt forever on her bosom –
   But stay, he's here.

> *[Enter Belvile dressed in Antonio's clothes.]*
> *Florinda* (aside):   'Tis not Belvile; half my fears are vanished.

In this situation, there is a proposition 'Antonio enters' which can be derived from the situation. Florinda incorrectly believes this proposition to be true (i.e. she thinks that the person entering is actually Antonio and not Belvile, and as a consequence will refuse to marry him). However, someone else – the author of the play and its audience – correctly disbelieve this proposition. This combination of correct and incorrect attitudes about the same proposition is characteristic of irony in general. The components we saw in verbal irony are all present, but somewhat differently deployed:

1   There is a proposition.
2   Someone incorrectly believes the proposition.
3   Someone else correctly disbelieves the proposition.

In verbal irony, the 'someone' who incorrectly believes the proposition is usually not made explicit but is just implied; but here, in situational irony, the believer is usually explicit. In contrast, in verbal irony, the someone else who correctly disbelieves the proposition is explicit – the speaker or writer; but in situational irony, the people who disbelieve the proposition are somewhat removed from the text – an author who is not a character, or a member of the audience. Thus situational irony focuses on the character who has an incorrect attitude of belief; verbal irony in contrast focuses on the speaker/writer who has the correct attitude of disbelief.

There are different kinds of situational irony, which to some extent depend on genre. The example cited above is an example of **dramatic irony**, in which a character on stage and involved in a dramatic action has a specific belief which the audience knows to be false. Typically, that incorrect belief will be about some crucial component of the plot, and hence the dramatic irony functions as a narrative mechanism. Another type of situational irony is **structural irony**, which is characteristic of prose fiction. Structural irony does not hinge on specific incorrect beliefs about specific incidents (as dramatic irony tends to do); instead, structural irony involves a collection of incorrect beliefs which are held by – and define – a fictional character. Irony is thus built into the structure of the narrative by being built into the character, and this character will often be the narrator; thus the narrative as a whole provides a wealth of propositions which are incorrectly believed by the narrator, but which are (implicitly) correctly disbelieved by the author and reader. Often a text is structurally ironic because it is told by an unreliable narrator, such as an uneducated child (Henry James, *What Maisie Knew* (1897), Mark Twain, *Huckleberry Finn* (1885)), someone mentally handicapped (book 1 of William Faulkner, *The Sound and the Fury* (1929)), or a foreigner (Tama Janowicz, *A Cannibal in Manhattan* (1987)).

Dramatic irony and situational irony are two kinds of structural irony, both of which have some resemblance to verbal irony in that the propositions come from texts which are produced by an author (who is the location of the correct disbeliefs, whether explicitly or implicitly). But the term 'irony' is also used to describe historical events which are non-textual and which have no author. This can be called **historical irony**, and is exemplified by phrases such as 'the irony of time' or 'life's little ironies'. Though there is no author here (unless we take time or life to be personified as authors of the ironies), there is typically the standard structure of irony: there is a false belief in a proposition (e.g. that a certain act will prevent a war) and at some later date a true disbelief in the same proposition (with historical perspective we can see that contemporary beliefs were not true).

14.3 Mechanisms of irony

What makes verbal irony different from lying? In all communication, I communicate both a proposition and my attitude towards that proposition. In both verbal irony and lying, I have an attitude of disbelief towards the proposition which I communicate. In verbal irony I communicate that attitude of disbelief (by various signals), while in lying I conceal my attitude of disbelief (i.e. I falsely communicate that I believe the proposition when in fact I don't). The difference between verbal irony and a lie is in the presence in verbal irony of evidence for the true attitude; hence for irony to be successful, the audience/readership must be able to recognize that there is a true attitude of disbelief towards a proposition expressed by the text. In principle, any kind of evidence might be used to indicate that there is a true attitude of disbelief towards the proposition; in this section we briefly consider some of the more common kinds of evidence.

One kind of evidence involves a contradiction between what the text tells us and what we already know. Unless there is good reason to abandon our previous beliefs, we will therefore adopt an attitude of disbelief towards the text. This is not enough on its own to give rise to irony, though: on its own, this might just generate a decision that the author has made a mistake. Thus we must be convinced that the author also shares the beliefs which we brought to the text. One way in which this might happen is if the beliefs are undoubtedly true and generally held; this is presumably how the irony in the 'slavery' extract above works. We know that slaves do not live in 'log mansions' and it is a reasonable assumption that everybody – including the author – knows this. In this case, the evidence for irony comes from the knowledge we bring to the text (rather than from the text itself, though the text might provide supporting evidence).

A second kind of evidence for irony comes from exaggeration and over-emphasis – as in 'the softest couches in the world' – with over-emphasis including hyperbole, emphatic (insincere) statements of belief, extensive use of superlatives, exaggerations in speaking (as in typical sarcasm). Here the irony might perhaps be revealed by drawing attention to an attitude of strong belief, and by stating it so emphatically that it undermines the belief. Over-emphasis as a mechanism of irony can be seen in the following passage from George Eliot's novel *Middlemarch* (1871).

> Some who follow the narrative of his experience may wonder at the midnight darkness of Mr Dagley; but nothing was easier in those times than for an hereditary farmer of his grade to be ignorant, in spite somehow of having a rector in the twin parish who was a gentleman to the backbone, a curate nearer at hand who preached more learnedly than the rector, a landlord who had gone into everything, especially fine art and social improvement, and all the lights of Middlemarch only three miles off.

There are basically two kinds of exaggeration here: first, expressions of extremity as in 'midnight darkness', 'nothing was easier', 'preached more learnedly than the rector', 'gone into everything', 'all the lights of Middlemarch', and second a repetitive list, stacking up to produce a long sentence. A proposition we can derive from this sentence is 'Given the learned social environment in which he lives, it is surprising that Mr Dagley (the farmer) has remained so ignorant'. We recognize an irony here – the author holds a true attitude of disbelief towards this proposition, but someone else (the implied 'some who follow the narrative' perhaps) holds an untrue attitude of belief. The irony is signalled, in part, by the exaggerations in the passage. (In addition, we probably also bring our knowledge of the world, and perhaps of the novel as it has previously developed, to contradict the proposition derived.)

Over-statement is an instance of a more general way in which a text signals the presence of irony, which is by some kind of disruption. In most texts it is possible to distinguish the **default** (i.e. normal) characteristics of the text from the disruptive characteristics. In a rhyming poem, the rhymes are the default case and any failure to rhyme would be disruptive; in prose, a rhyme would be disruptive in the context of a default lack of rhyme. (The terms 'unmarked' and 'marked' are sometimes used to characterize the default/ normal and disruptive elements of the text, respectively.) Looking for disruptions in a text is always a useful way of entering into and beginning to understand the workings of a text, and the manipulation of disruptions can be a powerful communicative tool. To indicate the presence of irony, the text can be disrupted in various ways. Internal inconsistency is one kind of disruption which is fairly characteristic of irony. A common example of this second type is where the **register** of the text changes unexpectedly; in this case, we say that the voice of the text is inconsistent. In Henry Reed's poem 'Naming of Parts' (1946), there are at least two registers: some of the lines are spoken as if by a military instructor and some as if by a dreamy romantic. Yet there is no explicit change of speaker. In this case, the irony comes from the fact that the two registers express different attitudes which contradict one another and yet the whole poem seems to come from a single source; thus one attitude must be false.

14.4 Uncertain ironies

Texts such as those by Northup or Eliot cited earlier clearly signal the presence of irony, and enable an easy attribution of the correct disbelief and the incorrect belief. This kind of straightforward irony is characteristic of realist texts, which these texts are. However, irony is not always as straightforward. In some texts, we cannot be sure whether to identify the presence of irony. In other texts we are presented with apparent evidence that there is irony, but are uncertain how to interpret it (specifically, how to attribute the correct disbelief and the incorrect belief).

Problems in identifying or interpreting irony can arise when author and reader are separated by major differences in what they know – if, for example, they are separated by major differences in time or place or culture. Because one of the ways of marking irony is for the text to contradict what we already know, the identification of irony can depend on our (culturally dependent) knowledge; if we knew nothing at all of slavery we would be less able to recognize the irony in Northup's text (though the exaggerations would still be a clue). In some cases, the fact that cultural or subcultural differences can be a barrier to irony can be exploited by an author. Dick Hebdige once proposed that the song 'Heart of Glass' by Blondie is capable of being read ironically (given a certain subcultural awareness) or non-ironically (in mainstream culture), thus maximizing its audience. Perhaps the barriers to cross-cultural interpretation of irony explain the claim which is sometimes made that people in a certain foreign culture 'lack the capacity for irony', because irony is difficult to recognize across cultures given its dependence on culturally-dependent knowledge. Nevertheless, given that irony is an exploitation of some very basic characteristics of human language, irony should be possible in every language and every culture, even if outsiders have difficulty in identifying or interpreting it.

The difficulties just mentioned are the consequence – often accidental – of cultural difference. But difficulties in the identification or interpretation of irony can also be built into the workings of a text. Thus it is possible to find texts which are apparently ironic (e.g. what is said contradicts what we know), where there is a narrator but where it is difficult to judge whether the narrator is the victim of a structural irony (i.e. a naïve narrator, unaware of the ironies) or whether instead the narrator is to be understood as producing verbal irony (and hence is aware of the irony); Samuel Beckett's fiction and plays often present a problem of this kind. Similarly, texts might have overt ironies where there are two opposing voices within them, each taking different attitudes towards a proposition, but where it is difficult to decide which of the two voices is the voice of truth. These problems are characteristically found in Modernist texts, where there may be many competing voices in a text.

As an illustration of some of the more complex possibilities of irony, consider part of Shelley's poem 'Ozymandias' (1819). This is a poem which – we assume deliberately – generates a number of unresolvable interpretive problems, among which is the identification and attribution of the irony in the inscription which is cited in lines 10–11:

> And on the pedestal these words appear:
> 'My name is Ozymandias, king of kings:
> Look on my works, ye Mighty, and despair!'

The inscription is found on a pedestal, surrounded by fragments of a statue and otherwise 'nothing besides remains' in the desert where it stands. If the inscription is to be interpreted as 'Despair because even my great works will come to nothing' then it is not ironic at all; it is correctly believed by all parties concerned. If alternatively the inscription is to be interpreted as 'Despair because my works are so great' then this proposition is falsely believed by Ozymandias, and correctly disbelieved by us (because the works have now vanished over the course of time). But even if we identify the text as ironic, there is still a problem of attribution, because it is not clear what attitude is taken by the sculptor, the person who has written these words on the statute: did the sculptor believe or disbelieve the proposition 'Despair because my works are so great'? It is not clear that these questions can be answered: whether there is an irony, and how exactly the attitudes are to be attributed. These uncertainties are characteristic of Shelley's work in general, and in particular of this poem, which is rich in uncertainties.

14.5 Why use irony?

Irony is a somewhat indirect method of communication; it requires the reader or hearer to take various interpretive risks in order to work out the intended meanings. Like other indirect methods of communication (for example, metaphor), its potential disadvantages can be outweighed by the special advantages which it brings. Some of the reasons for using irony are presented in this section.

Thus, irony might be used to express a particular world view, perhaps that we can never really be certain in our knowledge and beliefs. Even the simplest and most straightforward ironies (as in the Eliot text cited earlier) demonstrate the existence of incorrect certainties; and more complex ironies such as those found in Shelley's poem can create a sense of the impossibility of being certain of anything.

While irony can destabilize, it can also have stabilizing functions. Thus Eliot uses irony to confirm the authority of a particular voice (the narrator's own voice) as the voice of truth. Furthermore, because irony requires the reader to bring a certain kind of background knowledge to the text in order to make sense of it, irony can require the reader to make certain assumptions in order to interpret the text. Once we recognize the ironies in the Northup and Eliot texts, we have no real choice about what background knowledge (of slavery or about nineteenth-century British society) to apply to the text. Thus irony can have an ideological effect by forcing us to acknowledge certain 'truths'.

Irony might also have certain aesthetic consequences. Aesthetic experiences are kinds of experience characteristically set off by literary texts (and other kinds of artistic works). Little is known about how aesthetic experiences arise, but it is possible to make some hypotheses which might link the workings of irony to some of the types of aesthetic experience. First, irony can be a source of interpretive (hence psychological) complexity, whether resolvable or unresolvable. This type of psychological complexity might constitute aesthetic experience. It is also worth noting that many instances of even straightforward irony have somewhat indeterminate characteristics. If we take the Northup example with which we began, we might choose various slightly different propositions as the focus of the attitudes, we might decide on various strengths of attitude (is the proposition neutrally disbelieved or strongly disbelieved?) and might vary in who we attribute the propositions to (who exactly believes that slaves live in log mansions?). The experience of indeterminacy of this kind might also itself be a kind of aesthetic experience (as is argued by Sperber and Wilson, 1995).

ACTIVITY 14.1

The passage for this activity is the beginning of Oscar Wilde's play *The Importance of Being Earnest* (first performed in 1885).

1   Identify all examples of irony which you can discover in this text. For each one, try to decide whether it is verbal irony (i.e. the speaking character produces the irony deliberately), or structural irony (i.e. the speaking character is not aware of the irony generated by what they say). Make a note of examples where it is unclear whether the irony is verbal or structural.

2   For three of the examples listed in your answer to (1), indicate what the proposition is, who has a false belief in this proposition, and who has a true disbelief in it. In each case, what is the reason for the presence of the irony (e.g. what functions does it have)?

3   You may have found some cases where you are not sure of the presence of irony, or where you cannot decide whether the irony is verbal or structural. For each of these cases, does the uncertainty arise accidentally (as a consequence of the differences between you as a contemporary reader and the late nineteenth-century author and audience), or is the uncertainty built into the text? For built-in uncertainties of irony, what are their functions?

4   The extract is written to be performed. Suggest, for each case of irony, one way in which performance might affect it, either by emphasizing it further, by changing its meaning, or by reducing or even completely removing it.

First Act

Scene

Morning-room in Algernon's flat in Half-Moon Street. The room is luxuriously and artistically furnished. The sound of a piano is heard in the adjoining room.

   [*LANE is arranging afternoon tea on the table, and after the music has ceased, ALGERNON enters.*]

   A: Did you hear what I was playing, Lane?
   L: I didn't think it polite to listen, sir.
   A: I'm sorry for that, for your sake. I don't play accurately – anyone can play accurately – but I play with wonderful expression. As far as the piano is concerned, sentiment is my forte. I keep science for Life.
   L: Yes, sir.
   A: And, speaking of the science of Life, have you got the cucumber sandwiches cut for Lady Bracknell?
   L: Yes, sir. [*Hands them on a salver.*]
   A: [*Inspects them, takes two, and sits down on the sofa*] Oh! ... By the way, Lane, I see from your book that on Thursday night, when Lord Shoreman and Mr Worthing were dining with me, eight bottles of champagne are entered as having been consumed.
   L: Yes, sir; eight bottles and a pint.
   A: Why is it that at a bachelor's establishment the servants invariably drink the champagne? I ask merely for information.

L: I attribute it to the superior quality of the wine, sir. I have often observed that in married households the champagne is rarely of a first-rate brand.

A: Good heavens! Is marriage so demoralising as that?

L: I believe it IS a very pleasant state, sir. I have had very little experience of it myself up to the present. I have only been married once. That was in consequence of a misunderstanding between myself and a young person.

A: [*languidly*] I don't know that I am much interested in your family life, Lane.

L: No, sir; it is not a very interesting subject. I never think of it myself.

A: Very natural, I am sure. That will do, Lane, thank you.

L: Thank you, sir.
      [*LANE goes out*]

A: Lane's views on marriage seem somewhat lax. Really, if the lower orders don't set us a good example, what on earth is the use of them? They seem, as a class, to have absolutely no sense of moral responsibility.
      [*Enter LANE*]

L: Mr Ernest Worthing.
      [*Enter JACK. LANE goes out*]

A: How are you, my dear Ernest? What brings you up to town?

J: Oh, pleasure, pleasure! What else should bring one anywhere?

Reading

Fabb, N. (1997) *Linguistics and Literature*, Oxford: Blackwell, Chapter 10.

Furniss, T.E. and Bath, M. (1996) *Reading Poetry: An Introduction*, London: Prentice-Hall, Chapter 8.

Leech, G. and Short, M. (1981) *Style in Fiction*, London: Longman, pp. 277–80.

MacCabe, C. (1979) *James Joyce and the Revolution of the Word*, London: Macmillan.

Muecke, D.C. (1970) *Irony and the Ironic*, London: Methuen.

Sperber, D. and Wilson, D. (1986) 'Loose talk', *The Proceedings of the Aristotelian Society*, 1985/6, pp. 153–77.

Sperber, D. and Wilson, D. (1995) *Relevance: Communication and Cognition*, Oxford: Blackwell.

Unit 15

Juxtaposition

15.1 Verbal juxtaposition

Juxtaposition, in its most basic sense, simply refers to the placing of elements side by side. In communication the juxtaposition of meaningful elements is both a routine and essential practice in the composition of messages – literary or otherwise. Sentence construction, for instance, relies upon observing close constraints in the way words are put together and significant alterations in meaning can result from simple changes in the ordering or placement of items in a sentence.

The term juxtaposition, however, can also refer to a rhetorical technique which goes beyond the straightforward placement of communicative elements next to each other. In this more specialized sense, juxtaposition can be defined as:

> combining together two or more communicative elements so as to suppress the connections between them and emphasize the differences, thereby provoking some surprise or puzzlement at their close placement.

Some simple principles of juxtaposition can be illustrated at work in the following translations of seventeenth- and eighteenth-century Japanese Haiku.

Haiku 1

Harvest moon:
On the bamboo mat
Pine tree shadows.

Haiku 2

Wooden gate,
Lock firmly bolted:
Winter moon.

Each poem consists of three short lines, and in both cases the sense of the poem seems to rest on three separate elements – 'moon', 'mat', and 'shadows' in one; 'gate', 'lock', and 'moon' in the other. These elements are baldly juxtaposed in such a way that the links between them are not very obvious. Neither of the poems forms complete or coherent sentences and so the connections ordinarily present in sentences are not given. This means that the reader is required to make an effort to fill in the gaps and spell out the connections between the main elements. This effort is accentuated by the division of each poem into two sections around a major punctuation mark – a colon. In each case there is only an implicit connection between the elements on either side of the colon. Although it is possible to see a causal relation between a harvest moon and pine tree shadows, the lack of explicit connections forces the reader to make an imaginative leap. The connection between a locked wooden gate and a winter moon demands an even greater imaginative effort. In each poem there is a basic juxtaposition between a natural image with a human one – a harvest moon and a bamboo mat, a bolted gate and a winter moon – which creates a tension between the first and second part. Haiku poems typically revolve around a tension or puzzle produced by juxtaposing (without further explanation) a natural phenomenon with an event or object more closely related to the human world. This can be seen in two further examples:

Haiku 3

Spring rain:
Soaking on the roof
A child's rag ball.

Haiku 4

Overnight
My razor rusted –
The May rains.

These poems require the reader to supply a missing causal connection between their elements; thus they could be taken as implying something like:

A child's rag ball was soaking on the roof *because of* the spring rain
Overnight my razor rusted *because of* the May rains

But although this seems to 'explain' the poems, it does so by limiting their suggestiveness and reducing the multiplicity of possible connections between the elements. Leaving the precise relations between elements unexpressed seems actually to increase the communicative possibilities of these short poems; the very disparity of the elements which have been juxtaposed generates – in the absence of explicit connections – a kind of communicative charge.

Although these poems were originally written in Japanese in the seventeenth and eighteenth centuries, it is not difficult to find similar techniques at work in twentieth-century poetry written in English. Here is an example from Ezra Pound:

L'art, 1910

Green arsenic smeared on a egg-white cloth,
Crushed strawberries! Come let us feast our eyes.

In fact, it is not surprising that Pound's poems are reminiscent of haiku: this poem was written when Pound was a leading figure in the 'Imagist' movement (roughly 1910–20) in which a group of writers in Britain and the USA attempted to develop a new form of poetry which was strongly influenced by haiku (especially its use of stark, unexplained juxtaposition). This new form of poetry can be seen as an early example of modernism – a period (1910–40) of experimentation in all the arts in which the juxtaposition of very different elements was a characteristic technique. Much of T.S. Eliot's poetry (such as *The Waste Land*, 1922) juxtaposes a wide range of different kinds of linguistic material (quotations from Wagner's operas, biblical language, diaries, language heard in a public house, etc.). But, although juxtaposition was particularly common in the verbal and visual arts of the first half of the twentieth century, it is not confined to them; it may be found in texts (literary and non-literary) from all periods (as witness, for instance, the haiku discussed above). Wherever it is used, however, its effects are usually startling. A recent poetic example is found in the following poem by Margaret Atwood (1971):

You fit into me

you fit into me
like a hook into an eye
a fish hook
an open eye

15.2 Visual juxtaposition: film

The use of juxtaposition in order to set up a collision or tension between communicative elements is not limited to verbal texts. In a film, two very different scenes or images may be juxtaposed by immediately succeeding one another. The Soviet director, Sergei Eisenstein, argued that the way shots are combined into series is central to the way films work. In most films, it is not hard for the viewer to make the imaginative connection between images. The strand of cinematic development associated with commercial cinema and Hollywood uses a style of editing that aims at continuity and smoothness of transition between shots. In contrast, the aesthetic possibility of juxtaposition is an important organizing concept in certain kinds of film practice such as Soviet cinema in the years immediately after the Russian Revolution (1917). Early Soviet cinema, particularly that of Eisenstein, attempted to produce collisions rather than continuity between sequential shots in order to create quite startling juxtapositions. Eisenstein called this the principle of **montage** and argued that by introducing a gap or tension between successive images it was possible to generate meaning beyond that contained within the shots themselves. For instance, in two famous images from consecutive shots in Eisenstein's film *Battleship Potemkin* (1925) the first image shows a medium close-up of a woman's face wearing pince-nez or glasses, and the second image presents the same woman, but now the eye is bleeding and the pince-nez is shattered. The overall effect is that of a shot hitting the eye, even though the latter action is not explicitly displayed. These images are part of a larger episode, commonly referred to as the 'Odessa steps sequence', in which soldiers brutally attempt to put down a popular uprising. Images of boots marching down steps and of rifle volleys are intercut with images of a child's pram rolling unattended down the steps and a small boy being trampled underfoot (see Plates 1–4).

As well as creating a powerful sense of movement and confusion, these stark juxtapositions force the viewer to make the connection between the soldiers' actions and the suffering of the defenceless people. In this way, montage as a collision between images can here be seen as replicating larger contradictions between contending social forces. Indeed, juxtaposition for Eisenstein was part of a self-consciously Marxist and dialectical approach to film-making, not only emphasizing conflict between images but (like Bertolt Brecht in the theatre) also demanding the active interpretive engagement of the audience.

15.3 Serial and simultaneous juxtaposition

Juxtaposition in film, video and TV mostly works by exploiting a sense of surprise or shock achieved by juxtaposing successive images. Thus these media may be said to use temporal or serial juxtaposition. The images from Eisenstein's film *Battleship Potemkin* are good examples of serial juxtaposition, since their meaning depends on the very order in which the elements are presented; any change in the order either changes the meaning or results in nonsense.

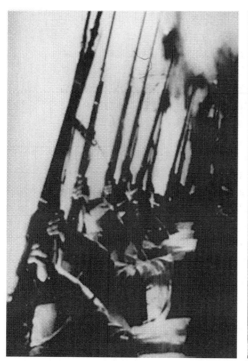

1

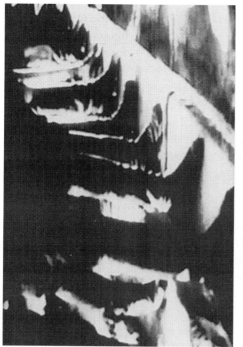

2

3

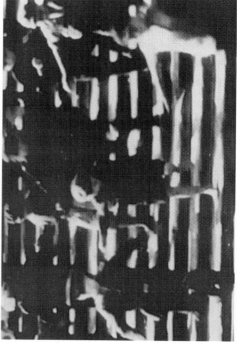

4

Plates 1–4 Images from the Odessa Steps sequence, *Battleship Potemkin*

Juxtaposition is also used in other kinds of media which are not sequential through time, but spatial (e.g. photographs, paintings, cartoons, etc.). Pictorial art is a case in point. A precise analogue to Eliot's technique of literary bricolage in *The Waste Land*, discussed above, may be found in pictorial art of the twentieth century. **Collage**, for instance, is an abstract form of art in which photographs, pieces of paper, string, etc., are placed in juxtaposition and glued to the pictorial surface. Surrealism, as exemplified in the work of Salvador Dali or René Magritte, often depicted quite unrelated items in the same pictorial space, creating an atmosphere of dream or fantasy. Here, for instance, is how Magritte described his famous painting (see Plate 5), *Time Transfixed* (1938), in which a steam locomotive emerges from an empty fire place on whose mantelpiece rests a clock with its hands at 12.43:

> I thought about painting a picture of a locomotive. Given that possibility, the problem was this: how to paint the picture in such a way that it evoked mystery ... the mystery that has no meaning ... The image of the locomotive is immediately familiar, so its mystery passes unnoticed. To bring out its mystery another immediately familiar and hence unmysterious image – that of the dining room fire place – was combined with the image of the locomotive ... suggesting the mystery of beings that normally strike us (by mistake, through habit) as familiar ...

In such cases, the juxtaposed elements are simultaneously present for interpretation, we take them in at a glance and the order in which they are read seems not to affect the overall meaning. We can therefore say that such media use simultaneous juxtaposition. As with verbal composition, such techniques – though prevalent – are not restricted to the twentieth century in its modernist phase. The pictures of the Flemish painter, Hieronymus Bosch (*c.* 1450–1516), depicting the delights of heaven and the horrors of hell, are full of startling – sometimes grotesque and fantastic – juxtapositions.

Any visual composition, of course, is likely to contain an organization of elements placed side by side. In this sense whatever occurs within the same visual frame has been 'juxtaposed', if only in rather weak terms. But, as we argued earlier, the notion of juxtaposition is more usefully applied to instances where the connection between elements seems arbitrary or not immediately obvious and where the reader or viewer is called upon to make the imaginative connection. Magazine advertising often uses juxtaposition in the sense we are using it here. The advertisement in Plate 6, for example, juxtaposes two basic elements within the image – a bottle of cognac and a diamond-encrusted watch.

At first sight there is no obvious reason why such objects should be put together. Indeed, the very absence of an obvious connection poses a puzzle to the reader, an enigma that requires some interpretive effort to solve. One way of connecting the items is supplied by the accompanying text in terms of the

Plate 5 *Time Transfixed* (La durée poignardée)
1938 – Oil on canvas, 147 x 98.7cm
Art Institute, Chicago (Joseph Winterbotham Collection)

time it takes to produce each object: 'It takes 1000 painstaking hours to create a half million pound watch. And 300,000 hours to make Hennessy X.O.' Since the brandy is said to take much longer to produce than the watch, we are presumably invited to assume that it is a more luxurious item and has more cultural value (even if it is less expensive) than the watch.

Since juxtaposition here invites the reader to compare (or contrast) the juxtaposed items, we can suggest that visual juxtaposition works in a similar way to **metaphor** (see **Unit 13**). This idea is borne out in the example in Plate 7, in which a gilt-framed art object is juxtaposed with a bottle of whisky.

There is no immediately obvious connection between paintings and scotch whisky. However, the title and subject of the painting prove to be 'THE FAMOUS GROUSE', which in turn operates as the trade mark for the brand of whisky being advertised. The art object and the whisky are therefore linked by virtue of their names and the shared image of the bird (as well as by the fact that grouse and whisky share the same 'country of origin'). These visual and verbal links invite us to transfer selected attributes of the art object to the commodity being advertised (just as a metaphor demands that we transfer selected attributes from vehicle to tenor). Since the painting has a title and a signature (in the bottom left-hand corner) and is exhibited in an ornate frame, we are invited to think that it has great aesthetic value and to transfer that quality to the whisky. The painting's title also tells us that the grouse is 'noted for its character and distinguished appearance', and we are expected to understand that this is also true of the whisky. As if to underline the parallel between painting/bird and whisky, the caption suggests that both maintain a certain quality 'in an age of change'.

In the examples of juxtaposition examined earlier, it was noticeable that juxtaposition operates by generating meanings that are somehow 'beyond' or 'between' the elements that are juxtaposed. In the haiku and imagist poems, the lack of a definite connection between images seems to open them up to a multiplicity of interpretations. However, when elements are juxtaposed in an advertising image, the accompanying text often plays an important role in fixing a preferred reading of the image. In the advertisements examined above, the captions prevent possibilities such as 'Hennesey is as tough as diamonds' or 'This grouse is looking for his whisky'. This suggests that juxtaposition is both a powerful and an unpredictable device to use, since advertisers often find it necessary to control the possible interpretations it might generate.

15.4 Some effects of juxtaposition

It is not possible to predict one single effect for all cases of juxtaposition, but we can point to a range of characteristic, sometimes overlapping, effects. We have already seen that juxtaposition tends to open up a plurality of possible meaningful connections between juxtaposed elements precisely because simple

Plate 6   Hennessy advertisement

and straightforward connections are omitted. Juxtaposition can also produce a characteristic sense of tension or incongruency, as in Pound's imagist poem given above: 'Green arsenic smeared on an egg-white cloth, / Crushed strawberries!'. This incongruency typically demands that the reader make some effort of comprehension.

Juxtaposition can therefore be thought of as a rhetorical strategy. We have already seen that in some instances juxtaposition works in a way similar to metaphor. This is supported by a humorous serial juxtaposition which is often used in films: the first image typically shows two people beginning to make love and is then cut to images of volcanoes errupting or fireworks exploding. The juxtaposition of the second image with the first asks us to imagine that there is a metaphorical relation between the couple's lovemaking and erruptions or fireworks (the second image becomes a metaphor for the first).

Some of the other effects of juxtaposition can be summarized as various kinds of **irony** (see **Unit 14**).

1 *Tragic irony*: An example of tragic irony may be found at the end of Shakespeare's *King Lear* (1606), where Edmund's dying attempt to revoke his command that Cordelia be murdered and Albany's supplication 'The gods

defend her!' is immediately juxtaposed with Lear's arrival carrying Cordelia dead in his arms:

> Edmund: He hath commission from thy wife and me
>   To hang Cordelia in the prison, and
>   To lay the blame upon her own despair,
>   That she fordid herself.
> Albany: The gods defend her! Bear him hence awhile.
> [*Edmund is borne off*]
> [*Enter Lear with Cordelia dead in his arms; Edgar, Captain and others following*]
> Lear: Howl, howl, howl . . . .

The juxtaposition of Cordelia's death (and Lear's reaction to it) with Albany's prayer ('The gods defend her!') reinforces the tragic effect here and ironically casts doubt on the very efficacy of prayer. Thus one of the effects of juxtaposition is to undermine or call into question one element through the immediate proximity of the other.

2 *Comic irony*: Sometimes the incongruity of the juxtaposition leads to a humorous effect. In radio broadcasting, mixing between alternative sources (e.g. live studio talk and pre-recorded announcements or commercials) can lead to laughably unintended juxtapositions, as in the following examples:

> 'It's time now, ladies and gentlemen, for our featured guest, the prominent lecturer and social leader, Mrs. Elma Dodge . . .' (*accidental cut to Superman*) . . . 'who is able to leap tall buildings in a single bound'.

> 'So remember, use Pepsodent toothpaste, and brush your teeth . . .' (*Cut in to cleansing product commercial*) . . . 'right down the drain!'

In these examples it is important that the cut-in text provides a grammatically well-formed completion of a sentence begun in the initial text, even though its topic in each case is discordantly at odds with that already established by the initial text. Humorous juxtaposition is often deliberately employed as a textual strategy in comic texts (as in the mixing of different **registers**: see **Unit 6, Language and context: register**).

3 *Destabilizing irony*: When elements from recognizably different texts are deliberately rather than fortuitously mixed in with each other, a sense of irony can be created which goes beyond calling one element into question by its juxtaposition with another. In the following example from *Ulysses* (1922), James Joyce intersperses the description of a place with fragments of a formulaic prayer:

Plate 7   The Famous Grouse advertisement

Stale smoky air hung in the study with the smell of drab abraded leather of its chairs. As on the first day he bargained with me here. As it was in the beginning, is now. On the sideboard the tray of Stuart coins, base treasure of a bog: and ever shall be. And snug in their spooncase of purple plush, faded, the twelve apostles having preached to all the gentiles: world without end.

'Drab abraded leather', 'base treasure of a bog', 'snug in their spooncase of purple plush' are phrases unlikely to occur outside the context of literary descriptions. On the other hand, the fragments 'As it was in the beginning, is now ... and ever shall be ... world without end' clearly belong to a prayer. These two types of text (or or the two registers they use) normally operate in very different contexts, the sacred and the secular, but here they are starkly juxtaposed. It would simplify matters if we could claim that this juxtaposition merely calls the prayer into question by inserting it into a secular context. But counterpointed, as they are in this passage, the sacred and the secular simultaneously call each other into question. One way of understanding the presence and relevance of the prayer fragments in the passage is to suppose that they comprise thoughts in the consciousness of the first person narrator (see **Unit 20, Narrative point of view**), but there is no explicit signal that this is the case, no reporting clause such as 'The unchanging nature of the room recalled to mind the oft-repeated formula like some ironic echo: "As it was in the beginning, is now ..."' In addition, the weaving together of these different strands of text blurs the boundaries between description of external objects and events and internal states of consciousness. But it also – and perhaps more interestingly – destabilizes the text, so that we are no longer certain where different parts of it are coming from. There is no longer a single, authoritative, narrative voice making clear to us where one element or fragment stands in relation to another.

15.5 Conclusion

Although simple juxtaposition is a general feature of communication, its special use as rhetorical device to startle the viewer or reader seems particularly noticeable in twentieth-century art forms, including both pictorial fine art and poetry. It also finds its way into film and advertising images as a pervasive technique for intriguing, mystifying and holding the viewer. It is a specialized invitation to read into the message meanings that are only there by implication because of the lack of an explicit connection between the elements that are juxtaposed. Its effects are multiple but a sense of irony, humour, surprise, or enigma is often produced in our reading of it. Like other literary and artistic techniques juxtaposition can be used (in the words of Magritte) to evoke 'the mystery of beings that normally strike us only as familiar'.

ACTIVITY 15.1 ━━━

1   Cut-up poems are made by juxtaposing elements drawn from two or more pre-existing texts in order to create effects of tension or incongruity. The following example is an extract from Adrian Henri's 'On the late late massachers stillbirths and deformed children a smoother lovelier skin job', which is presented as a 'Cut-up of John Milton Sonnet XVIII On the late Massacher in Piedmont / TV Times / CND leaflet'. ('CND' stands for 'Campaign for Nuclear Disarmament').

(a)   The seven-day beauty plan:
Avenge O Lord thy slaughter'd saints, whose bones
Will cause up to 1 million deaths from leukaemia
Forget not, in thy book record their groans
Now for the vitally important step. Cream your face and
        neck a second time
No American president world-famous for beauty creams
responsible for the freedom and safety of so many young
        offenders
TODAY'S MEN OF ACTION
The Triple Tyrant Macmillan Kennedy Watkinson
The West governments are satisfied as to the moral
necessity to resume Racing from Newmarket

(b)   This baby's eyes and nose had merged into
one misshapen feature in the middle of its
forehead, lost 6″ from Hips
sufferers can now wear fashon stockings
Early may fly the Babylonian wo
followed by
TOMORROW'S WEATHER
The Epilogue
close down.

(a)   Relying on features of language and style, try to identify the source of each phrase or line (i.e. whether it is from Milton's sonnet, the *TV Times*, or the CND leaflet).

(b)   Pick out three examples of juxtaposition and try to describe the effect of each one.

(c)   What is the overall effect of the use of juxtaposition in this poem?

2   Construct a cut-up poem of your own by (i) selecting two short texts (one
of which should be a poem); (ii) cutting them up into fragments; and (iii)
weaving them together in order to achieve irony, humour, surprise,
enigma, or effects which are similar to Henri's poem.

For the best results do not use two texts of the same type (two poems,
or two adverts, etc.). The reason for choosing a poem as one of your
source texts is to help establish a semblance of poetic form in your cut-
up poem, but the other text needs to be significantly different in order
to create effects of tension and incongruency. Use the same wording as
the original texts but you need not use the whole of each text nor follow
the original order.

When you have finished your cut-up poem, try to answer the following
questions:

(a)   What guided your choice of texts?
(b)   How did you decide where to divide them up into fragments?
(c)   What principles guided your attempt to reconstitute them as a cut-
up poem e.g. why did you use the material you included? Why did
you not use other material? Why did you juxtapose the material in
the way you did?
(d)   What kind of overall effect do you think you've achieved?

Reading

Burgin, V. (1976/1999) 'Art, common sense and photography', in S. Hall and J. Evans
(1999) *Visual Culture: The Reader*, London: Sage, pp. 41–50.
Eisenstein, S. (1979a) 'The cinematographic principle and the ideogram', in G. Mast and
M. Cohen (eds) (1979) *Film Theory and Criticism*, pp. 85–100.
Eisenstein, S. (1979b) 'A dialectic approach to film form', in G. Mast and M. Cohen
(eds) *Film Theory and Criticism*, Oxford: Oxford University Press, pp. 101–22.
Eliot, T.S. (1922) *The Waste Land*, in *Selected Prose*, Harmondsworth, Penguin.
Shklovsky, V. (1917/1988) 'Art as technique', in D. Lodge (ed.) (1988) *Modern Criticism
and Theory*, London: Longman, pp. 16–30.

Unit 16

Intertextuality and allusion

16.1 Allusion

An 'allusion' occurs when one text makes an implicit or explicit reference to another text. Some allusions are explicit; in an explicit verbal allusion an actual quotation is made and signalled with quotation marks. Other allusions are implicit; in an implicit verbal allusion, no signal is given and the original wording is changed to suit the new context. Thus the opening of Wordsworth's *The Prelude* (1805) alludes to the end of Milton's *Paradise Lost* (1667) without actually quoting from it:

> The earth is all before me: with a heart
> Joyous, nor scared at its own liberty,
> I look about, and should the guide I choose
> Be nothing better than a wandering cloud,
> I cannot miss my way.
>   (*Prelude*, I, 15–19)

> The World was all before them, where to choose
> Their place of rest, and Providence their guide:
> They hand in hand with wand'ring steps and slow,
> Through Eden took their solitary way.
>   (*Paradise Lost*, XII, 646–9)

16.1.1 Allusion as a means of establishing a relation to a cultural or literary tradition

Allusion serves to place a text within the textual network which makes up a cultural tradition. Because of this, allusion can be used simply as a way of adding cultural value to a text. This is a common device in advertisements. For example, in the *Observer* magazine of 8 May 1988, a Renault car is advertised with the caption 'A room of my own', and Cadbury's Bournville chocolate is advertised with the caption 'If Chocolate be the food of Gods, Heaven must be in Birmingham'. One of the reasons for making such allusions is that they are thought to invoke some of the cultural connotations of the source text and, by a process of transference, bestow them on the product being promoted: thus, in the first example (which has a picture of a woman in a Renault car), women are being encouraged to buy a Renault car by suggesting that it will grant them some of the independence which Virginia Woolf was seeking for women in *A Room of One's Own* (1929). Such allusions can also serve to flatter readers – giving those who recognize the allusion the illusion of being superior to those who don't even realize that an allusion is being made. The Cadbury's advertisement therefore implies that it is only 'highly cultured' people – those with the 'good taste' to recognize an allusion to Shakespeare (the first line of *Twelfth Night*) – who will fully appreciate Bournville chocolate.

As another example, consider the *New Scientist* magazine of 20 March 1999. Among the titles of articles are: 'Forever young' (article about the youthfulness of *New Scientist* readers), 'The long goodbye' (article about the extinction of the North Atlantic right whale), 'Complete control' (article about Bill Gates), 'Something rotten . . .' (article about bluebottles), 'For your ears only' (article about radio), 'Trouble in paradise' (article about ecological loss in Caribbean islands), 'Where no chip has gone before' (article about Motorola), 'Don't fence me in' (review of science books). Here the allusions are primarily to pop songs, films and television, or to very well-known passages in literature (again, try to identify sources for these), and the popular cultural references are mostly over twenty years old, reaching back to the 1970s or before. We might understand the consistency in the allusions as an issue of authorship, arising from the editor of the magazine (perhaps one person with a particular kind of knowledge writes the titles); at the same time this consistency of allusion also positions the reader by telling the reader who recognizes the allusions that this magazine is for him or her, and that he or she is a person of a certain age and with a certain range of cultural knowledge.

16.1.2 Varieties of allusion

Texts may allude to other texts in a variety of ways, of which these are the most common:

1   Through a verbal reference to another text (as in the way *The Prelude* refers to *Paradise Lost* through a similarity of phrasing).
2   Through epigraphs (an inscription at the beginning of the text). T.S Eliot's poem 'The Hollow Men' (1925) has an epigraph taken from Joseph Conrad's *Heart of Darkness* (1899/1902): 'Mistah Kurtz – he dead'; this invites the reader to look for a significant relationship between the poem

and the novel – which is perhaps that both texts suggest there is a hollow-
ness at the heart of European 'man' in the twentieth century.

3   Through names of characters: thus the name Stephen Dedalus, the central
character in James Joyce's *A Portrait of the Artist as a Young Man* (1914),
refers to Daedalus, a character in Greek mythology who 'made wings, by
which he flew from Crete across the archipelago . . . his name is perpet-
uated in our daedal, skillful, fertile of invention' (*Brewer's Dictionary of
Phrase and Fable*, p. 307).

4   Through choice of titles: thus the title of William Faulkner's novel *The
Sound and the Fury* (1929) is an explicit allusion to Macbeth's despairing
claim that life is nothing but 'a tale Told by an idiot, full of sound and
fury, Signifying nothing' (Shakespeare, *Macbeth* (1606): V. 5. 26–8).

16.1.3 Allusion in film, TV, and music

The process of allusion is not confined to literature and advertisements, but
may be found in most cultural and artistic forms. Music may allude to earlier
music (e.g. Stravinsky's allusions to Bach, or the Beatles' allusions to the French
national anthem and 'Greensleeves' in 'All You Need is Love'). A complex
example is presented by the band Big Daddy, who released a record called
Sgt. Peppers (1992) which is a reworking of the Beatles' record *Sgt. Pepper's
Lonely Hearts Club Band* (1967), but performed entirely using instruments and
musical styles of the 1950s. The Beatles' original 1967 record itself alluded
to, and reworked 1950s' music (among other kinds of music), and when Big
Daddy reperform it as a 1950s' record, styles originally alluded to now become
the dominant style of a song rather than simply an allusion within it. Woody
Allen's films frequently make allusions to literature and to other films: *Play It
Again Sam* (1972) is a striking example which makes a series of allusions
to *Casablanca*. Francis Ford Coppola's *Apocalypse Now* (1979) exists within a
complex network of allusions to Conrad and Eliot. It is in essence a rewriting
of *Heart of Darkness*, but towards the end the Kurtz character (played by
Marlon Brando) reads Eliot's poem 'The Hollow Men' – which reverses
the relationship between *Heart of Darkness* and 'The Hollow Men' noted
earlier. A combination of musical and narrative allusion together tell us that
the television series *Star Trek Voyager* (1995) is a version of *The Wizard of
Oz* (1939); the theme tune begins with a five-note motif which, stripped of its
initial note, is the beginning of the film's most famous song, 'Somewhere Over
the Rainbow', and the film's narrative is reproduced by the narrative of the
television series – about a ship captained by a woman, peopled by individuals
who represent accentuated traits but lacking certain qualities, swept into
another part of the galaxy, killing the 'witch' who brings them there and then
trying to get home. Even characters' clothing can be part of the set of allusions; the alien creature 'Neelix' is dressed and whiskered like a munchkin in
the film.

16.1.4 Allusion signals a relationship between texts

An adequate reading of a literary text will need to recognize the significance of the ways it interacts with earlier texts. We need to look for common ground between the texts. This involves trying to work out the similarities and differences between the two texts which are momentarily brought together by the allusion. By choosing the title *The Sound and the Fury*, Faulkner is presumably inviting us to compare Macbeth's nihilistic despair with the events and themes of his novel. In *A Portrait of the Artist*, the name Stephen Dedalus invites the reader to look out for parallels between the novel and the story of Daedalus: is there some connection with the notion of flight? Or is the emphasis on Stephen's aspirations to be an artist (skilful, fertile of invention)? or with failure (since Icarus, his son, dies)? or with the father–son relation (death of the son because the father's ingenuity fails)? A reading which approached the novel with this range of questions in mind would probably find that each of them is relevant in some way.

16.1.5 A way of reading allusions

Thomas Hardy's novels can often seem overloaded with allusions, but some of them are charged with a significance which an adequate reading cannot afford to pass by. In *Tess of the D'Urbervilles* (1891), for example, Alec d'Urberville, Tess's eventual seducer, makes an allusion which, if she had spotted it, might have allowed Tess to avoid her tragedy. Early on in the novel, Tess's impoverished parents send her to work for a rich family who they mistakenly think are related in some way. Tess's new employer, Mrs d'Urberville, who knows nothing of the supposed kinship, sets her to work looking after her poultry and bullfinches. One of the responsibilities involved in looking after the bullfinches is to whistle to them in order to 'teach 'em airs'. Alec, Tess's so-called cousin, spies her vainly attempting to practise whistling and takes this as an opportunity to flirt with her:

'Ah! I understand why you are trying – those bullies! My mother wants you to carry on their musical education. How selfish of her! As if attending to these curst cocks and hens were not enough work for any girl. I would flatly refuse if I were you.'

'But she wants me particularly to do it, and to be ready by tomorrow morning.'

'Does she? Well then – I'll give you a lesson or two.'

'Oh no, you won't!' said Tess, withdrawing towards the door.

'Nonsense; I don't want to touch you. See – I'll stand on this side of the wire-netting, and you can keep on the other; so you may feel quite safe. Now, look here; you screw up your lips too harshly. There 'tis – so.'

He suited the action to the word, and whistled a line of 'Take, O take those lips away'. But the allusion was lost upon Tess.

The editor of the Macmillan edition of Hardy's novel provides an endnote which tells us that Alec is alluding to the first line of the Page's song in Shakespeare's *Measure for Measure* (1604), Act IV, scene 1. But this information, in itself, is not enough to allow us to understand the full import of the allusion. Without an understanding of the significance of the song in the context of *Measure for Measure*, the allusion remains lost upon us as well as upon Tess. It is only when we compare the situation in *Tess* with the situation in the text being alluded to that the significance of the allusion becomes apparent. Peter Hutchinson (1983) makes a succinct analysis:

> The narrator may be suggesting that Tess is simply ignorant of the source ... If we too are ignorant of this, we may assume that the reference is merely a means of contrasting Alec's worldliness with Tess's simplicity and uncultured existence. This is certainly part of its function, but the fact that the narrator terms the whistling an 'allusion' may suggest that the original context of the song has some bearing on the present situation. In retrospect [when Tess has been seduced by Alec and abandoned by Angel Clare] we can see that it clearly does: the Boy sings these lines to Mariana when she has become a seduced and abandoned victim.

Thus the fact that the allusion is lost upon Tess proves fatal for her; for us as readers to understand the allusion will add to our sense of the text's tragic irony (once we know how the novel ends).

It is possible to identify at least three separate stages in this analysis of the allusion in *Tess of the D'Urbervilles*:

1   The first step is to recognize that an allusion has been made in the first place. In Hardy's novel, this is made easy because we are told that 'the allusion was lost upon Tess', but not all allusions are so explicit. To a certain extent the ability to spot an implicit allusion is largely dependent on the reader having read the text being alluded to (thus the reader will have the feeling of having read something vaguely similar and will proceed from there). But spotting an allusion is not so wholly dependent on chance as this suggests; it is often possible to detect the presence of an allusion because it will usually stand out in some way from the text that surrounds it – perhaps through differences of style or register (see **Unit 6**, **Language and context: register**). For example, Ernest Hemingway quotes the seventeenth-century poet John Donne in the title of his novel *For Whom the Bell Tolls* (1940), but we do not need to know this fact in order to recognize that the title uses a more archaic and 'literary' phrasing than Hemingway usually employs.

2   The second task is to trace the allusion. In the example from *Tess* the editor does this job for us, and in some instances we will be familiar enough with the allusion to go straight to the original text. But in most

cases we will have to do some detective work. Books in the reference section of most libraries will be of use in this (see **Unit 2, Using information sources**). If we have a hunch who the original author is, we might go straight to a concordance to the works of that author (though not many authors have had concordances made of their work). In most instances, however, the first recourse might be to a dictionary of quotations. For example, we could trace the allusion in *Tess* in the following manner: (a) decide which is the key word ('lips' in this case); (b) look up 'lips' in the index of the dictionary, and go to the page number indicated for the quotation and its source. If this fails, it's often a matter of educated guesswork: for example, the name Dedalus might seem vaguely 'classical' or 'mythical' and this might send us to *Brewer's Dictionary of Phrase and Fable* or to a Dictionary of Classical Mythology.

3   The third step involves a close reading of the section of the source text in which the word or phrase originally appears, together with some investigation of its significance in the text as a whole. At this stage you should try to work out the similarities and differences between the source text and the text being read. This should help you to establish why the allusion is being made and whether there is an ironic or parallel relation between the texts (see **Unit 14, Irony; Unit 11, Parallelism**). Only by such a careful consideration of the source text (as the example from *Tess* demonstrates) can we be aware of the full implications of an allusion.

16.2 Intertextuality

'Intertextuality' is used in literary criticism to describe the variety of ways that texts interact with other texts, and in particular to focus on the interdependence between texts rather than their discreteness or uniqueness. Allusion is a form of intertextuality which works largely through verbal echoes between texts; however, texts may also interact with one another through formal and thematic echoes.

16.2.1 Intertextuality through genre

The very idea of genre – that texts can be divided into different groups according to certain shared characteristics – necessarily involves a degree of interaction between texts (see **Unit 17, Genre**). No text is an island. Any poem, for example, will draw on certain poetic conventions which will distinguish it from prose (even if only to undercut or resist those conventions). The idea that texts belong to intertextual 'families' is even more true of the various sub-genres, such as that of the sonnet. The sonnet was developed in Italy and was introduced into English poetry in the sixteenth century. Its first practitioners in English generally followed the formal and thematic conventions established by Italian poets such as Petrarch: thus most sonnets have fourteen lines of iambic pentameter (close to Petrarch's endecasillabo meter) arranged into an elaborate rhyme scheme and have a male speaker who addresses his words to a woman he loves or is trying to woo. Although the thematic range of the sonnet has been greatly extended since then, the form continues to be associated with male passion. Thus Edna St Vincent Millay's sonnet 'I, being Born a Woman and Distressed' (1923), is intertextually related to the sonnets of the past not only because it conforms to the formal requirements of the sonnet, but because it reverses and flouts these thematic conventions:

> I, being born a woman and distressed
> By all the needs and notions of my kind,
> Am urged by your propinquity to find
> Your person fair, and feel a certain zest
> To bear your body's weight upon my breast:
> So subtly is the fume of life designed,
> To clarify the pulse and cloud the mind,
> And leave me once again undone, possessed.
> Think not for this, however, the poor treason
> Of my stout blood against my staggering brain,
> I shall remember you with love, or season
> My scorn with pity, – let me make it plain:
> I find this frenzy insufficient reason
> For conversation when we meet again.

Millay's speaker is clearly a woman who informs a man she has had sex with that she is so far from feeling eternal love for him that she feels no urge even to make conversation with him when they meet again. Part of the impact of the poem arises from the fact that the woman rejects the role conventionally ascribed to women in such situations. But its full impact can only be registered by a reader who realizes that it uses the sonnet form in order to transgress those thematic conventions we have come to expect in sonnets. Thus part of the meaning of the poem derives from the intertextual relationship it sets up between itself and the sonnet tradition.

16.2.2 Intertextuality through parody

A second way in which intertextuality occurs specifically through genre is in parody, satire, and mock forms. These sub-genres rely upon intertextual relations with other genres for their effect. For example, Alexander Pope's *The Rape of the Lock* (1712/14) depends upon the reader's familiarity with the conventions of the epic genre which it mocks. Thus the poem opens:

> What dire offense from amorous causes springs,
> What mighty contests rise from trivial things,
> I sing – This verse to Caryll, Muse! is due.

These lines echo the ritualistic opening gesture of the epic mode – an example of which can be seen in the opening lines of *Paradise Lost*:

> Of man's first disobedience, and the fruit
> Of that forbidden tree, whose mortal taste
> Brought death into the world, and all our woe,
> With loss of Eden, till one greater man
> Restore us, and regain the blissful seat,
> Sing heavenly Muse . . .

As its opening indicates, *The Rape of the Lock* uses these epic conventions in order to treat a 'trivial' social event as if it were an epic matter.

From these examples, we can see that part of the significance of a literary text exists not within itself but in the relationships it sets up with other texts. These examples also show that the intertextual dimensions of cultural texts can only have effects and meaning through the active knowledge which a reader brings to them. Thus Pope's poem has a much-reduced impact on readers unfamiliar with the tradition it parodies.

16.2.3 The changing role of intertextuality

Between the Middle Ages and the end of the eighteenth century education in Britain was limited to a privileged minority and was based on the study of the literature of ancient Greece and Rome (the 'classics'). Authors assumed that their readers would recognize allusions to the 'authorities' (the classics, Aristotle, the Bible), and tradition was valued at least as much as innovation. For example, in the 'neo-classical' period (roughly 1660–1790), authors demonstrated their respect for classical writers by writing thematic and formal imitations of them. Examples include Andrew Marvell (1681) 'An Horatian Ode' and Alexander Pope (1733–9) 'Imitations of Horace'.

In the Romantic period (roughly 1790–1830), however, with its emphasis on 'originality' in a period in which literacy and education in the vernacular (i.e. not using the classical languages) began to increase rapidly, the importance of the 'classics' as authorities began to dwindle. The relation of authors to past texts became less that of reverential imitation and more an attempt to break with the past. Wordsworth's allusions to *Paradise Lost*, for example, both acknowledge Milton's importance and register Wordsworth's rebellion against him.

16.2.4 Intertextuality and originality

The fact of intertextuality and allusion thus raises questions about originality: how far do literary texts originate in an author's mind and how far are they composed out of other literature? In Modernist literature (roughly 1910–40), allusion becomes a constitutive principle of composition. If T.S. Eliot's *The Waste Land* (1922) is read alongside the notes Eliot printed with it, we get a sense of the poem as a collage of quotations from and allusions to other texts. In the Postmodernist period (roughly 1960 to the present), writers such as Angela Carter (e.g. *The Magic Toy Shop* (1967)) and Umberto Eco (e.g. *The Name of the Rose* (1980)) seem to have set aside attempts to be original in the narrow sense in order to participate in an intertextual free-for-all in which the possibility that all writing is allusive and/or intertextual is celebrated for its own sake.

16.2.5 Post-structuralist accounts of intertextuality

Traditional literary criticism is often concerned with the texts which influenced a particular writer: influence is most usually established through tracing allusions. If an editor spots an allusion, he or she will typically say something like 'Keats is thinking of Shakespeare's *Venus and Adonis* here'. But this assumption begs a number of questions: how do we know that? What if the allusion were unconscious? Or accidental? Or created by the editor's own associations? What if texts inevitably interact and reading is necessarily an intertextual process? For post-structuralist theorists such as Julia Kristeva and Roland Barthes, all language usage is inevitably intertextual in several senses: first, because individuals do not originate or invent language – it always comes before us; and second, because without prexisting forms, themes, conventions, and codes there could be no such thing as literature at all. For Barthes, 'a text is . . . a multi-dimensional space in which a variety of writings, none of them original, blend and clash. The text is a tissue of quotations drawn from the innumerable centres of culture' (1977: 146). Such a theory of intertextuality is radically different from traditional understandings of the functions and significance of allusion.

ACTIVITY 16.1 ━━━━━━━━━━━━━━━━━━━━━━━━━━━━━━━

On first looking into Chapman's Homer

Much have I travell'd in the realms of gold,
    And many goodly states and kingdoms seen;
    Round many western islands have I been
Which bards in fealty to Apollo hold.

Oft of one wide expanse had I been told
    That deep-brow'd Homer ruled as his demesne;
    Yet did I never breathe its pure serene
Till I heard Chapman speak out loud and bold:
Then felt I like some watcher of the skies
    When a new planet swims into his ken;
Or like stout Cortez when with eagle eyes
    He star'd at the Pacific – and all his men
Look'd at each other with a wild surmise –
    Silent, upon a peak in Darien.

                     (John Keats, 1817)

George Chapman translated Homer's two epics from Greek into English. In 1611 he published *Iliads*, the story, in 14-syllable lines, of the fall of Ilium (Troy). In 1614–15 he published *Odysseus*, in 10-syllable lines, the story of Odysseus's long voyage home. Keats's sonnet is in praise of Chapman's translation.

The practice of looking for allusions falls into two parts: (a) identifying possible allusions in the text, and (b) knowing which reference sources might give a clue to each allusion. This exercise focuses primarily on the identification of possible allusions; you could extend it by looking up texts and reference sources which seem appropriate.

1   What literary texts might be worth consulting as a possible source of allusions in this poem? What kinds of allusion (in form, in meaning) might in principle be being made to those texts?

2   Identify possible geographical allusions in this poem. Why might geographical allusions be appropriate in this particular text?

3   Identify possible allusions to specific historical events in this poem. Why might these particular historical events be alluded to?

4   List the names of individuals in this poem. Where might you look to discover the significance of these names? What might you expect to find?

5   What phrases or sections of text in this poem might possibly be quotations or indirect verbal allusions to some other text? What makes these particular sections noticeable? How would you find out if they were allusions?

Reading

Barthes, R. (1968) 'The death of the author' and (1971) 'From work to text', in R. Barthes (1977) *Image – Music – Text*, Glasgow: Collins.

Bate, J. (1970) *The Burden of the Past and the English Poet*, London: Chatto & Windus.

Bloom, H. (1973) *The Anxiety of Influence: A Theory of Poetry*, Oxford: Oxford University Press.

Eliot, T.S. (1919) 'Tradition and the individual talent', in (1953) *Selected Prose*, Harmondsworth: Penguin.

Eliot, T.S. (1922/1953) *The Waste Land* (including Eliot's notes), in (1953) *Selected Prose*, Harmondsworth: Penguin.

Furniss, T. and Bath, M. (1996) *Reading Poetry: An Introduction*, London: Prentice-Hall, Chapter 13.

Gilbert, S. and Gubar, S. (1979) *The Madwoman in the Attic*, New Haven, CT: Yale University Press.

Hutchinson, P. (1983) *Games Authors Play*, London: Methuen, pp. 57–60.

Renza, L.A. (1990) 'Influence', in F. Lentricchia and T. McLaughlin (eds) *Critical Terms for Literary Study*, Chicago: University of Chicago Press, pp. 186–202.

Examples of the kinds of reference books useful in tracing allusions (see **Unit 2, Using information sources**): Concordances (e.g. to Shakespeare and to the Bible); *Dictionary of Quotations*; *Halliwell's Film Guide*; *Dictionary of Mythology, Folklore, and Symbols*; *Allusions in Ulysses*; *Dictionary of National Biography*; *Brewer's Dictionary of Phrase and Fable*, etc.

Aspects of narrative

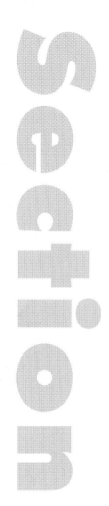

Unit 17

Genre

In its most general sense, 'genre' simply means a sort, or type, of text: thriller, novella, sonata, horror movie, musical, autobiography, prospect poem, etc. The word itself comes from Latin *genus*, meaning 'kind' or 'type' of anything, not just literary or artistic works. ('Genus' is still used to describe a technical sense of type, in the classification of species; and 'generic' is sometimes used to mean 'broad' or 'wide-ranging': 'including a whole type or class'.)

The term 'genre' presents serious difficulties, nevertheless, as soon as we begin to consider questions it raises about literary and other texts. Is there a fixed number of sorts of text? If so, on what basis could this be, or have already been, decided? Do formal elements of a text themselves signal what category, or genre, it will belong to? Or was the classification of genres simply ruled on by expert authorities at some time in the past? Or is classification a result of our own expectations or individual perceptions? And does classifying a text play any part in our appreciation or understanding of a text, or is labelling texts as instances of a genre merely something like butterfly-collecting?

These questions pose issues which stretch far beyond the obvious convenience of being able to sort texts into types, for instance for marketing, presentational, critical, or educational reasons. In fact, they raise deep questions about the relationship between fixed, formal properties of texts and relational properties which are the result of our historically and geographically located ways of seeing or thinking about them.

Attitudes vary towards creating texts which are recognizably within established genres. In some periods and places, it has been thought a valuable achievement to produce a good 'generic text', such as a detective thriller, a pastoral ode, a sonnet, or a stylized but not especially original pop ballad. In other circumstances, however, this aspiration is dismissed as simply an imitative and formulaic activity, lacking in individual creativity and imagination. In either case, what is worth noting is that genre contributes to what might be thought of as a higher-level social system or regime of literary and media production and circulation in society. But the historical differences suggest that this contribution is not fixed. Rather, the role played by genre alters, under pressure from whatever concepts of originality, taste and audience demand prevail during a given historical period. So understanding the role of genre involves not just working out how texts are classified and defined, but grasping how the distinctions on which systems of classification are based fit into larger, aesthetic and social frameworks governing how texts are created, used and evaluated (see **Unit 16**, **Intertextuality and allusion**).

17.1 Sorting texts into types

Notions of kind or type inevitably depend on a system of criteria for distinguishing members of one class from members of another. It is this aspect of genre which we examine first.

17.1.1 Classification on the basis of formal arrangement

The formal properties of texts (see **Unit 3**, **Analysing units of structure**) are often thought a suitable basis for classifying them. Sonnets have fourteen lines, and follow distinctive stanzaic and rhyme patterns (Petrarchan, Spenserian, Shakespearean, etc.). The more general distinction between poetry, drama and fiction (derived historically from Aristotle's classical distinction between lyric, epic or narrative, and drama) is also based on formal differences. Poetry typically involves rhythm and other kinds of sound patterning; fiction does not, at least not necessarily; but it does involve narrative. Drama involves characters speaking and acting in relation to each other. In Aristotle's *Poetics* (fourth century BC), distinguishing genres is primarily a matter of who speaks: lyrics are uttered in the first person; in epics or narrative, the narrator speaks in the first person, then lets characters speak for themselves; in drama, the characters do all the talking. Using formal distinctions in this way to classify texts is very common. But such classifications can nevertheless be difficult to sustain. What about verse drama? Or narrative poetry (as in ballads)? Or dramatic monologue? And the difficulties multiply as soon as other media are also taken into account.

17.1.2 Classification on the basis of theme or topic

Sometimes subject-matter is taken as a basis for genre. The pastoral, for instance, involves concern with country life; the whodunnit focuses on a concern with resolving an enigma in the narrated story; biography relates events in a life; science fiction explores possible future or alternative worlds; war poetry is concerned with war, and so on.

17.1.3 Classification on the basis of occasion

For most of its history, literature has not been a specialized discourse isolated from the rest of society and discussed in literature classes, in schools, colleges and universities. Rather, its involvement in public life, especially in various kinds of social ritual, has ensured that different sorts of texts which we may now regard as belonging to specialized literary types or genres have their origins in composition for or performance on specific sorts of social occasion.

Drama in classical times, for instance, was a social ritual with important cultural implications and effects. Subsequently, various dramatic genres developed, in particular historical contexts for special kinds of occasion: chronicle plays dealing with English history were popular in the sixteenth century in a period of patriotic fervour following the defeat of the Spanish Armada in 1588; and in the late sixteenth and early seventeenth centuries masques were forms of court entertainment combining poetic drama, music, dancing and elaborate costumes and staging, and linked together entertainment by means of spectacle with aristocratic participation in performance (for further discussion, see **Unit 26, Literature in performance**).

Poetic genres have developed in equivalent ways. An epithalamium is a poem written for – and proclaimed at – a public occasion in celebration of a victorious person (e.g. an athlete, a general). In the seventeenth century, the genre of elegy evolved into its current role as a consolatory lament for the death of a particular person. Ballads began as poems to be danced to, but evolved into two divergent traditions: the folk ballads of the oral tradition, and the urban broadside ballads circulated as single sheets or chapbooks which typically contained popular songs, jests, romantic tales and sensational topical stories.

Similar connections between genre and specific social occasions for ritual or entertainment may be seen in relation to song genres. Consider in this respect your experience of (or intuitions about) hymns, carols, love songs, songs on festive occasions such as birthdays, etc.

17.1.4 Classification on the basis of mode of address

Almost irrespective of specific social occasions or rituals, however, texts may still often be labelled on the basis of how they address their readers or audience. Some texts involve direct address, to a reader or audience (e.g. letters, newscasting). Others have a specific addressee named in the text, but are arranged to be overheard (e.g. odes, chat show discussion, most drama). Sometimes, within a single form, variation between modes of address takes place. Essays addressed to 'Dear Reader' are interpolated into narratives in some eighteenth-century novels (in ways that constitute what we will call later in this unit moments of genre switching or genre mixing). Or consider radio styles such as phone-in items and quiz interludes, embedded in larger talk-and-music formats.

17.1.5 Classification on the basis of attitude or anticipated response

Sometimes what a text is about overlaps with an attitude or emotion conventionally adopted towards its subject-matter. Pastoral often implies not just concern with country life, but also a reflective mode. Elegies – although first defined on the basis of the metre they used – became primarily concerned with lamenting deaths (and often take the form of pastoral elegies, delivered in the personae of shepherds). War poetry has a complex history both of jingoistic and anti-war traditions, although both strands tend to explore ideas of patriotism, moral values and loyalty.

A more complex example would be that of tragedy, which historically combines conventions about the main protagonist (the 'tragic hero', a character with a crucial flaw), about the catastrophic nature of the plot, and about the mode of speaking. Along with these, tragedy (at least in Aristotle's account) can be defined by a characteristic mode of audience response: what Aristotle called catharsis, a purging or purification by means of feelings of pity and fear aroused in the audience by the dramatic spectacle. Later developments of tragedy vary in each of these main respects. While classical tragedy involved kings and princes, modern tragedy commonly involves relatively anonymous, often socially alienated protagonists; modern tragedies also tend to involve little or no significant action, as opposed to the major political events and the destiny of nations which formed the usual concern of classical tragedy (see Williams, 1966). But it is arguable that what most allows a modern audience to consider a new text to be a tragedy is less its formal properties or subject-matter than the mood it creates or audience reaction it evokes.

17.2 Recognizing or deciding what genre a text is in

17.2.1 Genre as an expression of conventional agreement

Consider this question. How do you know whether a particular film is a Western? For example, is *Dances with Wolves* (1991), starring Kevin Costner, a Western? If we follow the methods just outlined we might try to decide this on the basis of aspects of the text and/or its reception. But an alternative way would be to look at other films which are conventionally agreed to be Westerns, and then compare *Dances with Wolves* with these. In that case, identification of genre would rely not on precise definition or analysis but on conventional agreement. Certain films are Westerns simply because people agree (without formal analysis) that they are Westerns. Particular genres may well emerge in this way – as names for perceived groups of texts, rather than for theoretically designed categories established on the basis of formal features. We might then say that specialist analysis only helps if it takes as its starting-point a degree of general consensus, rather than if it sets out to examine genre intrinsically, 'from first principles'. If this view is accepted, then to challenge or dispute conventional understandings of genre on the basis of expert, formal analysis is not to refine but to undermine the viability of the concept of genre.

17.2.2 Genres: prototypes and history

It may not be possible to determine the genre of a text by rigorous tests based on stable criteria. However, it is still possible to appeal to notions of family resemblance, common expectation, and prototypical cases.

Some genres, for instance, depend on specific texts which are thought to be exemplary cases: Sophocles's *Oedipus Rex* (*c.* 400 BC) is often appealed to as an exemplary tragedy, with other texts defined as tragedies to the extent that they are similar to this play. This view of genre, where a prototype is taken to exist, and where other texts are judged to be more or less close to this prototype, enables texts to be assigned to genres even when they do not have all the features of that genre. (In a corresponding way, an ostrich which cannot fly is nevertheless part of what we might call the 'bird' genre as a result of its partial resemblance to prototypical birds like sparrows or robins – which can fly.) In this sense it is possible for a text to be a horror film, even while evoking laughter rather than fear, if it makes use of conventions of the form; and it is possible for a text to be a novel even if it has no discernible narrative (as many experimental novels don't), as long as it works with or exploits our expectation that it should have a narrative.

Notions of the typical or 'prototypical' are themselves not fixed, however. Alongside difficulties presented by what appear marginal cases, we need to acknowledge that generic conventions come to us as a historical legacy, shaped and reshaped by the complex history of production and circulation of texts, as well as changing attitudes to them. What constitutes a typical novel in the twentieth century – even allowing for huge variation within the novel form – is not the same as what constituted a novel during the nineteenth or eighteenth centuries. (This insight allows the paradoxical observation that some novelists could be said to have been writing highly successful nineteenth-century novels at the very end of the twentieth century.)

How can we judge which texts are prototypes of a genre, though? We might think of a 1930s' Western like John Ford's *Stagecoach* (1939) as prototypical, and of revisionist Westerns produced from the 1950s onwards as finding part of their meaning on the basis of their deviation from that prototype. Or it may now seem that these more recent, revisionist Westerns have themselves become the typical type of Western; and so we could argue that the prototype has now changed, to something like Sergio Leone's *Once Upon A Time In the West* (1969). Genres are continually being redefined as social, working categories by actual practice, even when there is no deliberate or direct attempt to modify generic conventions.

17.3 Functions of genre

There seems to be a variety of ways of establishing notions of genre, then, in complex and changing relation both to formal properties of texts and to audience perceptions. But why should it matter whether we perceive texts as belonging to types or classes at all, and who in fact does? Why should a system of genres, at whatever level of explicitness it functions in any given situation, ever emerge in the first place?

17.3.1 Genre as a framework for a text's intelligibility

One view on these questions is that genres create an identifiable level of expectations that govern how a text will be understood or construed. In this respect, genre forms a major dimension of the tacit knowledge, or body of interpretative assumptions and techniques, that we draw on in reading. Our expectations in reading a text are structured at many different levels, from local inferences which fill in gaps between obviously related but not continuous details through to vague assumptions about overall point or significance. Genre in this view may dictate, for example, the degree of realism to be expected from a given type of text; or it may guide responses concerning the significance of costume, character, and choice of particular ways of speaking or moving. (Our notion of what genre we are watching or reading may help us anticipate, for example, whether a hero figure is likely to die or not.) We might accordingly say that genre provides a detailed schema, or kind of sign-posting or textual architecture, which gives instructions about how the text is to be read (see Bordwell, 1989).

17.3.2 Genre as a reflection of the nature of human experience

In some cases, texts have been classified into genres in order to reflect the relation they seem to enter into with fundamental human experiences. The distinction between tragedy and comedy is often made along these lines. The notion of archetypal genres (particularly associated with Northrop Frye) belongs here; for Frye, four selected genres (comedy, romance, tragedy, satire) correspond emotionally to the four seasons.

One problem with such views, however, is that they tend to have little to say about the emotional functions of less traditional or less high-cultural genres, such as the twelve-bar blues, the performance pop video, or the road movie. This kind of archetypal classification, that is to say, seems to take for granted a pre-existing, broad – 'generic' – distinction between serious forms (somehow corresponding to essential human experience) and other forms that are deemed to be non-serious (and presumably less worthwhile or significant).

17.3.3 Genre as a promotional device

Sometimes genres are part of a classification established in order to identify a textual product range. In this context, they signal an appeal to different audience tastes and wishes (for news, detective fiction, quiz shows, Indian 'masala movies', romance, potboilers, and so on). Genres in this way allow audiences to predict and plan kinds of experience for themselves, and to repeat, with local variation, kinds of pleasure or entertainment they have previously enjoyed. TV scheduling displays this type of thinking (indeed, the vocabulary of dividing schedules into segments consists largely of such a classification), as does the typical layout of bookshop or video rental store shelves.

17.3.4 Genre as a way of controlling markets and audiences

This view of the usefulness of notions of genre overlaps with the last. But it extends it, with the idea that genres do not so much reflect audience wishes as create them. In this sense, genres are part of a process of controlling the production of entertainment and directing culture markets. By trading on what has already been successful, formulae can be adopted which can be invested in with confidence. For some people, this view of genre as a set of planning or marketing categories represents a kind of conspiracy, bringing about a detrimental standardization of cultural products into predictable forms of differentiation. (The financing of Hollywood films, with notable exceptions, is often argued to follow this pattern.)

17.4 Defeated expectations: exploiting genre through collage and pastiche

Two common ways of combining genres together are **collage** and **pastiche**. In collage, different genres (or features of different genres) are placed alongside one another and so implicitly joined together. Such collage can be used, as it commonly is in modernist texts, to set up a dialectic, or process of contrastive judgement which results from the juxtaposition of different voices or quoted texts. (See **Unit 15, Juxtaposition**.) Pastiche (along with other genres, such as burlesque, mock epic and mock-heroic) is similar, in so far as it undermines or offsets a seemingly authentic speaking voice by bringing different styles together; but it does so by clearly signalling the element of imitation – especially incongruous imitation – often by merging conventions from one genre with subject-matter from another. Both kinds of genre mixing or genre layering are common in satire, whether in print, film, or radio and television sketches.

Techniques of this sort of genre mixing can lead to different kinds of irony. In the case of collage, something in the text – or in our expectations – signals that we are to respond to one of the genres in the compound as more powerful or persuasive than the other or others. It undermines or displaces those other genres or genre features, and so indicates some implied, often evaluative connection. In pastiche, tensions between subject-matter and the generic conventions followed can indicate satire, directed either towards the form adopted or the topic.

Ironies are not always fully controllable, however. Since irony relies on frameworks of expectations on the part of the reader or viewer, it can work against the author's intention, cutting two ways or remaining open-ended. In this sense, irony can escape from authorial control, leaving the text as an open dialogue between voices it juxtaposes, and resonances it brings in by way of allusion – with no stabilizing, dominant voice (see **Unit 14**, **Irony** and **Unit 24**, **Authorship and intention**).

17.5 Postmodernism and genre

When generic compounding and formulaic imitation make irony a dominant or continuous aspect of a text, they create one major dimension of **postmodernism**. Roughly, postmodernism is a set of cultural conditions believed characteristic of the contemporary period. In this period, exposure to language and media so saturates social experience that any act of communication inevitably involves a high degree of self-awareness of the genres in which the communication takes place. In many situations, such self-consciousness about the means of communication is played down. But what makes a text postmodern is that, rather than simply communicating its contents to you, it also refers to the ways of writing and reading texts which are being used, often undermining them by doing so. Because this notion of postmodernism applies both to styles of writing and to specific ways of reading texts, older texts can also be viewed in a postmodern way: a Romantic poem can be approached not as the expression of its author's spirit but as a text about the creation of itself as an example of the Romantic poetic genre.

Philosophically, postmodern thinking links features of irony and the instability of communication to a suggestion that direct access to human experience, unmediated by socially constructed genres of expression, is impossible. But this claim is presented not as alienation and despair, but as a cause for celebration. Postmodernist thinking aspires to producing new ways of enjoying, as well as finding a new agenda for, creative and interpretative activity. That agenda involves seeing how texts build on, subvert and play with conventions of established kinds of discourse and their contexts, rather than reaching out for personal or social messages. For these reasons, the notion of genre is foregrounded in most postmodernist work and criticism, especially as regards forms of pastiche or highly allusive writing. Attention to genre becomes a precondition of reading anything, since reading requires us to ask such questions as what references to conventional genres, or to particular other texts, are being made in a text. In a postmodern framework, you can only read a text by reading its relationships to a history of other texts, i.e. on the basis of its intertextuality (see **Unit 16, Intertextuality and allusion**).

17.6 Genre and ways of reading

As a skill of critical reading, the most obvious importance of the idea of genre involves seeing generic conventions in a text, rather than assuming the text to be a kind of immediate human expression or way of getting at social meaning or truth. Such awareness of the role of genre in shaping and presenting what we often think of as textual content means recognizing that human creativity, and the particular meanings texts create, are not fully 'original' but are built by exploiting existing, conventional resources or templates. This element of convention exists at the level of individual sentences, where words and constructions lie ready for use. It exists in terms of ideas: comparisons, themes and topics form stock resources within a society's repertoire of symbolic conventions. It also exists as regards the overall schema or template we impose for reading a text: its genre. Finding a pure truth of experience or of society may therefore be an impossibility: attempts to do so may speak as much (or more) about our networks of generic conventions as they do about anything beyond them.

ACTIVITY 17.1

This activity explores genre mixing by looking specifically at the genres 'travelogue', 'satire', and 'romance'. The activity's starting point is the possibility that the two texts selected might mix these genres. Both Jonathan Swift's *Gulliver's Travels* (1726) and Daniel Defoe's *Robinson Crusoe* (1719) – which are about travel, shipwreck and adventures which follow – could be put into the genre of travelogue. In the *Oxford Dictionary of English Literature*, however, *Gulliver's Travels* is described as a satire, while *Robinson Crusoe* is described as a romance. So it would seem that *Gulliver's Travels* might belong to two genres (satire and travelogue) and that *Robinson Crusoe* might also belong to two genres (though not the same two): romance and travelogue.

1   Make three lists under the following headings: 'travelogue', 'satire' and 'romance'. Each list should contain the following:

   (a)   the features which you think are necessary features or aspects of texts in each genre (you may have to divide up one or more of the genres into sub-genres; for example, you may feel that there are different kinds of romance);

(b) examples of texts which you think fit into each of the three genres. To get you started, we offer you the following dictionary definitions of each genre. But don't feel bound by these definitions; use your own knowledge and intuitions about the genres to help as well.

TRAVELOGUE: [*The Oxford English Dictionary*]: 'A lecture or narrative description of travel, illustrated pictorially'. (The word is first cited in 1903, but it could be taken to describe a genre which had existed unnamed earlier than this.)

SATIRE: [*Collins Concise English Dictionary*]: '(1) a novel, play, etc., in which topical issues, folly, or evil are held up to scorn by means of ridicule. (2) the genre constituted by such works. (3) the use of ridicule, irony, etc., to create such an effect.'

ROMANCE: [*Collins Concise English Dictionary*]: '(1) a love affair. (2) love, esp. romantic love idealized for its purity or beauty. (3) a spirit of or inclination for adventure or mystery. (4) a mysterious, exciting, sentimental or nostalgic quality, esp. one associated with a place. (5) a narrative in verse or prose, written in a vernacular language in the Middle Ages, dealing with adventures of chivalrous heroes. (6) any similar narrative work dealing with events and characters remote from ordinary life. (7) a story, novel, film, etc., dealing with love, usually in an idealized or sentimental way. (8) an extravagant, absurd, or fantastic account. (9) a lyrical song or short instrumental composition having a simple melody.'

2   *Gulliver's Travels* is said to be both a satire and a travelogue; *Robinson Crusoe* is said to be a romance and a travelogue. So we are faced with examples of texts which apparently fit into two genre categories at the same time. We can represent the possibilities of genre mixing using the grid on page 209, which has been left incomplete.

Fill in the empty slots in the grid, giving as many examples as you can think of for each choice. (Remember: each example represents another text which mixes the same genre elements as the text indicated, or which combines genre elements in the way specified by the pattern of 'Yes' and 'No' slots.)

3   Look at the list you made earlier of features for each of the genres. Can you explain, using this list, why certain links between genres should be possible? (For example, does the same or a related feature turn up in more than one genre?)

		Travelogue	Satire	Romance
1	Texts in two genres			
	Gulliver's Travels	Yes	Yes	No
	....	Yes	Yes	No
	Robinson Crusoe	Yes	No	Yes
	....	Yes	No	Yes
	....	No	Yes	Yes
2	Texts in all three genres			
	....	Yes	Yes	Yes
3	Texts in only one genre			
	....	Yes	No	No
	....	No	Yes	No
	....	No	No	Yes

4   Now consider how you chose texts to include in the grid above. Do all these texts mix genres in order to achieve the same sorts of effect? Or is it possible for two texts to mix the same genres – but for completely different reasons?

5   Is there any pattern to genre mixing, or is it just random chance that some texts mix genres and some do not? The kinds of pattern you might look for include whether there are certain historical periods when specific mixed genres become popular but then perhaps die out again.

6   What general conclusions, if any, can you reach about genre on the basis of this activity?

Reading

Aristotle (*c*. 400 BC) *Poetics* (many editions available, e.g. in Aristotle, Horace, Longinus (1965) *Classical Literary Criticism*).

Bordwell, D. (1989) *Making Meaning: Inference and Rhetoric in the Interpretation of Cinema*, Harvard: Harvard University Press.

Durant, A. and Fabb, N. (1990) *Literary Studies in Action*, London: Routledge, Chapter 5.

Frye, N. (1957) *Anatomy of Criticism*, Princeton, NJ: Princeton University Press, pp. 158–239.

Furniss, T. and Bath, M. (1996) *Reading Poetry: An Introduction*, London: Prentice-Hall, Chapter 11.

Jameson, F. (1985) 'Postmodernism and consumer society', in H. Foster (ed.) *Postmodern Culture*, London: Pluto, pp. 111–25.

Neale, S. (1980) *Genre*, London: British Film Institute.

Rosch, E. (1977) 'Classification of real-world objects: origins and representations in cognition', in P.N. Johnson-Laird and P.C. Wason (eds) *Thinking*, Cambridge: Cambridge University Press.

Watt, I. (1972) *The Rise of the Novel*, Harmondsworth: Penguin.

Williams, R. (1966) *Modern Tragedy*, London: Chatto & Windus.

Unit 18

Narrative

In this unit we look at narratives, stories about a series of events, usually in sequence and often with one event causing another. Where one event causes another we say that there is a causal connection between narrated events, and this causal connection functions partly to give unity to the narrative, and partly to enable the narrative to draw moral conclusions about the consequences of actions. In the simplest narrative texts, there is a single series of events with causal connections between them. More complex narrative texts might be compounded from simple narratives, with two or more simultaneous narratives (perhaps as plot and subplot), or with narratives in sequence which are only loosely connected, perhaps through sharing the same basic character (this is the structure of **picaresque** narratives).

18.1 Narrative form and narrative content

The content of a narrative is a collection of represented events, along with the participants in those events, and the circumstances of those events. The form of a narrative is the way in which those events are represented through a particular narrative medium (usually spoken or written language, and/or images). Many components of a narrative show a tension between content and form, as we see in this unit.

The distinction between content and form is realized in different ways for different aspects of narrative. When we consider the **narrative order**, we can distinguish between content order and form order. The **content order** is the order of events (in the sequence in which they supposedly 'really' occurred). In a verbal narrative (a narrative which uses language, whether spoken or written), the **form order** is the order of sentences. Each sentence can represent an event (i.e. a form-content match). In the simplest narratives, the order of sentences is the same as the order of events, and thus form order = content order. In fact, if there is nothing to tell us otherwise, we just assume that the orders are the same and hence that if we are told one thing after another then the second thing happened second. But it is also possible for the second of two sentences to describe an event which occurred earlier than the event described by the first sentence; this is a mismatch between form order and content order, with content being reordered. Flashbacks have this structure. Thus for example the film *Sunset Boulevard* (1950) begins with a body floating in a pool; the next images we see represent events which occurred earlier than the first image of the body in the pool. There are various terms used to describe the distinction between form order and content order in a narrative; one terminological distinction is between the 'plot' (= the form order of events, the order in which they are told) and the 'story' (= the content order of events, the order in which they supposedly happened).

A mismatch between form order and content order is an example of an **aesthetic strategy**, a strategy which might typically be used in creating an aesthetic object such as a novel, film, oral narrative, etc. It is never possible to pin down a single function for an aesthetic strategy; instead, it might perform any one of a number of functions. The strategy of mismatching content order and form order might be used to create enigmas (we are told the consequences before we are told how they were achieved), to create suspense (the order of events is interrupted by a flashback), to help organize our understanding of the content (crucial background history is delayed until we need to be told it), and so on. The Russian Formalists, a group of theorists working in the early twentieth century, focused their energies on an attempt to establish what makes a text 'literary'; one basic idea was that a text is literary to the extent that our attention is drawn to its aesthetic strategies. One very noticeable aesthetic strategy is a mismatch between form order (which they called *sjuzhet*, our 'plot') and content order (*fabula*, our 'story'); hence such a mismatch helps define a text as literary.

A mismatch between form and content can also arise for **narrative pace**. Events as they exist in the narrative content are paced regularly according to time (and history). Narrative form is not regularly paced because there is no requirement that a sequence of sentences describe a sequence of events which are equidistant in time. Hence, it is possible for the narrative form to compress or stretch out the temporal gaps between the narrated events. We get the effect of the narrative decelerating when things are described as occurring very slowly (an effect seen also in slow motion sections of films). And narratives can also accelerate or jump, with two events separated in the narrative content by major gaps in time placed next to one another. A strategy of this kind is used by Virginia Woolf in *To the Lighthouse* (1927). Various functions are possible for this aesthetic strategy which again exploits the difference between narrative form and narrative content.

Narrative coherence amounts to our recognition that we are being told one unified story – which means that we understand why we are told every event, we understand how events fit together, and if there are any sub-stories inside the main story these sub-stories make sense in terms of the overall story, perhaps as commenting on it (e.g. sub-plots in a Shakespeare play or a story one character tells another). An interesting test for coherence in a narrative is to try formulating the narrative as a whole as a single sentence, or even as a single word; this exercise can bring out quite abstract kinds of coherence (the title might carry out this function). One of the distinctions between form and content in a narrative is that form is inherently more coherent than content. If we take narrative content to be analogous to the way reality is, then we acknowledge its complexity, density and multiplicity; reality is a mess rather than a single coherent thing, and narrative content takes on this implied messiness. In contrast, the organization of narrative content by selection and ordering, which is part of the construction of narrative form, is the creation of order, a fitting together, a making sense, and in general a creation of coherence. Narratives tend to move from a lack to a resolution, a particular kind of beginning to a particular kind of end, but these are formal characteristics which give the narrative its coherence; the implied reality represented by the narrative (the narrative content) lacks any coherent movement from a particular kind of beginning to a particular kind of end – this is imposed upon it by the process of narration.

Finally, another possible kind of mismatch between narrative form and narrative content comes when we consider **narrative point of view**. Events in narrative content just occur; they do not occur from a particular point of view. But in a narrative, the selection of events and way in which they are described may all be governed by a choice of a focalizer, a single point of view. This point of view might be explicitly a narrator, a character who is supposedly involved in the events (and hence has a particular angle on them). The use of a narrator is an aesthetic strategy which, like all such strategies, can be used in various ways and for various purposes. Point of view might be switched in the course of the narrative (a technique systematically used by the author Philip K. Dick, or in the film *Rashomon* (1951) for example); the consequence might be that we become uncertain about the narrative content because it alters depending on point of view. And because narrators are fictional constructions, it is possible to invent narrators who are fantastic in various ways; so an animal may be a narrator, or a dead person (the body in the pool in *Sunset Boulevard* is also its narrator).

In this section we have seen that differences between narrative form and narrative content can be exploited in aesthetic strategies. In some cases, the narrative form is rigidly constrained but variation is possible in narrative content as in flashbacks, while in other cases it is the content which is constrained and the form which is unconstrained as in narrative pace acceleration and deceleration. In other cases, the narrative content simply lacks a characteristic which can be found in narrative form, such as narrative coherence and narrative point of view. In the next section we look at how events themselves, and the participants in those events, also show a tension between narrative form and narrative content.

18.2 The typicality of characters and events

So far we have looked at events in the narrative content, and how their representations are arranged in the narrative form. We now consider the events themselves. Here, too, there is a potential conflict between narrative content and narrative form. An event (narrative content) can be represented in a verbal narrative by a sentence (narrative form); our vocabulary is so large that we are able to represent an infinite variety of complex events in sentences. In this sense there is a good match between content and form. However, one of the characteristics of narratives is that the events are often stereotyped, with the genre of the narrative to some extent requiring certain kinds of typical event – a marriage, a murder, a chase, a disguise uncovered, a false accusation, etc. Types of event belong to the form of the narrative – they are among the components from which a narrative form is built. Hence there is a conflict for events between the tendency towards typicality (a formal characteristic) and the demands for individuality, uniqueness and realism which are associated with narrative content. A marriage in a narrative is both (supposedly) a specific marriage which really happens in all its complex and individual details in the fictional world; but at the same time it is a typical event with all its individuality stripped off, a building block of the narrative, perhaps as one of the components which helps end the narrative. Typical events in a narrative are called **motifs**. Folklorists catalogue motifs in folktales (naming and numbering them, tracing their occurrence across storytelling history).

Just as events in a narrative have both individuated and typical characteristics (which we have analysed as a distinction between narrative content characteristics and narrative form characteristics), so also characters in a narrative are both individual and typical. On the one hand, characters are representative of supposedly real people in the fictional world represented by the narrative; thus characters have a mimetic side to them (their narrative content). On the other hand, characters can also be seen as parts of the mechanism which drives the narrative from beginning to end; in this sense they can be labelled depending on their function in the narrative (this is the characters as elements of narrative form). This approach is particularly associated with Vladimir Propp, who suggested that typical characters in Russian fairy tales perform typical functions. Propp identifies a character function on the basis of the character's involvement in specific types of event; for example, for Propp, the **hero** is the character function of the character who, in the fairy tales under discussion,

> is forbidden to do something;
> is sent off to resolve a lack;

acquires a magical object;
fights the villain;
is marked (e.g. injured, or given something like a ring);
is pursued;
arrives somewhere unrecognized;
is married and ascends the throne.

Propp lists seven character-functions, not all of which are clearly useful in all narratives. However, one in particular, 'the donor', does appear to be found in many kinds of narrative. One specific character is often particularly important in enabling a narrative to move from lack to fulfilment. **Donor** (= giver) is the name given to this character, and typically the donor(-function) will give the hero(-function) some object which enables the hero to conclude the narrative by restoring the lack. In Propp's fairy tales the gift is often magical (a cloak of invisibility, or a special weapon), but if we move beyond fairy tales to more realistic narratives we still find that there may be something magical about the gift (e.g. it may function unexpectedly, like a Bible carried in a shirt pocket which deflects a bullet). A typical type of donor is an old person who gives the hero(-function) something in exchange for a favour. Sometimes the gift is simply information (as when the dying character in a thriller gasps out crucial information with her or his last breath).

When we seek Propp's character functions in more realistic texts we may need to adapt them in this manner, interpreting the name of the character function rather abstractly. Thus the 'princess' is just the character who is sought for by the hero, possibly because that character has been snatched by a villain. This means that the princess might, for example, be a kidnapped young boy; if the only family member otherwise involved is the boy's mother then she might be classified as 'the father of the princess'. This is the power of Propp's approach: it enables us to understand the characters functionally in terms of their role in the narrative rather than just realistically in terms of their identity.

Narratives permeate culture as a way of making sense, packaging experience in particular ways for particular groups and audiences. Thus as part of the self-representations and imaginings of a culture, an individual can be classified on the basis of some characteristic – race, ethnic group, gender, age, sexuality, size, skin colour, etc. It is interesting to look at the relationship between a particular classificatory characteristic of a character and the function played by that character in the narrative. For example, in many contemporary American films an African-American character has the function of donor. The donor typically has a minimal presence in the narrative (usually appearing briefly) but has a crucial role in enabling it to develop and come to a conclusion. In any particular film, we could interpret the use of an African-American donor as making a historical claim: that African-Americans function as donor for the development of the 'narrative' of the United States economy.

Or we could interpret it in terms of a contradictory position taken by the film with regard to racism since it enables racial discrimination at the level of employment (the actor gets a small part) while carrying a positive message at the level of meaning (without this African-American character the narrative could not be resolved).

18.3 The narrative arc: from lack to resolution

Narratives are typically about change. We can think of a change like this:

situation A   changes to   situation B

The changes are often brought about by human actions, and the notion that actions are causes which have effects is an important part of many narratives. Often in a narrative the changes that take place – particularly the important ones – can be understood in terms of situation A being a lack or disruption, which is restored or resolved by situation B. So we can think of many narratives as having arcs like this:

situation A   changes to   situation B
lack   leads to   restoration

The lack may occur when a family member leaves home; this lack may be restored when a family is reunited at the end (it need not be exactly the same people; the crucial point is that a lacking family is replaced by a restored family). Or the lack may be the theft of an object, which is hunted and finally recovered. The lack may be a personal lack; the hero or heroine may begin in ignorance and end in wisdom, or begin in isolation and end in community. There are many other variations on the pattern of lack and restoration, and the movement from one to the other is often the driving force of a narrative.

One very important aspect related to the unity and coherence of a narrative is its achievement of closure. **Closure** is the 'tying up' of the narrative, whereby loose ends are dealt with, problems solved and questions answered. The restoration of a lack is a form of closure. Few narratives are completely without closure (if they are, we think of them as experimental or avant-garde), though because most narratives involve plenty of lacks and plenty of restorations, there is typically some lack of closure – a few issues (though not usually central ones) may not be resolved. Sometimes the narrative ends with closure but at the very end of the text a new lack may open up again; the text in its conclusion opens up a new narrative (perhaps leading to a new text – a sequel – which will bring closure to the lack which begins that new narrative). The existence or non-existence of closure often reveals a moral or ideological position. For example, if a narrative can be closed by the major male and female characters getting married, the narrative potentially carries a message about the virtues of marriage. Along similar lines, we could look at what constitutes or causes a 'lack' or a disruption in the terms of a particular narrative: if the absence of the father at the beginning of a film constitutes its initial lack, then the narrative can be read to mean that nuclear families should stay together.

We can exemplify some of these points by looking at some aspects of the narrative of N. Scott Momaday's novel *House Made of Dawn* (1966), about a young American Indian man after the Second World War and his relationship with his culture; as in many narratives, the novel is concerned with an interior change in the hero from lack to fulfilment (in this case the change is emphasized by the fact that the narrative is constructed to parallel an all-night healing ceremony). The novel is divided up into a one-page prologue and four numbered sections. The prologue is echoed in the last page of the novel in that both parts describe a runner (the hero); they are somewhat distinct from the development of events in the narrative, and we could call one the orientation and the other the coda. After the orientation, the narrative begins with the return home of the hero from the war; we can interpret this as an inversion of the common opening in which the hero leaves home. Normally leaving home is seen as disruptive, but in this novel the hero is unable to fit into the home which he returns to, and so his return is the creation of a lack or a disruption. At the end of the novel, the hero walks out of the village, so providing a mirror-image of the beginning. But now he is integrated into the culture. In the prologue (the orientation) he runs alone; at the end he runs with others. These lacks and closures are to do with movement between the village and the surrounding landscape – a culture–nature opposition (see **Unit 11**, **Parallelism**); the closure of the novel involves the unifying of the two, a unity expressed in the title *House Made of Dawn*.

18.4 How narratives begin and end

We have looked at ways in which narrative form is a management of the narrative content which it represents. We now consider some of the ways in which the narrative form is a response to the context of narration, and in particular how narratives are started and finished. We can call the movement from lack to resolution the 'narrative proper'. The text of the narrative may begin before the lack is revealed, and may end some time after the lack is resolved. This extra material functions to lead into and out of the narrative proper. The hearer or reader must enter into a narrative, and must then exit from the narrative at the end, and there are characteristic strategies for achieving this entry and exit; we first consider some 'entry strategies' and then some 'exit strategies'.

Entry strategies include the title of the narrative and material quoted from elsewhere (an epigraph); these may function to set the leading idea of the narrative, the single notion which gives the narrative coherence. There may occasionally be an initial **abstract**, which is a summary of what is to come. Very often, the text begins by setting the scene; this is called the **orientation** of the narrative, and may include a representation of the place where the narrative is to take place and perhaps some initial details about the characters. Orientations can be stereotyped; fairy tales may begin with a stereotyped orientation 'Once upon a time there was . . . ', and many films begin with the camera travelling over a city towards a particular locality.

Exit strategies are ways of ending the text once the lack has been resolved. This material is generally called the **coda**; it can contain elements which mirror the abstract (e.g. a final summary) or the orientation (by describing some kind of departure from the scene). It can also be stereotyped, as in the fairy tale coda 'And they all lived happily ever after'. Codas sometimes fill a historical gap between an explicitly historical narrative content and now, the time of narrating and reading/hearing; thus a film might end by telling us what happened to various characters between the end of the narrative proper and now.

ACTIVITY 18.1

1   Choose a nineteenth-century novel. You will need to read the novel for this exercise. This activity can be understood in part as asking you to read different parts of a novel in different ways – a useful skill. Approaches to reading sometimes distinguish (a) **close reading**: reading every word carefully; (b) **skimming**: reading quickly through a whole text in order to get a sense of the whole, skipping chunks which you judge to be less crucial to your needs; (c) **scanning**: reading quickly while looking for particular things in the text. This exercise asks you to closely read the beginning and the end of the novel, while requiring you to skim the rest (so that you have a sense of the overall structure of the rest of the novel, while paying relatively little attention to detail).

2   Why does the novel have this particular title? In answering this, consider (a) whether the title is an aid in the interpretation of the novel, (b) whether it creates initial expectations which are important for the reading of the novel, (c) whether it has this title for marketing reasons.

3   (a)   Outline the structure of the beginning of the novel, distinguishing the following components (if they exist), or any other components you think are relevant: Title, prologue or abstract (introducing a text in an author's voice, perhaps summarizing some of what is to come), epigraph (= a quotation), orientation, beginning of the narrative proper, etc.

(b)   Comment on any continuities or blurred boundaries between these components.

(c)   If any of these components are absent, and you think there is some interest in their absence, comment on it.

(You will need to make your own decision about how far into the novel the 'beginning' extends.)

4   Does the ending of the novel relate in any ways to the beginning of the novel? Describe all the links you can find (you might expect e.g. a restoration at the end of lacks indicated at the beginning, and you might also find certain kinds of 'return' to the situation described at the beginning).

Reading

Briggs, K.M. (1970) *A Dictionary of British Folk Tales in the English Language*, London: Routledge & Kegan Paul.

Fabb, N. (1997) *Linguistics and Literature*, Oxford: Blackwell, Chapters 7 and 8.

Finnegan, R. (1992) *Oral Traditions and the Verbal Arts: A Guide to Research Practices*, London: Routledge.

Murray, J.H. (1997) *Hamlet on the Holodeck: The Future of Narrative in Cyberspace*, Cambridge, MA: MIT Press.

Onega Jaén, S. and Garcia Landa, J.A. (eds) (1996) *Narratology: An Introduction*, London: Longman.

Propp, V. (1968) *Morphology of the Folktale*, 2nd edn, Austin, TX: University of Texas Press.

Toolan, M. (1988) *Narrative: A Critical Linguistic Introduction*, London: Routledge.

Unit 19

Writing, speech and narration

19.1 Introduction

This unit is concerned with the differences between speech and writing as media of linguistic communication. It is also concerned with the problems and possibilities of reporting speech in narrative fiction. Several techniques have developed for reporting speech in narrative and these techniques have different communicative consequences, especially in terms of how we as readers interpret the relation of narrator to character.

19.2 Speech versus writing as media of communication

Speech is the primary mode of linguistic communication. As a species we are biologically adapted for speech but not for writing; and as individuals we learn to speak (largely unconsciously) long before we learn to write. Learning to write, in fact, only ever occurs as a result of conscious and deliberate instruction. All languages (with the notable exception of the various sign languages used by deaf people) have taken spoken form; writing as a mode of expression is by comparison relatively recent, and even now appears in comparatively few of the world's languages.

In literate societies, nevertheless, our ideas about language are formed largely by our conscious experiences of writing rather than by our everyday experiences of ordinary speech. Yet the two media are very different. Speech tends to operate in conditions of what we can call co-presence, particularly in face-to-face settings of an informal type where what we say has to be understood as we say it, often helped by facial expressions and gestures. In such situations, fine adjustments can be made to what we say in the light of immediate and continuous reactions from our interlocutor. Speech, then, is very much produced for the moment at hand, is evanescent and typically leaves no trace behind beyond what can be held in memory.

Writing, on the other hand, creates a relatively fixed and permanent product, which allows the separation of participants (writer and reader) in time and space. The process of composition may be lengthy, involving several stages and many revisions as the final product takes shape; and because the final product is relatively fixed, the process of interpretation may be extended, deferred and interrupted, involving several readings and re-readings.

These very different conditions under which speech and writing operate can be related to different features associated with the two modes of expression. These different features emerge most clearly if we compare a transcription of a fragment of everyday conversation with how it might have been if it had been composed as written text.

Speech [short pauses are indicated by (.)]:

> well you see (.) I'm sure it would have
> I'm sure it would have been possible
> if they had known anyone who was a post office engineer
> to install (.) a um er (.) rig
> so that the the (.)
> where you can actually dial from the from the from that phone (.)
> er and if you (.) but that could be you know locked away
> and the er something like that (.)
> so that you could actually dial from that one
> by-pass the coin mechanism

Writing

> I am sure it would have been possible, if they had known anyone who was a post office engineer, to install the type of pay-phone where you can, if you wish, use a key to by-pass the coin mechanism and still dial out.

Some of the noticeable features of speech that we typically do not find in writing are:

1   Pauses and pause-fillers (um/er/erm).
2   False starts, where a phrase or sentence is begun only to be replaced by something else ('... and if you (.) but that could be ...').
3   Self-corrections, where a phrase or sentence is begun and then re-cycled in an amended form ('... from the from that phone ...').
4   Repetitions, where a phrase is immediately re-cycled without alteration as part of building up to the larger utterance ('(.) I'm sure it would have I'm sure it would have been ...').

5   Response cues, where the recipient is invited to complete or supply for themselves the full sense of the utterance (' ... but that could be you know locked away and the er something like that ...').

The presence of such features goes some way to explaining why the transcribed spoken extract is longer than the equivalent written statement. They also create a misleading impression of lack of fluency – even sloppiness – in speech. They are, however, integral to the performance of speech in everyday circumstances. Pause-fillers, for instance, are spoken in a characteristic tone which helps to reinforce the signal they give that the utterance is unfinished and that a momentary hesitation at this point by the speaker should not be mistaken for the end of a turn at speech. Repetitions are a common feature of the beginning of a turn, where speakers are competing with each other to speak. Response cues ('you know', 'something like that') emphasize the active role of the listener in conversation, and the way in which background understanding and shared knowledge can be assumed between people talking to each other – so much so that it becomes odd, even condescending, to spell everything out in a completely explicit fashion. Since meanings are shaped, re-shaped and negotiated at the moment of speaking, speech can be seen as a much more dynamic and participatory mode of interaction than writing.

19.3 Speech and narrative

Story-telling – whether in a novel or an everyday anecdote – often relies on the expressive and dramatic potential of speech. Nearly all narrative relies on the presentation of material as if it were fragments of a spoken dialogue which is now being quoted for dramatic effect. But in written narrative the features of speech which we noted above – the false starts, the self-corrections, etc. – are rarely reproduced in this practice of apparent quotation. Instead, specific techniques have evolved in writing in order to introduce and mark the quotation of speech. This can be seen more clearly if we consider examples of narrative writing by small children where the conventions for embedding speech into written narrative have not yet been fully acquired. Thus, in the following opening to a story written by an 8 year old, it is difficult to distinguish who is talking to whom:

The Tidy House

One day a girl and a boy said,
Is it sping time?
Yes! I think so. Why?
Because we,ve got vister.
Who!

Jamie and Jason. Here they come.
Hello, our toby! I havont seen you for a long time.
Polkadot's outside and the sunflowers are bigger than us
Mark let's go and see.
OK.

(Carla, aged 8: cited in Steedman, 1981)

In this story, pieces of dialogue are not attributed in any clear way to specific speakers. Toby and Polkadot turn out to be, respectively, a dog and a rabbit belonging to the visitors. Not even the single use of the reporting verb ('said') in the first line successfully discriminates between the two possible speakers ('a girl and a boy'). Careful examination of spatial coordinates ('come', 'go', 'outside') suggests that Jamie and Jason are the visitors; if this is the case, Mark is probably the boy. Most of the dialogue, therefore, belongs in all likelihood to the girl and the boy, except for 'Polkadot's outside and the sunflowers are bigger than us', which seems to be said by one of the visitors. Thus, although it is possible to arrive at some sense of who is speaking to whom, it might be argued on the basis of this extract that distinguishing clearly between speakers is not important for young children – that speech for them is a medley of undifferentiated voices and that identifying exactly who owns which voice is not important to them. However, it is more likely to be the case that for the 8-year-old child the written mode of story-telling has not fully separated itself from oral story-telling: the child is still heavily dependent on oral strategies.

The spoken story, in this respect, has particular strategies available to it that have no direct equivalent in writing. One such strategy is for the spoken narrator to signal a change of speaker through a change in voice quality, as in the following example:

Trainee doctor's oral anecdote (on casualty)

They come bustin' through the door – blood is everywhere
on the walls
on the floor
everywhere
[raised pitch]
It's okay Billy it's okay we're gonna make it
[normal voice]
What's the hell wrong with you?
We look at him. He's covered with blood y'know?
All they had to do was take a wash cloth at home and go like this
[pause for wiping action]
and there'd be no blood . . .

Thus, in spoken narratives, and especially in everyday conversational anecdote, speakers can draw upon a range of expressive techniques, manipulating volume, pace, pitch and voice quality in order to distinguish the speech of one character from another. Indeed, pivotal moments in the action of spoken narratives are often marked by this kind of embedding of enacted dialogue involving the performance of different voices.

19.4 Types of speech presentation in prose fiction

The technical problem faced by the beginning authors of 'The Tidy House' above is learning to find ways of replacing the expressive possibilities of voice with techniques for quotation and for the presentation of speech and the identification of speakers in writing – techniques of the kind that developed in the history of the novel and the short story. It is these techniques that we will now consider. These techniques are, it must be stressed, highly conventionalized: they make little attempt, for instance, to replicate actual, 'real-time', conversational speech with all its apparent lack of fluency. They may be classified under the following major types.

19.4.1 Direct speech

Direct speech is enclosed within quotation marks and introduced by or presented alongside a reporting clause (*she said / declared / commanded / asserted*, etc.):

> She said: 'Well there's nothing I can say to that, is there?'
> He leaned forward and said: 'I'm going to give you another chance, Anna.'
>
> (Doris Lessing, *The Golden Notebook*, 1962)

19.4.2 Indirect speech

By comparison with direct speech, indirect speech is presented from a slightly different perspective, with a shift from the perspective of the speaker to that of the narrator. The piece of dialogue in direct speech from *The Golden Notebook*, given above, can be transformed into indirect speech simply as follows:

> She said that there was nothing she could say to that. He leaned forward and said that he was going to give her another chance.

Indirect speech differs from direct speech in the following ways:

1   quotation marks are dropped;
2   some kind of subordinating conjunction such as *that* is used;
3   there is a switch from 1st and 2nd person pronouns (*I, you*) to 3rd person (*she, he, they*);
4   there is a shift in the tense of the verb 'backwards' in time (e.g. from *is* to *was*);
5   temporal expressions shift backwards in time (e.g. *now* becomes *then*);
6   demonstratives shift from close to distant ones (e.g. *here* becomes *there*).

19.4.3 Free direct speech

In free direct speech the perspective of the narrator is minimized instead of being emphasized. The reporting clauses are dropped altogether, although the quotation marks are usually (though not invariably) preserved. The first line of dialogue in the example below could be treated as direct speech if 'They talked about his work' is taken as a reporting clause. But the remaining speech is in the free direct mode because of the absence of any other reporting clauses:

> They talked about his work. He specialised in leucotomies:
> 'Boy, I've cut literally hundreds of brains in half!'
> 'It doesn't bother you, what you're doing?'
> 'Why should it?'
> 'But you know when you've finished that operation, it's final, the people are never the same again?'
> 'But that's the idea, most of them don't want to be the same again.'
> (Doris Lessing, *The Golden Notebook*)

19.4.4 Free indirect speech

This is a mixed form, consisting partly of direct speech and partly of indirect speech, where – because of the suppression of some of the distinguishing signals – it is difficult to separate the voice of the narrator from the voice of the character. In the following short extract from Dickens's novel, *Dombey and Son*, we find backshifting of tense ('the motion of the boat . . . was lulling him to rest'), as well as some pronoun shift ('me' becomes 'him'); these characteristic features of indirect speech emphasize the presence of a narrator who filters the speech of characters. At the same time, some sections sound close to the direct speech of the character (e.g. 'how bright the flowers growing on them, and how tall the rushes!'):

> Presently he told her the motion of the boat upon the stream was lulling him to rest. How green the banks were now, how bright the flowers growing on them, and how tall the rushes! Now the boat was out at sea

but gliding smoothly on. And now there was a shore before him. Who stood on the bank!

(Dickens, *Dombey and Son*, Ch. 14)

It is a fairly simple matter, involving few changes, to switch the free indirect speech of this passage into direct speech, thereby emphasizing the perspective of the character:

Presently he told her:
'The motion of the boat upon the stream is lulling me to rest. How green the banks are now, how bright the flowers growing on them, and how tall the rushes! Now the boat is out at sea but gliding smoothly on. And now there is a shore before me. Who stood on the bank!'

Free indirect speech is thus an ambiguous mode in that it blurs the distinction between a character's speech and the narrative voice; this ambiguity has made it attractive to novelists from Jane Austen onwards. Some writers – such as Joyce in *Dubliners*, or Austen in *Emma* (1816) – are especially known as exponents of free indirect speech. As a technical device it offers writers a way of presenting words which seem to come from inside and outside a character simultaneously. Such words can be given the emotional weight of the character's perspective, while at the same time preserving a degree of narrative distance or ironic detachment from the character.

19.4.5 Thought and speech

In many respects, thought may be considered as a kind of 'inner speech'; and the major ways of presenting it are much the same as those reviewed above for external speech. Thus the different modes of presenting both speech and thought can be represented in a table which shows the different degrees to which a character's speech or thought can be filtered through the narrator:

FREE DIRECT SPEECH/ THOUGHT	UNFILTERED BY NARRATOR ('Come here tomorrow')
DIRECT SPEECH/ THOUGHT	SOME FILTERING (She said to him 'Come here tomorrow')
FREE INDIRECT SPEECH/ THOUGHT	MORE FILTERING (She said to him to come tomorrow)
INDIRECT SPEECH/ THOUGHT	MOST FILTERING (She said that he was to come there the next day)

Because of the connection between modes of presentation and relative close-ness to or distance from the viewpoint of the character or of the narrator, modes of presenting speech in prose fiction are more than mere technical accomplishments. Each possibility has a different effect, and seems to carry a different value ranging from allowing the character to speak as if in his or her 'own words' to filtering them through the perspective of the narrator. If, for instance, free indirect speech lends itself to the creation of ironic distance between the words of the character and those of the narrator, free indirect thought on the other hand can create a sense of empathy with the character. These different kinds of interplay between the voice of the narrator and the speech of a character make the issue of speech presentation important not just for its own sake but also for the way in which it connects with other topics such as **point of view** in fiction (see **Unit 20**).

19.4.6 Genre and the presentation of speech

Subtle differences in the presentation of speech can also serve as indicators of different **genres** of prose fiction (see **Unit 17**). Consider, for example, the following reporting clauses which frame direct speech (they are all drawn from within a few pages of each other in a single novel; the speech itself has been omitted):

> '. . . ,' she replied sharply
> '. . . ,' she stuttered
> '. . . ,' she wailed gaspingly
> '. . . ,' he murmured huskily
> '. . . ,' she asked as calmly as she could
> '. . . ,' he said with chilly emphasis
> '. . . ,' he countered silkily

Readers familiar with the genre will no doubt instantly recognize these as coming from popular romance (they are quoted from Susan Napier's *The Counterfeit Secretary: A Vivid Story of Passionate Attraction*, published by Mills & Boon (1986)). The way in which the manner of the speech has been fore-grounded in the reported clauses through adverbial phrases such as 'gaspingly', 'huskily', 'with chilly emphasis', and so on, is genre-specific to such popular romance. This can be seen by comparing these reporting clauses with the way speech is presented in the following short scene from Nancy Mitford's 'literary' novel *The Pursuit of Love* (1945):

> 'Allô – allô.'
> 'Hullo.'
> 'Were you asleep?'
> 'Yes, of course. What's the time?'

'About two. Shall I come round to see you?'

'Do you mean now?'

'Yes.'

'I must say it would be very nice. But the only thing is, what would the night porter think?'

'*Ma chère*, how English you are. *Eh bien, je vais vous le dire – il ne se fera aucune illusion.*'

'No, I suppose not.'

'But I don't imagine he's under any illusion as it is. After all, I come here for you three times every day – you've seen nobody else, and French people are quite quick at noticing these things, you know.'

'Yes – I see –'

'*Alors, c'est entendu – à tout à l'heure.*'

Both *The Counterfeit Secretary* and *The Pursuit of Love* are concerned with romantic relationships, and dialogue in both works is an important vehicle for registering fluctuations in degrees of emotional attachment. This makes the differences in the ways dialogue is handled all the more striking. *The Counterfeit Secretary* uses some free direct speech; but a great deal of the dialogue is direct speech, where information about the manner of the speaker is foregrounded in explicit narrative comment. *The Pursuit of Love* makes much more use of free direct speech, in which the words of characters have to achieve their own significance without being mediated by a direct comment from the narrator. Comparison between the two techniques suggests that, for popular romance, the shifting grounds of emotional attachment may be carried in the manner of the speech as much as by the speech itself. For readers of *The Pursuit of Love*, on the other hand, the ebb and flow of emotional confrontation is to be deciphered in the nuances of the very wording of the dialogue itself. Such differences function as formal markers of generic distinctness; they may also signal differences in attitudes towards language and meaning in the **implied readerships** of the two works (see **Unit 23**). The implied readership of *The Pursuit of Love* is, for instance, more class based than that of *The Counterfeit Secretary*. The extract from the former presupposes not only some knowledge of the French language (very much a minority skill in Britain in 1945, restricted mostly to the middle and upper classes) but also – for its humour to be intelligible – some acquaintance with the distance between French and English sexual mores of the time. Free direct speech, furthermore, may be seen as making greater demands of the reader, since the significance of the dialogue has to be extracted from the wording of the speech itself without interpretive signposts regarding tone and manner being supplied by the narrator. Thus, the differences in the narrative presentation of speech in prose fiction may correlate with broader distinctions between popular and minority genres.

19.5 Conclusion

In this unit we have explored how writing and speech – because of the very different circumstances in which they are produced – constitute very different modes of communication. We then considered how particular conventions have arisen in written story-telling, or prose narration, for the rendering of speech. Different techniques for presenting speech (as well as thought, as a kind of 'inner speech') were examined; and some suggestions were made as to the different effects associated with the different techniques. Finally, it was proposed that there may also be generic differences associated with the adoption of one mode of speech presentation rather than another.

—————————————————————————————— **ACTIVITY 19.1**

Since 'thought' may be considered as a kind of 'inner speech', the presentation of thought – for the purposes of this activity – is treated as similar to the presentation of speech. Direct speech, for example, is similar in its presentation to direct thought – except that the kind of reporting verb will be different.

> Direct speech: She said, 'Well there's nothing I can say to that, is there?'
> Direct thought: She thought, 'Well there's nothing I can say to that, is there?'

In the following extract from Doris Lessing's *The Golden Notebook*, two characters – Tommy and Anna – are having a confrontation. Tommy is the adult child of Anna's close friend; he is challenging Anna about her writing – specifically about her way of organizing her work in four notebooks.

> 'Don't put me off, Anna. Are you afraid of being chaotic?'
> Anna felt her stomach contract in a sort of fear, and said, after a pause: 'I suppose I must be.'
> 'Then it's dishonest. After all, you take your stand on something, don't you? Yes you do – you despise people like my father, who limit themselves. But you limit yourself too. For the same reason. You're afraid. You're being irresponsible.' He made this final judgement, the pouting, deliberate mouth smiling with satisfaction. Anna realised that this was what he had come to say. This was the point they had been working towards all evening. And he was going on, but in a flash of knowledge she said: 'I often leave my door open – have you been in here to read these notebooks?'

'Yes, I have. I was here yesterday, but I saw you coming up the street so I went out before you could see me. Well I've decided that you're dishonest, Anna. You are a happy person but ...'

'I, happy?' said Anna, derisive.

1   Identify the type of speech presentation in the following segments:

(a)   Anna ... said, after a pause: 'I suppose I must be.'

(b)   in a flash of knowledge she said: 'I often leave my door open – have you been in here to read these notebooks?'

Try to re-write each segment as indirect speech. Make a note of the changes that were necessary in order to do so. Compare the original with your re-written version: are there any differences between them in terms of meaning or effect? If so, make a note of what the differences are.

2   Identify the way of presenting speech used in the following segment:

'Yes, I have. I was here yesterday, but I saw you coming up the street so I went out before you could see me. Well I've decided that you're dishonest, Anna. You are a happy person but ...'

Try to re-write the segment as free indirect speech. Make a note of the changes you needed to make in order to do this. Compare the original with your re-written version: do they differ in meaning or effect? If so, how?

3   Identify the way of presenting inner-speech/thought used in the following segment:

Anna realised that this was what he had come to say. This was the point they had been working towards all evening. And he was going on, ...

Is there any ambiguity about how much of this extract is the character's thought, and how much is the narrator's report of, or comment upon, the events? If so, where does the ambiguity begin? How might you resolve this ambiguity? Try to re-write the passage as direct thought ('inner speech'). Compare the original with your re-written version: do they differ in effect? If so, how?

4   Substitute your re-written segments into the original, and read the whole (re-written) passage through again. Does it work as well as the original?

If not, why not? If you can offer an answer to this question, you have gone a long way towards understanding why the writer may have made those particular technical choices in the first place.

Reading

Brown, G. and Yule, G. (1983) *Discourse Analysis*, Cambridge: Cambridge University Press.

Leech, G. and Short, M. (1981) *Style in Fiction*, London: Longman, pp. 318–51.

Montgomery, M. (1995) *An Introduction to Language and Society*, 2nd edn, London: Routledge.

Ong, W.J. (1982) *Orality and Literacy: The Technologizing of the Word*: London and New York: Methuen.

Steedman, C. (1981) *The Tidy House*, London: Virago.

Toolan, M. (1988) *Narrative: A Critical Linguistic Introduction*, London: Routledge, pp. 90–145.

Unit 20

Narrative point of view

20.1 'Story' and 'narration'

In most theories of narrative two main dimensions or levels are identified. The first consists of the basic events or actions, in the chronological order in which they are supposed to have happened, together with the circumstances in which the actions are performed. This level is sometimes referred to as the **story**. The second level comprises the techniques and devices used for telling the 'story' to the reader. This latter level is sometimes referred to as **narration**. In effect, these two levels may be seen as corresponding to the distinction between the tale itself and the manner in which it is told – a distinction which is based upon our intuitive recognition that the same tale can be told in different ways. (See **Unit 18**, **Narrative**.)

20.2 Point of view and narration

The term 'point of view' in the discussion of prose fiction has been used in a variety of ways (see Fowler, 1986; Simpson, 1993). It can be used literally to refer to visual perspective – the spatial position and angle of vision from which a scene is presented. It can also be used, metaphorically, to designate the ideological framework and presuppositions of a text (e.g. 'the point of view of the emergent bourgeoisie', or 'a male perspective'). Finally, it can be used as a term for describing and analysing distinctions between types of narration – the different types of relation of the teller to the tale in any narrative. It is this relationship – between point of view and narration – that will be examined in this unit.

The simplest distinction that we can make in point of view is between two types of narration – a first person 'I-narration' and a third person 'THEY-narration'.

20.2.1 First person narration

First person narration may be found in a wide range of novels otherwise different in style and period. Novels such as Daniel Defoe's *Robinson Crusoe* (1719), James Hogg's *The Private Memoirs and Confessions of a Justified Sinner* (1824), Charlotte Brontë's *Jane Eyre* (1847), Mark Twain's *Huckleberry Finn* (1884), Philip Roth's *Portnoy's Complaint* (1967), Alice Walker's *The Color Purple* (1983), are all told in the first person. Indeed, in the case of *Robinson Crusoe*, the very chapter headings emphasize the use of the first person: 'I Go to Sea', 'I Am Very Ill and Frighted', 'I Sow My Grain', 'I Am Very Seldom Idle'. In this example, and in most of those listed above, the I-narrator is also the central protagonist of the tale, so that the person central to the action of the story is also telling it.

For instance, the 'Private Memoirs and Confessions of a Sinner' (which is the central narrative of *The Private Memoirs and Confessions of a Justified Sinner*, framed before and after by 'The Editor's Narrative', also narrated in the first person) begins as follows:

> My life has been a life of trouble and turmoil; of change and vicissitude; of anger and exultation; of sorrow and of vengeance. My sorrows have all been for a slighted gospel, and my vengeance has been wreaked on its adversaries. Therefore in the might of heaven I will sit down and write . . . I was born an outcast in the world, in which I was destined to act so conspicuous a part . . .

It concludes with the impending death of the sinner and a series of farewells:

> Farewell, world, with all thy miseries; for comforts and joys hast thou none! Farewell, woman, whom I have despised and shunned; and man, whom I have hated; whom, nevertheless, I desire to leave in charity! And thou, sun, bright emblem of a brighter effulgence, I bid farewell to thee also! I do not now take my last look of thee, for to thy glorious orb shall a poor suicide's last earthly look be raised. But, ah! Who is yon that I see approaching furiously – his stern face blackened with horrid despair! My hour is at hand. – Almighty God, what is this that I am about to do! The hour of repentance is past, and now my fate is inevitable – *Amen, for ever!* I will now seal up my little book, and conceal it; and cursed be he who trieth to alter or amend!

Thus, in the 'Private Memoirs and Confessions of a Sinner' the sinner's life is coterminous with the narrative which is told by him in the first person as the very figure who acts 'so conspicuous a part' in the tale.

First person narration, however, can be used in a quite different way where the narrative is told not by the central protagonist but by a subsidiary character. Indeed, the 'Private Memoirs and Confessions of a Sinner' is framed – as we have said – by just such a first person narrative, purportedly that of the editor and discoverer of the 'confessions' narrative that the sinner had completed just before his death.

Scott Fitzgerald's *The Great Gatsby* (1922) is a well-known case of the tale being told through the first person narration of a subsidiary character. Although Nick, the narrator, tells the story in the first person, he remains on the margins of the main events, which involve the central figure – Jay Gatsby himself – whose story is thus told from some degree of narrative distance. Here, for instance, is Nick describing Gatsby and Daisy, whose reunion he has helped – almost unwittingly – to make possible:

> As I went over to say goodbye I saw that the expression of bewilderment had come back into Gatsby's face, as though a faint doubt had occurred to him as to the quality of his present happiness. Almost five years! There must have been moments even that afternoon when Daisy tumbled short of his dreams – not through her own fault, but because of the colossal vitality of his illusion. It had gone beyond her, beyond everything. He had thrown himself into it with a creative passion, adding to it all the time, decking it out with every bright feather that drifted his way. No amount of fire or freshness can challenge what a man can store up in his ghostly heart.
>
> As I watched him he adjusted himself a little, visibly. His hand took hold of hers, and as she said something low in his ear he turned toward her with a rush of emotion. I think that voice held him most, with its fluctuating feverish warmth, because it couldn't be overdreamed – that voice was a deathless song.
>
> They had forgotten me, but Daisy glanced up and held out her hand; Gatsby didn't know me at all. I looked once more at them and they looked back at me, remotely, possessed by intense life. Then I went out of the room and down the marble steps into the rain, leaving them there together.

Nick's narration does contain some confident, almost poetic, assertions – usually about life: for instance 'No amount of fire or freshness can challenge what a man can store up in his ghostly heart'; or 'that voice was a deathless song'. But it is also full of circumspect observation ('I saw that . . .', 'As I watched him . . .', 'I looked once more at them . . .') where the truth of the events that are described is not certain: 'I saw that the expression of bewilderment had come back into Gatsby's face, *as though a faint doubt* had occurred to him'; or 'There *must have been* moments'; or 'and as *she said something low in his ear* he turned toward her with a rush of emotion'; or '*I think* that voice held him most'. Indeed, the two deaths that separately constitute the spring of the tragedy and its denouement happen, so to speak, 'off camera' since Nick is present at neither event.

First person narration, therefore, usually has in-built restrictions, especially when told from the viewpoint of a minor character, though even a central character will be ignorant about some of the things happening around him or her. Whatever its restrictions, however, it projects the reader clearly inside the consciousness of someone in the story giving us the events from a defined observer's position.

20.2.2 Third person narration

Third person narration, by contrast, can be used in such a way that we are not particularly aware of the role of the narrator, who remains outside the action of the tale. In such writing the narration seems to operate as a simple window on the events of the story; and, because the role of the narrator is carefully effaced, this mode of narration acquires a reputation for impersonal, but all-seeing, objectivity. The opening of *Lord of the Flies* (1954) by William Golding is of this type, in the way it introduces an unnamed boy, who is presented from the outside:

> The boy with fair hair lowered himself down the last few feet of rock and began to pick his way towards the lagoon. Though he had taken off his school sweater and trailed it now from one hand, his grey shirt stuck to him and his hair was plastered to his forehead.

As third rather than first person narration this presents quite different opportunities for readers to align themselves with the story. 'The boy with fair hair' is clearly presented to us at this moment as if observed from without. Indeed, it would be hard to re-cast any of this into first person from the boy's perspective: for instance 'my hair was plastered to my forehead' sounds odd precisely because the boy would simultaneously have to be the subjective agent of the narration and object of its scrutiny. He'd have to be looking at himself.

The opening passage of the novel continues (still in the third person) as follows:

> All round him the long scar smashed into the jungle was a bath of heat. He was clambering heavily among the creepers and broken trunks when a bird, a vision of red and yellow, flashed upwards with a witch-like cry; and this cry was echoed by another.

Although the narration remains in the third person the sensations described shift to being – in part at least – those of the boy. It could be the boy who feels the long scar in the jungle as a bath of heat, who sees the red and yellow of the bird and who hears its 'witch-like cry'. Indeed, these sentences do not sound as odd as the earlier part of the passage if transformed into the boy's first person narration: for instance 'All round me the long scar smashed into the jungle was a bath of heat' reads quite appropriately.

In this respect, third person narration is potentially more flexible and enjoys a technical advantage over first person narration. First person narrators have to provide a warrant for knowing the details that they narrate. But if the narrator is not defined and named, operating instead anonymously in the third person, the narrative does not have to provide a warrant for presenting everything and anything that is going on in the story whether it is inside the mind of a character or not.

Moreover, it is important to recognize that there are contrasting possibilities within third person narration, which we may sum up in terms of the following oppositions:

INTERNAL   versus   EXTERNAL

RESTRICTED KNOWLEDGE   versus   UNRESTRICTED KNOWLEDGE

20.2.3 Internal/external

The example of third person narration given above from *Lord of the Flies* begins by observing characters and events from outside (externally). But third person narration may also provide access to the (internal) consciousness of characters by telling us how they think and feel. Much of D.H. Lawrence's *Lady Chatterley's Lover* (1928), for instance, despite its title, adopts Connie Chatterley's perspective rather than that of her lover, Mellors. The following passage (despite its third person narration) is – with its emphasis on Connie's feelings – fairly representative of the novel as a whole:

> Now she came every day to the hens, they were the only things in the world that warmed her heart. Clifford's protestations made her go cold from head to foot. Mrs Bolton's voice made her go cold, and the sound of the business men who came. An occasional letter from Michaelis affected her with the same sense of chill. She felt she would surely die if it lasted much longer.
> Yet it was spring, and the bluebells were coming in the wood, and the leaf-buds on the hazels were opening like the spatter of green rain. How terrible it was that it should be spring, and everything cold-hearted, cold-hearted. Only the hens, fluffed so wonderfully on the eggs, were warm with their hot, brooding female bodies! Connie felt herself living on the brink of fainting all the time.

Although this passage, like the rest of the novel, is consistently in the third person, it is none the less devoted primarily to the inner sensations of the person it describes. Indeed, rhetorically it is structured around a simple, basic opposition in Connie's sensations between warmth and cold (equivalent to life and death). Significantly, it is difficult to read the penultimate sentence as the narrator's comment. It makes most sense as a piece of free indirect thought (see **Unit 19**, **Writing, speech and narration**) belonging in part at least to Connie herself. Third person narration, therefore, has the option of being internal or external, sometimes switching within the same text.

20.2.4 Restricted/unrestricted

A second distinction may be made in third person narration between narration with no restrictions on the knowable (so-called 'omniscient narration'), and narration with restrictions on the knowable. Indeed, in third person narration we tend to assume that narration is omniscient unless there are indications to the contrary, usually in the foregrounding of a character who – though given to us in the third person – offers a position from which events can be known. Consider the following passage from Henry James's short novel *Daisy Miller* in which the heroine is observed for us (by a subsidiary character, a young man named Winterbourne who is sympathetically attracted to Daisy) in conversation with an Italian companion ('her cavalier', or gallant), named Giovanelli:

> Winterbourne stood there: he had turned his eyes towards Daisy and her cavalier. They evidently saw no one; they were too deeply occupied with each other. When they reached the low garden-wall they stood a moment looking off at the great flat-topped pine-clusters of the Villa Borghese; then Giovanelli seated himself familiarly upon the broad ledge of the wall. The western sun in the opposite sky sent out a brilliant shaft through a couple of cloud bars; whereupon Daisy's companion took her parasol out of her hands and opened it. She came a little nearer and he held the parasol over her; then, still holding it, he let it rest upon her shoulder, so that both their heads were hidden from Winterbourne. This young man lingered a moment, then he began to walk. But he walked – not towards the couple with the parasol; towards the residence of his aunt, Mrs Costello.

In places this passage could be read as simple, omniscient, unrestricted third person. For instance, the following fragment, taken in isolation, seems to be from no one individual's perspective:

> The western sun in the opposite sky sent out a brilliant shaft through a couple of cloud bars; whereupon Daisy's companion took her parasol out of her hands and opened it. She came a little nearer and he held the parasol over her.

However, placed in a larger context this event is clearly framed from Winterbourne's perspective: 'he had *turned his eyes towards* Daisy and her cavalier. They *evidently* saw no one.' And, later, with the opening of the parasol, 'their heads were hidden from Winterbourne'. Restricting at crucial moments our observation of a central action to what a subsidiary character can see is an important structural device in the novel (as so often in James). Like Winterbourne we are left at this moment in the narrative in a state of uncertainty concerning the exact nature of Daisy's relationship (sexual or merely flirtatious?) with her cavalier (courtly gentleman or lover?).

Other indications of limited knowledge include phrases of doubt, such as 'it seemed/appeared/looked as if'. The following paragraph, for example, from a story by Nadine Gordimer, uses several signals of doubt (like 'no doubt', 'somehow' and the question form: 'Hadn't he written a book about the Bay of Pigs?'):

> The voice of the telephone, this time, was American – soft, cautious – no doubt the man thought the line was tapped. Robert Greenman Ceretti, from Washington; while they were talking, she remembered that this was the political columnist who had somehow been connected with the Kennedy administration. Hadn't he written a book about the Bay of Pigs? Anyway, she had certainly seen him quoted.

It is no accident, of course, that this kind of narrowing down of a potentially omniscient narration should come in a narration that aligns itself strongly with the consciousness of one character, even while remaining third person. It is important to recognize, therefore, that third person narration need not always embody objectivity. It can quite easily work from subjective, internal and restricted positions.

20.3 Focalization

We can see, therefore, that the distinction between first person and third person narration is not sufficient in itself to account for different types of point of view. An additional complication arises from the fact that most prose fiction is not stable or homogeneous in the point of view which it adopts, so that it can be quite misleading to describe a story as 'told externally in the third person' (which would imply that this was a consistent point of view throughout). Even Ernest Hemingway, who might be thought an exemplar of the external third person viewpoint, does in practice use a variety of modes of narration, often within the same text, which allow for subjective and internal points of view. Because of this instability in point of view, some accounts of narrative (e.g. Mieke Bal, 1985; Shlomith Rimmon-Kenan, 1983; and Simpson, 1993) have refined the account of point of view by developing the notion of **focalization**. Focalization refers to the way in which a text represents the relationship between who 'experiences' and what is experienced. The one who experiences is termed the **focalizer**, and who or what the focalizer experiences is then called the **focalized**. Focalization falls into two main types: external focalization, where an anonymous, unidentified voice situated outside the text functions as focalizer; and character focalization, where phenomena are presented as experienced by a character within the story.

It is possible then to map shifts and tendencies in focalization within any one text by using the following simple notation:

F'r	=	Focalizer
E	=	External
C	=	Character
1	=	1st Person
3	=	3rd Person
F'd	=	Focalized Phenomenon

Thus:

External Focalizer	=	EF'r
Character Focalizer (1st Person)	=	CF'r1
Character Focalizer (3rd Person)	=	CF'r3
Focalized Phenomenon	=	F'd

Take the following idealized examples of differing focalization from three hypothetical narrations:

(a) Despite closing the windows, I could hear noises from the beach all that sleepless night.
(b) Even with the windows closed, she could not shut out the noises from the beach.
(c) Even with the windows closed, the noises from the beach were audible all night.

In each example, 'noises from the beach' are the focalized phenomenon, hence [F'd].

In (a) 'I' is the focalizer, hence [CF'r1]. In (b) 'she' is the focalizer, hence [CF'r3]. In (c) no-one is identified as the focalizer and the noise is reported by an unidentified narrator from a position potentially outside the diegetic world of the fiction, hence [EF'r]. Thus, the focalization structure of the three examples may be rendered in notational terms as follows:

(a) CF'r1 ('I')   →   F'd ('noises from the beach')
(b) CF'r3 ('she') →   F'd ('the noises from the beach')
(c) EF'r   →   F'd ('the noises from the beach')

These examples, as if from separate narrations, have been constructed to display differences of focalization. In practice, focalization within a narrative text tends to shift from sentence to sentence and sometimes can alter even within the same sentence. In the later history of the novel it is hardly ever stable and consistent throughout a text. The advantage of the notation lies in the way it can be applied to display these focalization shifts in terms of who is experiencing what and how from sentence to sentence.

Crucial evidence for deciding who is focalizing is the presence or absence of verbs of experiencing such as 'look', 'see', 'touch', 'smell', etc. Consider the following example from Rosamond Lehmann's *The Weather in the Streets* (1936) (the sentences have been numbered):

> (1) She [Olivia] ran down to the next floor, telephoned for a taxi, then opened the door of Etty's bedroom, adjoining the sitting room. (2) Silence and obscurity greeted her; and a smell compounded of powder, scent, toilet creams and chocolate truffles.

In the first sentence Olivia and her actions are focalized from without by an unidentified focalizer. In the second sentence, however, the smell and the silence are impressions that belong to Olivia rather than to the external focalizer of the first sentence. The focalization shifts therefore from external focalization (EF'r) to character focalization (CF'r). This can be summed up as follows:

> Sentence 1: EF'r (unspecified) → F'd (Olivia)
> Sentence 2: CF'r3 (Olivia/She) → F'd (silence, smell, etc.)

Similar shifts can be detected in the following passage from the same book:

> (3) Between stages of dressing and washing she [Olivia] packed a hasty suitcase. (4) Pack the red dress, wear the dark brown tweed, Kate's cast off, well-cut, with my nice jumper, lime green, becoming, pack the other old brown jumper – That's about all.

Again, the extract begins as externally focalized, but in the second sentence there is a switch to Olivia's 'inner speech' or thoughts, as she does her packing (presented in **free indirect style**: see **Unit 19, Writing, speech and narration**). Moving into the character's consciousness in this way entails a change of focalization from external focalization to character focalization. Here again, we can summarize:

> Sentence 3: EF'r (unspecified) → F'd (Olivia packing)
> Sentence 4: CF'r1 (Olivia/my) → F'd (Olivia packing)

On this occasion, the notation helps to highlight, not just a shift in focalization, but the way in which Olivia in this passage comes to be the focalizer of her own actions. For a moment she is the object of her own subjective consciousness in a way that is both intimate and distanced. In ways such as these, the concept of focalization can become an important supplement to notions of point of view because it prompts close attention to the shifts, developments and balances within point of view within a particular text. *The Weather in the Streets,* for instance, moves between external focalization and character focalization which is centred primarily on Olivia, who figures sometimes as third person, sometimes as first person. These subtle variations help construct her as at once somehow both subject and object of the narrative.

Focalization can in this way be studied in terms of how it is realized from one sentence to another in a text. It may be observed at the level of the form of the text. But focalization at a deeper level is more than this. Patterns of focalization are at once the expression and construction of types of both consciousness and self-consciousness. In that respect, *The Weather in the Streets* is very much a novel of the first half of the twentieth century. It is quite distinct for instance from *Robinson Crusoe* even though Crusoe also figures as both subject and object of his own narrative. The relentless 'I' of Crusoe's narrative seems to present the human subject as individual, stable, unified and separate. The shifting patterns of focalization in *The Weather in the Streets*, on the other hand, seem to present an idea of subjectivity as split and dispersed at the very moment that it becomes possible to grasp it in a self-conscious way.

ACTIVITY 20.1

The following text is the complete version of a story by Hemingway. It is narrated in the third person and involves two main protagonists, a man and a woman.

A very short story

One hot evening in Padua they carried him up on to the roof and he could look out over the top of the town. There were chimney swifts in the sky. After a while it got dark and the searchlights came out. The others went down and took the bottles with them. He and Luz could hear them below on the balcony. Luz sat on the bed. She   5
was cool and fresh in the hot night.

    Luz stayed on night duty for three months. They were glad to let her. When they operated on him she prepared him for the operating table; and they had a joke about friend or enema. He went under the anaesthetic holding tight on to himself so he would not   10
blab about anything during the silly, talky time. After he got on

crutches he used to take the temperatures so Luz would not have
to get up from the bed. There were only a few patients, and they
all knew about it. They all liked Luz. As he walked back along the
halls he thought of Luz in his bed.   15

Before he went back to the front they went into the Duomo
and prayed. It was dim and quiet, and there were other people
praying. They wanted to get married, but there was not enough time
for the banns, and neither of them had birth certificates. They felt
as though they were married, but they wanted everyone to know   20
about it, and to make it so they could not lose it.

Luz wrote him many letters that he never got until after the
armistice. Fifteen came in a bunch to the front and he sorted them
by the dates and read them all straight through. They were all about
the hospital, and how much she loved him and how it was impos- 25
sible to get along without him and how terrible it was missing him
at night.

After the armistice they agreed he should go home to get a
job so they might be married. Luz would not come home until he
had a good job and could come to New York to meet her.   30

It was understood he would not drink, and he did not want
to see his friend or anyone in the States. Only to get a job and be
married. On the train from Padua to Milan they quarrelled about
her not being willing to come home at once. When they had to say
good-bye, in the station at Milan, they kissed good-bye, but were   35
not finished with the quarrel. He felt sick about saying good-bye
like that.

He went to America on a boat from Genoa. Luz went back
to Pordenone to open a hospital. It was lonely and rainy there, and
there was a battalion of arditi quartered in the town. Living in the 40
muddy, rainy town in the winter, the major of the battalion made
love to Luz, and she had never known Italians before, and finally
wrote to the States that theirs had been only a boy and girl affair.

She was sorry, and she knew he would probably not be able
to understand, but might some day forgive her, and be grateful to   45
her, and she expected, absolutely unexpectedly, to be married in
the spring. She loved him as always, but she realized now it was
only a boy and girl love. She hoped he would have a great career,
and believed in him absolutely. She knew it was for the best.

The major did not marry her in the spring, or any other time.   50
Luz never got an answer to the letter to Chicago about it. A short
time after he contracted gonorrhea from a sales girl in a Loop
department store while riding in a taxicab through Lincoln Park.

1   Read through the story and then try altering the mode of narration by transposing the text into first person narration from the woman's point of view. (Thus, 'Luz sat on the bed' becomes transposed to 'I sat on the bed'.)

2   Write down any peculiar or incongruous sentences that result from this transposition and try and detail the grounds on which they are peculiar.

3   Now transpose the text into first person narration from the man's point of view. (Thus, 'they carried him up on to the roof' becomes transposed to 'they carried me up on to the roof'.)

4   Note again any peculiarities or incongruities that result.

5   Which transposition of point of view has worked best and why? What does it suggest about the original, third person mode of narration? Did it involve an implicit bias; and if so, in favour of whom? What other textual mechanisms might support this bias?

Reading

Bal, M. (1985) *Narratology: Introduction to the Theory of Narrative*, Toronto: Toronto University Press.

Branigan, E. (1984) *Point of View in the Cinema*, New York: Mouton.

Fowler, R. (1986) *Linguistic Criticism*, Oxford: Oxford University Press, Chapter 9, pp. 127–46.

Furniss, T.E. and Bath, M. (1996) *Reading Poetry: An Introduction*, London: Prentice-Hall, Chapter 7.

Rimmon-Kenan, S. (1983) *Narrative Fiction: Contemporary Poetics*, London: Methuen, Chapter 6, pp. 71–85.

Scholes, R. (1982) *Semiotics and Interpretation*, New Haven, CT: Yale University Press.

Simpson, P. (1993) *Language, Ideology and Point of View*, London: Routledge.

Uspensky, B. (1973) *A Poetics of Composition*, Berkeley, CA: University of California Press.

Unit 21

Narration in film
and prose fiction

Narratives take many forms: stories are told in opera and in soap opera; in news and documentary; in poetry and in the theatre. At the beginning of the twenty-first century, however, two forms of fictional narrative dominate within the culture: the visual narrative forms of film (and television); and the prose forms of the novel (and short story). Not infrequently, the same stories circulate between the different media, so reinforcing the distinction developed in previous units between the story and its mode of narration. In this unit we explore this distinction further, by looking at some of the similarities and differences between narration in film and in prose fiction.

The early development of film as a medium is marked by effort to capture movement photographically. One of the curiosities of cinema's early history is the way in which this achievement quickly became devoted primarily not just to narrative, but to fictional narrative rather than, say, simply to song or spectacle; by the 1920s 'movies' or 'films' showing in 'picture palaces', 'film theatres' or 'cinemas' had become established as a rival to the novel or short story as a major source of narrative fiction.

Novels and prose fiction, however, have remained a constant source of inspiration to film-makers. Throughout its history film has drawn freely on available narratives that already existed in prose form: films such as *Gone with the Wind* (Victor Fleming: 1939), *The Maltese Falcon* (John Huston: 1941), *Moby Dick* (John Huston: 1956), *Trainspotting* (Danny Boyle: 1996), *Eyes Wide Shut* (Stanley Kubrick: 1999) were all adapted from novels. Since the inception of the Academy Awards more than three-quarters of the awards for best film went to films based on novels. Some novelists have proved particularly popular. There were, for instance, nearly 60 filmic adaptations of work by Dickens between the years of 1898 and 1915 alone (on average more than three a year), including eight versions of *Oliver Twist*. It has even been argued (see Wagner, 1975; and Spiegel, 1976) that certain film techniques (close focus, the flashback) were themselves anticipated in the writing of novelists such as

Dickens, Conrad and James and contributed in formal terms to cinema's rapid development as a narrative medium. Yet despite this history of interconnection, techniques of film narration and prose narration are in many ways quite different from each other; and these differences can be identified at various levels, from differences at the level of the institutions of literature and cinema to differences at the more formal level of the contrasting media themselves.

21.1 Institutional differences: literature versus cinema

Fictional narrative in prose and film has become institutionalized in quite different ways. Studio-based commercial cinema is a highly capitalized institution; the cost of making a commercial film for cinema can run to millions of dollars, using equipment that is costly and capital-intensive. Cinema is also a highly specialized industry, requiring a large number of skilled workers (camera operators, script-writers, editors, sound and lighting technicians, etc.); so the production process can only be understood as a highly collective one involving a large range of people in different capacities. An analogous perspective applies to the process of consumption. Although CD video and videocassette sales and rental for home viewing have complicated the picture, a major source of income for film studios remains 'box-office' receipts from public viewing in cinemas. Publicity and distribution networks provide for the screening of films in public auditoria where they are viewed by an audience that has assembled expressly for the purpose at advertised times.

By comparison, the novel, as an institution of cultural production, is not nearly as capital intensive or industrialized. Publishing houses may be large-scale commercial enterprises, but they often depend upon more than fiction for their commercial viability. Nor is the production process as heavily centralized as is the case with the film industry: printing, for example, is routinely sub-contracted. In addition, the production of the text of a novel is much more individualistic than the production of a film. Novels are 'authored' (see **Unit 24, Authorship and intention**) and, as such, they issue from a single, unitary source. Responsibility for the words on the page is always assumed to lie with the individual author. (There is nothing in the novel corresponding to the credit sequence in a film.) Authors are also much cheaper as a production entity than a film crew: millions of dollars do not have to be raised in advance in order to begin production on a novel. Significantly, consumption of the prose text mirrors its conditions of production. Again, it is highly individualistic, performed independently by discrete readers operating as autonomous entities.

21.2 Differences of media: film versus prose

The commercial film has evolved as a self-contained event, lasting about two hours, which accordingly needs to be intelligible at a single viewing. As a visual text, it is based upon the continuous projection of light through moving frames onto a screen, thereby providing a high-definition image typically accompanied by high-quality sound. As a result, it has to be viewed in semi-darkness, with direct appeal to the senses of hearing and vision; but also, typically, projection is continuous and without interruption for the course of the film. As a public event there is therefore no possibility, under normal cinematic conditions, for control by the viewer. Spectators in the cinema are in no position to vary or control the rate of viewing. Neither interruption nor review is permitted. The spectator is caught up by the event in a continuous process. Two key points emerge from this. First, the spectator's condition – viewing images in darkness – is similar to that of someone dreaming; this favours a high degree of projection of the self into the film, or identification with particular aspects of it. Second, as a self-contained but continuously projected event, film in mainstream cinema has evolved under a regime that values easy intelligibility.

The novel, by contrast, presents its stories in the medium of prose writing. This favours an individual mode of consumption. Reading a prose novel is usually a solitary act, which apparently allows greater degrees of discretion and control to the individual reader. Variable levels of attention are possible, as are differing rates of reading. It is possible to skip and to review. Readers, unlike cinema-goers, can set their own pace and choose to re-read at their own convenience.

21.3 Formal differences: verbal sign versus visual image

The most important contrast between film and prose, however, rests on the distinctive features of the two media and upon the different kinds of signification involved in them. Prose as a medium depends upon linguistic signs where the relationship between the material of the sign (sounds or letters) and that which is designated by them is quite arbitrary. The significatory medium – the letters on the page in the case of prose – has no necessary, obvious or natural relationship with the entities signified by them. There is no particular reason why the letters P-I-G should be inevitably associated with the concept of a four-legged creature that grunts and lives in a sty. The association depends simply upon convention – upon a tacit agreement between users of the sign. And decoding prose depends upon consciously learnt methods of interpretation. (See **Unit 8**, **Language and society**, for further discussion of the arbitrary nature of the linguistic sign.)

In film, by contrast, the signifying material (visual shapes projected in patterns of light and dark) has a much closer relationship to that which is signified. The film (or video) image resembles in visual terms the reality which it signifies or depicts, and so its relationship to reality seems more obvious, direct and easily intelligible. As a medium of representation, film is composed from iconic images – unlike prose, which is made up of linguistic signs.

21.4 Narration

This basic distinction between words and images is an important point of difference between the two media. Indeed, the differences between film and prose fiction can seem to reduce to a long-established distinction in the study of narrative between 'showing' (mimesis), on the one hand, and 'telling' (diegesis) on the other. It has even been suggested that narrative film can be thought of as 'story' without the level of narration – a tale without a teller. In what follows, however, it is suggested that film can be thought of as a narrative medium – even though the medium through which narration is accomplished is quite different from that of prose.

Despite the differences between them, some important points of resemblance between film and prose fiction remain. These resemblances are best revealed in terms of narration. In the first place, it is not true to claim that film is a non-narrated medium. It is not uncommon, for instance, for the soundtrack of a film to include elements of voiced over, first-person narration (as, for instance, in Steven Spielberg's *The Color Purple* (1985); or Francis Ford Coppola's *Apocalypse Now* (1979), where the writing behind the voiced-over narration is sometimes credited to Michael Herr, author of *Despatches*, also about the Vietnam War). More significantly and more persuasively, however, the way in which film is shot and edited together to construct a coherent and intelligible story follows certain basic conventions, amounting to codes of narration, or routine ways of telling, even when a personalized narrator is not evident. Film is not a completely transparent 'window' on the world of the tale: the film image should not be confused with reality. Despite their iconicity, film images are still 'signs', in that they recall or resemble a segment of reality elsewhere without being that reality itself. Moreover, the significance of a film image always exceeds what it literally depicts or denotes. This broader significance has many aspects, and is conferred on the image in several ways:

1   An image supplied by a shot derives significance from its place in series of shots. This is the classical principle of **montage** (see **Unit 15, Juxtaposition**) in which the sequential juxtaposition of one shot with another produces significance which goes beyond what can be traced to the individual shots themselves.

2   In mainstream cinema, the image is constantly supplemented by sound. Contemporary cinema typically uses immensely complex, multilayered soundtracks, which interweave several different types of sound, including music (e.g. 'motifs'), ambient or diegetic sound (e.g. traffic, rattling teacups, etc.), and voice/speech (both as character dialogue and voice-over narration).

The organization and sequencing of shots – especially in commercial cinema – are subject to powerful conventions. In the presentation of dialogue in the fictional film it is rare for characters to address the camera; rather, they are filmed in various degrees of profile addressing each other. This is such a binding convention that 'the look to camera' might almost be described in film terms as 'the forbidden look'. When it does occur, it typically breaks the illusion of naturalism. It is more common in art cinema (in films by Jean-Luc Godard and Ingmar Bergman, for example) than in mainstream cinema, though it may be found occasionally in popular television drama series (e.g. Glenn Gordon Caron's *Moonlighting*, 1985–9, Channel 4's *Sex in the City*, 1999, or BBC 2's *Rab C. Nesbitt*, 1992–9).

The practice of filming dialogue in profile is part of a larger set of conventions built up around an important organizing principle: the line of action. In its simplest form, for a scene involving two protagonists, this principle is based on an imaginary line drawn between the two characters. In mainstream cinema it is a basic convention to restrict consecutive shots in the same scene to only one side of this imaginary line. In theory, it might seem possible to set up shots from anywhere within a 360 degree circle around the space in which the filmed action occurs. In practice, however, shots are restricted to half this domain, in conformity with what then becomes known as 'the 180 degree rule' (see Figure 21.1).

In shooting a scene involving dialogue, film-makers have available to them a standard repertoire of possible shots. The most common amongst these are mid-shots, medium-close-ups, and close-ups. At or near the beginning of a scene will occur a mid-shot, in which both characters figure, in order to establish the line of action (sometimes called a two-shot or an establishing shot). As the dialogue proceeds, there will usually be a progressive focusing in on the individual protagonists, so that each is shown individually in close-up. At or near the end of a scene, a two-shot or mid-shot is often used as part of the process of bringing the scene to a close. Within the scene, then, the handling of close-ups is prepared for by the initial establishing shot which gives the line of action. Subsequent chaining together of the close-ups develops in a form of visual counterpoint: a shot of one speaker is typically replaced by a shot of the other in a technique commonly known as 'field/reverse-field' or 'shot/counter-shot'. In the clearest cases, the speaker is observed from a position near by, to one side or behind the listener; the position is then reversed when the speaking roles switch, the camera remaining all the time on one side of the line of action. The repertoire and combination of shots amount to a set of conventions for

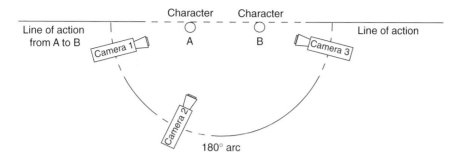

Figure 21.1 Two characters being filmed by cameras within 180° arc in conformity with 180° rule

making the events of the narrative intelligible. As a set of conventions they are comparable in some ways to showing and in some ways to telling. In the case of filmed dialogue, for example, they are analogous to (but clearly not the same as) the reporting clauses and other methods for the presentation of speech in fictional prose narratives. The sequence of stills in Plates 8–10, from David Lean's film of *A Passage to India* (1978), helps to show these conventions at work.

These basic conventions are, of course, honoured as much in the breach as in the observance. They have evolved as routines which provide flexible formats for making what is seen on screen coherent and intelligible; but they are not adhered to in a rigid fashion. The shot/counter-shot does not always follow the speaker. Sometimes it includes the reactions of the listener, hence the term 'reaction shots'. Generally, however, these routines provide background norms of presentation which help guide the spectator through the time and space of the narrative on the basis of tacit knowledge of the conventions.

The notion that conventions help to supply or guarantee intelligibility is crucial here. Conventions cue us to expect certain kinds of relationship between shots so that, for instance, if in one shot we, the viewers, see a character gazing out of frame, we then interpret the next shot (whenever possible) as depicting what that character could see from the position he or she occupies. Such apparently simple mechanisms for chaining shots together help to situate us as viewers in the temporal and spatial world of the fiction, and to draw us through the narrative. In this way the 'eye' of the camera, as reflected in the angle of shots and the way in which these shots are edited into sequence, is anthropomorphized, or made to seem human. As spectators, we see from positions that could be (and sometimes even are) those of protagonists in the fiction themselves.

It has been argued, in fact, that the position constructed for the film spectator (and the pleasures associated with being a spectator) resemble those of a voyeur – a claim that has been particularly discussed within feminist film

Plate 8 *A Passage to India*: two-shot

Plate 9 *A Passage to India*: field

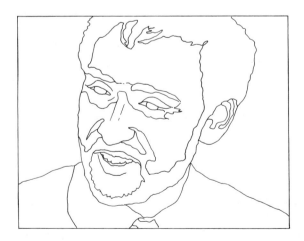

Plate 10 *A Passage to India*: reverse-field

theory but which has also been made the subject of conscious attention by film-makers themselves in films such as Michael Powell's *Peeping Tom* (1959) and Alfred Hitchcock's *Rear Window* (1954). One significant aspect of the notion of the voyeuristic spectator is that the camera does not just show the action of the story, like some simple recording device. It shows events in a way that is so constructed, and edited according to specifiable conventions, that it amounts – if not exactly to a narrator – then to some anthropomorphically defined, implied spectator. Indeed, for a feminist film theorist such as Laura Mulvey (1989) the eye of the camera is not merely anthropomorphic, but more specifically masculine, inasmuch as it routinely constructs women within cinema as objects of male desire (see **Unit 23**, **Positioning the reader or spectator**).

21.5 Differences between film and prose fiction

The novel, because it operates exclusively through the medium of the verbal sign, is sometimes considered richer in its texture than film. Its relationship to reality can seem more oblique, since the world which unfolds in the novel is not given directly but is developed by the narrator and recreated in an active and controlled process of reading which allows for reflection, comparison and the gradual construction of a coherent whole. Patterns of reference and cross-reference may be built up over several hundred pages; and the whole novel may take several hours to read (perhaps ten hours for an average length novel).

Film, by contrast, can seem more immediate, but perhaps at the same time less dense. In the case of a film adaptation of a novel, the ten hours of reading are condensed into two hours viewing; and this viewing is required to be intelligible at a single screening. This might suggest that film is somehow a less complex, less demanding medium than the prose novel. But it is worth remembering that film is a multilayered medium, working with a potent combination of two modalities of expression: image and sound. The image has powerful possibilities for condensing significance: descriptive detail, character, and action can be displayed simultaneously within the single shot, through codes of lighting, colour and composition, whereas prose is constrained by a sequential, piece-by-piece, mode of presentation. And the significatory possibilities of the image are further enhanced, of course, by the various kinds of sound that constitute the soundtrack. Because of their different conditions of presentation and consumption, then, films may condense narrative material but this does not inevitably entail simplification or mere reduction.

In conclusion, therefore, it is important to note that stories have a constructed nature, in which ever medium they are rendered. We have seen that film, no less than prose, depends on the operation of conventions, for example rules which guide the selection of shots and their combination. Such conventions range from those governing the depiction of dialogue to those governing the depiction of a chase or the intrusion into a scene of a sinister onlooker. These filmic conventions are just as crucial for narration in film as are those that govern the representation of thought or speech (see **Unit 19, Writing, speech and narration**) or the handling of **point of view** in prose fiction (see **Unit 20**). Prose is governed by conventions which are linguistic in character. What is less obvious – but no less true – is that film-makers also operate according to a kind of language: the language of film.

ACTIVITY 21.1

E.M. Forster's novel, *A Passage to India* (1924), was filmed under the direction of David Lean in 1978. In the following activity you are invited to prepare a shooting script from a passage of the novel and to compare it with a simplified shot sequence from Lean's film.

The extract from the novel reprinted below deals with a visit to a site of local interest – the Marabar Caves – by Aziz, an Indian doctor, and Adela Quested, an Englishwoman. Miss Quested is preoccupied with thoughts of her impending marriage to an English colonial officer, Ronny Heaslop. Dr Aziz, a widower, is also preoccupied – but with thoughts of a more mundane character to do with the organization of the trip, for which he feels responsible.

> Miss Quested and Aziz and a guide continued the slightly tedious expedition. They did not talk much, for the sun was getting high. The air felt like a warm bath into which hotter water is trickling constantly, the temperature rose and rose ... [Aziz] had never liked Miss Quested as much as Mrs Moore, and had little to say to her, less than ever now that she would marry a British official.
>
> Nor had Adela much to say to him. If his mind was with the breakfast, hers was mainly with her marriage ... There were real difficulties here – Ronny's limitations and her own – but she enjoyed facing difficulties, and decided that if she could control her peevishness (always her weak point), and neither rail against Anglo-India nor succumb to it, their married life ought to be happy and profitable. She mustn't be too theoretical; she would deal with each problem as it came up, and trust to Ronny's common sense and her own. Luckily, each had abundance of common sense and goodwill.
>
> But as she toiled over a rock that resembled an inverted saucer, she thought, 'What about love?' The rock was nicked by a double row of footholds, and somehow the question was suggested by them. Where had she seen footholds before? Oh yes, they were the pattern traced in the dust by the wheels of the Nawab Bahadur's car. She and Ronny – no, they did not love each other.

'Do I take you too fast?' enquired Aziz, for she had paused, a doubtful expression on her face. The discovery had come so suddenly that she felt like a mountaineer whose rope had broken. Not to love the man one's going to marry! Not to find it out till this moment! Not even to have asked oneself the question until now! Something else to think out. Vexed rather than appalled, she stood still, her eyes on the sparkling rock. There was esteem and animal contact at dusk, but the emotion that links them was absent. Ought she to break her engagement off? She was inclined to think not – it would cause so much trouble to others; besides, she wasn't convinced that love is necessary to a successful union. If love is everything, few marriages would survive the honeymoon. 'No, I'm all right, thanks,' she said, and, her emotions well under control, resumed the climb, though she felt a bit dashed. Aziz held her hand, her guide adhered to the surface like a lizard and scampered about as if governed by a personal centre of gravity.

'Are you married, Dr Aziz?' she asked, stopping again, and frowning.

'Yes, indeed, do come and see my wife' – for he felt it more artistic to have his wife alive for a moment.

'Thank you,' she said absently.

'She is not in Chandrapore just now.'

'And have you children?'

'Yes, indeed, three,' he replied in firmer tones.

'Are they a great pleasure to you?'

'Why, naturally, I adore them,' he laughed.

'I suppose so.' What a handsome little Oriental he was, and no doubt his wife and children were beautiful too, for people usually get what they already possess. She did not admire him with any personal warmth, for there was nothing of the vagrant in her blood, but she guessed he might attract women of his own race and rank, and she regretted that neither she nor Ronny had physical charm. It does make a difference in a relationship – beauty, thick hair, a fine skin. Probably this man had several wives – Mohammedans always insist on their full four, according to Mrs Turton. And having no one else to speak to on that eternal rock, she gave rein to the subject of marriage and said in her honest, decent, inquisitive way: 'Have you one wife or more than one?'

The question shocked the young man very much. It challenged a new conviction of his community, and new convictions are more sensitive than old. If she had said, 'Do you worship one god or several?' he would not have objected. But to ask an educated Indian Moslem how many wives he has – appalling, hideous! He was in trouble how to conceal his confusion. 'One, one in my own particular case,' he sputtered, and let go of her hand. Quite a number of caves were at the top of the track, and thinking, 'Damn the English even at their best,' he plunged into one of them to recover his balance. She followed at her leisure, quite unconscious that she had said the wrong thing, and not seeing him, she also went into the cave, thinking with half her mind 'Sight-seeing bores me,' and wondering with the other half about marriage.

1   Using this extract from the novel, select from it and, if necessary, adapt what you think should be the dialogue for the scene; then sketch alongside it, in a series of simple cartoons or pictures, how you think the scene should be shot in order to construct a shooting script.

2   Compare your shooting-script with the actual dialogue and simplified shot-sequence from the film in Plates 11–25.

3   What are the main differences between your shooting-script and the shot-sequence from the film? Do they involve different interpretations and realizations of the novel? If so, in what way?

4   What are the differences between the shooting-scripts and the extract from the novel? What specific aspects from the novel cannot directly be transposed into a film version? (Read the passage from the novel carefully and think back to what you have learnt about narrative prose fiction in the previous units.) What are the respective advantages and disadvantages of the two media?

Scene on the Kawa Dol (simplified shot-sequence reconstructed from David Lean's film of *A Passage to India*):

Miss Quested: It's almost a mirage.

11

Dr Aziz
May I ask you something
rather personal?

You were married, weren't
you?

12

Doctor Aziz: Yes, indeed.

13

Miss Quested: Did you love your wife when
you married her?

14

Doctor Aziz: We never set eyes on each
other till the day we were
married. It was all arranged
by our families. I only saw her
face in a photograph.

15

Miss Quested: What about love?

16

Doctor Aziz: We were man and woman.
And we were young.

17

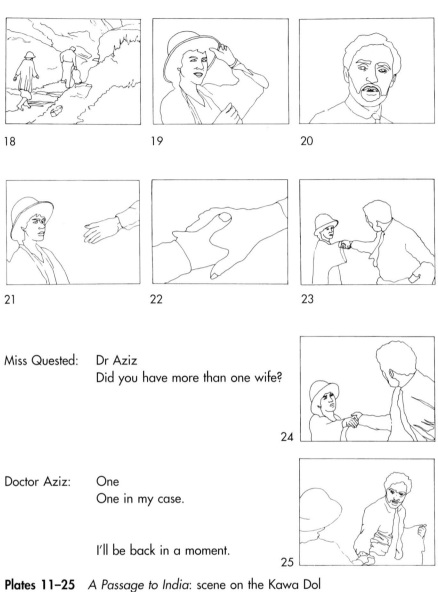

Plates 11–25 *A Passage to India*: scene on the Kawa Dol

Reading

Bordwell, D. (1985) *Narration in the Fiction Film*, London: Methuen.

Bordwell, D. and Thompson, K. (1979) *Film Art: An Introduction*, Reading, MA: Addison-Wesley.

Chatman, S. (1978) *Story and Discourse: Narrative Structure in Film and Prose Fiction*, Ithaca, NY and London: Cornell University Press.

Cook, P. (ed.) (1985) *The Cinema Book*, London: BFI.

Giddings, R., Selby, K. and Wensley, C. (1990) *Screening the Novel: The Theory and Practice of Literary Dramatization*, London: Macmillan.

McFarlane, B. (1996) *Novel to Film*, Oxford: Oxford University Press.

Mulvey, L. (1989) *Visual and Other Pleasures*, London: Macmillan.

Rifkin, B. (1994) *Semiotics of Narration in Film and Prose Fiction*, New York: Peter Lang.

Spiegel, A. (1976) *Fiction and the Camera Eye: Visual Consciousness in Film and the Modern Novel*, Charlottesville: University Press of Virginia.

Unit 22

Realism

'Realism' as a critical term is sometimes taken to signify a relationship between a text and reality which is felt to be immediate and direct. Examples of realism are typically chosen from genres such as 'the nineteenth-century novel', 'the Hollywood film', and 'popular fiction'. An alternative way of thinking about realism has developed within more recent critical theory, however, and that is to see it as marked out by the adoption of specific devices or formal techniques for producing a sense of the 'real'. Realism is thus a style which need not be considered to have any necessary reference to an external reality. It is possible, therefore, to make a distinction between **realistic**, commonly used to mean something like ' close to my version of reality' or 'life-like', and **realist**, in the more technical sense of conforming to conventions for passing something off as real, so that even future-fantasy or science fiction could be treated as examples of realism stylistically or formally. Realistic is an evaluation of a piece of prose whereas realist is an assessment of the formal elements of a prose narrative.

22.1 The traditional view of realism

Realism is both the name of a literary movement involving primarily novels which flourished between about 1830 and 1890 (including, for instance, George Eliot as one of the major British exponents), and a particular **genre** (see **Unit 17**) of writing in which certain formal features of realist texts are displayed. This was the view held by realist writers and many critics until recently. Within the traditional critical view it is possible to see realism in two ways: either as a direct imitation of the facts of reality, or as a special reconstruction of the facts of reality, which Eric Auerbach (1953) calls **mimesis**. In the first of these views of realism it is seen as a style of writing which acts as a simple window onto the world, mirroring events, almost as if the writing is a direct transcription of events in the real world. In mimesis, while the reader recognizes the vision of reality which is represented in the narrative, since it includes elements from external reality with which he or she is familiar, it is a more generalized or universalized version of reality than that which the reader habitually experiences, and it is this which is thought to be of most value.

In Unit 17 on genre, we looked at the possibility of listing characteristics of particular genres. In the traditional view, the characteristics of realism revolve particularly around its subject-matter and its message or moral intentions. The subject-matter of realist novels is generally concerned with what is considered in the West to be 'ordinary life' – centring on the home, on work and on human relationships. Most of the events described are not about heroic deeds but are, rather, the seemingly ordinary events within the lives of ordinary people, their emotions, their relationships, etc. One of the aims is to present ordinary people as complex and multifaceted. Although realist texts are about individual characters and their lives, their message – often developed in terms of a secular, socially based morality – is supposed be true for all readers.[1]

'ordinary' meaning 'middle class'

22.1.1 Language reality and representation

In such an approach to realism, there is not generally much attention to the language of the text; in fact the language is often seen to be non-self-reflexive, that is, it does not draw attention to itself as language. Rather, the language is treated merely as a transparent medium for the transmission of the message, as if it were capable of simply reflecting reality. However, it is clear that the relation between texts, particularly literary texts, and reality is far more complex than simply reflection or idealization. As Leech and Short state: 'The myth of absolute realism arises from a mistaken attempt to compare two incomparable things: language and extralinguistic realities' (1981: 152). Realist texts are, after all, only verbal constructs, and yet it is this essentially textual nature which is often ignored in traditional critical discussions of realism. It is for this reason that some critics have turned to analysing not the relation between words and the material world outside the text but the relations between words within the text.

22.1.2 How traditional realism shapes ways of reading

The traditional view, by which realist texts are assumed to describe the reality of a period or a place, is common in the criticism and teaching of texts, and is often tied into stereotypical views of the place of particular people in reality. Realism is firmly linked to stereotypical notions of authenticity, whereby certain experiences or individuals are deemed to be more 'real', or closer to 'life' than others. The so-called 'gritty' realism of a novel about working-class life in the inner city, for example, is often considered to be more authentic than a close examination of refined middle-class behaviour in north London. Many texts are assumed to be realist for these stereotypical reasons. For example, novels written by women are often interpreted, when they are included on university courses, as though they were autobiographical (drawing upon the stereotypical notion that women are restricted to the private sphere and to descriptions of the personal, intimate intricacies of relationships); novels by working-class writers are read as documentary accounts (according to a stereotype in which working-class people see everyday reality as it really is but are unable to transcend that view); or novels by Black writers are read as documenting personal struggles against oppression, rather than being concerned with larger, more universal issues which concern both white and Black people.

22.2 The structuralist view

Structuralist critics such as Roland Barthes (1986) and David Lodge (1977) have helped to shift attention from the relationship between the text and reality to the textual qualities of realism, and have shown that the notion of literary convention is very important in the construction of realist novels. In this view, whether or not a text is realist (that is, has the formal characteristics of realism) is not related to whether it is realistic (that is, whether it seems to the reader to approximate to some notion of reality), but to whether it uses conventional techniques to produce a 'reality effect'.[2]

22.2.1 Conventions

Literary texts are generally constructed according to a system of textual conventions or rules; our notion of which genre a text belongs to is largely founded on the recognition of the particular set of conventions that the text is drawing on (see **Unit 17**, **Genre**). When a writer decides to produce a realist narrative, there are already a set of conventions in place governing the choices to be made. For example, he or she will be constrained by a number of conventions which govern the production of such a narrative: (a) events in the text are arranged in a roughly chronological order; (b) there are 'round' or developed characters who develop throughout the narrative; (c) there is a narrator who will constitute a consistent position within the text; (d) there will be an ending which will draw the various strands and sub-plots in the narrative together, and so on. Point (c) is particularly important, as we will see. The presence of a reliable or omniscient narrator creates a hierarchy of discourse which seems to guarantee that at least one of the views of the events in the novels offers us a view of the 'truth' or the 'real'. Although these conventions of realism can be experimented with and altered, as they invariably are in novels, they nevertheless exist as the basis for the construction of the text.

22.2.2 Characteristics of realism

David Lodge (1977) suggests that realist texts achieve their effect not so much because they are like reality as such, but because they resemble in their conventions texts which we classify as non-fictional. He takes two separate descriptions of capital punishment, one by George Orwell entitled 'A Hanging' and one which appeared in *The Guardian* newspaper (he argues that Orwell's narrative is in fact a realist fiction, even though it is presented as if it were the account of an eye-witness). Lodge analyses the similarities between the realist fiction and the non-fictional report: (a) in neither case are features of language foregrounded so that they become the focus of attention; (b) the narrator does not draw attention to his/her role in interpreting events – the events, rather, seem to speak themselves or to present themselves to the reader without mediation; (c) there is an emphasis on detailed description of the context of the event (the exact time, place and setting) and of the preparation for the execution. It is almost impossible, Lodge argues, to distinguish one text from the other purely on the basic strategies that they adopt to depict the event. From this he concludes that realist texts draw on the same conventions used to construct non-fictional texts in order to convince the reader that they are describing reality. This strategy accrues some authority to realist texts. (Orwell's text is a rather extreme version since it reads like an authentic eye-witness account.) Lodge thereby suggests a working definition of realism in literature as: 'the representation of experience in a manner which approximates closely to descriptions of similar experience in non-literary texts of the same culture' (1977: 25).

In a similar way, as discussed in **Unit 19, Writing, speech and narration**, it is clear that dialogue is represented in literature, particularly in realist narrative, according to a set of conventions, rather than with reference to the way that people speak in real life. Many elements of actual speech are omitted when speech is represented in prose narrative (for example, hesitation, interruption, repetition, etc.) while other elements are included to signal to the reader that they are reading 'real speech' (for example, inverted commas, the use of colloquialism, etc.).

Other conventions which govern the production of realist narrative concern the inclusion of descriptive passages. Roland Barthes has noted that in most classic realist texts there is a proliferation of descriptive detail. Although narratives in general tend to include a descriptive section which sets the scene in which the actions take place, Barthes points to the presence in realist narratives of details which seem to be included for the sole purpose of signalling to the reader that it is 'the real' which is being described. For example, in the following extract from *The Well of Loneliness* by Radclyffe Hall (1928), some of the description serves the purpose of setting the principal character within a certain social class (the estate is 'well-timbered, well-cottaged'; there are two large lakes in the grounds; the house has 'dignity and pride', and so on), but other elements seem to be included in the text simply because of the conventions of realist texts:

> Not very far from Upton-on-Severn – between it, in fact, and the Malvern Hills – stands the country scat of the Gordons of Bramley; well-timbered, well-cottaged, well-fenced, and well-watered, having in this latter respect, a stream that forks in exactly the right position to feed two large lakes in the grounds. The house itself is of Georgian red brick, with charming circular windows near the roof. It has dignity and pride without ostentation, self-assurance without arrogance, repose without inertia; and a gentle aloofness that, to those who know its spirit, but adds to its value as a home.

The aside in the first sentence – 'between it, in fact, and the Malvern Hills' – serves no informational purpose as such, and functions simply to give a sense of the real. Similarly, the description of the house as being built of Georgian red brick and as having circular windows seems excessive. These elements of the passage may thus be seen to function as what Barthes terms **realist operators**, producing a **reality effect**, that is, the signal to the reader that this is a realist text, and helping to reinforce for the reader a sense that the text is well anchored to some recognizable reality.

Barthes also suggests that many realist texts implicitly draw upon a **cultural code**, which is a set of statements which must be decoded by the reader according to a set of conventions which the reader already knows, and shares with the writer. These are statements which appeal to background knowledge, stereotypes, so-called common-sense knowledge, and which either appear self-evident or which it is assumed that the reader will recognize and assent to. For example, *The Well of Loneliness* continues:

> To Morton Hall came the Lady Anna Gordon as a bride of just over twenty. She was lovely as only an Irish woman can be, having that in her bearing that betokened quiet pride, having that in her eyes that betokened great longing, having that in her body that betokened happy promise – the archetype of the very perfect woman, whom creating God has found good.

This description of Anna is presented as if the reader will instantly recognize that it fits the stereotype of the perfect woman. The reader is supposed to draw upon background assumptions about the loveliness of Irish women, and to recognize the elements about Anna's eyes and body which the text presents as self-evidently constituting perfection in women (that is, having quiet pride, embodying happy promise, and so on). It is presented as information that 'we all know'. In this way, in drawing on this kind of background knowledge we are, Barthes would claim, drawing upon the cultural code, using the term to indicate an organized repository of common-sense knowledge and stereotypes. It is through the cultural code that realist texts confirm certain conventional views of reality (which may have only slight correspondence with the way things actually are); in this way, realist texts are creating rather than reflecting realities, and one way of reading realist texts is to see them as shaping (rather than reflecting) our views of the real. Not only this, but they tend to reaffirm the status quo and the self-evident quality of stereotypical knowledge.

A further convention in realist texts is that they have narrative **closure** – that is, at the end of the narrative the problems which the text presents are resolved. In nineteenth-century realist novels plots are frequently resolved by death or marriage, and coincidence is a strong motivating factor in the way that most, if not all, of the loose ends of the plot are finally knitted together, so that the reader is left with no unresolved questions about the characters. In twentieth-century realist texts, the resolutions tend to be less complete and closure is one of the conventions which writers may feel that they can play with. Writers no longer feel it necessary to employ coincidence to such an extent to bring their narratives to a close. However, for many readers, narrative closure is pleasurable, and they may feel unsatisfied or cheated if a text leaves them with too many unresolved plot elements. (See **Unit 18**, **Narrative**.)

22.3 Realist film

Colin MacCabe (1981) has argued that realist films, rather than fully exploiting the potential of film as a medium, have largely restricted themselves to the conventions of realist novels.

22.3.1 Characteristics of realist film

MacCabe argues that one of the characteristics of realist film – like the realist novel – is that there is a **hierarchy of discourses** in relation to the truth; by this he means that there may be several narratives or points of view running at the same time throughout the film, and these narrative strands are not all equal in terms of the way that the audience is supposed to interpret and assess them. Instead, there is generally one character who is focused on in the narrative and who is presented as if in a privileged position in relation to truth; this is the character whose statements the audience is led to believe and whose point of view the audience is led to adopt. This can be most clearly illustrated by examining a section of the realist film *Saturday Night and Sunday Morning* (1960). The film is shot in black and white (which is associated with authentic realism and documentary) and the subject of the film is the life of white working-class people in Nottingham. In fact, it becomes clear that the discourse which is privileged within the hierarchy is that of the central working-class male figure; in the following sequence, illustrated by stills from the film (Plates 26–36), this

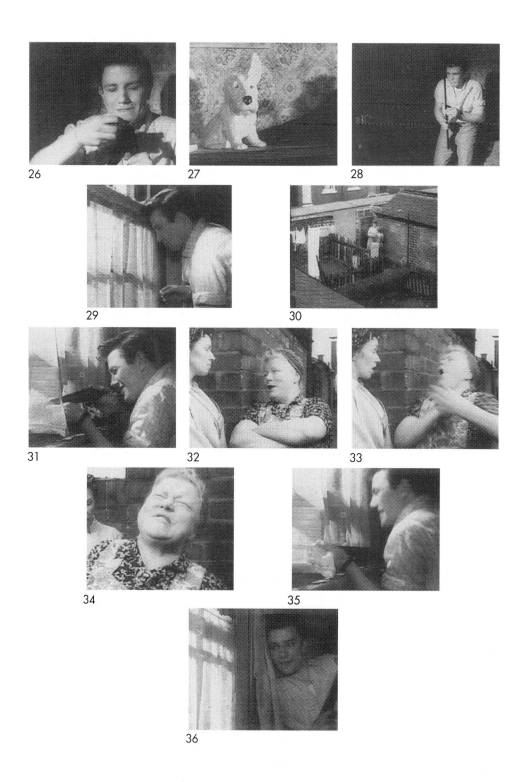

26

27

28

29

30

31

32

33

34

35

36

figure takes his revenge on an older woman who is portrayed in the film from his point of view.

The woman is represented as interfering and moralistic (when the hero sees a poor man breaking into a shop, he tries to help him escape, whereas her actions result in the man being arrested by the police). He decides to shoot her with an air-gun while she is talking to a neighbour on the street corner. The audience is led to collude with the actions of this character because of the way that his point of view is placed in a position of hierarchy in relation to the woman's point of view. We see him practising with his air gun and aiming at a china dog on the mantelpiece (still 27). Shots of him aiming at the woman are intercut with shots from his position of sight (stills 28, 29, 30, 31); the audience is thus led to see the shooting of this woman from his point of view. Although we view the woman from ground level (in stills 32, 33 and 34), the final evaluation of the event is created not by images of her pain, but by the male character's evident enjoyment of the event (stills 35, 36). The audience is thus encouraged to evaluate the event from his point of view and to assume that this is the position of truth. (One could try to rewrite this event and film it from the woman's point of view in order to foreground how much of the narrative is biased in favour of the male character's view of events. This would involve changing such elements as the position of the camera, the sequence in which shots are presented and the evaluation of events; see Toolan, 1991: 67–83 and Rimmon-Kenan, 1983: 71–85.)

MacCabe also introduces the term 'non-contradictory reality' to describe the way that realist film presents a seemingly self-evident and coherent vision of reality. There is nothing in this sequence of shots from *Saturday Night and Sunday Morning* to suggest that the situation could have happened in another way. There are very few discordant voices which question the moral view being presented here. Viewers are therefore being induced to take up what MacCabe calls a 'dominant position', that is, they recognize the hierarchies of discourses and align themselves with the one which seems to occupy the position of truth. In this case, spectators align themselves with the hero's point of view,

Plate 26 The camera focuses on Arthur Seaton in his room; he loads his air-rifle
Plate 27 Seaton practises by shooting the ear from a china dog on his mantelpiece
Plate 28 Seaton picks up his rifle
Plate 29 Seaton looks out of the window
Plate 30 Match-cut to a view out of the window to reveal what Seaton can see: the woman he dislikes talking on the corner
Plate 31 Cut back to Seaton aiming his rifle
Plate 32 Cut to a front view of the woman talking to a friend
Plate 33 The woman is shot in the backside
Plate 34 Close-up of the woman in pain
Plate 35 Cut to Seaton at the window grinning
Plate 36 Seaton moves away from the window so as not to be seen

positioning themselves alongside him and adopting a similar dominant position in relation to other characters in the narrative.

22.4 Marxism and realism

Marxist criticism attaches great importance to questions of realism, and the progressive or reactionary nature of realism has been much debated in Marxist circles. (This issue has also been debated within feminist circles. See for example, Coward (1986) for an overview.) For some critics, such as Georg Lukács (1962), realist novels can present to readers a vision of a greater harmony in the face of capitalist fragmentation; in this way, these novels can spur people to action, since they point out the problems within the present system, exposing the tensions between the individual and society in such a way as to foreground points of prevailing ideological contradiction. Lukács, indeed, championed the cause of realism against the rival claims of modernism, rejecting the latter on the grounds of its subjective, fragmentary and disconnected modes of representation, which he felt amounted to a retreat from society into pathological individualism. Bertolt Brecht, however, saw realist novels as a form of anaesthesia (Brecht, 1977). Readers become hypnotized by realist narrative and become uncritical of the values within the text and within the wider social system. As an alternative, he proposed a new form of art which would deny the reader the comforts of realist narrative and encourage her/him to act on the contradictions in capitalism. Lukács is thus closer to the traditional view, and Brecht closer to the structuralist view of realism.

ACTIVITY 22.1

The aim of this activity is to analyse two pieces of visual narrative and to identify the markers of realism and non-realism.

1   Choose two pieces of visual narrative, one which you would identify as an example of realism and the other an example of non-realism. Your two pieces should be from the same medium (e.g. from television, film, video, comic strip, photo-reportage, etc.). You will need to look closely and repeatedly at the texts, so if you choose a moving image you will probably need to have it on videotape.

2   Here is a reminder of some features which have been claimed to be characteristic of various different sorts of realist texts (for more detail see the unit):

(a) the subject-matter is generally drawn from 'everyday', 'ordinary' life;

(b) the characters are ordinary people presented as complex individuals who are shown to be capable of change and development;

(c) there is a moral position from which the events are viewed;

(d) there is a consistent point of view from which the events are evaluated (there may be more than one but they are consistent);

(e) the narrator presents a non-contradictory reality;

(f) the narrator does not draw attention to him/herself;

(g) the language used in the narrative does not draw attention to itself;

(h) events are arranged in roughly chronological order (there may be flashbacks, but the sequence of events is clear);

(i) the narrative reaches a clear resolution;

(j) there is detailed description of material objects (clothes, faces, furniture, etc.);

(k) there are realist operators (the inclusion of arbitrary details);

(l) the narrative includes an appeal to the cultural code (views which we are all supposed to share).

3   Examine the 'realist' text, and check which of these characteristics are present. Add any other general characteristics of realism which occur to you as you examine the text.

4   Now examine the 'non-realist' text and check which of these characteristics are absent. Cross off the list any characteristics which this examination suggests might be characteristic of all texts (not just realist ones).

5   For the two texts you have chosen, what are the reasons you might suggest for each text drawing on or rejecting the conventions of realism?

Notes

1   It should be noted that 'ordinary' here can often turn out to refer to middle-class characters, since most novels revolve around bourgeois characters. Although there is a tradition of working-class writing where the central characters are members of the working classes, generally even now it is the middle class who are mostly represented as the 'ordinary' and therefore universal individual.

2   These problems with the nature of 'reality' largely stem from theoretical work which questions the sense of a pre-existent reality to which all individuals have the same access and apprehension. Theorists who have questioned this notion of a pre-given, agreed upon reality which pre-dates our own individual experiencing and apprehension of it are Berger and Luckman (1966) and Michel

Foucault, most notably in *The Archaeology of Knowledge* (1989) and *The Order of Things* (1966).

Reading

Auerbach, E. (1953) *Mimesis: The Representation of Reality in Western Literature*, Princeton, NJ: Princeton University Press.

Barthes, R. (1986) *The Rustle of Language*, Oxford: Blackwell, pp. 141–8.

Berger, P. and Luckman, T. (1966) *The Social Construction of Reality*, Harmondsworth: Penguin.

Brecht, B. (1977) 'Against Georg Lukács', in T. Adorno, W. Benjamin, E. Bloch, B. Brecht and G. Lukács (eds) *Aesthetics and Politics*, London: New Left Books.

Coward, R. (1986) 'This novel changes lives: are women's novels feminist novels?', in M. Eagleton (ed.) *Feminist Literary Theory: A Reader*, Oxford: Blackwell, pp. 155–60.

Foucault, M. (1970) *The Order of Things: An Archaeology of the Human Sciences*, London: Tavistock.

Foucault, M. (1989) *The Archaeology of Knowledge*, London: Routledge.

Leech, G. and Short, M. (1981) *Style in Fiction*, London: Longman, pp. 150–70.

Lodge, D. (1977) *The Modes of Modern Writing*, London: Arnold, Chapter 3, 'Realism'.

Lukács, G. (1962) *The Historical Novel*, London: Merlin.

MacCabe, C. (1981) 'Realism and the cinema: notes on some Brechtian theses', in T. Bennet, S. Boyd-Bowman, C. Mercer and J. Woollacott (eds) *Popular Television and Film*, London: Open University Press and BFI, pp. 216–35.

Mills, S. and Pearce, L. (1996) *Feminist Readings/Feminists Reading*, 2nd edn, Hemel Hempstead: Harvester, 2nd edn especially chapter on Authentic Realism.

Rimmon-Kenan, S. (1983) *Narrative Fiction: Contemporary Poetics*, London: Routledge.

Toolan, M. (1988) *Narrative: A Critical Linguistic Introduction*, London: Routledge.

Section 6

Beyond the literary text

Positioning the reader or spectator

The relationship between the reader and the text in the process of producing meaning is a complex one. It cannot be said that one contributes more than the other, and much recent theorizing suggests a finely balanced negotiation between the two in terms of who or what determines the interpretation or meaning which the reader arrives at. Nevertheless, although it is clear that readers bring a great deal of background information with them which they use in order to construct a 'reading' of a text, the focus of this unit is on the way that texts address or position their readers. Texts address readers in a variety of ways, either by directly addressing them, or by indirectly encouraging them to agree with certain statements.

23.1 The implied reader

It is important to distinguish between the actual reader of any text and its **implied reader**. The actual reader is any person who reads the text, but the implied reader is an ideal or optimum figure which the text anticipates or constructs. In this sense, the implied reader is rather like a role which the real reader is being encouraged to adopt, providing a 'position' from which the real reader interprets the text. For example, in the following extract from Joseph Conrad's *Heart of Darkness* (1902), the main narrator (Marlow) makes the following statement:

> It is queer how out of touch with truth women are. They live in a world of their own, and there has never been anything like it, and never can be. It is too beautiful altogether, and if they were to set it up it would go to pieces before the first sunset. Some confounded fact we men have been living contentedly with ever since the day of creation would start up and knock the whole thing over.

Marlow is the main protagonist and narrator of this novel, and in general his views are not challenged by other views. It seems as if he as narrator and character is given a position from which the 'truth' of the situation is given (Rimmon-Kenan, 1983; Toolan, 1988). The role which the reader is called upon to adopt here – that of the implied reader – is in fact a male role: this is cued for the reader by the use of 'we men', a reference which includes Marlow and a group of men that comprises his audience on board a boat, together with the novel's male readers. It is also cued by the reference to 'women' as 'they', which signals to the reader that the narrator is referring to a group to which 'we' do not belong. The reader here may also be drawn into agreeing with what is said about women, since the statements are not modified in any way by qualifying phrases such as 'I think' or 'Maybe', or by counter-statements from Marlow's listeners. The narrator's views about women come from a position in which it is 'common sense', a 'matter of fact', that 'women ... are out of touch with truth', that 'they live in a world of their own', and so on. In this way, therefore, we can say that the (actual) reader of *Heart of Darkness* is drawn into a position (that of the implied reader) where the obviousness of these stereotypes about women may be taken for granted.[1]

23.2 Direct address

Most texts present themselves as ignoring the presence of a reader. Yet some texts do address the reader in a direct manner, for example, by calling her/ him 'dear reader' or 'you'. Advertisements in particular often address the reader in a very direct manner, as the following caption from an advertisement for Neutrogena Conditioner:

NOW YOU CAN CONDITION YOUR HAIR WITHOUT HEAVY OILS AND WAXES!

This calls upon the reader directly by addressing her as 'you' and by referring to 'your hair'. It makes assumptions about the reader that they can be included in a group of people who are concerned about the amount of oil and wax they use on their hair. Some texts also address only a small proportion of their potential audience, as in the following advert for the British Nursing Association, which appeared in *Cosmopolitan*, and began:

ISN'T IT TIME YOU RETURNED TO NURSING?

Since the advert appeared in *Cosmopolitan* – a women's magazine – it is reasonable to suppose that it addresses 'women in general'. And yet the address of the 'you', and thus the implied reader, is restricted to those women in *Cosmopolitan*'s readership who are qualified nurses who do not at present work in nursing. Thus, the real reader and the implied reader may not always match up. However, as will be argued in the next section, although the reader is relegated to the position of an 'overhearer', this still may have an effect on her/him, by encouraging them to agree with particular statements or ideas.

Direct address can also be found in novels. Mark Twain's *The Adventures of Huckleberry Finn* (1884), for example, begins with Huck as narrator introducing himself to the reader: 'You don't know about me, without you have read a book by the name of *The Adventures of Tom Sawyer*, but that ain't no matter.' The narrator of Herman Melville's *Moby Dick* (1851) begins by inviting the reader to 'Call me Ishmael' and then takes the reader on an imaginary journey, asking the reader to look and to respond to rhetorical questions. Sometimes, novels address the reader as 'reader' – the most famous example is perhaps the first sentence in the last chapter of Charlotte Brontë's *Jane Eyre* (1847): 'Reader, I married him.' Such strategies of direct address work to position the reader in relation to the text and to the narrator, although the precise implications of this need to be worked out in each case.

Even plays, which generally present the action and dialogue as if there were no audience or reader, may sometimes include a character who directly addresses the reader/audience. Such a character, sometimes operating as the chorus, is often detached from the play's action and acts as a type of narrator. The chorus in Shakespeare's *Henry V* asks the members of the audience to use their imagination to help the players present large-scale historical actions on the stage:

> . . . let us, ciphers to the great account,
> On your imaginary forces work.
> Suppose within the girdle of these walls
> Are now confined two mighty monarchies.

Yet, we need to be wary of assuming that all instances in which a text addresses someone in the second person (you) are directly addressing the reader. In poetry, for example, instances of direct address are more likely to refer to what is called the 'addressee' than to the reader. In other words, many poems are addressed to someone other than the reader.

23.3 Indirect address

While some texts address their readers directly by the use of 'you', others engage the reader in more subtle ways by the use of indirect address. An important aspect of the use of indirect address is the invocation of background knowledge and assumptions. All texts, even the most simple and explicit, assume some degree of shared knowledge between the reader and the producer of the text. Sometimes, these knowledges or ideas are presented as if the reader is bound to agree with them, or are based upon implicit assumptions which

Plate 37 Lil-lets advertisement

274

prove difficult to object to. For example, in the advertisement for Lil-lets tampons, (Plate 36) it is assumed that the reader will bring to bear quite particular background assumptions about menstruation. First, it is assumed that the reader will agree with the implicit assertion that periods are imprisoning (represented by the ball and chain), that menstruation is something which women want to be 'discreet' about, and that Lil-lets are a way out of this imprisonment (represented by Lil-lets as a key to the clasp on the chain). Even those women who do not in fact see their periods in such a negative way will, in order to make sense of the text, be led to draw on this shared knowledge about menstruation. (See Laws, 1990 for further discussion.)

23.4 Dominant readings

Recent theorizing of interpreting texts, particularly in cultural/media studies, has drawn on Stuart Hall's work on encoding and decoding (Hall, 1973; Van Zoonan, 1994). This assumes that the message which is encoded in the text by the author is not the same as the message which is decoded by the reader. However, it is possible to argue that there are clues to what might constitute a dominant reading, that is, the reading which seems to be self-evident; it is the one which is ratified by common sense or by other ideologies which are available within the society of the time. Thus, rather than simply assuming that the reader will have certain knowledges to make sense of the text, the dominant reading makes sense only through drawing on larger 'stories' circulating through society. For example, many texts have a dominant reading which accords with conventional notions of femininity. In the following advertisement for Lancôme, (Plate 37) the dominant reading is that women who want to look like the person depicted should use Lancôme eye make-up.

In order to make sense of this advertisement, we have to decode a range of elements: first, that the natural is good. This is signalled by the inclusion of reference to colours which are 'drawn from Nature herself' and named after natural substances (pebble grey, cedar wood). It is also signalled by the inclusion of the Lancôme trademark, which is a white stylized rose running horizontally across the image, linking the woman and the make-up. The **juxtaposition** (see **Unit 14**) of the woman, natural elements, the supposedly 'natural' make-up and the fact that Nature is referred to as 'her' produces a dominant reading of this text which offers itself for interpretation in ways which suggest the following kinds of connections between elements:

the make-up is coloured in the same way as nature;
natural ingredients are good;
feminine women have a special relationship with nature;
women who would like to be thought to be feminine will buy the make-up.

L'ORIGINE

Pebble grey, moss green, cedar wood, sienna brown. These are the subtle harmonies of original colour, colours drawn from Nature Herself.

LANCÔME PARIS

These are not statements which the text makes explicitly, but in order to make coherent sense of this very fragmented text the reader has to draw on these larger discourses about femininity and its relation to the natural. In this way, therefore, ideological assumptions which circulate and constitute systems of shared knowledge allow the preferred sense of a particular text to seem self-evident.[2]

While a text will normally proffer one particular preferred or dominant reading, there is always the potential for other, contrary readings of the same text, as will be explored later. But in order to make sense of the text as a coherent whole, the dominant reading is the one which readers can generally recognize easily and which they may therefore choose, unless they have political or personal reasons for challenging this reading.

23.5 Gender and positioning

The space or position that a text offers to a reader from which it makes most sense may be of various kinds, but one kind of position that has received particular attention of a critical and searching kind relates to the gender of the reader.

23.5.1 Positioning of the reader as male

Feminists such as Judith Fetterley (1981) and Elaine Showalter (1977) argue that, when women read literature, they often read as men, precisely because literature often constructs the implied reader as male. Thus, women readers often assent to background assumptions which are actually the shared assumptions of males, masquerading as a kind of general knowledge which 'we all know' to be true. So, for example, when women readers read the passage from Conrad cited above, they may read it without questioning the sexism contained in the text since it accords with stereotypical background assumptions.

Similarly, in film theory it has been argued (see Laura Mulvey, 1981) that women characters in many Hollywood films are posed as objects 'to-be-looked-at'.[3] The camera focuses on women characters from the perspective of male characters, and it is often a very sexualized vision of the women which is produced. This means that women spectators watching these films have to watch them as if they were male voyeurs. This may be a pleasurable experience for women spectators, but it may also make the woman spectator complicit with assumptions about women that she may not ordinarily share (see Stacey, 1994).

Plate 38 Lancôme advertisement

23.6 The resisting reader

At the same time, no account of the positioning of the reader would be complete without some attention to the way readers may also generate alternative readings. One influential approach to alternative readings is that developed by Judith Fetterley (1981) around the term **the resisting reader**, that is, a reader who does not accept the assumptions and knowledges which the text presents in the dominant reading, but resists them to construct an oppositional reading. Both male and female readers can read critically or oppositionally, as Jonathan Culler (1983) has shown, but it is often more in a woman's interest to read in this way. Thus with the Conrad text discussed earlier, a resisting reader will focus on the assumptions which seem to make the text intelligible (for example, by focusing on the use and effects of 'they' and 'we').

In the following extract from the song by Neil Hannon of The Divine Comedy (1997) it is possible to trace two distinct readings, a dominant reading and a resisting reading.

> If . . .
>
> If you were the road I'd go all the way
> If you were the night I'd sleep in the day
> If you were the day I'd cry in the night
> 'Cause you are the way the truth and the light
> If you were a tree I could put my arms around you
> And you could not complain
> If you were a tree I could carve my name into your side
> And you would not cry, 'cause trees don't cry
>
> If you were a man I'd still love you
> If you were a drink I'd drink my fill of you
> If you were attacked I would kill for you
> If your name was Jack I'd change mine to Jill for you
> If you were a horse I'd clean the crap out of your stable
> And never once complain
> If you were a horse I could ride you through the fields at dawn
> Through the day until the day was gone
> I could sing about you in my songs
> As we rode away into the setting sun
>
> If you were my little girl I would find it hard to let you go
> If you were my sister I would find it doubly so
> If you were a dog I'd feed you scraps from off the table

Though my wife complains
If you were my dog I am sure you'd like it better
Then you'd be my loyal four-legged friend
You'd never have to think again
And we could be together 'til the end.

The dominant reading of this song is shaped by a series of conditional propositions that involve the reader and the narrator in a series of statements which map out a position whereby the singer and the audience are assumed to share certain attitudes towards romance. The reader is directly addressed here, so that he or she has to decide as to whether he or she takes up the position of the 'I' or the 'you', the addresser or the addressee. However, the content of the song is not simple: at one and the same time, the singer articulates an excessively romantic form of love, while ironizing the grounds on which those romantic utterances are made. In some ways, the singer, in true postmodernist fashion, can be seen to be pushing the expression of romantic feeling beyond the realms of current discursive norms in that instead of comparing the person he loves to flowers and birds, he compares her to horses and dogs. In this lies the humour of the song since the singer uses the sort of language which is generally not permissible within romantic songs (for example, 'crap') and also makes statements such as 'If you were a man I'd still love you'. In this reading of the song, the singer is making excessive, humorous statements which the reader is expected to find ironizing and funny.

The resisting reading of this song would take issue with this position of postmodernist ironizing, since its playful instability seems to offer no basis from which to criticize the song. However, in this seemingly playful song, the woman is objectified just as in more openly sexist songs – she is represented as a loyal dog who is given scraps, a passive horse who is ridden, a tree on whom the singer carves his name, a drink which is consumed by the singer (albeit in this slightly distanced, conditional form). Perhaps the oddest line in the song is in the final stanza: 'If you were a dog I'd feed you scraps from off the table/Though my wife complains'. If the loved one were a dog she would be loyal and would 'never have to think again'. Female agency is deleted in this song, even though on the surface it seems to be gesturing towards a more playful and anti-sexist interpretation.[4]

Resisting readings may be produced for most texts, and may focus on the representation of a range of issues, such as race, class, sexual preference. For example, Cora Kaplan has questioned the way that white women have assumed that Alice Walker's *The Color Purple* refers to women in general rather than Black women in particular, and she challenges the universalizing discussions there have been of the book, which erase the discussion of race issues which the text raises (Kaplan, 1986). Lesbian readers might argue for a foregrounding of the elements in the text which focus on the female characters' love for one another (Hobby and White, 1991). In a similar way, some post-colonial theorists have begun to re-read canonical literary texts in order to focus on elements such as slavery and complicity in colonialism which earlier readers of the texts in the past have overlooked or tried to ignore (Said, 1993). Other post-colonial critics have analysed the way that Eurocentrism pervades much of the representational practices within Western culture (Shohat and Stam, 1994).[5] Adopting such an approach, the reader can first trace and describe the dominant reading of the text and then refuse this particular position in order to focus on other elements of the text. In this way, the reader is positively enabled and encouraged to assume power and responsibility in relation to the text and to the determination of its meaning. Instead of the traditional view of the reader as a passive recipient of information, the reader is enabled to construct meaning for her/himself.

ACTIVITY 23.1

Examine the advertisement for Flora margarine (Plate 38) and then try to answer the following questions:

1   What textual cues can you find which suggest that the advertisement is aimed at women rather than men?

2   What shared assumptions does the text presume that the reader has about men and boys?

3   What shared assumptions does the text presume that the reader has about women?

4   Is there anything strange about this advertisement in terms of its address and the potential consumers of the product? Can you think of other advertisements or texts which have this type of address?

Notes

1   It might be asserted that on the whole Marlow as a narrator is less than reliable, and therefore these statements cannot be taken at face value; however, his assertions about women do not seem to be subject to the same questioning as other statements which he makes in the novel.

2   There are further assumptions which are perhaps even more deeply embedded in the message of the text to do with race, and these are really at a higher discourse level of interpretation. The fact that Black models are rarely used in advertisements for beauty products entails that femininity, or at least the seemingly universal femininity which is referred to in this advertisement, is constructed as white femininity.

"He's just like his Dad."

Little boys can't wait to grow up like their dads. While dads, of course, are just little boys at heart.

With their dad's example – and a little encouragement from you – boys grow up enjoying the healthier ways of life.

They get to know about Flora margarine, too.

Flora's made with pure sunflower oil, so it's high in polyunsaturates and low in cholesterol.

The taste is one that men – and boys – seem to like. Light and delicate.

How soon will all your men be Flora men?

Flora. High in polyunsaturates
The margarine for men.

Plate 39 Flora advertisement

3   The model in the Lancôme advertisement we discussed previously has adopted the position of a woman who is to-be-looked at, in that she is not engaging in eye contact with the implied reader, but is presenting herself as an aesthetic object.

4   I would like to thank Keith Green and Jill LeBihan for bringing this example to my notice.

5   Eurocentrism is the form of thinking which takes as an implicit assumption that other countries are lacking in relation to a Western norm. This involves viewing other countries not in their own terms, but weighed against Western criteria, such as industrial development and scientific achievement, which, in other environments are not appropriate. Thus, small-scale self-sufficient communities in Latin America are judged to be lacking because they have not developed a certain type of technology appropriate to the Western world.

Reading

Booth, W. (1961) *The Rhetoric of Fiction*, Chicago: University of Chicago Press.

Culler, J. (1983) 'Reading as a woman', in *On Deconstruction*, London: Routledge & Kegan Paul.

Fairclough, N. (1989) *Language and Power*, Harlow: Longman.

Fetterley, J. (1981) *The Resisting Reader: A Feminist Approach to American Fiction*, Bloomington: Indiana University Press.

Hall, S. (1973) 'Encoding/decoding', reprinted in S. Hall, D. Hobson, A. Lowe and P. Willis (eds) *Culture, Media, Language*, London: Hutchinson.

Hobby, E. and White, C. (eds) (1991) *What Lesbians Do in Books*, London: Women's Press.

Kaplan, C. (1986) 'Keeping the color in *The Color Purple*', in *Sea Changes: Culture and Feminism*, London: Verso, pp. 176–87.

Laws, S. (1990) *Issues of Blood: The Politics of Menstruation*, Basingstoke: Macmillan.

Leith, D. and Myerson, G. (1989) *The Power of Address*, London: Routledge.

Mills, S. (ed.) (1994) *Gendering the Reader*, Hemel Hempstead: Harvester Wheatsheaf.

Mills, S. (1996) *Feminist Stylistics*, London: Routledge.

Mulvey, L. (1981) 'Visual pleasure and narrative cinema', in T. Bennett *et al.* (eds) *Popular Television and Film*, London: Open University/BFI, pp. 206–16.

Rimmon-Kenan, S. (1983) *Narrative Fiction: Contemporary Poetics*, London: Methuen.

Said, E. (1993) 'Jane Austen and empire', in *Culture and Imperialism*, London: Chatto & Windus, pp. 95–115.

Shohat, E. and Stam, R. (1994) *Unthinking Eurocentrism: Multiculturalism and the Media*, London: Routledge.

Showalter, E. (1977) *A Literature of their Own*, Princeton, NJ: Princeton University Press.

Stacey, J. (1994) *Star Gazing: Hollywood Cinema and Female Spectatorship*, London: Routledge.

Toolan, M. (1988) *Narrative: A Critical Linguistic Introduction*, London: Routledge.

Van Zoonan, L. (1994) *Feminist Media Studies*, London: Sage.

Unit 24

Authorship and intention

It is common for people to say that a text is created by an author (or by a group of authors). It is also a frequent extension of this point to say that an author (or group of authors) has a particular intention about how that text should act on a reader: how it should be interpreted. Together, concepts of author and intention are considered by many people to be central, even indispensable, notions: these ideas are believed to offer a necessary point of origin and guide to meaning for any given text. Indeed, it is generally our sense that a text (or art object) was designed by human agency which encourages us to believe that it will be worthwhile spending time interpreting it. Despite common-sense attractions, however, the concepts of author and intention are less straightforward than they seem.

24.1 The author

24.1.1 Views of the author's role and importance

What exactly is it that an author does in creating a text? One historically influential view is that the author is a sort of skilful craft worker, who draws on conventions at various different levels of a cultural tradition but always remains less important than the tradition in which he or she works. This view is associated with literary criticism and cultural attitudes in Britain broadly from the Middle Ages up to the eighteenth century. It places a high value on established ideas and styles, which are sometimes described as 'traditional', 'classical', or 'Neo-classical'.

Towards the end of the eighteenth century, however, the intellectual and artistic movement known as Romanticism offered a significantly different view. In that view, the author discovers material for creative work somewhere inside himself or herself. This shift of emphasis places the author, rather than the tradition, at the centre of the compositional process. The individual author, rather than the tradition, becomes the origin of the material (he or she makes it up to a greater extent than previously). And because of the concern with his or her own feelings and experiences, the author also becomes the guarantor of what might be called the text's authenticity ('authenticity' in this context combines the notion of genuineness or sincerity with other related values, including naturalness, worth, and purity). The resulting view of the author as being responsible for 'authorizing' the text became very influential in nine-teenth-century Europe. It survives today, in various forms and derivatives of the general notion of the 'Romantic artist', as a sort of popular 'common-sense' assumption about creativity.

Interest in the author (alongside interest in the style of a text; see **Unit 17, Genre**) contributes substantially to the pleasure in texts that many readers experience and also affects the value they are likely place on texts. Pleasure in a text, for instance, is often associated with some image of its author. Many people seek out further texts by the same person; and publishers and publi-cists encourage this by means of their promotional materials: 'by the author of . . .', 'from the people who brought you. . . '. The symbolic or cultural value of a text (expressed in aspects of the text's circulation – such as who reads it, where it is reviewed, and whether it is awarded prizes or is taught) often depends on who the author is. So does its economic value (generated through advances and royalties, as well as possibly by later media tie-ins). The centrality of the category of the author in modern text-producing cultural industries applies very obviously in the cases of painting and music (e.g. if a previously neglected painting is suddenly discovered to have been painted by a great 'master', then its aesthetic and commercial valuation may completely change). But it is also a major, if less often acknowledged, feature of print publishing (see **Unit 25, Judgement and value**).

Further issues arise with regard to how the author relates to other people's published texts, as well as to styles of writing which precede and surround him or her (what is commonly meant by tradition). Even in seeking to represent personal experience, a text producer is obliged either to repro-duce, modify or try to escape from a network of existing techniques and past examples. Debate on this aspect of the role of the author, and the kinds of creativity which are implicit in it, underwent further revision at the beginning of the twentieth century. The poet, dramatist and critic T.S. Eliot (1888–1965) attacked the Romantic conception of writing and the importance of the indi-vidual writer in his influential essay 'Tradition and the individual talent' (1919), by suggesting that the individual poet's mind is and should be subservient to a historically inherited greater 'mind', as constituted or carried by cultural tradi-tion. For Eliot, focus on a poet's individuality is therefore misguided. He proposes instead that we should distinguish between a poet's personal emotion and what he calls 'significant emotion, emotion which has its life in the poem and not in the history of the poet' (Eliot, 1919).

Eliot's thinking significantly affected a whole generation of writers and scholars. But despite his and other related critiques, key features of the Romantic view of the author and creativity remain central to many institutionalized ways of considering literature and other cultural forms. Consider, for instance, occasions when a text is included in a syllabus specifically on account of who its author is ('a piece of juvenilia, or early work, by one of the Brontës/Beatles'; 'a minor, occasional piece by George Eliot/T.S. Eliot', etc.). In such cases, authorship is the operative category, rather than, for example, a notion of intrinsic value, text-type or the issues a text deals with.

If we can see past this reverence for the author's identity, experience and intention, however, other ways of considering authorship become possible. Shifts in the perceived importance of the author can be examined in large-scale historical terms (see Foucault, 1988). This view allows us to see how far the focus on the author associated with the Romantics, for example, coincided with a broad social development in which questions concerning legal ownership of texts (e.g. laws concerning copyright) became increasingly important. It also allows us to consider how the proclaimed individualism of the Romantic artist was contemporaneous with a new concentration of European populations in cities as a result of the Industrial Revolution. We can also begin to see how changing notions of an author interlock with a more general development of interest in the individual which characterized Western thinking during the relevant period.

As we develop this more contextual way of thinking about authors, the category of authorship seems less to concern individual, creative agents than social patterns of thinking about creative agents. It also becomes possible to see individual authors as representative of social groups, and to trace relations between an author's life, works, and circumstances. If we can see how historical conditions shape the creation of texts through authors, then we might think of authors as bearers of specific social structures or forces. This is helpful if we can then investigate not only the particular authors and their works, but also textual production and circulation as a social practice which constitutes the cultural or representational element of the public sphere (and is therefore larger than any one individual).

By thinking of authorship as a social rather than individual category, we can show how the social field shapes, even produces, authors, rather than assuming that those authors who happen to be on the shelves are there purely on account of individual value or merit. Studying particular authors may then be joined with seeing, for example, how marginalized groups, such as female, black, working-class or gay writers, have had to struggle in order to represent particular, marginalized social experiences. One area in which such thinking has been particularly influential is feminist literary history. Feminist critics have shown how many women writers from the past have been lost to modern readers. One of the reasons for this is that it was once considered improper for women to be authors. Some eighteenth-century and even nineteenth-century women novelists were published anonymously, or under a man's name (e.g. Charlotte Brontë as Currer Bell), because of restrictive attitudes towards women writers at the time.

24.1.2 Can authorship always be identified?

An author of a text is not always directly known. He or she might have published anonymously, or under an adopted name. Such instances are worth considering more directly, because they expose a more general problem – i.e. that it is not always clear who authorship of a text should be attributed to.

Most texts pass through several hands before they reach their readers; and what the author originally wrote may have been changed by an editor, publisher or printer, or revised by someone else before or after the author's death. This might happen for many different reasons, including censorship, saving money by abbreviating the text, intervening editorially with the intention of 'improving' the text, and straightforward error (such as mistakes made in transcribing manuscripts by hand or setting up printing plates). Many such changes will be relatively trivial. In some cases, however, it is difficult to know exactly who wrote a text or some major part of a text. (This is especially the case with some of Shakespeare's late plays, such as *Pericles*, since much of Shakespeare's work was published after his death.)

Examples of unknown or questionable authorship are not uncommon in print media. But more emphatic illustration of the complexity of authorship is offered by texts typically created by a team or group of people, such as films, television programmes, theatrical performances, or music CDs. In these cases, contributions to a text are made by many people, including possibly actors, camera operators, lighting and set designers, script editors, make-up artists, directors, producers, etc. Often it is the director who is assumed to be a film's 'author', in the sense of having final artistic control. This view played a central part in the 'politique des auteurs' developed by the French Cahiers du Cinéma in the 1950s, and the related **auteur** theory of Andrew Sarris in the USA (see Caughie, 1981). In this view, the auteur of a film (an especially valued director) is considered to be the person who expresses his or her personal vision coherently across the corpus of films which he or she makes. Alfred Hitchcock is often cited as an example of an auteur under this definition. (For issues surrounding this view of directors, see **Unit 21**, **Narration in film and prose fiction**.)

The case of film and television mentioned here relates largely to classic, studio forms of production. (An analogy can be made here with mainstream music CD or record production: in that field, too, a number of different personnel and a complex division of labour are involved.) Studio forms of production are distinctive, among other ways, in having high entry-costs as regards the relevant technological means of production (not only equipment but also film and tape stock) alongside their other costs (including actor fees, etc.). Such entry-costs restrict access to production to companies and other organizations of a sufficient scale, and as a result offer limited opportunities for individuals to play the central part of 'author'.

Convergence of various means of media production around digital technologies, however, has implications for notions of authorship which are as yet untested (see **Unit 27, Ways of reading non-literary texts**). While instances of corporate production of contemporary media, including multi-media, clearly continue (consider, for example, the credit list on any commercial multi-media CD-ROM), a significant amount of individual production also takes place, in new kinds of individual desktop or home-studio production. Questions of authorship are at stake in these technological and cultural changes in two main ways. New questions arise as regards the precise role within production which constitutes authorship; and old questions are posed in new ways about how an author's assumed originality relates to other, preceding or contemporaneous texts (such as downloaded Internet materials, clip-art, and sampled sounds).

Two divergent visions of authorship struggle with each other in attempts to characterize these changes in media production. On the one hand, there is a view that, with changing media technologies, everyone will become an author (a view based on the increasing importance of interactive capabilities of media texts, and widespread opportunities for people to have home pages and post material on the Internet). But an alternative view suggests that, with changing media technologies, there will no longer need to be a clear-cut concept of authorship at all (a view based on the idea of cumulative text production, especially in hypertext forms: texts which constantly mutate as changes and additions are made to them by people who previously might have been thought of as readers rather than as, in effect, co-authors). Each of these visions of authorship, in its own different way, might seem to predict the end of the book as we know it. While it has been traditionally produced by an author or authors, the book is said by some thinkers to be on the verge of becoming less textually stable, less a document anchored to its author than a free-floating dialogue between contributing voices in a continuing conversation (for a counter-view, however, see Eco, 1996). However they measure up against what actually happens, these visions of the book of the future pose in a clear form central questions about the author's authority, as both point of origin and guarantor of a text's identity and meaning.

24.2 Authorship and voice

24.2.1 Narrator, implied author and persona

A text's author (the real person who wrote it) needs to be distinguished from its narrator (the imaginary person who narrates it). When we say that a text is written in the first person, we mean that its narrator refers to her/himself by using first person singular pronouns ('I', 'me', 'my', 'mine'). These pronouns are thought of as referring to the narrator, rather than to the author. As already mentioned in earlier units, Herman Melville's novel *Moby Dick* (1851) begins 'Call me Ishmael', and the novel is narrated (in part) by 'Ishmael' – from Ishmael's point of view rather than Melville's (see **Unit 20**, **Narrative point of view**). The term **persona** is often used to describe the first person narrator or speaker of a poem.

24.2.2 Autobiography, fiction, imaginative projection

One reason for distinguishing between author and narrator is that some texts may present us with a narrator who is subject to authorial irony or structural **irony** (see **Unit 14**) by being shown to be at some level unreliable – perhaps in terms of her or his ability to understand events or in terms of her or his moral position. For example Huck, the narrator of Mark Twain's novel *Huckleberry Finn* (1884), is presented from the beginning as being unable to understand his own situation fully, including the fact that he himself is a fictional character:

> You don't know about me, without you have read a book by the name of *The Adventures of Tom Sawyer*, but that ain't no matter. That book was made by Mr Mark Twain, and he told the truth, mainly. There was things which he stretched, but mainly he told the truth.

The novel was published in 1884, but it is set 'forty to fifty years previously' – that is, before the American Civil War led to the emancipation of American slaves. Huck is presented as sharing a conventional view that slavery is natural, even though this conflicts with his personal friendship for an escaped slave called Jim. As narrator of the novel, Huck explicitly expresses the moral confusion which results – worrying, for example, about Jim's plan to emancipate his children from slavery. Ironically, Huck is shocked by hearing Jim

> coming right out flat-footed and saying he would steal his children – children that belonged to a man I didn't even know; a man that hadn't ever done me no harm.

Huck subsequently recognizes that he would feel just as bad if he betrayed Jim to the authorities. So he abandons his attempt to resolve what for him is a moral dilemma. But if we suggest that Huck's predicament is a moral dilemma for the novel itself, or for its real author, then we confuse a number of different levels of reading. Huck's interior monologue is both comic and tragic in its limited viewpoint, and in its aping of the flawed logic and morality which helped sustain slavery. Since Huck can't see the irony which his own reasoning reveals, there seems to be a viewpoint being presented in the novel which is not available to Huck himself. (We might describe this viewpoint as a post-Civil War viewpoint, which exposes the ironic contradictions and limitations of a pre-Civil War narrator whose love for an individual slave does not allow him to see the problem with slavery in general.)

If we are to capture the sense that there is another point of view hidden behind Huck's – which allows us to glimpse a 'true' moral position behind Huck's ironized version – we need to have a concept such as that of an **implied author**. The implied author must be clearly distinguished from the real author, however, because the implied author is not the original cause of the text (i.e. its real producer) but rather an effect of the text – an impression which it produces (and so one of its meanings, which can be reached by undoing the text's ironies).

Even carefully distinguished, the notion of an implied author still intro-duces further complications into reading. In the first place, the implied author can only ever be a critical fiction, a rationalization of the impression we have in reading a novel (or viewing a film) that we are being confided in by some specific human consciousness. Thus the idea of the implied author already presumes an understanding of novels and films as a kind of intimate speech. You might say, therefore, that the implied author is more the product of a given way of reading than a way of reading in its own right. In addition, however sophisticated the interpretations permitted by the notion of the implied author may be, in the end the implied author works in the same way that recourse to a 'real' author does: it defines and stabilizes interpretive possibilities for a text by suggesting that readings of the text can be distilled into a coherent moral position and meaning controlled by an authoritative moral consciousness or intention.

24.3 Intention

Appeals to the author of a text (whether to a real or to an implied author) often serve, then, as a way of invoking intention in order to impose kinds of coherence and stability on processes of reading. Many readers feel anxious that, without an author presiding as guarantor of some fixity of textual meaning, there would be no boundary to the kinds of meanings which might be found, no way of judging whether we are misreading or over-interpreting, and no clear reason ever to stop reading the same text in endlessly different ways (see Eco, 1990).

But is this anxiety well founded? And if not, what factors other than authorial intention might serve to guide or limit interpretive processes? Discussion of such issues over many centuries typically identifies three elements which combine together in a complex division of communicative labour: authorial intention; conventional forms or codes of the text itself; and attribu-tions or ascriptions of meaning by readers (or viewers). Differing accounts of interpretation typically differ in the respective degrees of priority they accord to each of these three elements.

24.3.1 Author's intention

In the eighteenth century in particular, literary works were considered to be products of conscious intention. This assumption led to a particular way of reading, as encapsulated in one of Alexander Pope's couplets in his *Essay on Criticism* (1711): 'In every work regard the writer's end / Since none can compass more than they intend' (II, 255–6).

By the end of the eighteenth century, however, Romantic writers began to claim, by contrast, that authors are not always fully conscious of the meaning or implications of their own literary works, because their works were produced in moments of 'inspiration'. The Romantic poet William Blake, for example, claims that although Milton tells us that he set out to 'justify the ways of God to men' in *Paradise Lost*, in fact the poem itself reveals that he was actually 'of the Devil's party without knowing it'. Yet the apparent rejection of intention by some Romantic writers arguably still allows for interpretation to be anchored in authorial intention – so long as the author's intention is taken to include powers of imagination which are not always readily available for conscious reflection, even by the author himself or herself.

In the early twentieth century, the view that creation emerges out of a reserve of meanings not always available to conscious attention was given fresh impetus by psychoanalysis. Sigmund Freud, C.G. Jung, and others have suggested that we are never fully conscious of our intentions, because the unconscious mind can have an effect on what we say – and on what we don't say – without our being aware of it. For Freud and Jung – though in different ways – the unconscious mind plays a major part in artistic creativity alongside the conscious mind.

No agreed answer exists to the question of how far these complexities undermine appeals to authorial intention. In some traditions of criticism and theories of interpretation (e.g. in **hermeneutics**), intention has continued to play an important part in ways of finding validity or legitimacy for textual interpretations. Particular efforts have been made in some critical traditions to locate intention within the cultural horizons of the period and place in which the text was first produced. What is certain is that, in the light of psychoanalysis and other intellectual developments sceptical of authorial intention, straightforward confidence in the role played by intention in fixing meaning (for instance the kind of confidence implicit in Pope's couplet) can no longer be justified.

24.3.2 Intention and convention

One common argument against the notion that the author controls interpretation of a text comes from the sense that meaningful forms are shared, social property. They exist – and have an acknowledged meaning-bearing potential – before any particular speaker or writer uses them.

One literary development of this insight is that, since the means for making meaning are social and public, the meanings of texts (especially public texts) should be discoverable within the texts themselves rather than by searching beyond them for an author's intention. One particularly influential formulation of this view is W.K. Wimsatt and M.C. Beardsley's essay 'The intentional fallacy' (1946). Concentrating on poetry (though corresponding arguments might be made about novels, films, or other text-types), Wimsatt and Beardsley set out the following polemical points against the search for authorial intention:

1   In most cases it is not possible to find out what the poet intended.
2   We are primarily interested in how a poem works, not what was intended.
3   A poem is a public rather than a private thing because it exists in language – which is by definition social rather than personal. The author does not own the text once it has been made public, and therefore does not have eternal authority over its meaning.
4   A poem's meaning can only be discovered through its actual language, 'through our habitual knowledge of the language, through grammars, dictionaries, and all the literature which is the source of dictionaries, in general, through all that makes a language and culture' (Wimsatt and Beardsley, 1946).
5   'If the poet succeeded in doing [what he intended], then the poem itself shows what he was trying to do' (Wimsatt and Beardsley, 1946).

Notice that this last point slightly complicates Wimsatt and Beardsley's apparent critique of intentionalism. While no reliance is placed on intention in points 1–4, the view presented as point 5 seems to endorse interest in an author's intention – so long as that intention is looked for in the linguistic material of the text itself, rather than in diaries, anecdotes, or miscellaneous details of the author's life.

24.3.3 Intention and inference

The idea that linguistic and other cultural signs and practices are conventional and coded cannot fully account for how meanings are produced, however. No matter how richly coded such signs and practices may be, their social and conventional character cannot account for effects such as how vague expressions, ironic expressions, metaphorical patterns, and many other aspects of usage – not just in literature but in discourse generally – take on precise and readily perceived meanings in particular contexts which are nevertheless radically divergent from the conventional, 'coded' meanings they have in many other contexts. How could the complete reversal, or cancelling out, of clearly coded meanings happen in specific contexts, if interpretation is a matter of reading meaning straight off from form?

Acknowledging that discourse may mean something more or different from what the speaker consciously intends (as suggested by psychoanalysis) may not rule out authorial intention as an aspect of interpretation, either. Unintended effects of the kind psychoanalysis claims to discover occur along-side more routine processes of implying and inferring. Even allowing for unconscious slips or even for continuous slippage, therefore, those common meaning-effects still need to be accounted for – something which can seem difficult without some notion of how and why readers target their search for meaning.

Understanding the role played by inference in interpretation is crucial here. Communication can be said to occur (as it is in pragmatics, especially Relevance Theory) when a speaker or text-producer presents a general intention to communicate, together with linguistic or other material that can be taken by anyone whose attention is drawn to it as something potentially relevant to them. (The general intention to communicate itself is made mani-fest by the text-producer drawing attention to an act of speaking, writing, waving, or some other conventional gesture of communicating.) The person interpreting the discourse makes a presumption that the utterance or text has been framed in such a way that it will achieve relevant effects. As a result the interpreter's search for that relevance – a search which proceeds by focusing on assumptions accessed from the immediate context, from earlier parts of the text, and from background knowledge in some specific, culturally formed order of accessibility – quickly finds the meaning that the speaker is likely to have foreseen in formulating the utterance or text in that way rather than any other.

Such an account of interpretation combines aspects of 'coded' meaning with a further level of inference. Decoded meanings are used as input into an inferential process of filling-out and constructing a relevant meaning in the particular context modelled for the text by the interpreter. To the extent that the text-producer and interpreter share assumptions which can be activated in interpretation, the interpreter's computation of meaning is likely to resemble the author's intention. Where assumptions mobilized differ significantly, however – or differ in how they are mentally stored and therefore in the order in which they are accessed – then the interpretation produced will diverge from authorial intention. In the case of some texts or utterances (especially poetry, religious or mythical discourse, or other kinds of figurative, vague, or evoca-tive language), the search for relevant meanings will throw up a wide range of weakly implied meanings which border on meanings not intended by the author at all. And in constructing a reading of a text or utterance, of any sort, the interpreter can always also make inferences which will not have been in any way intended (or even foreseen) by the author. Such inferences lead to sorts of 'symptomatic' interpretation which generate meanings for the text that are highly relevant to the reader – and possibly of great interest in the reader's context – regardless of what the author may or may not have been trying to say.

24.4 Is the author dead?

Consideration of these three different aspects of reading – which overlap and intercut in complex ways – opens up radically different perspectives on the role of intention in constructing meanings for a text.

From a post-structuralist perspective, Roland Barthes addressed such concerns in an influential essay called 'The death of the author' (1968). In this essay, Barthes develops the insight that 'to give a text an Author ... is to impose a limit on that text' into a polemical case against interpretive closure and in favour of more open-ended reading. Barthes's key arguments in this essay are worth comparing with Wimsatt and Beardsley's above:

1   The author is, by definition, absent from writing (in contrast with speech, which generally implies the presence of the speaker).
2   A text is not a unique artefact, emerging through a kind of immaculate conception from a writer's brain. Rather, the conventions and language which make up the text (any text) are available to the writer precisely because they have been used before (see **Unit 16, Intertextuality and allusion**). A text is 'a tissue of quotations', 'a multi-dimensional space in which a variety of writings, none of them original, blend and clash'.
3   A text's meaning is accordingly produced in the act of reading, not of writing. To open up reading as a productive practice, in which the reader is freed from the process of discovering, or pretending to discover, what the author intended, Barthes claims that far greater attention needs to be given to reading. 'Classic criticism has never paid any attention to the reader; for it the writer is the only person in literature.'
4   Encapsulating these arguments, Barthes concludes that 'the birth of the reader must be at the cost of the death of the Author'.

Barthes's position inverts the established idea of the author conferring meaning and authority on a work. He suggests instead that the author is a construct created in order to fill an empty place where such certitude or authority might be located. In claiming this, Barthes simultaneously transforms the idea of literary or cultural tradition from being a selected body of earlier work available as a stable resource behind the text into a potentially infinite network of links and echoes between texts of all kinds. Barthes's aim in this essay, as in much of his other writing, is in part to celebrate not only the more dispersed and improvisatory ways of reading he advocates, but also to endorse particular styles of writing which especially lend themselves to such reading.

The continuing influence of his essay, however, points to the fundamental nature of the questions he poses: questions about the symbolic role played by the author and by authorial intention in imposing a kind of law on what would otherwise be a freeplay of discourse.

ACTIVITY 24.1

The following text was written, anonymously, in France during the thirteenth century. In form, it is a motet (a musical composition for two, three, or four voices, with each voice singing different words). The text – whose author remains unknown – was translated from Old French by Carol Cosman.

> I am a young girl
> graceful and gay,
> not yet fifteen when
> my sweet breasts may
> begin to swell;
>
> Love should be my contemplation,
> I should learn its indication,
>
> But I am put in prison.
> God's curse be on my jailor!
>
> Evil, villainy and sin
> did he
> to give up a girl like me
> to a nunnery;
>
> A wicked deed, by my faith,
> the convent life will be my death
> My God! for I am far too young.
>
> Beneath my sash I feel the sweet pain.
> God's curse on him who made me a nun.

This activity concentrates on questions about who the author of the text might be (allowing for an informal use of the word 'author' to describe production of a text in the circumstances that are likely to have existed). You may find evidence as to the writer's identity in features of the text, in the description given at the beginning of the activity, or in what you know or can guess about historical circumstances of thirteenth-century France and about people of the time and the sorts of opportunities open to them.

1 Give any evidence which you can find (or can construct for yourself) for thinking that the speaker of the text is also the author.

2 Give any evidence which you can find (or construct for yourself) for thinking that the speaker of the text is *not* the author.

3 Are there aspects of your response to the poem which you believe are affected by the fact that it is (a) anonymous, (b) written for more than one voice, (c) written in the thirteenth century, (d) a translation by a specific, named translator?

4 Now temporarily assume that the author is not, in any direct way, the speaker. Present any evidence which you can find (or construct) in support of the idea that the author was: (a) a woman; (b) a man.

5 Below are simple descriptions of two hypothetical authors. For each, describe how believing that this was the identity of the author would change how you read the poem (and the effects the poem has on you):

(a) imagined author X = a 25-year-old male
(b) imagined author Y = a 15-year-old female

Pay particular attention to sorts of effect you think may have been intended or anticipated by the author of the text, and sorts of response you are making to the text which could not have been anticipated by the text's author.

Reading

Abrams, M.H. (1953) 'The orientation of critical theories', in D. Lodge (ed.) (1972) *20th Century Literary Criticism*, Harlow: Longman, pp. 1–26.

Abrams, M.H. (1988) *A Glossary of Literary Terms*, 5th edn, New York: Holt, Rinehart & Winston, Inc. Entries entitled 'Persona, Tone, and Voice', and 'Point of View'.

Barthes, R. (1968) 'The death of the author', in D. Lodge (ed.) (1988) *Modern Criticism and Theory*, London: Longman, pp. 17–72.

Burke, S. (ed.) (1995) *Authorship: From Plato to the Postmodern: A Reader*, Edinburgh: Edinburgh University Press.

Caughie, J. (ed.) (1981) *Theories of Authorship: A Reader*, London: Routledge & Kegan Paul and the British Film Institute.

Eco, U. (1990) *The Limits of Interpretation*, Bloomington: Indiana University Press.

Eco, U. (1996) 'Afterword', in G. Nunberg (ed.) *The Future of the Book*, Berkeley, CA: University of California Press, pp. 295–306.

Eliot, T.S. (1919) 'Tradition and the individual talent', in D. Lodge (ed.) (1972) *20th Century Literary Criticism*, Harlow: Longman, pp. 334–44.

Foucault, M. (1980/1988) 'What is an author?', in D. Lodge (ed.) (1988) *Modern*

Criticism and Theory, London: Longman, pp. 197–210.

Moi, T. (1985) *Sexual/Textual Politics*, London: Methuen, pp. 21–69.

Newton-de Molina, D. (ed.) (1976) *On Literary Intention*, Edinburgh: Edinburgh University Press.

Todd, J. (1987) *A Dictionary of British and American Women Writers, 1660–1800*, London: Methuen.

Wimsatt, W.K. and Beardsley, M.C. (1946) 'The intentional fallacy', in D. Lodge (ed.) (1972) *20th Century Literary Criticism*, Harlow: Longman, pp. 334–44.

Judgement and value

Many kinds of writing might be designated as 'literature'. In the past, definitions of what counts as literature have been much broader than our present definitions, at times taking in non-fictional works, travel writing, essays, political and religious texts, and so on. However, not all literature excites critical interest and comment. Literary critics have usually assumed that the texts which seem to repay special attention, by many readers over a long period of time, thereby gaining the status of 'classics', do so because they are somehow intrinsically valuable. And it is these classic texts which – by virtue of their special value and the amount of criticism and commentary which they generate – come to comprise the 'canon' of Great Literature.[1] This canon tends to form the core of syllabuses in schools, colleges and universities. Judgements about the value of texts, therefore, can clearly be seen to be at the heart of literary studies. Also, for many critics, assessing the value of a text is also seen to be a crucial part of the role of the critic.

25.1 Characteristics of valued texts

It was against this background of assuming that certain texts were more valuable than others that critics such as F.R. Leavis set out to judge which texts are valuable and which are not (Leavis, 1962). Value, in such a view, is seen as a quality residing within texts themselves. And critics of this persuasion have generally stressed the importance of characteristics such as complexity, aesthetic unity, literary language, subject-matter, and canonical status.

25.1.1 Complexity and unity

Literary texts which are assumed to be of special value are generally characterized by complexity of plot, structure, language, and ideas. Indeed, complexity is often used in this context as a synonym of value. But complexity can be of a number of different kinds. In novels, complexity typically involves not only a skilfully constructed main plot, but often the co-existence of this plot with sub-plots which mirror and highlight the events and themes in the main plot. The structure of a specially valued poem is held to be complex in ways which repay close attention; for example, the poem may be structured as a complex sequence of **parallelisms** (see **Unit 11**). The more the reader studies the poem, the more he or she is aware of the poet's skill in composing it in this way. The language of valued literary texts is also typically assumed to be complex: writers do not simply choose 'ordinary' words, like the words we use for conversation, but words which have resonance, historical associations, beauty, or 'rightness' for the particular context. The reader is encouraged to assume that writers of valued texts laboured painstakingly to choose exactly the right word, since each word forms part of a larger complex structure. Nor can the ideas of a poem or novel be taken as haphazardly chosen: they too form complex patterns or structures, either being echoed by other ideas in the text or reaffirmed in the form of general themes. The complex interweaving of elements of language, structure, plot, ideas and so on, can be seen to constitute the aesthetic unity of the text. Through carefully studying the text, the reader will consequently find that all of its elements contribute to the same overall structure, and is thereby likely to consider the poem to have achieved value, or even greatness. Alternatively, if by applying the same criteria the reader is not able to discover a complex but unified pattern in the text, that text will not be regarded as the highest kind of literature, and will be judged to be flawed.

25.1.2 Language

We assume that writers of canonical texts are craftspersons – that they are in command of their writing, and that they are skilled in ways that other writers are not. Of special interest, as regards the question of value, is the attention paid to the language of valued texts. Language in valued texts is described as being elegant, witty, patterned, controlled; in short, the author is considered to have taken care in her or his choice, and the reader takes pleasure in the skill which the author displays. Literary language, for critics such as the Russian Formalists, is seen to constitute a separate type of language where authors consciously play with the possibilities of expression in order to produce verbal art that has specific aesthetic qualities (Shklovsky, 1965).

25.1.3 Subject-matter

The subject-matter of valued texts is generally considered to be serious, dealing with moral and philosophical topics of acknowledged importance. Valued texts are supposed to give the reader an insight into fundamental questions which are of universal concern, such as the nature of evil, the corrupting effect of money, the value of love, and so on, and to rehearse the dilemmas of moral and ethical choice. For this reason, comic texts are rarely accorded status unless they appear to discuss such supposedly universal themes. Because valued texts are held to deal with such universal themes, which are of concern to all people, they are also thought to have qualities of durability. Shakespeare's works, for example, are deemed valuable because they are believed to have significance not only for his time but for all time. When texts discuss evidently universal questions, they are unlikely to be at the same time texts which discuss specific political questions in any detail. Political polemic (open and heated critical discussion) is generally taken to be at odds with literary worth, and is often seen to detract from the universalizing aim of great literature (satires are often valued for their observations about humankind in general, rather than for their more specific criticisms of particular societies).

25.1.4 The canon

As has been suggested above, the canon is the group of texts considered to be of most value. These are the books which are generally taught in schools, colleges and universities (though the canon is constantly changing, especially in schools). Although many new universities have largely dispensed with the notion of the canon, and offer courses on non-canonical writing, many more traditional universities still structure their syllabus around a chronological study of the canon. Despite changes in the canon, however, when students are asked to list members of this elite grouping, the results are generally very similar: the first writers on the list are usually Shakespeare, Chaucer and Milton; after these, a certain amount of debate generally occurs on whether to include such writers as Dryden, Lawrence, Pope, Swift, Joyce, Wordsworth, Keats, Shelley, Jonson, Dickens, Hardy, Burns, Woolf, Austen, Eliot, and the Brontës. These writers share certain characteristics. First, most of them are male (indeed it is not unusual for some students' lists to include only male writers). Second, they are generally from the middle- or upper-class, and are all white. Third, they are all dead. To be included in the canon, writers must be seen to have written valuable texts; but is it merely a coincidence that these writers also belong to essentially the same socio-economic, racial and gender group? As soon as you ask one question about the canon, others arise. Who decides whether someone is in the canon and who is not? And how is it that most students of English literature know, to a greater or lesser extent, who is included and who is not?

Most traditional critics do not consider that there are any agencies involved in decisions about who is in the canon and who is not; the selected texts are simply clearly better than others. You might like to consider, however, a range of agencies which make and enforce decisions about canonical status. Within the school context, because of the introduction of the National Curriculum, the choices about which authors and books are included on the syllabus are largely taken by government agencies.[2] In universities, individual lecturers, ratified by other staff, university bodies and external examiners, make decisions about which books should be studied. They also largely make up the researchers and critics who work on canonical writers, and publish learned articles or introductions for students to canonical texts. This system of 'commentary', as Michel Foucault calls it, ensures that certain texts remain the focus of attention and stay in print (Foucault, 1986). Outside of the educational domain, there are publishers who commission critical books from academics writing on particular authors, and who also label certain books as 'Classics'; libraries who buy such books; and individual readers who accept this version of canonicity. In the light of this, you might like to ask yourself some questions about your own course of study: for example, do you study Shakespeare; how many texts are there by contemporary writers, women writers, working-class or Black writers? Underlying the way that your course is constructed may be notions about value which may come to the fore when you consider your answers to these questions.

25.2 Some recent critical perspectives on value

Modern literary theorists have professed much less certainty about questions of literary value. While many of them have considered that certain texts do seem to be better than others, others have considered that value is simply a means of excluding certain texts. A range of differing views on questions of judgement and value now exists.

Roland Barthes (1986), for example, was innovatory in analysing not only texts which are canonical, but also texts drawn from popular literature, like Ian Fleming's *Goldfinger* (1959). Barthes does consider, however, that there are important differences among texts; and he is concerned in much of his writing to describe those differences. But rather than assuming that value resides within the text, he shifts attention to the 'pleasure of the text'; instead of being a scholarly enjoyment of the seeming control of the writer over her or his material, the process of reading, for Barthes, involves a more sexualized pleasure. In particular, Barthes identifies the different types of pleasure to be gained from reading realist texts (see **Unit 22**, **Realism**) compared with other texts. He calls realist texts 'readerly', because in reading such texts the reader begins not to be aware of the fact that he or she is reading, and starts to get caught up in the pleasure of narrative. But Barthes prefers 'writerly' texts, which are those texts (such as experimental and avant garde texts) which force the reader to 'work' (and 'play') more in order to make sense of them. With writerly texts, attention is drawn to the process of writing; we are unable to become 'lost' in the narrative in the same unthinking way as with readerly texts. Thus, although Barthes claims to be opposed to constructing hierarchies, there does seem to be a value judgement made between readerly and writerly texts. Despite this,

his writing on the pleasure of the text does question the traditional notion of canonical texts as somehow intrinsically more valuable than others, and suggests that the reader plays an important role in attributing value to a text.

Marxist critics are often much less clear about whether the notions of value and evaluation are useful. Terry Eagleton (1976, 1983), for example, attacks the concept of the canon, arguing that texts become canonical precisely because they serve to support the ruling ideology. He does not want to dispense, however, with the notion of value completely, since he also thinks that there are literary texts which question or 'escape' ideology, and so force the reader to consider her or his position and perhaps lead to a form of consciousness-raising. Within the Women's Movement, for example, feminist novels written by Fay Weldon, Janette Winterson, Toni Morrison, Margaret Atwood and Angela Carter have been very important in bringing about changes in women's thinking. These literary texts have brought about a questioning of certain ideological assumptions about the position of women, and could therefore be considered valuable for that reason.

Michel Foucault (1986) takes a more sceptical position, questioning the idea of attributing value to texts at all. He argues that literary texts are really empty texts, containing less rather than more than other texts. They display, as he puts it, 'enunciative poverty'. With literary texts, critics have to work hardest, in order to fill gaps which the text leaves gaping open. It is critics themselves, writing scholarly articles and books on canonical writers, who repeat over and over the message which the text itself failed to tell. Foucault also questions the notion that the writer is totally in control of what is written. He draws attention to the importance of other factors in the writing process, such as the common-sense knowledge of the time, literary traditions, and the economic and literary pressures which led the writer to write within certain genres or styles, and on certain subjects.

25.3 Value and genre/media

So far, we have been considering issues of value and judgement mainly in relation to literary texts. But criteria of value are also important for the way that we view other genres and media. For example, when watching a film which has been made of a book (for example, *The Color Purple*, *Vanity Fair*, or *The Company of Wolves*), many people express the view that the film did not measure up to the book. Perhaps this judgement stems less from the merits of either the particular book or film, than from implicit assumptions about the relative cultural merits of films and novels in general (see **Unit 21**, **Narration in film and prose fiction**). Because film is a more recent medium, more popular, and seemingly 'parasitic' on the novel, many people assume that it is of less value than literature. The same can be said of songs, when judged against poetry. We may memorize the lyrics of a pop song which we like but we are less likely to analyse those lyrics in the same way that we might analyse a poem by Shakespeare, although recently the study of the lyrics of certain songwriters such as Bob Dylan has gained a certain credibility in academic circles (Day, 1988). Nor would we generally expect to analyse a popular song in an English literature class, since songs, particularly pop songs, are rarely given canonical status.

If you look back to our initial description of the canon, you will see that many of the writers who were included were poets rather than novelists or dramatists. Poetry is often seen as a more valued genre than prose. Poetry appears to call for closer attention than prose. Within poetry itself, further distinction is often made between poetry and verse. Verse is sometimes regarded as poetry less skilfully written or less profound than 'poetry'. A recent book of poetry by a feminist group, the Raving Beauties, called *In the Pink* (1983), was labelled by critics as 'verse' rather than 'poetry'; and much of the poetry written by working-class writers is also (dismissively) labelled verse.

25.3.1 Literary texts and popular culture

Within literature departments, canonical literary texts are generally considered superior to the fictional texts which many of us read to relax in our spare time: romances, detective novels, thrillers, comics, and so on.[3] But we might like to ask why the judgement is made in this way. The pleasures we gain from canonical and popular literary texts may be different, because we read them in different environments and for different reasons, but it is debatable what benefit comes from saying that one type of text is therefore better than another.

25.4 Judgements of value marginalize texts

Rather than considering the valuing process as something which simply focuses on what is good, we might instead say that evaluation functions to prevent books from being read. The fact that we study mainly canonical texts in school and higher education, for example, may mean that we do not give the same analytic or critical attention to the texts we read at home. This has the more general effect that the critical skills of literary analysis which we learn at school and university tend not to be used once we leave those institutions.

25.4.1 Women's writing

Feminist critics such as Elaine Showalter (1977) and Dale Spender (1986) have shown that women in the past have conventionally been discouraged from writing literary texts. There are several factors which led to women not considering writing to be an appropriate occupation. First, women were not allowed access to the literary and general education needed to write literary texts;

so it was primarily women of the upper classes, such as the Duchess of Newcastle, who wrote before the eighteenth and nineteenth centuries (when women began to write in large numbers). Second, writing was seen by society at large as a form of self-display, which could compromise the sexual reputation of women. Writing in the seventeenth century, for example, Katherine Philips was horrified when she found that some friends had published her poetry, since she was worried that her reputation would be ruined. Many women writing even during the nineteenth and twentieth centuries have done so under the cover of a male pseudonym (such as George Eliot, Georges Sand, Currer Bell) or else have given their name in a way which does not expose the author's gender (P.D. James, A.S. Byatt). As well as avoiding being accused of indecent behaviour, such writers are responding to the problem that their texts are likely to be judged as inferior simply on the basis of their sex. Indeed, Elizabeth Bishop's executors would only allow her poems to be included in an anthology of women's poetry if there was a statement made that she did not wish to be categorized as a woman poet (Adcock, 1987). Some critics even go so far as to argue that women cannot produce literature because their creative energies should be reserved for child-bearing (see Battersby, 1989). Women have been encouraged to see certain styles or less valued genres of writing as their domain (such as autobiography, religious and sentimental verse, letter writing, and so on) and, through a process of circular logic, their writing has been viewed as inferior because they have written within these genres. Women's poetry dealing with emotional responses to situations such as enforced partings, tragic death of loved ones, and so on, has been labelled 'sentimental' by many critics. Because many women poets of earlier centuries have written poems concerned with certain types of subject-matter, their work is considered less important – a contrast which is particularly clear between the work and reputations of Elizabeth Barrett Browning and Robert Browning, for example.

It is only since the 1980s, when women's studies courses began to become very common in Britain, that women's writing has been adequately represented within the curricula of schools and universities. The inclusion of women's writing, both in separate courses and within mainstream courses, was and still is the subject of sustained pressure and argument by feminist critics working within schools and universities. Many of the arguments about this under-representation have focused on the lack of availability of such texts, and thus it can be seen that external agencies such as publishers play a vital role in decisions about canonical status.

25.4.2 Black writing and literature in English

There has been a great deal of writing by Black people in English. Some of this writing is by Black British people, such as Caryl Phillips, Barbara Burford and Jackie Kay; some is by writers from countries which were colonized by

Britain, such as Chinua Achebe, Ngugi wa Thiong'o, and Buchi Emecheta, who have English as one of the languages available for literary writing. This literature in English is now beginning to be studied within schools or institutions of higher education. Because of a growth of interest in this writing and the post-colonial situation in general, there are now university departments devoted to the study of Black writing and literature in English. However, before the 1980s university departments of literature tended to concentrate on canonical literature and therefore had little time for other writing. It seems that traditional value judgements about what literature should be like have often excluded Black writing, in much the same way as they have often excluded women's writing.

25.4.3 Working-class writing

So few working-class writers make their way onto the syllabus of literature departments that it would be possible to believe that working-class people do not produce literature. If you were asked to name a working-class writer, you might cite D.H. Lawrence or Robert Burns. But there are very many other working-class novelists and poets, such as Margaret Harkness, Lewis Jones, Harold Heslop, Ethel Mannin, Ellen Wilkinson, James Hanley, and Robert Tressell. Writings by these authors seem to meet all the criteria of complexity, seriousness, and so on, and within the traditional value system they should be considered alongside canonical literature. Alternatively, it is possible to argue that they should be studied separately, rather than assuming that they should be considered to be of value only if they conform to models of bourgeois literature. It might be argued that in schools and universities students should study a full range of writing and not simply the writing of one particular class grouping.[4]

25.5 Alternatives to the canon

For many critics, it is difficult to imagine doing without the notion of a canon. It is for this reason that, when the canon has been challenged, critics have often attempted to set up a new one. Thus, Elaine Showalter, because of the exclusion of women writers from the mainstream canon, felt it necessary to set up an alternative canon exclusively for women writers. It must be stated, however, that this canon only included writing by white women. For many teachers, it also appears unthinkable that a syllabus could be constructed without some kind of canon. But since canons inevitably exclude writers as well as include them, we should now consider alternatives to the canon.

One alternative is to refuse to take part in the valuing process at all, and to simply give descriptive accounts of texts. Much structuralist criticism is based on the principle that it is possible to analyse the structure of a work without necessarily referring to the skill of the author, or suggesting that the work is therefore better than any other work. Another approach is, instead of studying canonical literature, to analyse a wider body of work, 'writing' or 'discourse'. From such a perspective, literary texts are still studied, but only within the context of other texts such as advertising, scientific texts, film, TV, popular literature, and so on. In this way similarities across genres and media can be analysed (in much the same way that we have adopted in this book). A third approach is, instead of analysing any given work as the product of an isolated genius, to analyse the socio-political and literary pressures on the writer to write in particular ways. While not reducing the writer to an automaton, this process recognizes that there are many factors which determine the way that the text is written which lie beyond the control of the writer or her/his conscious intentions. Finally, some critics have turned from the studying of literature to an analysis of the valuing process itself; they examine, as we have done here, why it is that certain texts are studied rather than others.

ACTIVITY 25.1

Read the two extracts below. The first is from a Mills & Boon novel, *Stolen Summer* by Anne Mather; the second is from *Women in Love* by D.H. Lawrence.

1   Which text do you think would generally be seen as of more value?

2   Make a note of differences between the two texts which might lead to their being considered of different value. (Pay special attention to the language of the texts; what you imagine to be their intended audience; critical reception; subject-matter, and so on.)

3   Make a note of similarities between the extracts which might lead you to question the notion that one of the texts is of more value.

Passage A

They were silent, enjoying the feel of the sun warming their bodies. 'Angharad . . . ?' She heard him gently speak her name. 'Yes?' She turned to him and gave a little gasp, freezing quite still. His face was only inches from hers, his blue eyes gleaming as they gazed at her mouth. Instinctively, her lips parted for his kiss, responding to it when it came as she had always responded; transmitting all the love in her heart. It was a gentle, almost lazy kiss, and all too soon it was over, and Saul was pulling her into the crook of his shoulder and settling down to sleep. Angharad could not sleep herself. She was far too aware of his near-naked body touching hers. She could feel his warmth burning through the thin cotton of her dress, and his heartbeat was close to her ear. Her head was filled with the musky scent of his aftershave as she lay still, tense and aware, aching with the need to reach out and touch him, to have him respond to her caresses.

(Anne Mather, *Stolen Summer*)

Passage B

'Is it you Ursula?' came Gudrun's frightened voice. He heard her sitting up in bed. In another moment she would scream.

'No, it's me,' he said, feeling his way towards her. 'It is I, Gerald.'

She lay motionless in her bed in sheer astonishment, too much taken by surprise, even to be afraid.

'Gerald!' she echoed in blank amazement. He had found his way to the bed, and his outstretched hand touched her warm breast blindly. She shrank away ...

He had come for vindication. She let him hold her in his arms, clasp her close against him. He found in her infinite relief. Into her he poured all his pent-up darkness and corrosive death, and he was whole again. It was wonderful, marvellous. It was a miracle. This was the ever-recurrent miracle of his life, at the knowledge of which he was lost in an ecstasy of relief and wonder. And she, subject, received him as a vessel filled with his bitter potion of death. She had no power at this crisis to resist.

(D.H. Lawrence, *Women in Love*)

Notes

1   'Canon' is a term which derives from Christian theology and refers to a set of writings which are considered to be genuine; in the literary context it refers to the set of authors who are considered to be great writers. See the section 'Questioning the canon', in Walder (1991), for a discussion of the term.

2   Before the National Curriculum, choices about which books and authors to include were largely determined by examination boards and individual teachers. It may be argued that, while the choice of authors for study now often includes some non-canonical writers, the number of authors chosen has been greatly restricted.

3   This is clearly not the case in Cultural Studies departments, nor in those English literature departments which have been influenced by theoretical work in cultural studies.

4   It might also be argued that gay and lesbian writing should be studied too (Bristow, 1992; Hobby and White, 1991).

Reading

Adcock, F. (ed.) (1987) *The Faber Book of 20th Century Women's Poetry*, London: Faber & Faber.

Barthes, R. (1986) *The Rustle of Language*, Oxford: Blackwell.

Battersby, C. (1989) *Gender and Genius: Towards a Feminist Aesthetics*, London: Women's Press.

Bristow, J. (ed.) (1992) *Sexual Sameness: Textual Differences in Lesbian and Gay Writing*, London: Routledge.

Culler, J. (1975) *Structuralist Poetics*, London: Routledge & Kegan Paul, especially Chapter 11, 'Structuralism and the qualities of literature' pp. 255–65.

Day, A. (1988) *Jokerman: Reading the Lyrics of Bob Dylan*, Oxford: Blackwell.

Eagleton, T. (1976) *Criticism and Ideology*, London: Verso, especially Chapter 5, 'Marxism and aesthetic value', pp. 162–87.

Eagleton, T. (1983) *Literary Theory: An Introduction*, Oxford: Blackwell, especially Chapter 1, pp. 10–16.

Foucault, M. (1986) 'What is an author?', in P. Rabinow (ed.) *The Foucault Reader*, London: Peregrine, pp. 101–20.

Hobby, E. and White, C. (eds) (1991) *What Lesbians Do in Books*, London: Women's Press.

Leavis, F.R. (1962) *The Great Tradition*, Harmondsworth: Penguin.

Leavis. F.R. (1978) *The Common Pursuit*, Harmondsworth: Penguin.

Raving Beauties (1983) *In the Pink: The Raving Beauties Choose Poems from the Show and Many More*, London: Women's Press.

Shklovsky, V. (1965) 'Art as technique', in L. Lemon and M. Reis (eds) *Russian Formalist Criticism: Four Essays*, Lincoln, Nebraska, pp. 3–24.

Showalter, E. (1977) *A Literature of their Own*, Princeton, NJ: Princeton University Press.

Sontag, S. (ed.) (1982) *Barthes: Selected Writings*, London: Collins.

Spender, D. (1986) *Mothers of the Novel*, London: Pandora.

Walder, D. (ed.) (1991) *Literature in the Modern World*, Oxford: Oxford University Press.

Unit 26

Literature in performance

Ask almost anyone what the main kinds of literature are and they will say novels, poems, and plays. (For discussion of literary types, see **Unit 17, Genre**.) Listing these three kinds together can nevertheless obscure questions about exactly what literature is. Is literature simply the historical accumulation of particular printed books? Or is it some practice, or body of insights or values, which is commonly stored in books but whose most important characteristics are nevertheless not to be found in the books themselves, but experienced instead in some other form (as may be suggested by the case of dramatic performance)?

One important aspect of this issue is medium – the distinction, for example, between print and speech (as explored in **Unit 19, Writing, speech and narration**). Much of the discourse which makes up what we usually think of as literary works is fixed as written text, even if one of our habitual ways of reading such writing is to imagine it as speech. But other kinds of discourse, especially those which notate speech for performance (as in the case of drama and of poetry to be read aloud), have to be recreated on each occasion of a work's performance. We should therefore ask: is there a performance dimension to what we think of as literature?

26.1 Text and performance

Consider this widely discussed problem: if nowadays people, especially young people, consume narrative and drama more in films and on television than in books or on the stage, and lyricism more in pop lyrics and other forms of recorded speech than in books, does it follow that literature is dying?

There are two main reasons for thinking that this question cannot be asked satisfactorily in this way. One reason is that texts traditionally recognized as being literary sometimes take oral, rather than written, form (as we can see in the case of poetry readings, audio cassettes of novels, and stage plays). The second reason is that conventionally literary texts can also be closely associated with other media, especially music (in the form of song). Literature may therefore not consist essentially of written discourse, even if it has strong connections with 'writing' both as a transcription or representation of earlier speech, and as a cue to speech which is to follow the written representation.

26.1.1 Oral literature

In many oral societies (that is, societies which do not employ writing as a system of representation), stories and lyricism are presented in memorized and extensively improvised speech performances. Such standardized oral forms are often called 'oral literature', a term which can at first seem paradoxical: the word 'oral' means to do with the spoken; by contrast the etymology of 'literature' in *litterae* (Latin: 'letters') suggests a central preoccupation with, or existence in, the written form. Composition of oral literature in oral societies often takes place as a communal practice of improvisation. It is only with transition to a substantially literate society – especially one which develops institutions of print literacy – that the modern category of the author emerges (see **Unit 24, Authorship and intention**).

Oral composition takes place not only in those societies which may seem remote from 'literary' production (though even in the late twentieth century only a small minority of languages in the world have a written form). The classical Greek culture of Homer of around the eighth century BC – which is often considered a key moment in the development of Western, writing-based literature – emerged prior to the development of writing (see Ong, 1982). The elaborate patterning of poetic language found in Homer's epics, the *Iliad* and the *Odyssey*, appears to have been developed over many generations by performing bards. Writing was not commonly used at the time for literary purposes, so these bards recited without the aid of a written text. Instead of composing and memorizing fixed works, they built up a large stock of verbal formulas that enabled them, by altering and recombining elements to suit the context, to improvise long poems more or less spontaneously. In this way, the poems which are attributed to Homer may be substantially a written record – a transcript – of earlier, oral production.

Yet practices of oral composition are not necessarily historically remote. Nor do they take place exclusively in those cultures that do not use writing. Oral traditions may be found in industrialized, especially multicultural societies where they flourish alongside conventionally written literatures. In Britain, poets, especially poets with Caribbean origins or links (e.g. Grace Nichols or John Agard), recite in ways that emphasize oral tradition and performance as well as publishing poetry collections in print. Story-telling traditions, often including extemporization from Africa, the Indian sub-continent, and among Native Americans, co-exist with promotional readings from published novels by authors in bookshops and at literary festivals. Several generations of performed 'pop' poetry have also existed in Britain: Liverpool poets (alongside Merseybeat pop music in the 1960s); Punk poets during the 1970s; and recently a growing number of alternative, improvisatory poetry performance clubs on both sides of the Atlantic.

26.1.2 Literature and sound

Oral performances often involve more than simply the human voice. They may involve other kinds of sound (as well as images and design). Speech on the stage or in clubs – as in face-to-face situations – is combined with other signals (including facial expression, gesture, and posture). In film and television narrative, speech may be accompanied by a soundtrack made up of backing music and sound effects, some of which emerge from the represented field of action (so-called 'diegetic' sound), while other effects are superimposed as a separate layer, not audible to characters within the action but only to the audience, as a kind of reinforcement of or commentary on what is going on ('non-diegetic' sound).

Just as 'oral literature' is a paradoxical term, so too is 'lyricism'. The muses of Classical Greece were thought to preside over various verbal arts, each of which was accompanied by types of music or instrument: flutes, choral songs and dance, and music on the lyre (leading directly into the word 'lyric'). In medieval France, lyric forms such as the canzone and rondeau were developed by troubadours and trouvères for singing; and in Germany the early singing lyricists were called minnesingers. During the sixteenth and seventeenth centuries in Britain, the term lyric was applied to verse that was sung (as in madrigals or the songs of poet-singers and composers like Thomas Campion or John Dowland), but also increasingly to verse that was not sung.

In the late twentieth century, popular music combines lyricism with new forms of accompaniment. Mostly, combinations of words and music take the form of singing. But, growing out of traditions of toasters and other DJs (especially in the Caribbean and among African-Americans), forms of highly accentuated speaking have come to prominence in mainstream media. Rap vocals typically emphasize rhythmic complexity or syncopation of speech over melody or harmony. Linking these popular traditions with more conventionally literary expectations, some poets perform with backing bands (as Linton Kwesi Johnson and Benjamin Zephaniah have); and some singer-songwriters have been widely considered to be poets (Bob Dylan, Suzanne Vega, etc.). Such performers blur conventional boundaries between verbal and other (audio and audio-visual) arts, as well as boundaries between high and popular culture.

26.2 Understanding orality and literacy as regards literature

Complications about what literature is in terms of medium can lead into two conflicting myths. What might be called a myth of orality is created when special value is placed on the presumed power of speech to offer direct expression of the self, unmediated by the secondary system of writing, and to produce a unique intimacy or communion between speaker and hearer or hearers. Often, such oral expression is also assumed to reinforce an imagined, organic or fundamentally united society. It is not uncommon among poets, for instance, to aspire to such immediacy of poetic speech (and the integral role in society for the poet which goes with it), rather than suffering the presumed alienation which attaches to written traditions. In drama, plays in print can be viewed as notations brought to life only in performance. Rehearsals are then seen as adaptations or interpretations of the text, not just an enactment of it: actors' steps are blocked out; lines are not only learned, but changed and deleted. Dramatic literature on this view – and other literature in a corresponding, if less visible way – is regarded as spoken performance and action, which is merely echoed in the notational form of writing.

This myth of orality collides, however, with a conflicting myth about writing. Until the advent of films and sound recording, there was no way of replicating a performance permanently (rather than reproducing it in a transcribed form). By contrast with the fleeting or ephemeral nature of speech, a book is somehow forever. Written and printed texts become revered historical documents and are often assumed to be of higher cultural status than hearsay, or reports of speech. Special authority is attached to religious, legal and constitutional documents. (Consider in this context also the use of the word 'canon' to describe collections of literary, as well as religious, works.) Because of such reverence for written texts, any alteration to a historical text is likely to be considered disrespectful and inappropriate, by comparison with more respectable efforts to discover its original meaning.

These two viewpoints (which may be considered myths to the extent that they are powerful but not fully sustainable stories about speech and writing) contrast strikingly. Despite their divergence, however, they coincide to some extent in the act of reading itself. Even considered narrowly as construing words on a page, reading has many properties of a performance: the text is used as a sort of notation to be realized in a performed interpretation; it has a specific duration, in that reading is a time-based activity; and it varies between different performers and occasions (as different readings are produced). Yet while reading may be performance, it may be thought still only performance in miniature by comparison with a poetry reading or dramatic performance: in those cases, the written, notated form is not just performed, from the page, by an individual reader, it is linked up with other sign-systems (such as body language and gesture, lighting, costume, props, make-up, and special effects), and directs a number of people through the more complex interactions of a public occasion or institution.

26.3 Meanings of performance

As used in this unit so far, performance is a highly general term, and opens up two main dimensions of contrast between literature in print and literature in performance. In one contrast, performance signals 'live action', performed on a unique occasion and unrepeatable in exact form, as opposed to written literature's stability as a permanent and repeatable representation. In the other contrast, performance may be either live or recorded; its distinctive feature is that, unlike written literature's use of a narrower repertoire of punctuation, typeface, and other graphic features, performance draws simultaneously on a wide range of sign-systems. Each of these contrasts is now considered in more detail.

26.3.1 'Live' and recorded

'Live' speech – performed language – includes public speaking, reciting poems, making phone calls, teleconferencing, phone-in radio shows, live action sports coverage, and stage-drama. Some types of such 'live' speech are scripted in advance; other kinds are improvised on the spot. In either case, what is important about performance of such speech is that it is specific to a given occasion, and momentary. Performance relies on particular agents or performers for its existence; and if you miss something, e.g. because of background noise, then you can't recover what you haven't heard by turning back a page or winding back the tape. Often it is interactive, like dialogue: what is said is replied to and conversation moves on. When we think of texts, on the other hand, we typically think of more fixed representations, without immediate opportunity for reply: a written or printed document; a film, audio or video cassette; a CD or CD-ROM; a document file or minimally interactive, informational web-page.

The distinction between live and recorded speech doesn't coincide neatly with the distinction between speech and writing. Rather, many performed and broadcast texts combine modes associated with both speech and writing. Speech becomes 'writing' when it is recorded; it can then be stored, played back identically, and also copied and distributed. Conversely, kinds of writing (in this sense of permanent and reproducible texts) tend towards imitating speech in the case of talking clocks and message services, Internet chatrooms, and continuously updated data displays such as airport flight announcement boards and interactive, live web-sites.

Because 'speech' and 'writing' in these extended senses are superimposed on each other, what we understand by live performance alters. Uniqueness of occasion may be regarded as a special value, rather than merely an inevitable aspect of the experience (as it was before writing, printing, or audio and visual recording). Multiple, uniform copies of an original are easily produced and distributed and this can affect both the economic and symbolic value of a single 'original' or limited edition. Such changes have deep and continuing effects on our discourse environment, especially as regards what is considered textual value and what constitutes an art-work.

26.4 Performance's repertoire of signs

The various sign-systems which accompany speech in performance can all be analysed. Each field of stylistic choices (between bright or soft lighting, or between different coloured backgrounds at a political rally, etc.) involves a grammar (see **Unit 3, Analysing units of structure**). Units can be identified and rules of possible combination for them described (as Roland Barthes and others attempted to do in order to develop a culturally critical semiology, or science of signs). Conventional meanings for units can be ascertained, which are then employed (but also undermined and deviated from) in patterns of usage and for particular, local effects (see **Unit 12, Deviation**).

26.4.1 Speech and dialogue

Performed speech differs from written text. Most obviously, tempo, pauses, accent, and intonation (collectively, what are called language's prosodic and paralinguistic systems) add emphasis and signal a speaker's attitudes towards what is being said. In the theatre voices have to fill a large auditorium, and so a specialized, theatrical kind of projected speech tends to be produced: speech which is often declamatory, ritualistic, or incantatory in ways which overlap with song (and with recitative in opera). In different periods, efforts to mirror conversational styles in theatrical performances have varied. But even where dialogue does closely simulate speech (as in many films), such speech is always imitated stylistically, never matched precisely, as becomes quickly evident if you compare the extent of pauses, repetitions, and local incoherence in real conversation with the polished nature of dialogue, sifted so that dramatically significant details can be emphasized (for a discussion of differences between conversation and written dialogue, see **Unit 19, Writing, speech and narration**).

Intonation, accent, and qualities of voice are not the only meaning-bearing aspects of performed speech. In addition, utterances which make up dramatic dialogue – like conversation in this respect – signal verbal actions: of ordering, apologizing, greeting, promising, requesting, etc. These verbal actions are called performatives, or more generally speech acts: each speech act of this kind has a conventional force (though the words don't necessarily indicate directly the force they will have on a given occasion of utterance). Specific patterns of speech acts move dramatic situations and action forward; in fact in many cases verbal acts are the key actions of a play (e.g. threatening something, professing love, renouncing a kingdom). By investigating the speech acts performed in dramatic dialogue, it becomes possible to formulate generalizations about a speaker's role in a given situation (e.g. one character consistently requests or gives orders; another consistently apologizes). In recent stage-drama, nevertheless, it has been as much the breakdown of communication and inarticulacy of characters as the successful handling of situations which has been the focus of interest – how speech acts go astray or fail to work (especially in writing by such dramatists as Samuel Beckett, Tom Stoppard, or Harold Pinter).

26.4.2 Characters

Speech, then, is central to the performance of poetry and drama. A great deal of theatre works, in fact, without much use of scenery or special effects, relying almost entirely on the performance of speech. In dramatic monologues in poetry, too, such as Robert Browning's 'My Last Duchess' (1842), the particular importance of speech in creating an image of the speaker is clearly shown: a first-person voice is created which suggests a specific speaker (the Duke), depicts a specific situation (the last Duchess has been murdered on the Duke's personal order on account of his suspicions about her), and evokes a particular period and place – all separate from the poet's own circumstances – without use of any theatrical effects at all.

Dramatic monologue may in this respect be thought of as an isolated segment of dramatic dialogue, whose performance involves impersonation, or acting out the complex features we think of as indicating subjectivity. In many styles of drama (especially attempts at psychological realism, as in Strindberg or Ibsen), great effort is made to achieve the consistency of verbal style that can make a character believable, alongside distinct physical attributes and mannerisms.

However convincing they may appear, nevertheless, created characters need to be distinguished from the author. The overall point of view created in a play as a whole, for instance, must lie beyond what any one character says, and can only be determined by examining the interaction between all the characters as expressed in the action as much as in dialogue and direct speeches to the audience (even apparently self-revealing cases of **soliloquy**).

26.4.3 Acting

For actors themselves, emphasis may not be placed particularly on how various conventional signs which indicate character work. The Russian theatre director Konstantin Stanislavsky (1863–1938), for example, developed the attention to verbal subtlety for which he is noted by demonstrating how an actor could, by focusing on a deep emotional experience in the past, stimulate a similar emotional state in the present and channel it towards the requirements of a particular scene. Stanislavsky's approach is reported from a different perspective by the linguist Roman Jakobson, in an anecdote about an actor being required at audition to depict forty distinct situations simply by saying the Russian words for 'This evening' (Jakobson, 1987: 67). In modified form, some of Stanislavsky's ideas have become more familiar since the 1940s in what is called 'method acting'. In this approach, an actor tries as far as possible to draw on personal experience and emotion as the basis for the character being portrayed.

By emphasizing 'being someone', method acting illustrates a more general point. It reflects the aspiration in much dramatic performance towards representing characters in a naturalistic way. This aspiration contrasts with an alternative notion of characterization associated with the German dramatist Bertolt Brecht (1898–1956). Brecht preferred to see characters as representatives of classes and of struggle between classes. He required actors to stand outside the parts they were playing, in order to present more dispassionately the arguments of a play (and so to 'show someone' rather than 'be someone'). By such means Brecht sought what has been called an 'alienation' effect, in which an audience's sense of illusion is disturbed in order that they should attain sudden states of awareness and readiness for social action.

26.4.4 Theatre

While much of the force of dramatic action is carried by speech, what most visibly distinguishes theatrical productions from one another are the various design resources they adopt. Production conventions reflect a complex history of the theatre as a social institution, and have emerged from an interaction between very different influences, including that of liturgical drama; carnivals, festivals, and performances in market squares; private, participatory court masques; and conventions of public theatres over several centuries. In modern theatre productions, as a result, a wide range of resources is available, ranging from costume, lighting, and sound effects to ramps, archways and trapdoors for entrances and exits.

Such techniques can seem simply a matter of performance style. But they also contribute to important dimensions of drama in at least two ways. First, differences between production techniques display production values, or priorities set for spending money from a finite budget, given a diversity of different demands. (Production values also need to be examined as regards editions of books; but they tend to be more visible in performances because of the physical presence of so many of the practitioners and production elements.) Should the production spend its money on a small number of expensive star actors? Or cheaper actors but a lavish set? On specially composed accompanying music, or on purchasing exhibition rights for existing music? Production values in this way mark an intersection between compositional and institutional aspects of performance.

Second, particular kinds of staging construct a relation which is set up between the audience and dramatized action, involving a continuum from active audience participation through to accentuated separation of the audience from the performing area. Such relations are reflected in stage shapes, such as theatre-in-the-round or the three-quarter round ('thrust') stage, which offer lines of viewing across the acting area (and also more scope for joining in). Such arrangements contrast with use of the proscenium arch, or hole in an end-wall through which an audience views the dramatic action. The arch simultaneously separates spectators from the action and also frames the performed action in a way that more narrowly specifies the audience's point of view (both literally in terms of sight and also in terms of the interpretive position on what is going on which the audience is encouraged to adopt). In this respect, the proscenium arch may be regarded as a significant precursor of cinema layout, which combines darkness and the notion of an invisible viewer into a distinct form of spectatorship.

26.5 Excerpt from Shakespeare

The various performance considerations discussed so far determine the texture of a dramatic production continuously, rather than being occasional or special features. How far such considerations extend back into the planning and composition of a play can be illustrated by considering an extract from a minor scene in Shakespeare's *Antony and Cleopatra* (c. 1607) that is set apart from the play's big speeches or main action. The scene depicts a group of sentries on night-watch between two major battles.

[*Music of the hautboys is under the stage*]

2 Soldier: Peace! What noise?
1 Soldier: List, list!
2 Soldier: Hark!
1 Soldier: Music i'th'air.
3 Soldier: Under the earth.
4 Soldier: It signs well, does it not?
3 Soldier: No.
1 Soldier: Peace, I say! What should this mean?
2 Soldier: 'Tis the god Hercules whom Antony loved
           Now leaves him.
1 Soldier: Walk. Let's see if other watchmen
           Do hear what we do.
2 Soldier: How now, masters?   [*Speak together*]

ALL: How now? How now? Do you hear this?
1 Soldier: Ay. Is't not strange?
3 Soldier: Do you hear, masters? Do you hear?
1 Soldier: Follow the noise so far as we have quarter.
            Let's see how it will give off.
ALL: Content. 'Tis strange.
            [*Exeunt*]

                                    (*Antony and Cleopatra*, IV, 3, 13–30)

The excerpt presented here differs from the earliest printed versions. It has
been modernized, as can be seen from the following, corresponding lines from
the First Folio edition (1623):

2: Peace, what noife?
1   Lift lift.
2   Hearke.
1   Muficke i'th'Ayre.
3   Vnder the earth.
4   It fignes well, do's it not?

Such modernization of the language extends even to the title itself: Antony is
spelled both as 'Anthony' and 'Anthonie' within the same Folio edition. The
presentation of lines as verse, together with the act and scene divisions,
have been regularized by later editors; and because of language change, some
vocabulary items invite editorial assistance ('hautboys' are oboes; 'list' means
'listen'; 'signs well' means 'is a good omen'). If we are to revere the authenticity and authority of Shakespeare's text, therefore, as opposed to considering
it simply as notation which gives access to the drama, then we need to
remember that the textual identity of a written text can itself involve complicated questions.

Even in the brief extract quoted, different types of speech act are evident,
with different roles in the unfolding action: questions, commands, and assertions. In the line to be said by 'All', the utterance is collective rather than
individual. This use of collective rather than individual speech not only reflects
a more ritualized, conventional speech style (that of a sort of chorus), rather
than depiction of any particular character; it also indicates what sort of characters the sentries are. Major historical figures, such as Antony or Cleopatra,
are contrasted here with an unnamed group of type-characters. Generally,
before the twentieth century, such characters feature in drama in one of three
ways (or some combination between these ways): as part of a broad social
tableau; in order, collectively, to express popular sentiment; or as servants and
dependants of the protagonists. Significant dramatic action, by contrast, focuses
on figures who exhibit conflict, tension, contrast and emotion (that is, 'dramatic'
elements); such characters are typically members of the monarchy or nobility

– indeed, the play's title itself draws attention only to Antony and Cleopatra's tragedy. (This dimension of tragedy in particular – that tragic things only happen to certain social classes – is questioned and radically changed in modern tragedy, see Williams, 1966.)

But if the sentries aren't on stage as characters in their own right, what are they doing there? Collectively they signal a counterpoint of moods (between the urgency of battle and periods of quiet between battles, as well as between the staged darkness of night and light of morning). The scene may also serve practical needs of performance, including actors resting or changing costume and stage props. In addition, the soldiers' conversation invites dramatic irony. When the sentries ask whether the omens are good, the outcome of the subsequent battle is anticipated; but it is also suggested that Antony's guardian deity, Hercules, is deserting him (see **Unit 14**, **Irony**).

26.6 Modern productions

Larger questions also need to be asked: why should a drama about Antony and Cleopatra (historical figures from nearly two thousand years ago) be put on the stage, either in Shakespeare's time (the first few years of the seventeenth century) or since? Because performances take place at a particular time and for particular audiences, they have to meet the challenge of being in some way relevant to those audiences. Newly composed plays respond to this challenge by updating styles and tackling new subjects, as well as by repeating successful formulas (see **Unit 17**, **Genre**) – though there is also a corresponding history of subjects not considered performable, including controversies about depictions of sexuality, religion, certain political topics, particular kinds of language, on-stage nudity, etc.

At different times, Cleopatra's life and her relationship with Antony have formed the basis for many literary works, including John Dryden's play *All for Love* (1678) and George Bernard Shaw's *Caesar and Cleopatra* (1906), besides Shakespeare's own play. A number of film and television versions have also been made. In addition to drawing on the traditional status of earlier stories, writers in different periods create new kinds of relevance for them by combining the re-telling of a conventional narrative with re-interpreting its themes or significance (see **Unit 16**, **Intertextuality and allusion**). But this still leaves the question of fresh productions of already existing plays, where dialogue, symbolism and point of view might be thought already determined by the words on the page. Why do theatre companies re-work Shakespeare's *Antony and Cleopatra* in modern productions?

One common answer is associated with the Polish critic Jan Kott. Countering earlier orthodoxies which emphasized the immortality or universality of Shakespeare, Kott stressed a continuing renewal and redirection of plays in new productions directed at specific cultural moments, making

Shakespeare always 'our contemporary' (Kott, 1967). Performances of Shakespeare's *The Merchant of Venice*, for instance, were presented in Nazi Germany both to express and to encourage anti-Semitism, while aspects of Shakespeare's history and Roman plays have been presented as allegories of political power in a number of modern totalitarian states. A wide range of such connections between Shakespeare's plays and changing social circumstances is conceivable.

What Kott outlines can be seen as a general characteristic of dramatic performances: that they exploit the notation provided by a written text in order to engage with an audience's contemporary search for relevance based on that audience's background knowledge, experience, beliefs, and desires. It is highly likely, therefore, that the publicity notices for the 1999 production of Shakespeare's *Antony and Cleopatra* in the newly reconstructed Globe Theatre, London – which seem to combine usually antithetical styles of humanist essay and tabloid feature – are quite different from how the play was presented on the occasion of its probable first performances at the original Globe Theatre around 1607–1608:

> In the power struggle following Julius Caesar's death, the great warrior and champion of Rome, Antony, becomes the irrational betrayer of his Roman honour, deserting his wife and making war on Octavius Caesar. [...] Is his love for the reckless and intoxicating Queen of Egypt, Cleopatra, foolishly human or transcendent and redemptive?

26.7 Speaking parts and technologies of reproduction

Conventions of performance are not static. As well as affecting dramatic speech, costume, and scenery, such changes also reflect the particular delivery systems available for what might be called performed literature (see **Unit 21, Narration in film and prose fiction**). If film and television can be seen to achieve more successfully some of the effects previously sought by stage drama (e.g. intimate speech spoken intimately rather than in stage voice, or facial expression depicted in close-up), then other questions follow. What directions will performance move in, now that performed speech can be textualized (as it is in film, audio cassettes and easily edited digital sound files)? How far will stage drama continue to seek illusionistic or naturalistic effects?

One alternative to naturalism can be found in the theatrical tradition derived from Brecht, which assumes that when contradictions, rather than an illusion of reality, are exhibited in a performance, members of the audience are obliged to pause and reflect. Another alternative can be found in the absurdist tradition derived from Ionesco, Beckett, and others, in which cause and effect are dissolved, language and character become empty games, and dramatic performance explores unspecified, surreal or allegorical settings. Alongside these possibilities, drama may focus increasingly on the act of performance itself, including its historical connections with dance, juggling, mime, and spectacle.

ACTIVITY 26.1

In this activity we return to the drama of the late Elizabethan period in order to ask questions about the changing significance (and scope for interpretation) of plays.

In 1595 the playwright, literary patron and translator Mary Herbert Sidney, Countess of Pembroke (1561–1621), published *The Tragedy of Antonie*, 'done into English' from a French original by Robert Garnier. (The translation had been published earlier, in a slightly different version and with a different title, in 1592.)

The play tells the story of Antony and Cleopatra, focusing on Cleopatra's side of the story. The excerpt below is from Act V when, after hearing of Antony's death and facing imminent capture at Alexandria, Cleopatra takes leave of her children before committing suicide. Characters in the excerpt are listed at the beginning of the play as: Cleopatra herself; Eras and Charmion, described as 'Cleopatra's women'; and 'Cleopatra's children'.

Cleopatra:	Farewell, my babes, farewell, and bend to force of fate.
	With pity and pain, myself with death enclosed.
	My breath doth fail. Farewell for evermore;
	Your sire and me you shall never see more.
	Farewell, sweet care, farewell.
Children:	Madam, adieu.
Cleopatra:	Ah this voice kills me. Ah, good gods, I swoon!
	I can no more, I die!
Eras:	Madam, alas!
	And will you yield to woe? Ah, speak to us!
Euphron:	Come, children.
Children:	We come.
Euphron:	Follow we our chance.
	The gods shall guide us.
[*Exit Euphron and the children*]
Charmion:	O too cruel lot!
	O too hard chance! Sister, what shall we do,
	What shall we do, alas, if murdering dart
	Of death arrive while that in slumbering swoon
	Half dead she lie with anguish overgone?

Eras:	Her face is frozen.
Charmion:	Madam, for god's love
	Leave us not thus; bid us yet first farewell.
	Alas, weep over Antonie; let not
	His body be without due rites entombed.
Cleopatra:	Ah, ah!
Charmion:	Madam.
Cleopatra:	Ah, me!
Charmion:	How faint she is!
Cleopatra:	My sisters, hold me up! How wretched I,
	How cursed, am; and was there ever one
	By fortune's hate into more dolours thrown?

(Act V, 1, 73–94)

1   Consider each speaking-turn in the extract in terms of what act it performs
(e.g. question, command, assertion, etc.). Does the distribution of such
speech acts between the various characters suggest anything about the
main interest of the drama at this point (remember: this is only a short
extract from a longer scene)? Do any of the characters speak less than
you would have expected? Do any speak more?

2   Now distinguish different, more general types of dramatic speech. Use a
contrast between (relatively) individualized, naturalistic speech and
more conventional or ritualized speech. Note features that lead you to
consider any given utterance as being towards one end or the other of
this spectrum. (For help with this task, see **Unit 6**, **Language and context:
register**.)

3   Identify aspects of the excerpt which might present particular problems
in a modern performance (e.g. things that are difficult to say, or uncon-
vincing in the tone evidently required). Do these points of potential
difficulty for a modern production tell us anything about language
change? Or about changing dramatic conventions? Or about changes in
audience expectation or taste?

4   Which of the following strategies would it be appropriate to use to try to
overcome the difficulties you have identified in question 3?

   (a)   Change the words of the dialogue, editing out whatever causes the
         difficulties?
   (b)   Encourage actors to overcome difficulties with sensitive pauses and
         intonation, while keeping exactly to the written text?
   (c)   Treat the passage ironically, presenting it as mock-serious or as in
         some other way 'theatrical'?

Can you think of other interpretive production strategies that might be appropriate here?

5   Now consider the following information about Mary Sidney, as background to the remaining tasks.

> Mary Sidney was part of a famous literary family. She was related to other celebrated Elizabethan literary figures, including Sir Philip Sidney, her brother (whose style she is sometimes thought to have tried to imitate after his death in 1586), and also to Mary Wroth. Among other writers besides Mary Sidney and Shakespeare who composed plays dealing with the Antony and Cleopatra story during the period, the writer Samuel Daniel – an associate of Sir Philip Sidney – wrote a companion piece to Mary Sidney's, called *Cleopatra*. At the beginning of his play, Daniel celebrates the private, aristocratic performance of plays as opposed to public performance in the theatre. In the essay, 'Seneca in Elizabethan Translation' (1927), T.S. Eliot comments that 'It was after Sidney's death, that his sister, the Countess of Pembroke, tried to assemble a body of wits to compose drama in the proper Senecan style, to make head against the popular melodrama of the time.'
>
> In 1575, following the established social behaviour of her class, Mary Sidney married Henry Herbert, Earl of Pembroke. She was 15, he was 50. When the Earl of Pembroke died in 1601, Mary Sidney took on the public behaviour of a conventional widow. But court correspondence suggests that she then had a long affair with a physician, Sir Matthew Lister, ten years younger than herself, before being buried, finally, alongside her husband in Salisbury Cathedral when she died in 1621.
>
> Mary Sidney is credited as the translator of this play ('done into English'), rather than as its author. This is despite substantial changes made to Robert Garnier's *Marc Antoine* (1592) in her translation. (Remember: Shakespeare didn't invent the stories for all his plays either.) Patron, editor, and translator were all more accepted roles for a woman than that of playwright; Mary Sidney could not have put the play on in public as her own invention without risking her reputation. Even so, by standards of the day Sidney is thought to have presented herself at court less as a wife and mother of four than as a literary thinker in her own right.
>
> Among the ways Mary Sidney changed Garnier's play are the following: she used blank verse rather than the more formulaic alexandrine metre of the original; in doing so, she seems to make Cleopatra a more believable and sympathetic protagonist, rather than a stereotypical stage villainess; she also foregrounds women

characters in the play generally, and presents them more sympathetically than in other, roughly contemporaneous versions of the story.

6   Assuming that such information (which comes from commonly available reference sources, and is partly interpretive, partly speculative) is well founded, compare the following three views about modern productions of the play:

(a)   This complicated background should be incorporated into modern performances; Mary Sidney is in important ways 'our contemporary', and this should be shown when the play is produced.

(b)   Emphasizing modern elements in historically remote plays risks reducing the past to a reflection of the present. Instead, modern productions should signal, rather than disguise, the historical remoteness of the play, so that its performance offers an opportunity to engage with aspects of a historically distant world.

(c)   These two views are not contradictory; they can be reconciled. (Describe as far as you can how you believe this might be done.)

7   At least two recent films based on new scripts – rather than productions of existing dramas – deal directly with women's social position in Elizabethan public life. One is *Elizabeth* (dir. Shekhar Kapur, 1998), which deals with political unease during the early years of the reign of Elizabeth I, including the queen's relationship with Essex and the threat of rebellion. The other film is *Shakespeare in Love* (dir. John Maddon, 1998; script co-written by Tom Stoppard). The latter film suggests that Shakespeare's writing of *Romeo and Juliet* may have been linked to an actual love affair. In the light of your answers to question 6, how do you think explorations of such themes in films devised and produced at the end of the twentieth century can compare with re-reading history through new productions of plays written during the period itself? (You can answer this question in general terms even if you haven't seen either of the two films.)

8   Finally, is there any alternative to performances which take into account features of the present as well as features of the time of composition (whether ten years ago or one thousand years ago)? What criteria might be formulated for a historically 'authentic' performance of a text? (Use similarities and differences between the case of plays and that of cover versions of records as a loose analogy, if you find this helpful.)

Reading

Cerasano, S.P. and Wynne-Davies, M. (1996) *Renaissance Drama by Women: Texts and Documents*, London: Routledge.

Jakobson, R. (1987) *Language in Literature*, Cambridge, MA: Belknap Press of Harvard University Press.

Kott, J. (1967) *Shakespeare Our Contemporary*, London: Methuen. First published in Polish in 1964.

Ong, W.J. (1982) *Orality and Literacy: The Technologizing of the Word*, New York and London: Methuen.

Williams, R. (1966) *Modern Tragedy*, London: Chatto & Windus.

Unit 27

Ways of reading
non-literary texts

In this book we have examined ways of reading texts mostly of a literary kind. We have assumed that recognizing the intricate or unusual ways in which literary texts are organized contributes to, and enhances, our understanding of them; we have also thereby in effect assumed that literary texts are a special kind of text. Yet at the same time we have made passing reference throughout the book to non-literary examples, such as railway passenger announcements, legal texts, adverts and film images. We have done so in the belief that our understanding of the workings of a literary text is complemented by understanding how texts in general work – and vice versa. In this unit, therefore, we wish to explore in a little more detail some of the areas of convergence and divergence between literary and other types of text, and to examine, more systematically, strategies for the analysis of non-literary text (focusing particularly, for illustrative purposes, on newspaper headlines).

27.1 Literary and non-literary texts

Section 3 of this book, Analysing Poetic Form, suggests that literary texts differ from non-literary texts by virtue of the nature and extent of their linguistic patterning. In literature – particularly in poetry – extra patterning occurs, for example, through parallelism, alliteration, rhythm and rhyme. In addition, literature breaks with the patterns of everyday linguistic usage through deviant syntax, strange vocabulary or specialized layout. In short, literature is the domain of pattern-making and/or pattern-breaking.

This kind of approach to the distinctive nature of literature, however, stresses particularly its poetic dimension. A complementary approach that emerges in Section 5, Aspects of Narrative, places greater emphasis on the different functions of literary discourse when compared with everyday discourse. Typical functions of everyday discourse include representing the world in descriptions, averrals, assertions, etc., and modifying or affecting the behaviour of others in commands, requests, instructions, etc.: either words are being used to refer to states of affairs in the world or an attempt is being made to change states of affairs in the world through words. Literary discourse, however, functions neither to describe the world that exists nor immediately to affect it. Its function seems to be to narrate and describe a *possible* world – a world that might, but does not necessarily, exist – in such a way as to 'make strange' or 'defamiliarize' the world of everyday experience.

Even so, it is difficult to make a hard and fast distinction between texts which are literary and texts which are not. Some features that we associate strongly with literature and which have been the focus of units in this book also occur in other kinds of discourse. Take, for instance, **parallelism** – the focus of **Unit 11** – which is an obvious feature of the following lines from an untitled poem by Shelley:

> One word is too often profaned
> For me to profane it;
> One feeling too falsely disdained
> For thee to disdain it;
> One hope is too like despair
> For prudence to smother;
> And pity from thee more dear
> Than that from another.

At a syntactic level the first four lines are built up from a repetition of a basic pattern as follows:

> One –X– (is) too –Y– –Z–ed
> For –M– to –Z– it;

(where X = noun; Y = adverb; Z = verb stem; and M = personal pronoun).

This very tight patterning is relaxed in the last four lines of the poem; and, indeed, the last two lines are different enough in their patterning for them to be interpreted as some kind of semantic reversal of, or at least a contrast in meaning with, the poem's opening. This elaborate kind of organization – supported, of course, by other kinds of parallel patterning such as rhyme, rhythm and alliteration – is just the kind of device which we associate with literature in general and the poetic function in particular.

Yet very similar kinds of artful patterning can be found in other kinds of discourse. Take, for instance, the following portion of a political speech from a general election campaign:

We are ruled by a government
whose rhetoric is resolution
but whose reality is industrial ruin,
whose rhetoric is efficiency
but whose reality is collapse.
Their rhetoric is morality.
Their reality is unemployment,
which splits and scatters families.

The verbal parallelism in this speech is similar to that in the poem, here used
for strongly contrastive purposes:

whose rhetoric is A
but whose reality is B
whose rhetoric is C
but whose reality is D

In addition to the noticeable syntactic patterning, we also find extra sound
patterns, for instance in the half-rhymes of *reality* (used three times) with *efficiency* and *morality* and the alliteration of *r*uled, *r*hetoric, *r*esolution, *r*eality,
*r*uin, as well as the semi-alliteration of *s*plits and *s*catters.

A similar patterning of sound and syntax may also be found in the
following piece of magazine advertising copy, promoting fragrance:

The perfume you wear says a lot about you.
The range we have says something about us.
Nothing triggers memories as strongly as scent.
Just a hint of a familiar fragrance brings back that time,
                                    that place,
                                    that person.

Names are forgettable.
Even photos fade.
But perfume lingers.

Again the text is structured around syntactic patterns – 'that time, that place,
that person', 'photos fade . . . perfume lingers' – sometimes reinforced by alliteration and semi-alliteration – '*f*amiliar *f*ragrance . . . *ph*otos *f*ade'.

Advertising, political rhetoric and poetry would seem, on the face of it,
to be very different kinds of discourse and so it may be surprising to find similar
verbal strategies at play in all of them. On further consideration, however,
it is possible to see continuities between these different kinds of discourse.
They all depend to some extent upon heightening the language to make it more
memorable or effective. Perhaps not surprisingly, then, similar strategies

of parallelism and repetition can be found in religious language. Take the following well-known lines from the Old Testament:

1   To every thing there is a season, and a time to every purpose under the heaven:

2   A time to be born, and a time to die;
     A time to plant, and a time to pluck up that which is planted;

3   A time to kill, and a time to heal;
     A time to break down, and a time to build up;

4   A time to weep, and a time to laugh;
     A time to mourn, and a time to dance ...

(Ecclesiastes 3: 1–4)

Each of the verses 2, 3, and 4 (and the verses that follow the extract) are built primarily on parallel structures ('a time to X, and a time to Y'), involving a contrast (birth versus death, planting versus uprooting, killing versus healing, tears versus laughter, mourning versus dancing). The contrasts are accentuated by the parallelism, but each parallelism is itself in turn made parallel with another: for instance, 'A time to weep, and a time to laugh' is made parallel with 'A time to mourn, and a time to dance'. Similar patterns may be found in related books of the Old Testament, where they are used to reinforce a statement of similarity on the one hand or difference on the other. Many of the statements in the Book of Proverbs, for instance, take the form of two parts, as in the following:

The false witness shall not go unpunished,
the man who utters lies will meet his end.
(Proverbs 19: 9)

Here the second part matches, with only small modification, the sentiment of the first part in a common pattern which can be called synonymous parallelism. Also common, however, are cases of antithesis or contrast:

A merry heart doeth good like a medicine:
But a broken spirit drieth the bones.
(Proverbs 17: 22)

These examples come from a section of the Old Testament sometimes described as the 'wisdom literature', in which ethical principles for everyday life are being presented in an accessible and memorable form. The structuring (preserved from the original Hebrew by the translators of the King James Bible four centuries ago) is, to some extent at least, a mnemonic device, extremely important in cultures where teaching depends heavily upon oral transmission rather than writing, as would have been the case in Palestine four or five millennia ago. But similar principles of structuring by parallelism still inform various kinds of oral performance today. The lines from Ecclesiastes above, for instance, formed the basis of a pop lyric sung by the Seekers. Or consider the following passage from Martin Luther King's famous speech before the Lincoln Memorial roughly four decades ago:

> I have a dream that one day even the State of Mississippi,
>> a desert state, sweltering with the heat of injustice and oppression,
>> will be transformed into an oasis of freedom and justice.
> I have a dream that my four little children will one day live in a nation
>> where they will not be judged by the colour of their skin
>>> but by the content of their character
> I have a dream today . . .

Broad parallelisms link the components of the dream. But within the separate statements there are also minor parallelisms, which are themselves structured around contrast and antithesis: thus 'the colour of their skin' is contrasted with 'the content of their character', 'injustice and oppression' contrasted with 'freedom and justice'. In the peroration of King's speech the biblical cadences become more obvious, culminating with his seamless incorporation into the speech of a passage almost verbatim from the Old Testament (cf. Isaiah 40: 3–5) (see **Unit 16, Intertextuality and allusion**):

> I have a dream that one day every valley shall be exalted,
>> Every hill and mountain will be made low,
>> The rough places will be made plain,
>> And the crooked places will be made straight,
>> And the glory of the Lord shall be revealed,
>> And all flesh shall see it together.

Recordings of the speech make clear just how strongly interactive the occasion was. The audience constantly punctuated King's words with their reactions and frequently expressed their sympathy with, and approval for, what he was saying, both by applauding and also by calling out 'Yeah, Yeah' and (significantly) 'Amen'. Indeed, part of King's accomplishment as a public speaker was to blend the rhythms and the idiom of a preacher (he was a Southern Baptist minister) with the appeal of a political orator, crafting his words in such a fashion that the audience found it easy to respond to them. This is not just a matter of expressing the right sentiments for the moment at hand; it is also a question of shaping them into structures which signal where responses by the audience would be appropriate – through repetition and parallelism with contrast. Interwoven with biblical echoes, and delivered with wonderful variations in volume, pace and rhythm, the parallel patterning not only heightened the effect of the words but also signalled exactly where responses and reactions would be appropriate.

329

We are forced to recognize, therefore, that the very features which signal the literariness of a text may also appear in religious texts, advertising, political speeches and in other kinds of verbal text, such as pop lyrics, jokes, and so on: the literary or poetic impulse does not restrict itself to novels, plays or poems but feeds into many types of verbal activity – especially the promotional discourses of advertising, the persuasive discourses of politics and the ethical discourses of religion, where engagement with the reader and rhetorical impact are at stake. For this reason it makes sense to think not only about the analysis of literary texts – as we have primarily done in this book – but also to consider ways of exploring the significance of non-literary texts.

27.2 Critically analysing the non-literary text

Every text can be considered from three perspectives:

1 what it is about;
2 to whom it is addressed;
3 how it has been composed.

27.2.1 Language constructs social reality

Our experience of the world is shaped for us by the terms and by the patterns that our language provides. Partly this is a question of vocabulary. The emergence of particular vocabulary items in a language helps to bring aspects of reality into focus for its speakers, and a shift between vocabulary items or expressions may reflect or produce a redefinition of that reality. The historical shift in the USA in the latter half of the twentieth century between expressions such as *nigger*, *Negro*, *Black*, and *African-American*, for instance, represents a shift from a vocabulary of race to a vocabulary of ethnic identity with profound consequences for the way people view each other. Indeed, at a more abstract level anthropologists have argued that different languages carve up the continuum of experience in different ways, offering to their users different versions of the world which we inhabit. Russian, for example, divides up the colour spectrum with twelve basic colour terms, whereas English segments the same domain with eleven, using only one basic colour term for 'blue' in place of the two items available in Russian. In an Australian aborigine language called Pintupi there are ten discrete expressions for types of hole, many of which can only be translated into English by means of elaborate paraphrase: *katarta*, for instance, neatly sums up something which in English we can only express as 'the hole left by a goanna when it has broken the surface after hibernation'. Thus, in speaking a particular language we become party to an agreement to organize reality in one way rather than another: reality – as codified in the shared vocabulary of our language – is socially constructed for us.

It is not just vocabulary, however, that shapes our experience of the world. The patterning of sentence structure, as we saw in **Unit 8**, **Language and society**, can also put a particular 'spin' on reality. Compare for instance the following headlines:

(a)   ELEVEN RIOTING BLACKS SHOT DEAD BY POLICE
(b)   POLICE SHOOT ELEVEN BLACKS DEAD IN RIOT

Both sentences seem to record the same information. But most readers find the first sentence implicitly more sympathetic to the police than the second. Since the vocabulary of the two sentences is virtually identical, how is the difference achieved? The difference of emphasis is achieved not so much in the *choice* of words themselves but through **word order**, or syntax. By virtue of their different syntax, the first sentence foregrounds the action of rioting by blacks, whereas the second sentence foregrounds the action of shooting by police. Both in its syntax and in its vocabulary, therefore, language constructs reality for us and represents the world to us in quite determinate ways.

27.2.2 Language and social relations

At the same time as language constructs a social reality for us, it also constructs and shapes our social relationships. When we speak or write, we speak or write *about something* but we also speak or write *to someone*. Consequently, every time we speak or write we articulate our social identity in relation to the social identity of the hearer or reader: as Valentin N. Vološinov (1973) has pointed out, every utterance is a bridge between self and other. One way in which this works is through the choice of address terms, or more generally in the way that the text codifies the position of its addressee (see **Unit 23**, **Positioning the reader or spectator**). The incumbent of the White House is not addressed in press conferences as 'Bill' or 'Al' or 'George', but as 'Mr President', or 'Sir', or even 'Mr President, Sir'. Similarly, exchanges in the Westminster Houses of Parliament have elaborate codes of address in which speakers in the lower house refer to each other as 'the Right Honourable Lady' or 'my Right Honourable Friend' and to members of the upper house as 'my noble Lords'. Such formulations, involving titles and honorifics, encode social distance, formality and status in graduated ways. Title (Mr President) is more formal than Title + Last Name (President Clinton) – which in turn is more formal than First Name (Bill). Collectively, such formulations constitute a system of modes of address. Selecting from within the system is a way of defining (and re-defining) the nature of the relationship between speaker and hearer, addressor and addressee. In addition to direct address, of course, as we noted in **Unit 23**, **Positioning the reader or spectator**, the audience is also addressed by implication. In effect, texts project or invoke 'a position' – a framework of beliefs and common understanding – from which they make sense.

Both types of address – direct and indirect – work hand in hand. Consider, for instance, Henry Fielding's novel, *Tom Jones* (1749), which frequently uses direct address to define and re-define the relationship of the narrator to the reader:

> We are now, reader, arrived at the last stage of our long journey. As we have therefore travelled together through so many pages, let us behave to one another like fellow-travellers in a stage coach, who have passed several days in the company of each other; and who . . . mount, for the last time, into their vehicle with chearfulness and good-humour . . .
>
> And now, my friend, I take this opportunity (as I shall have no other) of heartily wishing thee well. If I have been an entertaining companion to thee, I promise thee it is what I have desired.
>
> (Book XVIII, ch.1)

Notice that 'the reader' is not only addressed as such but is also being consti-tuted, both directly and indirectly, in quite specific terms as singular ('thee'), as equivalent to a companion or friend, as capable of being 'chearful' and 'good-humoured', and so on. Indeed, the positive, ideal traits of sociability, benign good-humour, tolerance, and conviviality that are so much espoused in the narrative world of the novel are also projected outwards onto its implied addressee.

The mode of address in *Tom Jones* is worlds apart from the less formal, offhand, but strictly impersonal opening of Forster's *Howards End* (1910):

> One may as well begin with Helen's letters to her sister.

Thus, every text, spoken or written, through its modes of address organizes social relationships. This is achieved partly through address terms (gentle reader, Mr President, etc.). We should note also that language organizes social relations by means of its capacity to perform actions in words in relation to the addressee (see **Unit 26, Literature in performance**). Through words we can question, command, state, challenge, promise, insult, offer, invite, request, and so on. Many of our most important institutions depend upon using words to perform quite specific actions, whether it be in the context of a marriage cere-mony, Parliamentary debate, a job interview, or union negotiations.

27.2.3 Language as text

As we saw in **Unit 6, Language and context: register**, language as text is affected by a number of situational variables. Crucial to the operation of text is the selection of the medium through which it operates. Perhaps the most impor-tant contrast is between speech and writing – or, more generally, between language designed for consumption in the here and now in conditions where the addressor and addressee are co-present to each other, and language designed for transmission across time and space using some kind of permanent or semi-permanent inscription or record. Spoken language adopts looser principles of organization than writing, so that conversational texts are full of hesitations, false starts, grammatical mistakes, and unfinished sentences. Speakers tend to use the active rather than the passive voice and the proportion of content words is lower than in writing. Sentences tend to be simple or compound rather than complex: in other words, clauses tend to be linked in a simple fashion using 'and', 'but', or 'so'.

Written text tends to be organized in a tighter fashion. The proportion of content words is higher than in speech and more of the sentences are complex in their construction, using links such as 'if . . . when . . .', 'whereas', 'because', 'since', 'therefore', 'consequently', 'however', 'moreover'. The passive construction occurs more frequently in writing than in speech. Basically, written text has to be more self-sufficient as communication than spoken text because it cannot rely upon the rich additional cues that face-to-face communication has available, such as tone of voice, facial expression, gesture, and so on – cues which supplement the meaning of the words themselves. And, of course, in spoken communication the process of interchange between interlocutors provides opportunities for ongoing clarification so that meanings can be left implicit and clarified only where the interlocutors should find it necessary.

27.3 Analysing non-literary discourse: the example of news headlines

We will now look at the operation of these three dimensions in practice by examining the headlines for the leading front-page story over a two-day period in the British press. The material is drawn from 25–26 March 1999, at the beginning of NATO's air campaign to prevent the violent expulsion by Serbs of Albanians from their homes in Kosovo. The onset of the campaign was of great significance, immediately in terms of the lives of Albanians and Serbs involved, and more generally in terms of prevailing international relations and the possible international repercussions. The coverage of the war in broadcast and print media was extensive and prompted major questions – both at the time and subsequently – about news coverage of armed conflict. Such questions were mostly about factual accuracy, bias, propaganda and truth ('is truth the first casualty of war?'), although there were also debates about vocabulary – about the accuracy and appropriacy of terms like genocide, mass murder and ethnic cleansing.

It is not within the scope of the following discussion to address the problem of the moral rightness of the war or the truthfulness of the news reporting. However, even focusing only on headlines from the press will raise questions about the ways in which the events of the war were constructed.

27.3.1 News headlines: constructing reality

Consider first of all the following headlines from broadsheet newspapers.

(a) THE ONSLAUGHT BEGINS (*The Guardian*)
(b) SERBS REMAIN DEFIANT AS THE MISSILE ATTACKS GO ON (*The Guardian*)
(c) NATO VOWS TO BOMB SERBS UNTIL RESISTANCE IS DESTROYED (*The Scotsman*)
(d) NATO SPLIT OVER AIR CAMPAIGN (*The Times*)
(e) 'NO SANCTUARY' WARNS NATO AS SERBS ARE BOMBARDED AGAIN (*The Independent*)
(f) MILOSEVIC TAKES SWIFT REVENGE AS NATO JETS RENEW ONSLAUGHT (*Daily Telegraph*)
(g) BELGRADE ROCKED BY BOMBS AS BRITISH JETS JOIN NATO ATTACK (*Daily Telegraph*)
(h) AIR STRIKES BEGIN AS BLAIR SAYS 'WE MUST END VILE OPPRESSION' (*The Independent*)

In **Unit 8, Language and society**, we distinguished four main types of verbal process, three of which occur in these headlines:

1   Material action processes as exemplified by verbs such as 'to bombard', 'to rock'. Material action processes of this type require an **agent** to perform the action. Whatever is on the receiving end of the action may be described as the **affected**.

2   Verbal processes, such as 'to say', 'to warn' or 'to vow', where the originator of the process is categorized as the **sayer** and what is said as **verbiage**.

3   Relational processes, such as 'to be', 'to become', 'to remain' through which an **attribute** is associated with an entity known as a **carrier**.

Now consider the following clauses from headlines which marked the opening of the bombing campaign in Serbia:

> The onslaught begins
> Air strikes begin
> . . . missile attacks go on
> . . . NATO jets renew onslaught

In these clauses the verbs 'begin', 'go on' and 'renew' encode **relational processes** of inception, duration and renewal. The action of 'bombing Serbia from the air' is encoded in plural nouns such as 'attacks', 'strikes' and in the noun 'onslaught'. What the clauses generally and significantly do not encode is who actually 'strikes' or 'attacks' whom.

This can be contrasted with the identification of the sayer in the following **verbal processes**:

> 'No sanctuary' warns NATO
> Blair says 'We must end vile oppression'
> NATO vows to bomb Serbs

Here we have verbal processes ('vow', 'warn' and 'say') which encode a role for major protagonists in the conflict: NATO and Blair appear in the role of sayer.

The other major protagonists in the conflict, Serbs/Belgrade, are encoded in the following clauses:

> Serbs are bombarded again
> Belgrade rocked by bombs
> NATO vows to bomb Serbs

In these cases 'bombard', 'rock' and 'bomb' are **material action processes** in which Serbs/Belgrade figure as the affected. It is noticeable, however, that these clauses are passive constructions and thus the agent of the processes, though easily recoverable from context, is not explicitly encoded.

Indeed, throughout the headlines there is a lack of explicitly encoded agency. The clearest exceptions to this are in the following clauses:

> Milosevic takes swift revenge
> British jets join NATO attack

'Milosevic' is the agent in 'Milosevic takes swift revenge', while 'British jets' are the agent in 'British jets join NATO attack'. In neither case, however, does the clause clearly encode the affected in human terms.

The overall picture that emerges from this analysis is of an event beginning or continuing (The onslaught begins/Missile attacks go on/Air strikes begin), in which Serbs are affected (Serbs are bombarded again/Belgrade rocked by bombs) by unspecified agents, and in which NATO and Blair give voice (NATO vows/NATO warns/Blair says), but in which the actions performed by one side on the other are not explicitly articulated together in any one clause.

Thus behind a headline such as THE ONSLAUGHT BEGINS lies recoverable content along the lines of 'NATO's onslaught on Serbia begins'. And behind NATO JETS RENEW ONSLAUGHT lies recoverable content along the lines of 'NATO jets renew onslaught on Serbia'. Behind BELGRADE ROCKED BY BOMBS lies content along the lines of 'NATO rocks Belgrade with bombs'. Indeed, the expanded proposition behind many of the headlines is 'NATO (/British) jets/missiles bomb Belgrade (/Serbs/

Serbia)'. This proposition, however, tends not to be encoded in full and it tends to be relegated to subordinate clauses

AS SERBS ARE BOMBARDED AGAIN
AS NATO JETS RENEW ONSLAUGHT
AS BRITISH JETS JOIN NATO ATTACK
AS MISSILE ATTACKS GO ON

There are various possible explanations as to why the participants and the processes are presented in a truncated fashion and a subordinate position in these headlines. The simplest and most straightforward account would point out that, on the one hand, war is a complex reality and, on the other, there are limits to the space that a headline can occupy. Sub-editors, therefore, instinctively delete recoverable elements from the underlying proposition in order to save space. At first sight, therefore, it is difficult to call such reductions into question as other than simple space-saving devices. In practice, however, there is a consistency about the reductions which leads to what might be called a 'dis-articulation' of the relations between parties to the process and the readership is insulated from the actions carried out in its name. When such formulations are routine, it becomes harder to recognize the way in which ordinary citizens are implicated in the actions of their government. Nor is it true, in any case, that short headlines are incapable of articulating the relations between parties to the conflict. As one tabloid newspaper succinctly, but more explicitly, expressed it: OUR BOYS BOMB BELGRADE. Alongside an example such as this, the headlines discussed above seem somewhat euphemistic. (Even this last example, while more bald than the others, could be seen as potentially euphemistic if Belgrade is interpreted as a metonymic expression for Serbia.)

Two points need emphasizing. When there is regular, persistent and consistent patterning of choices of the kind identified above, there are potential consequences for the way in which reality is represented. However, patterns in the process of representation may arise without them necessarily being dependent upon a conscious and deliberate strategy to represent or misrepresent events one way or another. Patterns may simply and easily – perhaps too easily – reproduce a 'natural', or 'common-sense' or taken-for-granted way of putting things. To call them into question is not necessarily to identify a concerted attempt at propaganda, merely to ask if aspects of reality become overlooked or suppressed by these patterns; are there other ways, we may ask, of representing events that should be considered?

Second, the issue of how the war was represented is a separable issue from the rights and wrongs of military intervention by an international force in the Balkans. So, to raise questions about the language in which events are represented *may* entail taking a position on the events themselves, but the one does not follow automatically from the other. Separable from the question of the rights and wrongs of the event are questions of the politics of representation: who says what to whom and how. Informed democracies depend upon citizens who recognize the ways in which they are implicated in the actions of their governments and who understand how to influence them. And so informed democracies depend upon a press that clearly articulates the connections between citizen, government and action.

27.3.2 News headlines: reaching readerships

The headlines which we have considered above all come (with the single exception of OUR BOYS BOMB BELGRADE) from the British national daily broadsheet press, which consists of six or seven titles with combined sales of about 3m copies in the UK. In contrast, the tabloid press in the UK with a similar number of titles sells about 11m copies daily. A mass circulation tabloid paper such as the *Sun*, selling about 3.7m copies daily, tends to have a very different readership than *The Times*, which it outsells by a factor of about 5:1, even though they are published by the same organization. The difference in approach to their readerships may be seen by contrasting tabloid with broadsheet headlines. Where *The Times* printed NATO SPLIT OVER AIR CAMPAIGN the *Sun* printed CLOBBA SLOBBA.

To develop this point further, consider the following examples from the tabloid press for the 25–26 March

(i) ONSLAUGHT (*The Express*)
(j) FIRESTORM! (*Daily Mail*)
(k) NOWHERE TO HIDE (*Sun*)
(l) STILL THEY MURDER US (*The Scottish Express*)
(m) JUSTICE (*Daily Record*)
(n) ONSLAUGHT (*Daily Mail*)
(o) CLOBBA SLOBBA (*Sun*)

The differences between these tabloid headlines (i–o) and those of the broadsheets (a–h) are clear and striking. Where the broadsheets use a full sentence, the tabloids will not uncommonly use a single word. Compare, for instance, ONSLAUGHT in the *Daily Mail* and *The Express* with THE ONSLAUGHT BEGINS in *The Guardian* (or as the *Daily Telegraph* more elaborately encodes it MILOSEVIC TAKES SWIFT REVENGE AS NATO JETS RENEW ONSLAUGHT). The brevity of the tabloid headlines in comparison with those in the broadsheets makes them sound more like emotive comments, reactions or captions than descriptions of events. Indeed, often the tabloid headline only makes sense if we read it as a non-attributed quotation belonging by inference to one of the parties to the event. Thus, *The Express* headline, STILL THEY MURDER US, belongs by inference to Kosovan refugees.

For tabloids, emotion about an event takes precedence over the event itself. For broadsheets, the event takes precedence over emotion. In this respect, tabloids may be seen as displaying a preference for spoken melodrama (sensationalism and excessive emotion), whereas broadsheets are more rooted in written epic (the narrative of events that are important to a nation). Thus, the relationship of tabloid and broadsheet headlines to their putative audience would seem to be very different. Fundamentally, they adopt different modes of address to their respective readerships. In their headlines they project differing frameworks of interest, with the clear implication that the habitual reader of, for instance, the *Daily Mail* or the *Sun* will be looking for different emphases in its account of the world than those offered by *The Guardian* or the *Independent*.

27.3.3 News headlines: formatting the news

The differences between tabloid and broadsheet newspapers work on many different levels: the two types of newspaper represent the world in different ways, for instance, and they appeal to different readerships. Most obviously, however, they adopt very different physical formats. Broadsheets, as the name clearly signals, are large-size newspapers with pages approximately 24×15 inches, roughly double the measurement of tabloid newspapers, whose pages are approximately 15×12. Tabloid headlines, however, despite the smaller page, use considerably larger font than broadsheet headlines: the height of the typeface in a tabloid headline can measure as much as 1½ inches, as opposed to half or three-quarters of an inch in a broadsheet headline. Using roughly half the size of page but at least twice the font size in headlines means there are very different constraints on tabloid sub-editors than upon broadsheet sub-editors. Tabloid sub-editors have to squeeze larger letters into a smaller space with the consequence that front-page tabloid headlines, as we have seen, are rarely more than four words long and frequently are less. Indeed, four out of the seven front-page tabloid headlines listed above consist of a single word. Sentences that are only one or two or at most a few words long are necessarily elliptical: they lack basic constituents. The shorter the sentence in a tabloid headline, the likelier it is that it will lack a verb. It is this kind of compositional strait-jacket that contributes to the impression we noted above of tabloids projecting emotion as much as, if not more than, a sense of event. Without a verb a sense of the news being about events is difficult to sustain. As we have seen already, what remains reads more like a spontaneous comment or reaction (JUSTICE; FIRESTORM! CLOBBA SLOBBA).

The composition of the headlines is therefore affected by the overall design of the page and the prior constraints that govern it. Tabloid headlines in particular are usually juxtaposed with a large picture which dominates the page. The headline, FIRESTORM!, for instance, is placed above a picture of a night scene showing buildings burning in Belgrade that occupies perhaps a

Plate 40 *The Guardian*, 26 March 1999

Plate 41 *The Daily Telegraph*, 26 March 1999

Source: Telegraph Group Ltd, London 1999

Plate 42 *The Daily Mail*, 26 March 1999

Plate 43 *The Express*, 26 March 1999

Plate 44 The *Sun*, 26 March 1999

third of the page. The headline, JUSTICE, is juxtaposed with a large image of a NATO fighter plane.

The interaction between word and image on these pages is inescapable and provides a significant dimension of the meaning of the headline. For instance, although the headline STILL THEY MURDER US occurs without quotation marks, it is placed underneath a picture of a Kosovar child whose words they become by virtue of the juxtaposition. The elliptical quality of tabloid headlines and their context dependency, the way in which their meaning is supplemented from the interaction with other aspects of the page, help to emphasize their pseudo-spoken qualities and sets them off from those of the broadsheets.

Broadsheet headlines, using smaller typeface, may stretch right across the front page of the newspaper, so the potential for a fully formed sentence is much greater. As we saw earlier, the main constituent elements of a sentence or clause are all there in the broadsheet headlines. Each headline encodes a process in a verb (such as 'warn', 'begin', 'join', 'remain') and, for each process, at least one entity or participant is also encoded. Although we have noted a tendency in broadsheet headlines to elide the full range of participants to a process, the clauses are more or less syntactically complete. Some minor function words – such as definite articles, pronouns, or auxiliary verbs – are occasionally left out: [*THE*] SERBS REMAIN DEFIANT AS THE MISSILE ATTACKS GO ON; or NATO [*IS*] SPLIT OVER [*THE*] AIR CAMPAIGN. But such omissions do not markedly affect the meaning.

One of the noticeable features of the broadsheet headlines we have considered, especially in comparison with tabloids, is the way in which the extra space allows them often to be composed of two clauses rather than one, as in the following examples:

MILOSEVIC TAKES SWIFT REVENGE
AS NATO JETS RENEW ONSLAUGHT (*Daily Telegraph*)
BELGRADE ROCKED BY BOMBS
AS BRITISH JETS JOIN NATO ATTACK (*Daily Telegraph*)
AIR STRIKES BEGIN
AS BLAIR SAYS 'WE MUST END VILE OPPRESSION' (*The Independent*)

The temporal coding of broadsheet headlines is rather unusual. Nearly all the two-clause headlines which we have considered are connected by means of a temporal expression, the most common being 'AS'. In each case the temporal structure consists of presenting two separate events as if in simultaneous occurrence: *a* at the same time as *b*. Thus, for example, (a) the air strikes are beginning, at the same time as (b) Blair is saying that we must end vile oppression. Also noticeable is the consistent use of the present tense. Strictly speaking, the air strikes have already happened by the time the report is composed and certainly by the time the newspaper reaches the reader. A more literal encoding of reality might say: THE AIR STRIKES HAVE BEGUN AFTER BLAIR SAID 'WE MUST END VILE OPPRESSION'.[1]

Partly, of course, as we noted earlier, it is a simple question of brevity: 'begin' is shorter than 'have begun'. But it is also a question of immediacy: news, by definition, deals with 'the new', with very recent events. Indeed, the temporal codings of broadsheet headlines treat the news as happening in a timeless present in which the events of yesterday occurred simultaneously with each other and are treated as somehow continuous with 'the now' of today. One of the clearest grammatical markers of a broadsheet headline, then, is the use of the present tense. 'British jets join NATO attack' sounds like a headline, whereas 'British jets joined the NATO attack' would sound like history.

However, when events happen in a timeless present it is difficult to plot the relations between them. The emphasis on immediacy and simultaneity obscures notions of succession and temporal sequence. And, without a sense of temporal sequence, causal relations – which are often crucial – are lost.

Conversely, the presentation of temporal sequence tends to imply causality. It is noticeable above, for instance, that rewriting the broadsheet headline to suggest a temporal sequence in which Blair's announcement precedes the beginning of the air strikes implies a stronger relationship between the two events: indeed, it foregrounds the implication that air strikes began in order to end oppression.

There is, therefore, an interaction between the physical shape of the page and the kinds of meanings which they carry. The smaller tabloid page is dominated by its headline and its associated picture: it is a graphic and pictographic experience. The larger broadsheet front page may also be dominated by its headline but it is harder to take in at a single glance and is less dependent on an accompanying picture. Instead it works as an introduction to or summary statement about the story printed beneath it. Thus, the tabloid page tends to assume a moral or emotional position about the news, while the broadsheet page seeks to report it.

It may appear that we are claiming that these distinct approaches actually derive from the different formats, but such a claim would be simplistic. Certainly, the difference in the shape and size of the page is one kind of grid which helps to 'shape' printed news, rather like the difference in format between a half-hour programme and a one-hour programme helps to shape different kinds of television news. But it is not a determining factor. There is, for instance, no reason in principle why the smaller page *in itself* should result in such a drastically shorter headline. After all, a tabloid headline could be as wordy as a broadsheet's if the print size were reduced in proportion to the size of the page. This, however, would make it less readable at a glance. And ultimately newspapers produce copy for sale. At the point of sale a tabloid newspaper presents the whole of its front page to a prospective buyer, whereas a broadsheet paper (folded on the news-stand) only presents half. It is likely that tabloid readers include a higher proportion of those who read the paper occasionally – who are 'spot buyers'. For this reason the front page with its headline and picture must act like a hook to draw the reader to the paper; hence the exaggeratedly large typeface. In the case of the broadsheet newspaper, however, readers tend to be habitual buyers and the role of the headline is rather different – to hook the reader, having bought the paper, into the story.

A recent study of the popular press (Hartley, 1996) has argued that

> Journalism is ... *the* textual system of modernity ... a gigantic archive of textuality, a huge store of human sense-making, unselfconsciously generated by and documenting the social, personal, cultural and political interactions of contemporary life, while at the same time displaying its own particular properties and characteristics, its own patterns, histories, quirks and accidents. It is therefore a resource which has to be studied in its own terms, but which can also be used to pursue questions about matters outside of itself; questions about meanings, for instance.

In our discussion, we have tried to show, by looking at the patterning of language choices in two sets of front-page headlines from a two-day period, how meanings can become limited or channelled in particular directions. Restricting ourselves to the domain of print journalism and to examples of front-page headlines from a two-day period, we developed illustrative generalizations in three key areas of meaning. First of all, we considered language as a mode of representation and we noted how, in reporting the bombing campaign in the Balkans, the British broadsheet press tended towards what might be termed an intransitive version of events: in other words, the broadsheets were rarely able in their headlines to articulate the full connection between protagonists to the conflict. Second, by comparing the verbal structure of broadsheet headlines with tabloid headlines we suggested that rather different readerships were being addressed by them: at the risk of oversimplifying the differences, tabloid headlines project meanings which are implicit by comparison with the more explicit codings of the broadsheets. Thus, the differences between tabloid and broadsheet headlines are predicated upon a sense of quite different reading publics. Finally, we suggested that different graphic and pictographic design formats of tabloid and broadsheet helped to reinforce the different verbal strategies of the two types of newspaper.

These three dimensions may be summed up under the headings **modes of representation**, **modes of address** and **modes of composition**. It is, of course, not always easy to keep these dimensions separate. Choices in one dimension have repercussions in other dimensions. For instance, a tendency towards ellipsis in all headlines may be driven by the compositional requirements associated with limited space. However, the particular kinds of ellipsis that take place have consequences for modes of address and modes of representation. Thus, tabloid headlines, restricted to one or two words, read like direct quotation or like comments or reactions (with consequences for modes of address); and generally headlines lack precise references to time or to the sequence of events (with consequences for modes of representation). None the less, despite the overlap between them, these three analytical dimensions provide useful angles of vision from which to examine any text, or group of texts. They provide ways of exploring layers of significance in text.

In effect, these three analytic dimensions extend ways of reading beyond literature to other types of discourse. Literary texts are highly significant texts of the culture. They can show the fractured qualities of experience as well as giving shape to it. Not only do they embody frameworks of belief, they also dramatize the tensions and the gaps between one framework and another. It is appropriate that much of this book has been devoted to ways of analysing works that have claims to canonical status within the culture – whether these be exemplified by established canonical figures such as William Shakespeare (four references), John Milton and James Joyce (three references apiece), or the more contested figures of Aphra Behn, Dorothy Parker, or Ee Tiang Hong (see **Unit 25**, **Judgement and value**). These authors, however, are figures from the first age of mediated culture – from the age of the printed book. From the fifteenth to the twentieth centuries, mediated culture was principally a literate culture, constituted primarily in books, which provided a major means for the wide circulation of values, experiences, and frameworks of meaning and belief. We now live, however, at the dawn of the second age of mediated culture in which texts circulate in electronic form in increasingly diverse media. Lyric poetry is available on vinyl, tape and CD as well as in books. Fictional narratives are available on broadcast television, on videocassette and on video CD as well as in books, theatre or cinema. 'News' is available on satellite and cable TV, on radio and the Internet. The technical possibilities of mediation have become astonishingly complex and are subject to accelerating rates of change. Cultural and communicative forms, however, endure and change at a slower pace; and analytical techniques developed for one mediated context now prove valuable in another. Ultimately, the concern of *Ways of Reading* is with the analysis and interpretation of cultural and communicative form, not only as it occurs in books, but also in other mediated and unmediated contexts. Headlines are just one case of one kind of communicative form that plays a significant role in our culture; and as such – like the form of a novel or poem – its properties can be usefully displayed. Indeed, like a novel or a poem, it is most important that they should be critically examined rather than taken for granted.

ACTIVITY 27.1

1   Try to identify which ten of the following headlines come from the front pages of tabloid newspapers and which ten come from broadsheet newspapers. Answers are given in the Appendix, pp. 350–1.

(a)   STUPEFYING ARROGANCE
(b)   CHANNEL 4 IN NEW DOCUMENTARY FAKE ROW
(c)   CAN WE BELIEVE ANYTHING WE SEE ON TV?
(d)   RAF TORNADOS JOIN IRAQ ATTACK
(e)   YOU'RE A FOOL M'LUD
(f)   NANNY FACES JAIL AFTER ADMITTING KILLING BABY
(g)   MENINGITIS: NEW VACCINE
(h)   EMERGENCY DECLARED AS MENINGITIS CLAIMS THIRD VICTIM
(i)   SLEEP WELL
(j)   TV STAR DANDO MURDERED BY SINGLE SHOT
(k)   WELFARE: THE CRACKDOWN
(l)   I KILLED BABY CAROLINE, SAYS NANNY
(m)   VIOLENT PAST OF KILLER NANNY

    (n)   TEACHERS' ANGER AT PAY BY RESULTS

    (o)   HODDLE ON DEFENSIVE AS HIS SUPPORT RUNS OUT

    (p)   RAF PILOTS BLITZ IRAQ

    (q)   BRITISH JETS ROAR INTO ACTION

    (r)   ASSASSINATED

    (s)   US CLAIMS SUCCESS AS IRAQ IS HIT BY HEAVY NEW WAVE OF AIR STRIKES

    (t)   ROBBIE BOOZE BLITZ AT THE RITZ

2   List the grounds on which you were able to decide which headlines were tabloid and which were broadsheet. Were any examples difficult to identify as tabloid or broadsheet?

3   Consider the following contrasting openings to front page news stories and match them with the appropriate headlines given below.

> CHANNEL 4 IN NEW DOCUMENTARY FAKE ROW
>
> CAN WE BELIEVE ANYTHING WE SEE ON TV?
>
> RAF TORNADOS JOIN IRAQ ATTACK
>
> RAF PILOTS BLITZ IRAQ
>
> ASSASSINATED
>
> TV STAR DANDO MURDERED BY SINGLE SHOT
>
> I KILLED BABY CAROLINE, SAYS NANNY
>
> VIOLENT PAST OF KILLER NANNY

(1a) 'A Channel 4 documentary that purported to investigate how Manchester's gangsters got hold of illegal guns and which resulted in the imprisonment of a man for seven years was faked in key parts, an . . . investigation has revealed.'

(1b) 'A gritty prime time Channel 4 documentary contained faked scenes, it was admitted last night.'

(2a) 'A nanny who yesterday admitted shaking a six month old baby to death was sacked from four previous jobs, twice for violence to babies in her care.'

(2b) 'A nanny yesterday admitted shaking to death a six-month-old baby in her care, rekindling calls for a national register of nannies to be set up by the Government to protect children and their parents.'

(3a) 'As the sun went down over the Kuwaiti sands last night, 12 British Tornados roared into the skies to strike into the heart of Iraq.'

(3b) 'British Tornados joined the bombing raids on Iraq last night in a second day of attacks, causing devastating damage to President

Saddam Hussein's most important military facilities.'

(4a) 'Jill Dando, one of Britain's best-known broadcasters, was shot dead yesterday on her doorstep in West London. A single shot to the head killed the woman who was familiar to millions as the self-confident presenter who asked for the public's help in tracking down criminals on the BBC's *Crimewatch* programme.'

(4b) '*Crimewatch* host Jill Dando was killed by a single gunshot to the head, it emerged last night. The telly golden girl was left screaming in a pool of blood on her doorstep.'

4   Some openings in question 3 are from tabloids and some from broadsheets. List some of the verbal features that help you to distinguish one from the other.

5   Translate the following headline and opening from the *Daily Telegraph* into tabloid style.

ENGLAND EXPELLED FROM FIVE NATIONS
The five nations rugby championship was in disarray last night following the expulsion of England in a long-running row over television rights.

6   Which style do you prefer – the style of the broadsheet *Daily Telegraph* or the style of your tabloid version? Why?

Note

1   That this was the probable order of events may be derived from that fact that Government press briefings are scheduled early enough in the day to be in time to influence evening broadcast news bulletins, whereas the first bombing of Serbia took place during the hours of darkness. If Blair or his office issued a statement it would be earlier than 8.00 p.m. The bombings began no earlier than 10.00 p.m.

Reading

Atkinson, J.M. (1984) *Our Masters' Voices: The Language and Body Language of Politics*, London: Methuen.
Bell, A. (1991) *The Language of News Media*, Oxford: Blackwell.
Bell, A. and Garrett, P. (eds) (1998) *Approaches to Media Discourse*, Oxford: Blackwell.
Corner, J. (1995) *Television Form and Public Address*, London: Arnold.
Fairclough, N. (1995) *Media Discourse*, London: Arnold.
Fowler, R. (1991) *Language in the News*, London: Routledge.

Hartley, J. (1982) *Understanding News*, London: Routledge & Kegan Paul.

Hartley, J. (1996) *Popular Reality*, London: Arnold.

Hoggart, R. (1958) *The Uses of Literacy*, Harmondsworth: Penguin.

Jakobson, R. (1961) 'Concluding statement: linguistics and poetics', in T. Sebeok (ed.) *Style in Language*, Cambridge, MA: MIT Press.

Kress, G. and Van Leeuwen, T. (1998) 'Front pages: the (critical) analysis of newspaper layout', in Λ. Bell and P. Garrett (eds) *Approaches to Media Discourse*, Oxford: Blackwell, pp. 186–220.

McLuhan, M. (1964) *Understanding Media: The Extensions of Man*, London: Routledge & Kegan Paul.

Tolson, A. (1996) *Mediations*, London: Arnold.

Trew, T. (1979) 'Theory at work', in R. Fowler *et al. Language and Control*, London: Routledge & Kegan Paul.

Vološinov, V.N. (1973) *Marxism and the Philosophy of Language*, New York: Academic Press.

Appendix: notes on activities

Unit 1 Asking questions

The author, Ee Tiang Hong, is a Malaysian writer, who was born in Malacca in 1933 and educated at Tranquerah English School and High School, Malacca. Until his death in the early 1990s, he lived mostly in Australia.

Tranquerah Road: the road is an extension of Heeren Street, in Malacca.
Kampong Serani: 'Portuguese Village', in the suburb of Ujong Pasir.
Limbongan: a suburb adjacent to Tranquerah. The Dutch used to moor their vessels off the coast here.
Kimigayo: the Japanese national anthem.
Nihon Seishin: 'Japanese Soul'.
Greater East Asia Co-Prosperity Sphere: the Japanese scheme to unify Asia, during the Second World War.
Meliora hic sequamur: the motto of the Malacca High School ('Here let us do better things').
Merdeka: 'Independence'.
Negara-ku: 'My Country', the Malayan, and then Malaysian, national anthem.
pontianak: a succubus, or evil spirit.
jinn: genie; evil spirit.
Omitohood: a Buddhist benediction ('Om Mane Pudmi Hum'), in the Hokkien Chinese dialect.

Unit 3 Analysing units of structure

The first sentence should read:

Following Nancy's death Sikes tries to escape the hue and cry.

The order of the sentences given in the published companion is:

15, 11, 3, 8, 9, 2, 6, 12, 4, 7, 1, 14, 5, 10, 13.

Unit 27 Ways of reading non-literary texts

These are the tabloid headlines.

(a)   STUPEFYING ARROGANCE
[*DAILY MAIL*]

(c)   CAN WE BELIEVE ANYTHING WE SEE ON TV?
[*DAILY MAIL*]

(e)   YOU'RE A FOOL M'LUD
[*DAILY RECORD*]

(g)   MENINGITIS: NEW VACCINE
[*DAILY MAIL*]

(i)   SLEEP WELL
[the *SUN*]

(k)   WELFARE: THE CRACKDOWN
[*DAILY MAIL*]

(m) VIOLENT PAST OF KILLER NANNY
[*DAILY MAIL*]

(p)   RAF PILOTS BLITZ IRAQ
[*DAILY MAIL*]

(r)   ASSASSINATED
[the *SUN*]

(t)   ROBBIE BOOZE BLITZ AT THE RITZ
[the *SUN*]

These are the broadsheet headlines.

(b)   CHANNEL 4 IN NEW DOCUMENTARY FAKE ROW
[*THE GUARDIAN*]

(d)   RAF TORNADOS JOIN IRAQ ATTACK
[*THE TIMES*]

(f)   NANNY FACES JAIL AFTER ADMITTING KILLING BABY
[*THE TIMES*]

(h)   EMERGENCY DECLARED AS MENINGITIS CLAIMS THIRD
VICTIM
[*DAILY TELEGRAPH*]

(j)   TV STAR DANDO MURDERED BY SINGLE SHOT
[*THE GUARDIAN*]

(l)   I KILLED BABY CAROLINE, SAYS NANNY

                            [*DAILY TELEGRAPH*]

(n)   TEACHERS' ANGER AT PAY BY RESULTS

                            [*THE INDEPENDENT*]

(o)   HODDLE ON DEFENSIVE AS HIS SUPPORT RUNS OUT

                            [*THE INDEPENDENT*]

(q)   BRITISH JETS ROAR INTO ACTION

                            [*DAILY TELEGRAPH*]

(s)   US CLAIMS SUCCESS AS IRAQ IS HIT BY HEAVY NEW WAVE
OF AIR STRIKES

                            [*THE INDEPENDENT*]

References

Abrams, M.H. (1953) 'The orientation of critical theories', in D. Lodge (ed.) (1972) *20th Century Literary Criticism*, Harlow: Longman, pp. 1–26.

Abrams, M.H. (1988) *A Glossary of Literary Terms,* 5th edn, New York: Holt, Rinehart & Winston.

Adcock, F. (ed.) (1987) *The Faber Book of 20th Century Women's Poetry*, London: Faber & Faber.

Aitchison, J. (1972) *Teach Yourself Linguistics*, London: Hodder.

Anderson, E.A. (1982) *English Poetry, 1900–1950: A Guide to Information Sources*, Detroit: Gale Research Company.

Aristotle (1965) *Classical Literary Criticism*, Harmondsworth: Penguin.

Atkinson, J.M. (1984) *Our Masters' Voices: The Language and Body Language of Politics*, London: Methuen.

Attridge, D. (1982) *The Rhythms of English Poetry*, Harlow: Longman.

Attridge, D. (1995) *Poetic Rhythm: An Introduction*, Cambridge: Cambridge University Press.

Auerbach, E. (1953) *Mimesis: The Representation of Reality in Western Literature*, Princeton, NJ: Princeton University Press.

Baker, N.L. (1989) *A Research Guide for Undergraduate Students (English and American Literature)*, New York: MLA Publications.

Bal, M. (1985) *Narratology: Introduction to the Theory of Narrative*, Toronto: Toronto University Press.

Barber, C. (1976) *Early Modern English*, London: André Deutsch.

Barthes, R. (1968) 'The death of the author', in D. Lodge (ed.) (1988) *Modern Criticism and Theory*, London: Longman, pp. 17–72.

Barthes, R. (1977) *Image – Music – Text*, Glasgow: Collins.

Barthes, R. (1986) *The Rustle of Language*, Oxford: Blackwell.

Bate, J. (1970) *The Burden of the Past and the English Poet*, London: Chatto & Windus.

Battersby, C. (1989) *Gender and Genius: Towards a Feminist Aesthetics*, London: Women's Press.

Bell, A. (1991) *The Language of News Media*, Oxford: Blackwell.

Bell, A. and Garrett, P. (eds) (1998) *Approaches to Media Discourse*, Oxford: Blackwell.

Belsey, C. (1980) *Critical Practice*, London: Routledge & Kegan Paul.

Berger, P. and Luckman, T. (1966) *The Social Construction of Reality,* Harmondsworth: Penguin.

Bergvall, V., Bing, J. and Fried, A. (eds) (1996) *Rethinking Language and Gender Research: Theory and Practice*, London: Longman.

Bloom, H. (1973) *The Anxiety of Influence: A Theory of Poetry*, Oxford: Oxford University Press.

Booth, W. (1961) *The Rhetoric of Fiction*, Chicago: University of Chicago Press.

Bordwell, D. (1985) *Narration in the Fiction Film*, London: Methuen.

Bordwell, D. (1989) *Making Meaning: Inference and Rhetoric in the Interpretation of Cinema*, Harvard: Harvard University Press.

Bordwell, D. and Thompson, K. (1979) *Film Art: An Introduction*, Reading, MA: Addison-Wesley.

Bourdieu, P. (1991) *Language and Symbolic Power,* Oxford: Blackwell.

Branigan, E. (1984) *Point of View in the Cinema,* New York: Mouton.

Brecht, B. (1977) 'Against Georg Lukács', in T. Adorno, W. Benjamin, E. Bloch, B. Brecht and G. Lukács (eds) *Aesthetics and Politics*, London: New Left Books.

Briggs, K.M. (1970) *A Dictionary of British Folk Tales in the English Language*, London: Routledge & Kegan Paul.

Bristow, J. (ed.) (1992) *Sexual Sameness: Textual Differences in Lesbian and Gay Writing*, London: Routledge.

Brown, G. and Yule, G. (1983) *Discourse Analysis*, Cambridge: Cambridge University Press.

Burgin, V. (1976/1999) 'Art, common sense and photography', in S. Hall and J. Evans (1999) *Visual Culture: The Reader*, London: Sage.

Burke, S. (ed.) (1995) *Authorship: From Plato to the Postmodern: A Reader*, Edinburgh: Edinburgh University Press.

Burton, D. (1982) 'Through glass darkly: through dark glasses', in R. Carter (ed.) *Language and Literature: An Introductory Reader in Stylistics*, London: George Allen & Unwin, pp. 195–214.

Cameron, D. (1985) *Feminism and Linguistic Theory*, London: Macmillan.

Cameron, D. (ed.) (1990) *The Feminist Critique of Language*, rev. edn, London: Routledge.

Cameron, D. (1994) 'Words, words, words: the power of language', in S. Dunant (ed.) *The War of the Words: The Political Correctness Debate*, London: Virago, pp. 15–35.

Cameron, D. (1995) *Verbal Hygiene*, London: Routledge.

Cameron, D. and Coates, J. (1989) *Women in their Speech Communities*, London: Longman.

Caughie, J. (ed.) (1981) *Theories of Authorship: A Reader*, London: Routledge & Kegan Paul and the British Film Institute.

Cerasano, S.P. and Wynne-Davies, M. (1996) *Renaissance Drama by Women: Texts and Documents*, London: Routledge.

Chatman, S. (1978) *Story and Discourse: Narrative Structure in Film and Prose Fiction*, Ithaca, NY and London: Cornell University Press.

Cook, P. (ed.) (1985) *The Cinema Book*, London: BFI.

Corner, J. (1995) *Television Form and Public Address,* London: Arnold.

Coward, R. (1986) 'This novel changes lives: are women's novels feminist novels?', in M. Eagleton (ed.) *Feminist Literary Theory: A Reader*, Oxford: Blackwell, pp. 155–60.

Coward, R. and Black, M. (1981/1990) 'Linguistic, social and sexual relations: a review of Dale Spender's *Man Made Language*', in D. Cameron (ed.) (1990) *The Feminist Critique of Language*, London: Routledge.

Crowther, B. and Leith, D. (1995) 'Feminism, language and the rhetoric of television wildlife programmes', in S. Mills (ed.) *Language and Gender: Interdisciplinary Perspectives*, London: Longman, pp. 207–26.

Culler, J. (1975) *Structuralist Poetics*, London: Routledge & Kegan Paul, especially Chapter 11.

Culler, J. (1983) 'Reading as a woman', in *On Deconstruction*, London: Routledge & Kegan Paul.

Daly, M. (1978) *Gyn/ecology*, London: Women's Press.

Day, A. (1988) *Jokerman: Reading the Lyrics of Bob Dylan*, Oxford: Blackwell,

Dunant, S. (ed.) (1994) *The War of the Words:The Political Correctness Debate*, London: Virago.

Durant, A. and Fabb, N. (1990) *Literary Studies in Action*, London: Routledge.

Eagleton, T. (1976) *Criticism and Ideology*, London: Verso.

Eagleton, T. (1983) *Literary Theory: An Introduction*, Oxford: Blackwell.

Eco, U. (1990) *The Limits of Interpretation*, Bloomington: Indiana University Press.

Eco, U. (1996) 'Afterword', in G. Nunberg (ed.) *The Future of the Book*, Berkeley, CA: University of California Press, pp. 295–306.

Eisenstein, S. (1979a) 'The cinematographic principle and the ideogram', in G. Mast and M. Cohen (eds) *Film Theory and Criticism,* Oxford: Oxford University Press, pp. 85–100.

Eisenstein, S. (1979b) 'A dialectic approach to film form', in G. Mast and M. Cohen (eds) *Film Theory and Criticism*, Oxford: Oxford University Press, pp. 101–22.

Eliot, T.S. (1919) 'Tradition and the individual talent', in D. Lodge (ed.) (1972) *20th Century Literary Criticism*, Harlow: Longman, pp. 334–44.

Eliot, T.S. (1922/1953) *Selected Prose*, Harmondsworth: Penguin.

Erlich, V. (1969) *Russian Formalism: History – Doctrine*, The Hague: Mouton.

Fabb, N. (1994) *Sentence Structure*, London: Routledge.

Fabb, N. (1997) *Linguistics and Literature*, Oxford: Blackwell.

Fabb, N. and Durant, A. (1993) *How to Write Essays, Dissertations and Theses in Literary Studies*, London: Longman.

Fairclough, N. (1989) *Language and Power*, Harlow: Longman.

Fairclough, N. (1992) *Discourse and Social Change*, London: Polity Press.

Fairclough, N. (1995) *Media Discourse,* London: Arnold.

Fawcett, R. (1980) *Cognitive Linguistics and Social Interaction*, Heidelberg: Julius Groos.

Fetterley, J. (1981) *The Resisting Reader: A Feminist Approach to American Fiction*, Bloomington: Indiana University Press.

Finnegan, R. (1992) *Oral Traditions and the Verbal Arts: A Guide to Research Practices*, London: Routledge.

Foucault, M. (1970) *The Order of Things: An Archaeology of the Human Sciences*, London: Tavistock.

Foucault, M. (1978) *The History of Sexuality*, vol. 1, Harmondsworth: Penguin.

Foucault, M. (1980/1988) 'What is an author?', in D. Lodge (ed.) (1988) *Modern Criticism and Theory*, London: Longman, pp. 197–210.

Foucault, M. (1989) *The Archaeology of Knowledge*, London: Routledge.

Fowler, R. (1986) *Linguistic Criticism*, Oxford: Oxford University Press.

Fowler, R. (1991) *Language in the News*, London: Routledge.

Fox, J.J. (1977) 'Roman Jakobson and the comparative study of parallelism', in C.H. von Schooneveld and D. Armstrong (eds) *Roman Jakobson: Echoes of His Scholarship*, Lisse: Peter de Ridder Press, pp. 59–90.

Fox, J.J. (ed.) (1988) *To Speak in Pairs: Essays on the Ritual Languages of Eastern Indonesia*, Cambridge: Cambridge University Press.

Frye, N. (1957) *Anatomy of Criticism*, Princeton, NJ: Princeton University Press.

Furniss, T. and Bath, M. (1996) *Reading Poetry: An Introduction*, London: Prentice-Hall.

Fussell, P. (1979) *Poetic Meter and Poetic Form*, New York: McGraw-Hill.

Garvin, P. (ed. and trans.) (1964) *A Prague School Reader in Aesthetics, Literary Structure and Style*, Washington, DC: Georgetown University Press.

Giddings, R., Selby, K. and Wensley, C. (1990) *Screening the Novel: The Theory and Practice of Literary Dramatization*, London: Macmillan.

Gilbert, S. and Gubar, S. (1979) *The Madwoman in the Attic*, New Haven, CT: Yale University Press.

Gregory, M. and Carroll, S. (1978) *Language and Situation*, London: Routledge & Kegan Paul.

Hall, S. (1973) 'Encoding/decoding', reprinted in S. Hall, D. Hobson, A. Lowe and P. Willis (eds) *Culture, Media, Language*, London: Hutchinson.

Hall, S. and Evans, J. (1999) *Visual Culture: The Reader*, London: Sage.

Halle, M. (1987) 'A biblical pattern poem', in N.D. Fabb, A. Durant and C. McCabe (eds) *The Linguistics of Writing: Arguments between Language and Literature*, Manchester: Manchester University Press.

Halliday, M.A.K. (1978) *Language as Social Semiotic: The Social Interpretation of Language and Meaning*, London: Arnold.

Halliday, M.A.K. (1996) *An Introduction to Functional Grammar*, 2nd edn, London: Arnold.

Harner, J.L. (1993) *Literary Research Guide: A Guide to Reference Sources for the Study of Literatures in English and Related Topics*, 2nd edn, New York: Modern Languages Association of America.

Hartley, J. (1982) *Understanding News*, London: Routledge & Kegan Paul.

Hartley, J. (1996) *Popular Reality*, London: Arnold.

Hawkes, T. (1972) *Metaphor*, London: Methuen.

Hayes, B. (1995) *Metrical Stress Theory*, Chicago: University of Chicago Press.

Hobby, E. and White, C. (eds) (1991) *What Lesbians Do in Books*, London: Women's Press.

Hoggart, R. (1958) *The Uses of Literacy*, Harmondsworth: Penguin.

Hutchinson, P. (1983) *Games Authors Play*, London: Methuen.

Jakobson, R. (1961) 'Concluding statement: linguistics and poetics', in T. Sebeok (ed.) *Style in Language*, Cambridge, MA: MIT Press.

Jakobson, R. (1987) *Language in Literature*, Cambridge, MA: Belknap Press of Harvard University Press.

Jameson, F. (1985) 'Postmodernism and consumer society', in H. Foster (ed.) *Postmodern Culture*, London: Pluto, pp. 111–25.

Jeffers, R. and Lehiste, I. (1979) *Principles and Methods for Historical Linguistics*, Cambridge, MA: MIT Press.

Kachru, B. (1982) *The Other Tongue: English across Cultures*, Oxford: Pergamon.

Kaplan, C. (1986) 'Keeping the color in *The Color Purple*', in C. Kaplan, *Sea Changes: Culture and Feminism*, London: Verso, pp. 176–87.

Kidd, V. (1971) 'A study of the images produced through the use of the male pronoun as generic', in *Moments in Contemporary Rhetoric and Communication* 1: 25–30.

Kirkham, S. (1989) *How to Find Information in the Humanities*, London: Library Association.

Kott, J. (1967) *Shakespeare Our Contemporary*, London: Methuen. First published in Polish in 1964.

Kramarae, C. and Treichler, P.A. (1996) *A Feminist Dictionary*, Illinois: University of Illinois Press.

Kress, G. and Van Leeuwen, T. (1998) 'Front pages: the (critical) analysis of newspaper layout', in A. Bell and P. Garrett (eds) *Approaches to Media Discourse*, Oxford: Blackwell, pp. 186–220.

REFERENCES

Lakoff, G. and Johnson, M. (1980) *Metaphors We Live By*, Chicago: University of Chicago Press.

Lakoff, R. (1975) *Language and Woman's Place*, New York: Harper Colophon.

Laws, S. (1990) *Issues of Blood: The Politics of Menstruation*, Basingstoke: Macmillan.

Leavis, F.R. (1962) *The Great Tradition*, Harmondsworth: Penguin.

Leavis, F.R. (1978) *The Common Pursuit*, Harmondsworth: Penguin.

Leech, G. (1969) *A Linguistic Guide to English Poetry*, London: Longman.

Leech, G. and Short, M. (1981) *Style in Fiction*, London: Longman.

Leech, G. and Svartvik, J. (1975) *A Communicative Grammar of English*, 2nd edn, London: Addison-Wesley, Longman.

Leith, D. (1983) *A Social History of English*, London: Routledge & Kegan Paul.

Leith, D. and Myerson, G. (1989) *The Power of Address*, London: Routledge.

Lemon, L.T. and Reis, M.J. (eds) (1965) *Russian Formalist Criticism*, Lincoln: University of Nebraska Press.

Lentricchia, F. and McLaughlin, T. (eds) (1990) *Critical Terms for Literary Study*, Chicago: University of Chicago Press.

Lodge, D. (ed.) (1972) *20th Century Literary Criticism*, Harlow: Longman.

Lodge, D. (1977) *The Modes of Modern Writing: Metaphor, Metonymy and the Typology of Modern Literature*, London: Edward Arnold.

Lodge, D. (ed.) (1988) *Modern Criticism and Theory: A Reader*, London: Longman.

Lodge, D. (1992) *The Art of Fiction*, Harmondsworth: Penguin

Lukács, G. (1962) *The Historical Novel*, London: Merlin.

MacCabe, C. (1979) *James Joyce and the Revolution of the Word*, London: Macmillan.

MacCabe, C. (1981) 'Realism and the cinema: notes on some Brechtian theses', in T. Bennet, S. Boyd-Bowman, C. Mercer and J. Woollacott (eds) *Popular Television and Film*, London: Open University Press and BFI, pp. 216–35.

McCrum, R., Cran, W. and McNeil, R. (1986) *The Story of English*, London: Faber & Faber and BBC Publications.

McFarlane, B. (1996) *Novel to Film*, Oxford: Oxford University Press.

McLuhan, M. (1964) *Understanding Media: The Extensions of Man*, London: Routledge & Kegan Paul.

Martin, E. (1997) 'The egg and the sperm: how science has constructed a romance based on stereotypical male–female roles', in L. Lamphere, H. Ragone and P. Zavella (eds) *Situated Lives: Gender and Culture in Everyday Life*, London: Routledge, pp. 85–99.

Mast, G. and Cohen, M. (eds) (1979) *Film Theory and Criticism*, Oxford: Oxford University Press.

Miller, C. and Swift, K. (1979) *Words and Women*, Harmondsworth: Penguin.

Mills, J. (1989) *Womanwords*, London: Longman.

Mills, S. (1987) 'The male sentence', *Language and Communication*, pp. 189–98.

Mills, S. (ed.) (1994) *Gendering the Reader*, Hemel Hempstead: Harvester Wheatsheaf.

Mills, S. (1996) *Feminist Stylistics*, London: Routledge.

Mills, S. and Pearce, L. (1996) *Feminist Readings/Feminists Reading*, 2nd edn, Hemel Hempstead: Harvester Wheatsheaf.

Moi, T. (1985) *Sexual/Textual Politics*, London: Methuen.

Montgomery, M. (1995) *An Introduction to Language and Society*, 2nd edn, London: Routledge.

Muecke, D.C. (1970) *Irony and the Ironic*, London: Methuen.

Mulvey, L. (1981) 'Visual pleasure and narrative cinema', in T. Bennett *et al.* (eds) *Popular Television and Film*, London: Open University/BFI, pp. 206–16.

Mulvey, L. (1989) *Visual and Other Pleasures*, London: Macmillan.

Murray, J.H. (1997) *Hamlet on the Holodeck: The Future of Narrative in Cyberspace*, Cambridge, MA: MIT Press.

Neale, S. (1980) *Genre*, London: British Film Institute.

Newton-de Molina, D. (ed.) (1976) *On Literary Intention*, Edinburgh: Edinburgh University Press.

Ngugi wa Thiong'o (1986) *Decolonising the Mind: The Politics of Language in African Literature*, London: Currey.

Nowottny, W. (1962) *The Language Poets Use*, London: Athlone Press.

O'Barr, W.F. and Atkins, (1982) 'Women's speech or powerless speech', in S. McConnell-Ginet, R. Borker and N. Furman (eds) *Women and Language in Literature and Society*, New York: Praeger.

Onega Jaén, S. and Garcia Landa, J.A. (eds) (1996) *Narratology: An Introduction*, London: Longman.

Ong, W.J. (1982) *Orality and Literacy: The Technologizing of the Word*, New York and London: Methuen.

Propp, V. (1968) *Morphology of the Folktale*, 2nd edn, Austin, TX: University of Texas Press.

Quirk, R. and Greenbaum, S. (1973) *A University Grammar of English*, Harlow: Longman.

Raving Beauties (1983) *In the Pink: The Raving Beauties Choose Poems from the Show and Many More*, London: Women's Press.

Richards, I.A. (1936) *Philosophy of Rhetoric*, Oxford: Oxford University Press.

Rifkin, B. (1994) *Semiotics of Narration in Film and Prose Fiction*, New York: Peter Lang.

Rimmon-Kenan, S. (1983) *Narrative Fiction: Contemporary Poetics*, London: Methuen.

Rosch, E. (1977) 'Classification of real-world objects: origins and representations in cognition', in P.N. Johnson-Laird and P.C. Wason (eds) *Thinking,* Cambridge: Cambridge University Press.

Sacks, S. (ed.) (1979) *On Metaphor*, Chicago: University of Chicago Press.

Said, E. (1993) 'Jane Austen and empire', in E. Said, *Culture and Imperialism*, London: Chatto & Windus, pp. 95–115.

Scholes, R. (1982) *Semiotics and Interpretation*, New Haven, CT: Yale University Press.

Shklovsky, V. (1917/1988) 'Art as technique', in D. Lodge (ed.) (1988) *Modern Criticism and Theory*, London: Longman, pp. 16–30.

Shohat, E. and Stam, R. (1994) *Unthinking Eurocentrism: Multiculturalism and the Media*, London: Routledge.

Showalter, E. (1977) *A Literature of their Own*, Princeton, NJ: Princeton University Press.

Simpson, P. (1993) *Language, Ideology and Point of View*, London: Routledge.

Sontag, S. (ed.) (1982) *Barthes: Selected Writings*, London: Collins.

Spender, D. (1980) *Man Made Language*, London: Routledge & Kegan Paul.

Spender, D. (1986) *Mothers of the Novel*, London: Pandora.

Sperber, D. and Wilson, D. (1995) *Relevance: Communication and Cognition*, Oxford: Blackwell.

Spiegel, A. (1976) *Fiction and the Camera Eye: Visual Consciousness in Film and the Modern Novel*, Charlottesville: University Press of Virginia.

Stacey, J. (1994) *Star Gazing: Hollywood Cinema and Female Spectatorship*, London: Routledge.

Steedman, C. (1981) *The Tidy House*, London: Virago.

Strang, B. (1970) *A History of English*, London: Methuen.

Tannen, D. (1991) *You Just Don't Understand: Women and Men in Conversation*, London: Virago.

Thompson, G. (1996) *Introducing Functional Grammar*, London: Arnold.

Thompson, J. (1971) *English Studies: A Guide for Librarians to the Sources and their Organisation*, London: Bingley.

Thwaites, T., Davis, L. and Mules, W. (1994) *Tools for Cultural Studies: An Introduction*, London: Macmillan.

Todd, A. and Loder, C. (1990) *Finding Facts Fast: How to Find Out What You Want and Need to Know*, Harmondsworth: Penguin.

Todd, J. (ed.) (1985) *A Dictionary of British and American Women Writers, 1660–1800*, Totowa, NJ: Rowman & Allanheld.

Todd, J. (ed.) (1989) *A Dictionary of British Women Writers*, London: Routledge.

Tolson, A. (1996) *Mediations*, London: Arnold.

Toolan, M. (1988) *Narrative: A Critical Linguistic Introduction*, London: Routledge.

Trew, T. (1979) 'Theory at work', in R. Fowler *et al. Language and Control*, London: Routledge & Kegan Paul.

Uspensky, B. (1973) *A Poetics of Composition*, Berkeley, CA: University of California Press.

Van Zoonan, L. (1994) *Feminist Media Studies*, London: Sage.

Vološinov, V.N. (1973) *Marxism and the Philosophy of Language*, New York: Seminar Press.

Walder, D. (ed.) (1991) *Literature in the Modern World*, Oxford: Oxford University Press.

Watt, I. (1972) *The Rise of the Novel*, Harmondsworth: Penguin.

Widdowson, H.G. (1975) *Stylistics and the Teaching of Literature*, London: Longman.

Widdowson, H.G. (1992) *Practical Stylistics: An Approach to Poetry*, Oxford: Oxford University Press.

Williams, R. (1966) *Modern Tragedy*, London: Chatto & Windus.

Williams, R. (1973) *The Country and the City*, London: Chatto & Windus.

Williams, R. (1988) *Keywords: A Vocabulary of Culture and Society*, London: Collins.

Wimsatt, W.K. (ed.) (1972) *Versification: Major Language Types: Sixteen Essays*, New York: Modern Language Association and New York University Press.

Wimsatt, W.K. and Beardsley, M.C. (1946) 'The intentional fallacy', in D. Lodge (ed.) (1972) *20th Century Literary Criticism*, Harlow: Longman, pp. 334–44.

Wimsatt, W.K. and Beardsley, M.C. (1949) 'The affective fallacy', in D. Lodge (ed.) (1972) *20th Century Literary Criticism*, Harlow: Longman.

Woolf, V. (1979) 'Women and writing', in D. Cameron (ed.) (1990) *The Feminist Critique of Language*, London: Routledge.

Wray, A., Trott, K. and Bloomer, A. (1998) *Projects in Linguistics: A Practical Guide to Researching Language*, London: Arnold.

Subject Index

Index of texts discussed